Ticket Scalping

Ticket Scalping

An American History, 1850–2005

KERRY SEGRAVE

McFarland & Company, Inc., Publishers
Jefferson, North Carolina, and London

LIBRARY OF CONGRESS CATALOGUING-IN-PUBLICATION DATA

Segrave, Kerry, 1944–
    Ticket scalping : an American history, 1850–2005 / Kerry
Segrave.
        p.   cm.
    Includes bibliographical references and index.

    ISBN-13: 978-0-7864-2805-2
    ISBN-10: 0-7864-2805-8
    (softcover : 50# alkaline paper) ∞

    1. Ticket scalping — United States — History.   I. Title.
HD9999.T523U575   2007
381'.4579 — dc22   2006030959

British Library cataloguing data are available

Cover design by Mark Durr

Manufactured in the United States of America

McFarland & Company, Inc., Publishers
    Box 611, Jefferson, North Carolina 28640
    www.mcfarlandpub.com

Table of Contents

Preface

The scalping of tickets to American entertainment events has been a problem since at least 1850 and probably well before that. Prominent figures in the entertainment world from Jenny Lind to Charles Dickens to Oscar Hammerstein to Flo Ziegfeld to Billy Joel to Bruce Springsteen have been bedeviled by the speculator and most tried to deal with the problem in one way or another. None had any success.

This book looks at the practice of ticket scalping in the United States from 1850 to 2005 and covers all forms of entertainment, from theatre events to sports to rock concerts. Scalping a ticket involved selling the seat to someone for a price different from the original box office price; almost always that second price included a premium of some amount. Over that period the status of the speculator has been that of a pariah and public sentiment has been overwhelmingly against the practice. Laws too numerous to count have been enacted at the state and local level. Many of those statutes have fallen after being declared unconstitutional; many have stood. Yet none has had much of an effect even though over a century and a half many people have been arrested and convicted of speculating. While a rare few have drawn jail sentences, most have been fined a relatively small sum of money.

War has been declared on scalpers many times by managers and producers of events with private security guards and local police officers pressed into action to defeat the evil. Initially the speculators were small-time, independent operators or "sidewalk men," as they were called. They got tickets to scalp by hiring mostly young boys to stand in box office lines for them and buy seats. As time passed the ticket agency or brokerage — starting off in the lobbies of fashionable hotels — came to dominate the scalping field as the sidewalk men became less important. Still, public ire tended to focus on the sidewalk men who were much more visible.

When government probes of the practice became fashionable there were many dramatic revelations of the extent of the practice. Also revealed by such probes was the extent of the collusion between the managers and producers of entertainment events and the sellers of the tickets. Such collusion had existed since at least 1850 and evidence of its existence had been sporadically reported over time.

While morality was sometimes mentioned as a reason to oppose the practice, by the dawn of the 21st century such ideas had been largely forgotten. Scalping was then undergoing a slight revision to a more positive status as the economic mantra of free markets was used by the increasing number of supporters of the practice. This, then, is a history of an institution as American as apple pie.

1

The General Situation, 1850–1899

"The prosperity of the present [theatrical] season appears to have greatly increased their number [scalpers], and if possible added to their ugliness."

New York Times, 1856

"It is nevertheless true that gangs of hardened ticket-speculators exist and carry on their atrocious trade with perfect shamelessness."

New York Times, 1876

When ticket scalper David M. Neuberger appeared before a New York City Council committee in 1908 to argue against a proposed regulation of his trade he told the aldermen that ticket speculation began in 1850 when famed singer Jenny Lind first came to New York to perform.[1]

Actually, the practice must have existed before 1850 because Lind discussed the issue in that year. When she was stopped in a New York hotel in the fall of 1850, preparing for her concerts later that year, Lind wrote a letter to concert promoter P. T. Barnum, dated October 24, 1950. In that letter, with respect to ticket prices, she said, "You know that I have always been in favor of having lower prices to my concerts, and you have invariably expressed your willingness to make them so far as could safely be done and at the same time prevent speculators from taking advantage of the reduction." The "Swedish nightingale," as the international superstar was popularly known, went on to add in her letter, "Will you permit me to suggest that Tripler Hall is immensely large and that with proper precaution you might certainly avoid selling tickets to speculators and at the same time put the prices within reach of the people at large. If you can do so you will greatly oblige me." Barnum replied that he was happy to oblige her request, ultimately pricing the tickets for the Lind concerts at $3, $4, and $5.[2]

Journalist Robert Sylvester observed in 1949 that scalping plagued even author Charles Dickens during his second American tour in the 1860s when $5 seats for the Dickens's readings were sold on the black market for as much as $50.[3]

During a police crackdown on scalping in 1870 an unidentified theatrical man "of some years experience," reflected that speculation in the sale of theatre tickets was started in New York City by a man named Joseph Siegrist who for some years was said to have done a brisk trade in the sale of tickets to amusement seekers, together with his business as a steamboat ticket agent. Upon the death of Siegrist (1818–1892) it was observed, "For thirty years he was a ticket speculator, and could always be seen in front of the old Academy of Music in the prosperous day of Italian opera." Although it was said he made a fortune in his years of scalping, Siegrist reportedly died "comparatively poor."[4]

During this period ticket scalping was a widespread practice both in the entertainment business and in the railroad business. Throughout most of this period the term "scalping" was applied only to the black market trade in railroad tickets while the term "speculating" was applied to the practice in the entertainment and amusement areas. There was virtually no overlap in the use of the terms. One of the earliest usages of the word "scalping" applied to theatre tickets occurred in a news account in September 1887. After that "scalping" slowly became the term of choice for the practice in all areas, with the term "speculator" gradually fading from common usage.[5]

An 1856 article summarized who was playing at various entertainment venues in New York City, one of which was the Academy of Music. Wrote the journalist, "By the way, we would suggest to the management of the Academy the actual necessity of driving the ticket speculators from the steps of their building. The pertinacity with which these gentlemen persist in thrusting reserved seats in your face is intolerable. The prosperity of the present season appears to have greatly increased their number, and if possible added to their ugliness." The reporter went on to add that it may have been impossible to prevent those "vociferous gentlemen" from obtaining tickets, "but it cannot be beyond the resources of the Academy to kick them out of the lobby and off the steps into the street."[6]

Such criticism could arouse a venue's management and a couple of years later the Academy of Music published an advertisement in which coming attractions were listed and in which a Mr. Ullman (possibly the manager) addressed part of the ad "To the Public." That part of the message declared, "Mr. Ullman, from a sense of justice, deems it his duty to publicly announce that the several proprietors of those places where irregular and illicit ticket offices had been established by speculators have withdrawn their permission." Scalpers of the time often conducted their business in the doorways of stores close to the venue (especially if the venue was in the midst of one of its periodic campaigns to shoo them away from its own lobby area and/or front steps and sidewalk) and sometimes even conducted business within a nearby store, presumably paying something to the shopkeeper. Ullman's message concluded with a warning, "Public attention is likewise called to the fact that during the great rush a number of counterfeit tickets had been sold by itinerant ticket speculators to respectable persons, who, of course, were denied admission."[7]

An editorial in 1874 was not entirely opposed to the speculator. That writer felt the ticket scalper was likely to be a greater nuisance than ever for the 1874-1875 theatrical season — although he gave no reasons as to why that would be so — and argued the theatre managers should keep their number to a moderate level at their venues, as opposed to trying to eliminate them completely, "for there are times when one or two such men, known to be of good character, might prove useful." He explained that he had noticed two or three such people in the lobby of Wallack's Theatre who had been there ever since the venue had been built and, "They do not sell spurious tickets, or demand an unreasonable profit on their tickets." On the other hand, if their numbers surpassed the moderate level, the situation became unpleasant. "But when the sidewalk or lobby is lined with speculators — as at the Lyceum Theatre for instance — the nuisance becomes intolerable.... The managers of the Lyceum Theatre should see to this," he argued. "The ticket speculator need not be absolutely suppressed, but he should not be allowed to persecute people who wish to enter a theatre."[8]

Two years later another editorial described the pervasiveness of the practice in 1876, noting, "It is nevertheless true that gangs of hardened ticket-speculators exist and carry on their atrocious trade with perfect shamelessness. These speculators may be seen in front of every theatre on the evening of a performance." This editor singled out the theatre-going public for even more blame, calling those who bought a scalper's wares his accomplices "and that they are directly responsible for his continued exertions, and the success which rewards his life of crime ... it is evident that the public who buy the speculator's tickets ought also to be suppressed...." Held in contempt by this editor were people who bought black market tickets and then wrote letters to the editor complaining about the practice and wondering why it was not stopped. "Thus the guilty accomplice diverts attention from himself and retains the respect and confidence of virtuous managers, while the wicked speculator counts his ill-gotten gains and cares not how much his accomplice may publicly denounce him, provided he privately buys his tickets," he declared. In the editor's opinion the best way to stop such transactions would be to enact a municipal ordinance forbidding any person from selling tickets on the sidewalk unless he had a city-issued license to do so — for, say, a license fee of $100. However, he admitted such an ordinance would never be enacted and resigned himself to the idea, "Perhaps, after all, the matter must be left in the hands of the public who must decide whether or not to buy poor seats at the box-office at $1.50 or good seats from the speculator at $2."[9]

Several years passed before another editorial comment appeared in 1883, at which time it was observed that with the opening of the 1883-1884 theatrical season complaints by play-goers were heard anew that they were unable to obtain seats to a successful play unless they purchased them from sidewalk speculators or at the ticket offices then found in many New York hotels, also at a premium. After remarking that the subject had been discussed time after time in newspapers but it still turned up each year as a hot issue, the editor said that there was a class of theatre-goers who preferred to pay a premium to avoid the trouble of standing in line, "But most people prefer to buy goods at the market price, whether the goods are theatre tickets or not...." Also mentioned by the editor was that the charge that any reputable manager in New York was in league with scalpers and received a share of their profits had never been proved, although it was often reiterated. He saw no reason the ticket sellers at newsstands in downtown hotels should retail tickets for no profit but, "With the sidewalk speculators the case is different. They are of no real use to the public, because they carry on their business within a few feet of the regular ticket-offices, and the only good excuse that the public has for patronizing them is that good seats cannot be obtained at the offices." Seemingly, the editor accepted the notion that managers could not effectively refrain from selling tickets to speculators, because of their use of proxies, and so on, "But the managers can, with the aid of the police, prevent the speculators from disposing of their tickets in front of the theatres. That would go far to check the nuisance, and if all playgoers would then refuse to buy tickets except at the accredited offices the cause of complaint would be removed altogether."[10]

Typical of complaining letters to the editor was an angry one from "R.C.H." in 1885 in which he argued there were more scalpers around than ever before. On several occasions he had gone to the Fifth Avenue Theatre where he tried unsuccessfully to get tickets for "*The Mikado.*" He described his experiences as follows, "I have visited the sidewalk in front of this theatre, and in no instance have I found less than nine speculators in front of the Broadway entrance, and on Friday evening, Sept, 4, I counted 13, seven in one row and six in the other, ranged each side of the door, faced inward, so that every person entering had to run through this double file of howlers and be annoyed by their ill-mannered importunities." R.C.H. also expressed a sentiment held by many would-be ticket buyers when he asserted, "The truth of the matter in relation to this sidewalk business is that the managers are in sympathy with it, and probably share the profits with the speculators."[11]

Just two days later a reporter produced an article about the theatre managers' failure to curb speculators in front of their houses. According to him the only manager who had succeeded in doing so was Augustin Daly, but he also felt that after hearing everything that Daly went through to drive away the traffic few other managers would likely follow suit. Daly reportedly had to fight not only the scalpers but also the public because not a day went by during the

Daly campaign in the 1884-1885 theatrical season without half a dozen complaints from Daly patrons that they could not find any speculators and they were unable to buy seats at the box office due to the great crowd of people. Condemned by this reporter was Daly's course in "depriving" the public of something it considered to be a great convenience as there were just as many people who used the scalpers as there were who complained about them. "There are a great many people in New York who never think of buying seats in advance, and who, in point of fact, do not know they are going to the theatre until the last moment before starting." As far as the reporter was concerned Daly had "accomplished unquestionably a complete victory" in eliminating sidewalk trade from around his venue. Daly's method was to keep two or three men posted in front of his house at all times, to watch the speculators. As soon as one of them disposed of a ticket Daly's spotter followed the purchaser to the venue entrance and gave the ticket-taker a prearranged signal whereupon the holder of the seat was stopped at the door. At the same time the ticket-taker made a note of the seat number so the ticket could not be presented again later that evening. Of course, many such refused patrons became very hostile and engaged in shouting matches with the staff.[12]

In an 1893 editorial it was observed that the "annual futile cry of the public" against theatre ticket scalping was going up and newspapers were urged to renew the fight against "this species of petty extortion." However, this editor felt it was a hopeless fight because the only agency that, practically speaking, could end the practice was the aggrieved public itself and that agency refused to act. "So long as people will buy tickets from sidewalk speculators so long the speculators will thrive and share their spoils with such managers as are willing to stoop to this kind of business." One leading manager, unidentified, who was said to have driven scalpers from the doors of his house said one would be surprised how large was the class of playgoers willing to pay 25 cents or 50 cents extra to a scalper, on top of a ticket that usually sold for $1.50 tops. "There is a certain class of men — especially in the 'swell' crowd — who regard it as a compliment to their female companions to pay the extra price rather than join the common herd at the box office," explained the manager. "It gives them the opportunity to show their carelessness of money, real or assumed, before the eyes of their sweethearts and to make an impression on the common people. These men not only encourage the evil of speculation, but they really demand its continuance."[13]

Nor was scalping limited to America. Theatre-goers in Paris, France were so annoyed by scalpers at the very end of the nineteenth century that a crusade was organized against the practice. Early in 1900 the police conducted a raid and arrested several ticket vendors on the ground of interfering with traffic. Fines and imprisonment were said to have been imposed on them. According to a news account, "the existence of this evil in Paris is mainly due to the number of tickets allotted authors nightly, who sell them to agents and the latter greatly annoy the public at the theatre entrances. The police intend to break up this practice."[14]

Scalping of tickets to sporting events was also common in this era, mainly involving boxing matches and college football games. A July 1882 fight at New York's Madison Square Garden between John L. Sullivan and England's Tug Wilson was said to have drawn the biggest fight crowd in America, a sell-out of 10,000 that included a "who's who" of famous people. Tickets were priced at $1 and $2 but, "Ticket speculators were in force, and they had no difficulty in disposing of tickets at from $3 to $5 each." Accounts of boxing matches regularly mentioned, in a routine way, that scalpers could be found at the event. But the remarks were limited to no more than a single sentence. That is, the existence of speculators working boxing matches seemed to not irritate or annoy anybody, contrary to the reception scalpers received in almost any other entertainment area.[15]

During a horse racing season at Morris Park, New York, in 1891 trouble developed at the track over certain admission tickets that had been given out in the city to people who had allowed ads for the race meet to be placed in their stores. Placing ads in store windows was then one of the most popular ways to advertise upcoming events, plays, circuses, race meets, and so on. Typically the shopkeeper received a couple of free tickets to the event for hosting the sign in his window. Implicitly or explicitly the understanding was that those tickets would not be sold to scalpers, and would be void if sold or used by anyone except the person to whom they were given. But, of course, they were sold regularly. In this example, speculators had reportedly scoured the city and bought as many of those tickets as they could find for a small sum. Speculators hawked them for $1 each (that was less than the price of the admission ticket if it was purchased at the track box office) but when there "was good evidence" that holders other than the original recipients were trying to use the tickets the holders were refused entry.[16]

If boxing was somewhat nonchalant in its attitude toward scalping, college football was not. A few days before the Princeton-Yale game was played at the end of November 1890 at Eastern Park, Brooklyn, both teams agreed they had left the sale of seats entirely to the managers of Eastern Park. That management had been criticized because a "comparatively limited number" of people had been charging more for tickets than the advertised price of $1 for general admission and $2 for a reserved seat. Management spokesman George Chauncey explained there were lots of general admission seats available for the advertised price of $1 with the problem limited to black market transactions on some reserved seats. He thought that people accustomed to buying tickets from scalpers would not complain at paying an extra price. According to Chauncey, about 6,200 reserved seats had been sold with about 800 of those passing through speculators' hands. Just a few days before the game, explained Chauncey, management added 1,500 chairs, loaned by the Coney Island Jockey

Club, thus extending the number of reserved seats by that number and they were put on sale at the regular price of $2 at the ticket agencies on a first-come, first-served basis and to guard against their falling into the hands of scalpers, "the sale will be under the personal supervision of an officer of the club, and purchasers will be restricted to four seats each."[17]

Three years later, just before another Princeton-Yale game, it was reported the contest was expected to develop a lot of student speculators because they "have gone into the business this year even stronger than usual and the general public will be the sufferers." Chief complaint in the article was about student greed. Students at both campuses had been able to buy seats for $1.50 in the uncovered stands and $2 for seats in the covered stands. A total of 3,400 covered seats and 1,000 uncovered seats in total had been assigned to the two colleges. When students sold their tickets directly to others they charged $8 for the uncovered stands and $10 for the covered stands. Some students sold their seats to the hotel agencies, apparently for lesser amounts. C. F. Matthewson, chairman of the committee in charge of distributing seats, declared his group had done all it could to prevent it, "even putting the students on their honor not to buy for speculation or for speculators when they took the seats they said they needed for personal use." A conclusion drawn in the article was that "the blame lies wholly with these young men"— that is, the students.[18]

One year later intense interest was directed to the Yale-Princeton game slated for December 1, 1894. No seats were left many days prior to the game except through scalpers at exorbitant prices. Scalpers, once again, had managed to secure blocks of them through the aid of the students at Yale and Princeton, each of whom was entitled to two seats, if he cared to buy them. Many who had no intention of going to the game came forward to buy their seats anyway, and turned them over to speculators "at a handsome profit." Reserved seats (face value of $1.50) were being hawked on the black market at $5 and up.[19]

Just prior to the November 1899 Yale-Princeton clash management announced it was releasing several hundred choice reserved seats at the regular price in an effort to defeat the high prices charged by scalpers as they circulated the report that they alone had good tickets for sale.[20]

People in this period were regularly harassed by the police, and sometimes arrested for scalping. Legislators at the local and state level frequently got involved as they tried to regulate ticket selling.

2

Laws, Arrests, Police, Courts, 1850–1899

"They are impudent beyond endurance and press their wares upon each new arrival with an audacity and a persever-ance...."

New York Times, 1883

"The speculators in tickets have been recognized by the city authorities for nineteen years by the imposition of a license. This, I contend is an admission of the legitimacy of their business."

David M. Newburger, 1899

Captain Ira Garland of the New York Police Department ordered the arrest of four men in September 1868 who had allegedly been scalping tickets at the Olympic Theatre, in response to a complaint of disorderly conduct made against them by the manager of that venue. However, a judge dismissed the complaint on the ground the evidence did not sustain the charge, and the accused were discharged.[1]

Police in New York conducted a raid on the evening of August 19, 1870, on ticket speculators who operated near Booth's Theatre. Before the doors opened a "large number" of police were posted on 23rd Street and on Sixth Avenue, extending their ranks far beyond the house on either side, "so that the sidewalk speculators could offer no tickets for sale within a block of the doors." Finding themselves thus completely foiled none of the men attempted to dispose of their tickets, with the management reported to be "entirely successful" in its goal of having all the patrons purchase their seats at the box office. No arrests were made at Booth's. Similar measures were also taken that night at Niblo's Garden venue "with like results, the speculators being thwarted by the same quiet tactics which forced their up-town brethren from the field."[2]

A couple of nights later it was reported that quiet ruled as theatres had gotten rid of the speculators because policemen guarded the doors of the different venues and had orders to arrest anyone found selling tickets. It was opening night of the new season at the Olympic Theatre, which had a long line patiently waiting at the box office. Surveying the situation were three New York policemen and one private security guard, placed there by management, all around the entrance, with the result that no one was allowed to scalp tickets within 50 feet of the building. Speculators did not attempt to sell although, reportedly, "groups of them stood around the doors and cursed their hard fate in being prevented from making use of the opportunity to reap a golden harvest."[3]

One of the events that led to the police crackdown at Booth's, and other venues, took place on August 17. On that night Charles Appley, an alleged scalper, was arrested on the complaint of John H. Magonigle, business manager of Booth's Theatre, who charged Appley with "using insulting, abusive, opprobrious and threatening language, making a noise, and disturbing the public peace" in the vestibule of the venue.[4]

When Appley appeared in court on August 23 the courtroom was said to have been crowded with ticket speculators, although by this time the story had changed to one wherein Appley was refused admission to the house when he presented a ticket he had allegedly bought from a scalper. Magonigle told the court he refused to admit Appley, although the ticket was genuine, because a man he employed as a spotter outside the house informed Magonigle that Appley bought the seat from a speculator. Once he was refused admission to the house, continued the business manager, Appley used loud and abusive language in order to be admitted. For his part, Appley admitted having bought the seat from a speculator but denied using abusive language or acting up in any way. However, two witnesses gave testimony that agreed with Magonigle's account. As a result the presiding magistrate found Appley guilty of disorderly conduct tending to a breach of the peace and ordered him to keep the peace for 12 months, on the forfeit of $300.[5]

Later in 1870 it was reported that in spite of the recent efforts of theatre managers to suppress speculation, "it thrives as vigorously as ever." On November 26, 1870, George Sistere purchased two double tickets for admission to the rehearsal of the Philharmonic Society at the Academy of Music, for a total cost of $16, from a street vendor on the representation that he would secure front row seats. The street vendor from whom he made the purchase, George, stated he only made a $1 profit from the transaction, and that no objection would be made to the admission of Sistere to the venue. But when Sistere presented his tickets to the doorman on November 26 he was refused admission to the Academy of Music. To add to his chagrin he discovered his tickets had a face value of just $6 in total. Sistere reported the matter to the police, with George being arrested.[6]

In April 1872 Justice Cox held an examination in the case of Joseph Tooker, manager of the Sabbath concerts at the Grand Opera-house, against James Brown and his assistants, Mr. Carmon and Mr. Feichtner, alleged ticket speculators, for creating a disturbance in the lobby of the house on the previous Sunday. Brown showed the court his written and stamped lease to sell tickets for which he paid J. F. Cole, the lessee of the building, $200, and he said that, therefore, Tooker had no right to stop him from selling as he did on the previous Sunday. Tooker declared he had no written lease for his use of the Opera-house on Sundays and that the seats Brown and his assistants were selling were purchased from him at his box office. Brown asserted he would appear and sell seats on the coming Sunday while Tooker was equally adamant that he would prevent him from doing so. A report the next day said, without giving details, that the differences between the two sides had been amicably settled.[7]

A brief account in April 1873 recorded, also with little detail, that a ticket scalper had been arraigned in Municipal Court in Boston on a complaint charging him with violating a Boston by-law by standing in Howard Street and selling tickets to the Howard Atheneum while not being licensed to do so by the Board of Aldermen of that city. That unidentified man was convicted and fined.[8]

Attempts to enact New York State laws regulating scalping were unsuccessful during this period. Around 1870 the New York City theatrical managers made what was called a "very strong effort" to get a bill passed by the State Legislature to abate what they considered a nuisance and an infringement of their right to regulate the sale of their tickets. Under their proposal the bill provided that persons selling tickets on the sidewalks in front of a theatre could be punished by fine or imprisonment unless the consent of the manager of a venue had been obtained. Mainly through the exertions of a senator who represented New York City, the proposal was defeated as the unnamed senator decided the penalty was too severe. As well, it was generally thought that such a proposal would not have been constitutional.[9]

Almost 15 years later, in 1884, a bill to suppress theatre ticket scalping was introduced in the New York State Assembly at Albany by Mr. Farrell of Kings. It made it unlawful "for any person to buy or sell, traffic or speculate in any ticket or other evidence of the right to admission, either with or without reserved seats, to any place of instruction or amusement in any town or city of this State for the purpose of making a profit over and above the price or prices for which such ticket or evidence of the right of admission to such place was issued by the manager or proprietor of such place or his agent, or the promoter of any such entertainment to be given in such place." Penalty under the proposal was to be a fine of not less than $25, or more than $100, or by both fine and imprisonment at the discretion of the court. That proposal failed to become law.[10]

Efforts to enact legislation were more successful in other jurisdictions, although it was arguable whether they ever had much effect on the practice itself. One jurisdiction that did enact a formal rule was New York City. After a long discussion at a meeting of the New York City Board of Aldermen on December 14, 1880, an ordinance was passed requiring theatre ticket speculators to procure licenses and wear badges. The license fee was set at $50 for the first year and $25 for renewals.[11]

Less than a month later, on January 11, 1881, two alleged theatre ticket scalpers, Philip S. Paulscraft and Leon Stedeker, were arrested by the police on the complaint of Leigh Lynch, cashier of the Union Square Theatre, and accused of violating the recently passed ordinance that regulated ticket speculation. Arraigned in the Jefferson Market Police Court, the pair came before Justice Flammer, who called for the ordinance. When a police officer produced a slip cut from the *City Record* (an official record of City Hall doings) counsel for the defense objected to that being received as legal proof of the existence of the ordinance. Flammer decided there was no legal evidence before him of the passage of such ordinance and therefore discharged the accused.[12]

Some 15 months after passage of the ordinance, the Law Committee of the New York Board of Aldermen met and heard the views of a number of theatrical managers concerning the proposed abolition of the measure. Wesley Sisson of the Madison Square Theatre expressed strong opposition to the current system, calling it an outrage to the public and stating that the business of scalping should be punishable by law instead of "permitted and encouraged" by the law that allowed licensing of vendors. John Stetson of Booth's Theatre called speculators a nuisance and wanted to see them eliminated, although he admitted to being in favor of allowing hotel agencies to sell seats at a "small advance" over regular prices to accommodate the traveling public. John Schoeffell of the Park Theatre also opposed the licensing by-law and urged the measure be repealed.[13]

At another hearing on the issue a week later, still in April 1882, a speculator who appeared spoke of collusion. Leon Stedeker spoke in opposition to any idea of rescinding the ordinance (speculators generally favored the licensing measure sensing it gave a legitimacy they previously lacked) noting that scalpers had already paid $2,800 to the City Treasury and besides, most theatrical managers kept a man in the lobby to sell seats at an advanced price. Stedeker said he used to sell tickets in the lobby of Daly's Theatre and had to pay to the manager $1.90 for every $2 ticket ($1.50 face) he sold. Two speculators, he said, were employed at Booth's Theatre by a Mr. Guernsey and men were employed for the same purpose by the managers of all the theatres except the Germania and the Thalia. Mr. Lonsdale, manager of the Standard Theatre, told the Law Committee the chief objection to speculators was that they crowded the lobby and that he did not believe any law against them would be effective. At his venue, admitted Lonsdale, a man was employed to sell tickets at an advance, a procedure that was utilized to prevent outsiders from running up the prices of good seats to an "exorbitant figure."[14]

Lester Wallack, of Wallack's Theatre, was another who argued the New

York City license law was ineffective and that the scalpers who frequented his venue injured his business. Therefore, he launched a suit against them hoping to drive them away from the theatre and its immediate vicinity. Upon affidavits made by him and Theodore Moss, treasurer of Wallack's, Judge Donohue, in Supreme Court Chambers, granted a temporary injunction on May 20, 1882, restraining John Kenny, John Turnbull, Henry Mackey, William Hack, Peter Tiemann, and Robert Anderson from scalping tickets in front of his venue. According to those affidavits it was the practice of the defendants to assemble in front of the venue and to annoy its patrons by causing a crowd to gather, thus obstructing the street and the theatre entrances. They may have been licensed to sell tickets, argued the suit, but not to stand in front of theatres and thereby injure business. A main argument of the action was that although the city could license people to sell theatre tickets, it could not through its licenses give them the right to sell in such a manner and at such places as to do injury to the rights of other persons, and that if they did such injury they violated their licenses.[15]

Defendants in the Wallack suit argued the real purpose of the legal proceeding was to get rid of them entirely, if possible, so that two men, Augustus Hamilton and Charles Hovey, would be left in full control of ticket scalping at Wallack's Theatre. Those men, said the defendants, were in collusion with the plaintiff and split the profits from scalping with him. They admitted Wallack had begun an action to restrain Hamilton from selling tickets but asserted that suit was not in good faith because since Hamilton had been served with a preliminary injunction, they alleged, he had stood in the main vestibule of the venue and directed people to buy seats from Hovey. Wallack had launched no legal action against Hovey.[16]

On the last day of 1882 speculator William Beck was arrested at the Casino Theatre for not wearing his badge (he was licensed) so that it could be seen by the public, as required by the measure. He was held in lieu of $100 bail. When he was arrested Beck had $35 worth of unsold tickets on his person.[17]

Joining in with the people opposed to the licensing measure was an editor of the New York Times who remarked in a September 1883 editorial that during the previous week he had observed seven speculators at one west side theatre, and no less than five at a different venue, on several occasions. "It is useless to deny the fact that these men are nuisances to the great mass of the public," grumbled the editor. "They are impudent beyond endurance and press their wares upon each new arrival with an audacity and a perseverance...." He blamed the Board of Aldermen for the situation because they had licensed them. "Any theatre manager who interferes with their business would immediately be punished," added the editor. "The remedy for this nuisance lies primarily with the Board of Aldermen."[18]

Despite the hearing and the turmoil the New York licensing measure stood. Still, the Law Committee of the Board of Aldermen revisited the issue and reported in April 1884 that, in its opinion, the interests of entertainment venue patrons, and the proprietors thereof, would be best served by repealing the ordinance authorizing speculation of theatre tickets on public streets. Accompanying the report was a resolution repealing the ordinance, but not preventing the sale of theatre tickets at places other than the theatre. At the committee hearing about 40 scalpers were present, most of whom had something they wanted to say. A licensed scalper named Murphy said he bought his tickets from the box office when business was poor but for a successful play he had to get them where he could. Sometimes, he explained, he bought them from the lobbyman, who got his supply from the venue manager, and paid him a percentage of his profits on the sales. Leon Stedeker favored a high license fee, say $500 instead of the current $50 for the first year, and added that scalpers not affiliated with venues had to obtain their seats from hotel agencies and from the lobbymen. Speculators were divided on the issue of the license fee; some favored a high license fee, some wanted to maintain the current level.[19]

Statistics from the Mayor's office in New York City revealed that in 1883, 31 scalpers took out new licenses at $50 each and 43 renewed their licenses at $25 each. In 1884 there were 12 new licenses issued along with 40 renewals, showing an apparent fall of 22 in the number of men engaged in the business.[20]

Two reports concerning scalping were presented in March 1885 to the New York Board of Aldermen by its Law Committee. The majority report recommended the repeal of the licensing ordinance, that in future the sale of theatre tickets be confined to the box office, and that no advance on the advertised prices be permitted. The minority report simply recommended the present ordinance be continued in force. Aldermen adopted the minority report.[21]

Meanwhile sporadic attempts to enforce the measure continued. Richard Rourke was arrested in July 1885 in front of the Casino Theatre for peddling tickets without a license. A few days later in court he was fined $10 by Police Justice Ford.[22]

Leon Stedeker, president of the protective association recently formed by scalpers, was arrested in front of the Fifth Avenue Theatre in December 1885, on the complaint of Charles Burnham, venue treasurer, that he was selling tickets in front of the venue and blocking access. Stedeker was released on bail and when he appeared in court the next day at the Jefferson Market Police Court Burnham said he had no complaint to make. In response, Stedeker insisted that a complaint be made and said he would make it a test case as to the rights of licensed speculators to sell seats in front of places of amusement. Justice Smith told him, "But there's no one here to make a complaint against you. You're discharged." Said the scalper, "I don't want to be discharged. I waive examination and elect to be tried at the General Sessions." Replied Smith, "You can't waive an examination when there's no complaint against you." And so Stedeker was discharged, a disappointed man.[23]

Edward Welsh, James Tuomey, and Thomas Dalton were arrested in March

1886 for peddling tickets in front of Harrigan's Theatre, although it was not reported if they were licensed or not. When they were arraigned a few days later before Justice Power at the Jefferson Market Police Court, Dalton stated the proprietor of the venue kept a ticket speculator in the lobby who sold tickets furnished by the management. Also, Dalton claimed he and his companions had as much right to sell the tickets in the street as the house speculator had in the lobby. Apparently Justice Power thought so, too, and discharged the men.[24]

Several years passed before the issue was raised again before the New York City Council. In March 1891 the Law Committee of the Board of Aldermen held a hearing on an ordinance proposed by Alderman Harris in which it was provided that no licenses should be issued to speculators after the present licenses expired. Additionally, the proposal made it a misdemeanor for anyone to sell tickets in the lobby of a theatre without the permission of the proprietor.[25]

Once again the issue surfaced in June 1895, when New York Alderman Hall proposed an ordinance wherein no licenses would be granted to scalpers after the current ones expired. At a meeting of the Aldermen that proposal was defeated by a vote of 20 to nine. Before the vote Hall read letters from many theatre managers endorsing the proposition. But Alderman Wund said, at the public hearing held on the issue, that 60 people appeared to speak against the proposed resolution and not one appeared to speak in favor of it.[26]

The Law Committee held still another hearing on the subject, in October 1899, on a proposed ordinance requiring scalpers of theatre tickets to stand at least 100 feet from the entrances to venues while plying their trade. That ordinance was drafted at the request of several theatre owners but, said a reporter, sentiment was obviously against it and the proposal would certainly fail. Speaking for the speculators at the hearing, David M. Neuburger explained, "The speculators in tickets have been recognized by the city authorities for nineteen years by the imposition of a license. This, I contend, is an admission of the legitimacy of their business."[27]

One of the earliest state laws was the one enacted in Pennsylvania, on the books at the start of 1884. Described as an act to prevent the selling and vending of theatre tickets on the public streets and highways, it read as follows, Section 1. "It shall not be lawful for any person or persons to sell, barter, or exchange, or offer for sale, barter, or exchange upon the public streets or highways or in front of any theatre or place of amusement and entertainment tickets of admission to such theatre or place of amusement and entertainment." Section 2. "Any person or persons violating the provisions of this act of the Assembly shall be deemed guilty of a misdemeanor and, on conviction, shall be punished by a fine of $50 and imprisonment, not exceeding three months, or either or both for every such offense."[28]

When seats went on sale in September 1887 in Chicago for an engagement starting a week later at the Chicago Opera House the event was so popular that

200 people lined up overnight before the first day of public sales. Despite what were described as "strenuous efforts" to keep tickets out of the hands of speculators, including imposing a purchase limit of four seats per person for each evening of the two-week run, it was admitted scalpers did obtain a few. Due to that situation and other events, an ordinance against theatre ticket scalping was introduced at the meeting of the Chicago City Council and referred to committee. That proposed measure made the selling, or buying with intent to sell, either on the street or at any place except the usual office of a venue, of a ticket or tickets to any theatre or place of amusement, a misdemeanor punishable by a fine of from $20 to $200. Observed a reporter, "There is a doubt about the constitutionality of the law, which would be classed as a police regulation, but its enactment and enforcement would make theatre ticket scalping in Chicago an impossibility."[29]

For the most part, in this period scalpers were small operators who usually worked the streets alone, obtaining tickets any way they could. Ticket agencies or brokers, usually found in hotels, also existed at this time but were less dominant than were the street vendors. And, of course, the street peddlers were far more visible, and annoying, to everybody.

3

Scalpers, 1850–1899

"I have used my utmost endeavors to put down ticket spec-
ulators ... and the most powerful influence has been brought
to bear upon the Police authorities to clear the sidewalk of
the Academy of Music, but without success."

J. H. Mapleson, 1881

Lining up in person at box offices for tickets was a staple scalper tactic of the era, illustrating perhaps that the business was not very big. One man told a reporter in 1869 of his experience in trying to get tickets for the Philharmonic Concerts at an unnamed venue. He arrived at the box office at 8 A.M.—the sale was advertised to start at 9 A.M.—only to find some 15 people ahead of him in line, "That among these were several well-known ticket speculators, some of whom took then, some twenty boxes." As a result it was soon announced that all boxes were sold, with many disappointed people still in line.[1]

An 1870 account of the situation argued the sidewalk speculators could be divided into two groups: those who followed the trade as a means of daily support and main source of revenue, and those who only took to scalping due to unusual circumstances, that is, part-timers. According to this report the number of men who followed the trade as their main source of income was about 20, most notable of whom was a Mr. Brown who was said to have amassed over $10,000 by and through his business. Brown reportedly offered Jarrett and Palmer $2,500 for the exclusive right of selling his tickets on the street in front of their theatre. In the words of a journalist, Brown "is represented to be strictly honorable in his dealings, and has his regular patrons, who, being confident that they can get the best seats in the house from him, and, as a rule, better than they can get on personal application at the box office, willingly pay him the advance of fifty cents which he asks." Naively he added the 50 cent advance was "a price to which he and those of his class always adhere, except when the scarcity of the tickets exposed for sale, brought about by the great rush for them, makes it difficult to get them or forces the speculator himself to pay a premium to obtain a supply to meet the demands of his traffic." As to the other class of black market vendors, the part-timers, this account dismissed them as men who threw discredit upon the regulars. It was those men, who, thinking only of the current moment, gouged their customers with high prices, compared to the regulars who never did such a thing except under the most pressing circumstances. Those part-timers, it was explained, were also the ones that used obnoxious tactics in their efforts to sell, "Cajolery and even bullying is often resorted to in their attempts to rid themselves of their wares at a premium."[2]

Line-ups by scalpers at box offices for tickets soon developed into a tactic where the more ambitious speculators employed an increasing number of proxies to stand in line for them. On the morning of October 1, 1880, at 8 A.M. at Booth's Theatre in New York tickets first went on sale for the performances to be given by actor Sarah Bernhardt, then a huge superstar. Well before midnight on September 30, a line up had formed and it was led, said a reporter, "by a squad of ticket speculators whose faces are as familiar as the three-sheet posters in front of the theatres" advertising Bernhardt as a coming attraction. Tickets for Bernhardt's 24 performances were sold only in sets for the whole series, at $60 each per set, with purchasers limited to a maximum buy of 10 sets. The front part of the line, said a news account, "consisted of men who are seen every night at some of the theatres offering the best seats at a slight advance upon box-office prices, and of the class known as ticket speculators" with the remainder of the line being composed of "shabby boys and half-grown men" — that is, proxies. According to the police most of the men and boys held their positions in line all night. One speculator approached a reporter and offered to sell him good tickets for $4 each for a single performance even though he had not yet acquired them. Just before 8 A.M. Fred Rullman, said to be a well-known speculator, arrived at the box office and replaced the man who had been first in line. Some of those in the line, apparently with no prearranged deal with a scalper, offered their place in line for prices ranging from $5 down to $2. When the box office opened Rullman bought his 10 sets of seats for $600. The next two dozen or so in line also each bought and paid for 10 sets and each dropped them into Rullman's satchel as they left the window. Sales of seats for Bernhardt's performances in the first hour the box office was open were said to have totaled $24,000, of which $15,000 or so came from Rullman and his assistants.[3]

A few months later, in February 1881, a man who signed himself as "Verity" wrote an angry letter to the editor in which he described his experiences in trying to buy seats for the opera at the Academy of Music box office. Verity protested vehemently against the "fraudulent manner" in which sales were conducted and that the approach to the Academy box office was "lined by a gang of speculators who infest this locality and it is an impossibility for purchasers, particularly ladies, to reach said office without being subjected to their rude and impertinent appeals for patronage." Even if one did reach the box office, Verity continued, no good seats were available even days prior to the desired performance, and one was then chagrined to be referred to the speculators by the box office staff. All those things, explained Verity, had personally happened to him many times and to other people he knew.[4]

Following Verity's outburst a letter in response came from J. H. Mapleson, director of the Academy of Music. Said the director, "Ever since I have had the direction of the Academy of Music I have used my utmost endeavors to put down ticket speculators ... and the most powerful influence has been brought to bear upon the Police authorities to clear the sidewalks of the Academy of Music, but without success." As to the assertions his box office staff affably directed people to scalpers or that he countenanced the imposition of the situation on patrons, he dismissed as "utterly false." However, he added, "but the public, nine cases out of ten, prefer to go to the ticket speculator rather than have the trouble of waiting in the cue...."[5]

Later in 1881 scalpers and their proxies spent the night in line in front of the Academy of Music in Brooklyn to be among the first in line for the sale of seats that began the following morning for Madame Patti's concert, to be held several days later. A large number of $5 seats were bought by the scalpers, with several of the speculators turning around and selling them on the spot for as much as $10 each to people too far back in the line to get the ticket locations they wanted.[6]

A throng of men and boys lined up overnight in front of Wallack's Theatre in November 1882 to get seats for a Lily Langtry performance when the box office opened at 8 A.M. the next morning. Men in the line were scalpers while the boys were all employed by them. The first speculator to show up did so at 5:30 P.M. the day before. One speculator explained to a reporter that because no one was allowed to purchase more than four seats, he had employed six messenger boys, at 30 cents an hour, to line up all night long.[7]

When sales opened early in January 1883 in St. Louis for a concert by singer Mme. Nilsson, the line of purchasers that first day was said to have been composed mainly of speculators or their agents, with the first day's sales reaching $3,000 and most of those seats going to scalpers. Over the following eight or so days the scalpers reportedly succeeded in getting rid of most of their tickets ($3 face) at prices ranging from $6 to $10 each. It was estimated their aggregate profits reached from $5,000 to $8,000. At the last minute it was announced the concert was cancelled — Nilsson had developed a sore throat — and it was then that ticket holders were annoyed to learn they would only get a refund of $3 per ticket.[8]

Approximately nine boys hired by scalpers lined up for three days in September 1883 before ticket sales started at the Star Theatre in New York for performances by British actor Henry Irving. When a reporter spoke to the boys he was told that a man had hired them to hold places in line but they refused to name him. W. W. Tillotson, a spokesman for Mrs. Abbey, promoter of the Irving performances, acknowledged that undoubtedly the people in line were hired by speculators but, "All that a manager can do in this matter is to limit the number of tickets to be sold to any one man, and Mr. Abbey has placed the limit at 10. The Star Theatre holds, I think, about 1,500 people, and there will be plenty of good seats, even supposing every speculator in the City secured his first choice."[9]

Seats for Irving's performances (24 in all) were limited to a maximum of 10 sets of 24 each, for $60 per set. Single tickets were also available at $3 each. Messenger boys (their day job) were paid 30 cents an hour to line up while a number of older boys were paid $5 a day and supplied with meals and cigars. One speculator was said to have invested over $10,000 in buying seats. As in the past, several boys in the line were not tied directly to a scalper but were there freelance, hoping to sell their place to some latecomer — for example, a private buyer who did not want to go to the end of the line. On the first day of sales some 511 ticket sets were sold, for a gross of $30,660 with 80 percent of them, reportedly, taken up by speculators.[10]

A civil lawsuit was brought in May 1885 by scalper Leon Stedeker against theatre owner Augustin Daly to recover $33 for tickets to Daly's Theatre after the ticket holders were refused admittance to the venue. Barney Aaron testified he met Stedeker on March 23 and was asked by him to purchase for him two tickets to Daly's. Stedeker gave Aaron $3 with which the latter went to the box office, bought the seats, and gave them to the scalper. At the box office Aaron was asked for his name and gave it. Robert McVeaney testified that on the evening of March 23 he bought two tickets from Stedeker for Daly's but the doorman refused him admission, explaining the refusal was because the seats had been bought from a scalper. McVeaney returned to Stedeker who directed him to go to the box office and demand the cost of the tickets. He did so, but the money was refused. Then Stedeker refunded the money to McVeaney. However, Daly's refused to refund the cost of the tickets to the scalper. Stedeker explained that he often purchased tickets through others, such as with Aaron in this case, because he was often refused any seats when he went in person, being a well-known speculator. No outcome of the case was reported.[11]

Counterfeit tickets were sometimes sold to unsuspecting purchasers as a scalper tactic, but it was not too common. The Arion Society held a ball at Madison Square Garden in February 1895 and found itself victimized by phony tickets. Some 400 of the $10 tickets were accepted at the door before the swindle was uncovered. Another 300 turned up later with counterfeit items and were refused admission. Virtually none of those people paid another $10 at the door to get in; as a result the $9,000 profit the Arion Society expected to make dwindled down to $2,000. Three speculators were arrested that night as they had continued to openly carry on the selling of spurious tickets in front of the

Garden. Richard Weinacht, president of the Society remarked that if his group ever gave another ball "we shall make it a strict rule not to accept any ticket purchased on the sidewalk."[12]

Violence among the scalpers was not unknown. James F. Hyde shot William Turnbull dead in front of the Fourteenth Street Theatre in New York on March 22, 1890. Both men were speculators and the cause of the shooting was an altercation arising out of the pursuit of their calling. According to Hyde, a great crowd of people were gathered around the box office and Turnbull was annoying them by trying to sell them seats. Hyde, who, said a reporter, "has the speculating privileges of the house" tried to shoo his rival away. One word led to another and then Turnbull punched Hyde and knocked him down. Then he kicked his prostrate opponent and jabbed at his eye with the point of his umbrella, making a wound on Hyde's cheek. Hyde struggled up and they tussled some more before Hyde drew a pistol and shot Turnbull. A policeman arrived and took Hyde into custody. A reporter described Hyde as "one of the best known ticket speculators in New York, and has heretofore borne an excellent reputation among all classes of theatrical people" whereas Turnbull "had an ugly and quarrelsome disposition. The management of the Fourteenth-Street Theatre say that he has caused them more trouble than all other ticket speculators combined." A few days later at an inquest into the death of Turnbull the jury delivered a verdict of self-defense on the part of Hyde.[13]

Over this period the fixed site office for selling tickets (away from the venue box office), hotel agencies initially, grew tremendously. The first established theatre ticket agency in New York, according to an 1870 news item, was the one still then in operation at the St. Nicholas Hotel, which had been run for about five years by Harry Powers although he was no longer involved with the agency. No start date for that agency was given. Reportedly, that agency was encouraged by the hotel proprietor as it was considered a great convenience by hotel guests. By its hotel lease that agency was restricted to charging a maximum of a 50 cent advance over the box office price for the seats. Those seats offered at hotel agencies were usually among the best in the venue. Early hotel agencies, and any others located at fixed sites not in hotels, did not confine themselves solely to theatre tickets but also sold "cards of admission" to all kinds of entertainment events such as balls, lectures, readings, and so on. Similar ticket agencies to the one at the St. Nicholas were said to have been established by 1870 in all the principal hotels in New York City. Virtually all those agency proprietors, though, made ticket vending an adjunct of other business such as the sale of notions, magazines, stationery, and so forth. Those agencies, it was claimed by a reporter, were recognized by theatre managers, encouraged by them, and given special privileges. Among the privileges were "pick" of the house for seats and the right to return all unsold tickets to the venue for a refund, provided they did so at least a few minutes before the show began.[14]

By 1893 a newspaper editor observed that while the street speculator could theoretically at least be eliminated, one type that could not be was "the hotel speculator," also believing theatrical managers were completely in his power. Originally, argued the editor, the large hotels were furnished with seats to sell as an accommodation to the traveling public, and of course they charged a "small advance" over the box office price, which the editor described as reasonable and just. But the original scheme had grown to "gigantic" proportions, "and the managers are powerless in the grip of the hotel speculator. Hotel after hotel has established its theatre ticket office and demanded the choicest seats for its patrons." If the manager refused to comply, he faced the prospect that other and more compliant houses than his own would be recommended to the guests of the hotel who were looking for an evening's entertainment. Some of the managers were said to demand a share of the profits from those hotel agencies, but the editor felt the shrewd ones did not because they knew their houses would be recommended over the others because the hotel got more profits. "In any event, the hotel seller is master of the situation, the managers are completely within his power, and they can not fairly be criticized for being accessory to this form of speculation," concluded the newsman.[15]

War on speculators was declared regularly by theatre managers as they tried various strategies to eliminate the practice. Sometimes they actually meant it; sometimes it was just rhetoric, delivering to the general public and the media what they felt was wanted to be heard while actively, but quietly, they colluded with the scalpers.

4

War on Scalpers, or Collusion, 1850–1899

"I will admit that I was drawn into a business connection with speculators, but I am done with them now."
Mr. Goodwin, manager, Walnut Street Theatre, Philadelphia, 1882

"But as to managers being in with ticket speculators, why of course we're in with them. Why shouldn't we be?"
Harry Miner, theatrical manager, New York City, 1883

"The abuse can never be cured wholly until the people refuse ever to buy seats from speculators, and it is not reasonable to suppose that such a heavenly state of things will ever come to pass."
Daniel Frohman, Lyceum Theatre, New York City, 1893

One of the earliest tactics used by theatrical managers to combat scalping was employment of the auction system. A special notice advertisement placed in the newspaper for the New York entertainment venue Niblo's Garden (the ad was signed by James M. Nixon) in September 1860 explained that because of the high demand for seats for an upcoming performance by a Mr. Forrest, and wanting to give everybody a fair and equal chance, 250 of the desired orchestra seats were to be sold by public auction in the vestibule of the theatre. All of the remaining seats would be sold to the public at the box office at the usual prices — Family Circle 25 cents, Parquet and Dress Circle, 50 cents. "I have been induced by a desire that the masses should have to pay no more than usual to see the renowned tragedian," Nixon explained in the ad. "I have, furthermore, determined that during Mr. Forrest's engagement, and at all times, ticket speculators shall be excluded from the theatre and its vicinity. I do not intend my patrons shall be imposed upon in any way I can prevent, and I hereby warn all from buying tickets except at the office."[1]

Seats for opening night at Wallack's new theatre were sold on December 29, 1881, at auction by John H. Draper, auctioneer. It attracted a crowd of about 400 men, many of them said to be Wall Street brokers. Draper explained that in order to not give speculators too much of an opportunity, no more than 10 seats would be sold to any one bidder, and the 10 seats purchased together had to be in the same row (scalpers usually preferred to buy, say, two tickets in the middle of a row and go back row by row rather than buy all across a single row). Top prices paid for seats at the auction were $16 and $15, going down to $10 as the rows available got farther back. Wallack's new theatre opened in the first week of January 1882 with a production of *School for Scandal*.[2]

An auction of tickets for the Music Festival in May 1882 at Chickering Hall in New York was an event where it was said the scalper "abounded," with Fred Rullman and Mr. Tyson singled out by name. During the course of the sale, said a reporter, about 1,000 seats were sold with about half going to speculators. Also noted as a feature of the auction were the seat purchases made by the Festival managers, ostensibly for people in Boston, Philadelphia, and elsewhere. "The regular speculators, however, were rude enough to insinuate that the managers were engaging in a little private speculation game of their own," asserted the account.[3]

Another common measure adopted by venues was the one in use as the 1870-1871 theatrical season opened. Most of the venues that opened placed in front of their doors signs warning the public "that tickets purchased from sidewalk speculators will be refused at the door." Such refusals, of course, led to many angry confrontations between ticket holders and door staff. One war of words at Booth's Theatre in 1870 led to the theatre manager causing the arrest of the would-be patron on the charge of disorderly conduct. At issue was whether a theatre could refuse a citizen admission when the latter had bought his seat from a sidewalk speculator or from "any other man." Managers claimed scalping was an evil they wanted to do away with on behalf of their patrons and argued they had a right to say who could stand in front of their houses to sell tickets, or who could stand there for any other purpose. Speculators countered that the managers wanted to speculate themselves, by preventing others from engaging in the business they thereby enjoyed a monopoly, and their real desire was to increase their gains, as opposed to benefiting the public. As far as they were concerned they had a right to purchase as many tickets to a performance as they pleased and to dispose of those tickets any way they pleased.[4]

Management of the Barnum and London traveling circus show determined to end scalping of their tickets in 1881 when they were performing in Bridgeport, Connecticut. Thus, it was decided to issue new and different tickets for each performance, and that all would be dated, even though the new method involved the outlay of $30 to $40 a day for new tickets. Reportedly the plan worked well. When the new tickets were used for the first time on May 20, 10 to 15 scalpers were around the venue but agents for the show stood on the streets and warned people not to buy from those men as the tickets would not be accepted at the door. By nightfall the speculators were said to have been ready to surrender. One of them went to the Barnum management, said he had 700 tickets in total that he had got in Brooklyn, and if the managers would buy them back he would sign a paper agreeing to stop following the show. Another speculator had 200 tickets and was prepared to accept the same terms. "The result was that the whole gang were called in and their tickets taken back and paid for, and all signed an agreement to give up the business," observed a journalist.[5]

Philadelphia's leading theatrical managers— Goodwin, Haverly, Zimmerman, Hall, Pugh, Carncross, Gallagher, and Mrs. Drew — joined forces to declare "war" against the ticket speculators at the beginning of 1882. All were supposedly opposed to the "loud-mouthed peddlers who infest the lobbies of their theatres, and declare they will do everything in their power to prevent them from securing tickets to resell." Hall, manager of the Lyceum Theatre, was bitterly opposed to the scalpers and had been at war with them all season, although he admitted he found it useless to try and prevent them from securing seats and that he had no power to drive them from the pavement in front of his venue. The moment a scalper appeared in front of his house, one of his box office employees went out to the sidewalk, explained Hall, "and sells at regular prices side by side with the professional peddler, who charges fancy prices." Gallagher, who managed the Grand Central Theatre, was then being sued by speculator William J. Beecher for malicious prosecution stemming from an incident a week earlier. To circumvent Beecher, who had bought his tickets in the afternoon, Gallagher issued tickets of a different color at night and refused to honor Beecher's, with the result that four or five people who had bought seats from the scalpers were refused entry. One thing led to another and after "some unpleasantness" Gallagher ordered "his special officer" to arrest Beecher. Taken to the police station he was, however, immediately discharged as the prosecutor declared there was no substantial case against him.[6]

The situation in Philadelphia and the response to it by theatrical managers there drew praise from an editor with the *New York Times* who especially liked the plan of selling side by side against the scalper. He added, "No action on the part of theatrical managers will be assured of such cordial public sympathy and support as a sincere and combined effort to abate the nuisance and injustice of ticket speculation." As to the argument regularly advanced by managers that scalpers could not be stopped from obtaining tickets because of tactics such as using proxies, this editor wondered if such an assertion were true since it was not likely scalpers could thrive "within the lobbies and about the entrance of theatres were the managers to combine against them or seek to keep their business within the limits of propriety and public comfort." Although the editor believed that a man who had bought a ticket had the right to sell it at a profit if he could, "he should not be allowed to make a nuisance of himself in the bargaining."[7]

An 1885 news story proclaimed that speculators had become extinct at the Fifth Avenue Theatre because manager John Stetson instituted a complicated system of writing down a purchaser's name and seat number on the ticket and in a book (generating two separate records). When people arrived for a performance records were compared and while the system required twice as many people to be working in the box office and tied up the lobby somewhat, it was effective. However, not everybody was happy with the result because, said a reporter, "Meanwhile not a night goes by without more or less angry protests at the box office against the absence of speculators"—nearly everybody who came late and could not get good seats wanted to know why there were no speculators around. An exasperated Stetson exclaimed, "You can't satisfy some people no matter how hard you try. These folks would not have speculators, and now they won't get along without them. I should like to know what a man is to do under these circumstances."[8]

On October 27, 1885, Theodore Moss (treasurer of Wallack's Theatre), accompanied by ex–Judge A. J. Dittenhoefer as his legal counsel, met with New York Police Captain Alexander S. Williams and presented him with a petition (signed by the owners and tenants of buildings in the immediate area of his venue) to remove all people engaged in selling tickets from in front of Wallack's. Williams said he could not comply because all the ticket vendors had regular licenses. Dittenhoefer argued the city's Common Council had no right to legalize a nuisance. Pointed out to Williams was the fact that Moss then had in force an injunction that restrained several specific scalpers from monopolizing the sidewalk in front of and in the neighborhood of Wallack's but that Moss did not want to take that course toward all sidewalk speculators because it would involve "a hundred suits." And besides, Moss did not see why he had to go to the bother of adopting such measures against men who were "simple nuisances." Police Commissioner Stephen French deferred the matter by saying he wanted competent legal advice.[9]

In the mind of one reporter at least that position by Moss represented a complete reversal, for "Mr. Moss has long been regarded as the most tenacious supporter of the general idea of ticket speculation. In both of the theatres bearing the name of Mr. Lester Wallack private speculators have always been run by Moss, and upon all great engagements a very large amount of money has been cleared in that direction." Still, this newsman felt that with Moss joining Daly in a war on scalping there was little doubt that nearly all the other managers in the city would join in. At that time Daly's Theatre issued tickets with a paragraph printed on the back stating a ticket would not be honored if it was bought from a speculator.[10]

From that meeting with Police Captain Williams, Moss came away with the idea that in the future scalpers would be kept away from his venue and/or arrested. But later in 1885 they appeared in force on several nights. One night, when Moss said four scalpers were operating in front of his house, he asked police officer Genore, present near the house, to stop them but Genore said he had seen no soliciting and declined to arrest them. That caused Moss to send an urgent message to police headquarters asking for a superior executive officer to attend at his venue, but he was told that none of the officers he had named were then at the station.[11]

Wallack's continued its war on speculators a year or two later, led by a different individual with the venue, Colonel McCaull. According to one account he drove scalpers away completely from his venue in the summer of 1886 but they had returned in August 1887, after a year's absence, when a sold-out opera playing at Wallack's drew them back as they were able to sell tickets for as much as $5 ($1.50 face). That development caused McCaull to wage war anew on the black market vendors. Posters containing a warning in large letters advising the public not to buy seats from speculators as they would not be honored at the door were conspicuously displayed around the theatre. A petition to the police (seemingly like the earlier one) to keep the street clear fell on more receptive ears this time and resulted in "a force of police to carry out the wishes of the petitioners." In the end the scalpers were excluded entirely from the block in which the venue stood and forced to ply their trade from far away. Also, McCaull assigned a spotter to stand beside each speculator and warn potential customers not to buy as they would be denied entry. One speculator was said to have been forced to sell his tickets back to McCaull for face with the latter only agreeing to the transaction because they were good seats and he did not want to see them wasted since people were nightly turned away from the box office due to sell-outs.[12]

A year after that, with scalpers seemingly once more gone from Wallack's during that time, they returned to the venue while it hosted a very successful production of *Prince Methuselah*. One morning the venue's business manager, Mr. Stevens, noticed people buying seats at the box office that he knew to be working in the interest of scalpers who did not want to show up in person. Determined to eliminate them, Stevens stationed a squad of men in front of the venue with instructions to warn any people approached by the speculators not to buy from them as those tickets would not be honored. Also, two policemen were obtained and placed on guard. When the scalpers began to arrive, one of the policemen drove four or five of them away and they did not return. Others stood farther away and worked "quietly."[13]

With respect to the tactic employed by many venues whereby notices were posted that seats bought from scalpers would not be accepted, a journalist commented cynically in 1889, "The manner in which ticket speculators stand in front of the signs at the Metropolitan Opera House, which declare with great positiveness that 'No tickets purchased on the sidewalk will be accepted at the door,' and sell the bits of pasteboard with perfect security that they will be accepted, is decidedly amusing to persons who have purchased tickets ahead."[14]

In obedience to a summons issued by Police Justice O'Reilly, at the request of licensed ticket speculator Edward McDermott, against Carl Herman, business manager of New York's Standard Theatre, the latter appeared in court in March 1889 to answer the complaint made by the speculator who charged Herman illegally interfered with him in his business. McDermott said that a few days earlier when he was selling seats at the venue entrance a private detective employed by the house management told one of his customers not to buy from the speculator as the tickets would be refused by the doorman. Nevertheless, the man bought two tickets for $5 ($1.50 face each) from McDermott and then was indeed refused entry to the theatre. McDermott was compelled to refund the money. That action by the theatre management in refusing the tickets, argued McDermott, was an unwarranted interference with his business. He further declared the tickets for the best seats in the house were sent to the hotels to be sold there for $2 each, a 50 cent advance over the box office price, and that he bought his tickets from the hotel agencies for $2 and resold them for $2.50, making a profit of 50 cents per ticket. Herman said management had been greatly annoyed by the speculators and had refused to sell them seats and had printed on the tickets and posted notices in the lobby that seats purchased from sidewalk speculators would be refused.[15]

Justice O'Reilly said, in his opinion, management had no right to refuse admission to holders of tickets issued by the theatre, no matter from whom they were purchased and told Herman that McDermott, being a licensed speculator, must be permitted to exercise his calling under his license, for which he paid a fee to the city, and must not be interfered with so long as he did not infringe upon the terms of his license and did not violate any law. O'Reilly told McDermott that if any person interfered with him while he was in the peaceable and legal pursuit of his business he would, on a complaint, issue a warrant for such person or persons.[16]

A number of speculators and theatrical managers and doorkeepers met on May 1, 1889, ostensibly to talk, discuss, and peacefully settle "business matters" connected with the issue of ticket sales. But they were unable to amicably adjust their claims and a fist fight erupted between the two groups, with one of the more severely injured being Louis Waldron of the Broadway Theatre, "who was beaten and kicked in the face."[17]

When theatre operator Edward Harrigan appeared at a hearing held by New York's City Council to consider the issue of speculator licenses in 1891, he argued scalpers were a nuisance and should be abolished. Efforts had been made, he said, to prevent their getting tickets but they just sent proxies— typically messenger boys— to the box office who said they were buying the seats for theatre parties. Alderman Noonan asked Harrigan if it was not a fact that managers frequently sold the privilege of their lobbies to speculators. While admitting it was done sometimes he explained he kept such a man in his lobby to "protect" patrons from being imposed upon by outsiders, but his man was instructed never to charge more than a 50 cent advance on a seat. "This statement caused some merriment," among the aldermen, remarked a reporter. Lawyer George Wahle, for the scalpers, led Harrigan to acknowledge in some instance the profits of speculators were shared by the managers. Three scalpers declared separately that they had never known more than $1 extra to be added to the price of a ticket in front of Harrigan's. To that assertion Alderman Noonan countered he had been obliged to pay $8 for two tickets ($1.50 face each) in front of Harrigan's Theatre.[18]

Daniel L. Frohman, manager of New York's Lyceum Theatre, remarked at the start of 1893 that for the previous three years he had been doing all he could to break up the "nuisance" of the man on the sidewalk and to make things as agreeable as possible for the public in the matter of ticket selling. All through that period he had displayed signs at the entrance to his venue, he explained, that tickets sold on the sidewalk would not be accepted at the door "but today, for the first time, I have advertised in the newspapers that speculators are not allowed at the Lyceum Theatre, and that all the seats are sold to the public at the box office," admitting it was possible for unknown scalpers, or proxies, to buy small quantities of tickets. To keep the black market vendors away from adjoining property, which the theatre did not own, Frohman got permissions from those owners to remove any speculators. He kept two men in the front of the venue on the watch for scalpers and he often went there himself to stand watch. When he spotted people about to buy seats from a speculator he went over and said, "I am Mr. Frohman, the manager of this theatre, and I must warn you that those tickets will not be received at the door." In Frohman's view the people who did not mind scalpers and who bought from them were in the minority; the majority wanted to buy seats at regular prices at the box offices and they should prevail. Seats at his venue were sold up to three weeks in advance as a matter of course and up to six weeks in advance to anyone who applied.[19]

With respect to the selling of Lyceum tickets at hotel agencies, Frohman declared he limited the number available through such outlets and that more than 80 percent of the seats were retained at the box office and sold from there. He argued it was right and proper to put a certain number of seats on sale at hotels for the convenience of their guests, "But I make it a rule to keep the number of seats given to Mr. Tyson less than he calls for. This is right because it preserves the right proportion between the seats offered at the hotels and at the box office. More persons are turned away from the box office because there are no seats left for them than are turned away from the hotels for the same reason." According to Frohman, the Lyceum absolutely refused to enter into any agreement with the hotels in the way of sharing any extra profits from the sale of seats at advanced prices. "There is no collusion between speculators of any sort and myself against the general public, as most persons are ready to believe, but it is unfortunate that in a number of instances the box offices of theatres do deal with speculators for the sake of the extra profit, which the public has to pay," remarked the showman. Claiming he did all he could to give the public first chance at the box office, Frohman concluded, "The abuse can never be cured wholly until the people refuse ever to buy seats from speculators, and it is not reasonable to suppose that such a heavenly state of things will ever come to pass."[20]

Little more than a year later scalper Alfred B. Sullivan attempted to take legal action against Frohman. He tried to secure an arrest warrant against Frohman but having failed, proposed to make some move in the Supreme Court. Frohman assumed Sullivan was being financed and encouraged by the "syndicate" of speculators. The basis of Sullivan's attempted legal action was that by declining to accept tickets from people who had purchased them from him Frohman made his license, for which he paid a fee to the city, worthless. A firmly held belief by Frohman was that no license held by a scalper could force the Lyceum to accept tickets for which more than the regular price had been paid by the holder. "Sullivan has threatened to make trouble for me since I began the war on the speculators. He didn't like the presence of my sandwich [board] man on the sidewalk, warning the public that his tickets would be refused at the door," explained Frohman. He was determined to control the sale of tickets at the Lyceum and do what he could to eliminate scalpers "until a properly authorized court advises me that I have no right to interfere with the speculators. By this time the Lyceum Theatre had a large illuminated sign in front of the house that warned the public against patronizing the speculators.[21]

In September 1894 James Scott of Beaver Falls, Pennsylvania, bought a ticket for Daly's Theatre on the street in front of the venue, was refused entry, and become upset to the point he was forcibly ejected from the house and placed under arrest. Scott was charged with disorderly conduct but was discharged in the Jefferson Market Police Court the following day when Daly's representative in court, Arthur Rehan, declined to press a complaint. A number of speculators in court went away disappointed because they had hoped to launch a test case on a manager's right to refuse a genuine ticket. It was precisely because Daly's did not want to furnish the material for such a test case that the venue declined to pursue the complaint. Richard Dorney, venue business manager, declared, "There are but a very few tickets in the hands of speculators. Those, I suppose, were purchased one or two at a time. The speculators asked permission to sell what tickets they had to tonight, but we refused to grant permission. Mr. Daly will not tolerate speculation in tickets." Dorney added Daly made no extra profit on the seats that were sold at the hotel agencies; six seats for each performance were placed on sale at Gilsey House, six at the Windsor Hotel, and 10 at the Fifth Avenue Hotel.[22]

Oscar Hammerstein was another showman who waged war on scalpers; in his case it was in front of the Olympia in New York in June 1896. About 10 speculators were lined up along the sidewalk offering tickets for the roof garden show. They were charging as much as $7 for $1.50 seats and up to $20 for $6 boxes. Determined to stop it, Hammerstein stationed several of his own men on the sidewalk to follow people who bought seats from scalpers and point them out to the door staff, who denied them entry. William D. Mertons bought four tickets for his party from a scalper and after he was refused admission called over a policeman and had speculator William Collister arrested. Taken to the police station, the authorities refused to hold him when Collister showed them the license he had from New York City permitting him to speculate in tickets. Hammerstein also had placards placed in conspicuous places around the venue saying that tickets purchased from speculators would be valueless.[23]

Efforts by ticket speculators to secure all the desirable seats at Allen's Grand Opera House in Washington, DC, in 1896 were broken up by Allen himself. A line of scalpers had formed and been standing in front of the box office before tickets were placed on sale for a popular show. Scalpers had planned to corner the market but Allen dispersed the line and placed a limit on each man's purchase. He announced that one person could not buy at one time more than 10 seats, and only one of them could be an aisle seat. According to a news account if Allen had not taken that action all the best seats in the Grand Opera House would have fallen into the hands of speculators and the public would have been at their mercy. Hawkins Taylor, a speculator, secured first place in line and then hired two men at $3 a day to hold the place for him, one during the day and the other at night. One night the fellow was approached by another scalper who offered the place-holder $25 for the spot. Thus, Taylor's night man sold out and when Taylor arrived with the day man in the morning he found his first place was lost. Taylor went to the police and demanded the other scalper be arrested but was informed that no legal offense had been committed.[24]

More direct evidence of collusion was not hard to come by in this time period. When that unidentified man went to a New York venue in 1869 to get tickets for the Philharmonic Concerts only to find himself behind a line of some 15 well-known scalpers who proceeded to buy all the best seats as soon as the box office opened, he could not help but wonder. Since the scalpers were known and readily recognized did that not indicate the box office staff was equally aware and "these latter persons are in collusion with the speculators in their scheme to impose upon the public?" Commented a reporter, "it is not easy to believe that such facts can exist, especially as what is now charged is but a repetition of abuses that were allowed to be perpetuated last season."[25]

An April 1875 letter to the editor signed "Acorn" grumbled there was no such thing as ticket speculators because the true name for the men permanently stationed in the outside lobbies of the main theatres was that of "outside" ticket-sellers, since they "worked" for the venues. It was a sentiment held by many at the time. According to Acorn the four leading theatres were Wallack's, Booth's, Daly's, and the Union Square with the system being the same at all four. That is, the outside man was supplied with a certain number of tickets at the same time they were placed on sale at the box office, covering the same time period. At the end of each night he settled up with the house. Usually that outside man added a 50 cent advance to the box office price. For the privilege of making 50 cents per ticket at the Union Square Theatre the outside man paid them $40 per week, $60 at the Fifth Avenue Theatre. At Wallack's Theatre the profits were said to have been divided equally between the outside man and the venue. In all cases the extra money went directly to the theatre management, as opposed to the producers of the show and/or the talent involved in the performance, who were sometimes paid a percentage of the box office receipts. However, added Acorn, no profit was made by any one connected with the theatres from tickets sold through the hotel agencies. Those brokers bought from the venue at regular prices, kept the 50 cent advance they imposed, and returned unsold tickets to the house each night for credit. A seat at most major theatres then went for, roughly, $1.50 at the box office. Acorn argued the situation was especially bad at Booth's and Wallack's, where good seats were just never available at the box office no matter when one arrived there or however far in advance one wanted seats. At one popular show, said Acorn, "It is no exaggeration to say that Booth's outsider sold for that performance 600 tickets, making a very neat profit of $300, to be divided between himself and the management...."[26]

In the face of Philadelphia's leading theatrical lights joining forces to declare war on the scalpers in 1882, a reporter jibed, "This stand on the part of the managers has excited a great deal of comment today, and as some of the reformers are known to have made a regular practice of supplying the speculators with tickets and sharing the profits, many persons are inclined to think the crusade is a 'put up job.'" Mr. Haverly's agents at his new Chestnut Street Theatre were said to have allowed Thomas Carman and two or three other speculators to obtain about 300 choice seats for an event to be staged just a few days after the war on scalpers was declared. Goodwin, of the Walnut Street Theatre admitted, "I will admit that I was drawn into a business connection with speculators, but I am done with them now. The system offends my best patrons and I make little or nothing by practicing it."[27]

Surveying that Philadelphia situation an editor with the *New York Times* remarked, "It is known that in the past managers have often sanctioned ticket speculation, and have shared in the profits of the imposition which it works on theatre-goers." He felt the imposition of speculators "becomes intolerable when there is reason to believe that the manager reaps a profit from such transactions."[28]

An early example of how ticket agencies and theatrical producers worked together to ensure concerts took place, and where the former had a significant say in what was produced, could be seen in 1882 when J. Mapleson of the Academy of Music engaged Italian opera star Adelina Patti to perform in New York in a season commencing in October that year. Under the contract Mapleson agreed to pay Patti $4,400 per night for her services with a cash payment to be made to her at the start of her season of $42,000, a sum that was both a deposit and a guarantee. Mapleson probably could not have met those high expenses were it not for the fact that in April, six months before Patti's first performance, Tyson and Fred Rullman, "the two largest ticket speculators in the world" gave guarantees that they would take in total over $50,000 worth of tickets for Patti's concerts.[29]

A letter to the editor from "Stay At Home" in December 1883 complained he had gone to the Star Theatre the day before to buy a seat for *Richelieu* but found there was nothing closer than 19 rows from the orchestra, a situation that was true for every night of the engagement. And after a speculator in the lobby offered him a ticket for a "greatly advanced price" he became irate. "In order to get more out of their patrons, do they rent their lobbies to speculators, who swindle such impatient people as have not the self-control to stay at home?" he thundered. Personally, he refused to buy seats from scalpers and see his money go to a class "whose relations to the drama are only a disgrace to it." Rather than patronize them, he urged people to agitate for legislation to "abate the nuisance" and to stay at home until it was obtained. That letter set off a storm of controversy about collusion that generated a number of news articles and many letters to the editor over the remainder of the month.[30]

A couple of days later a reporter went to the Star Theatre, passing three or four speculators on the way in. At the box office he asked for the best seats but was told the best available were in the 17th row back from the orchestra and there was nothing better on any night for the coming two weeks— all orchestra seats were $1.50 at the box office. On the next afternoon the same reporter got the same story at the box office except that the 22nd row was then the best available. Scalpers in the lobby offered him seats in the 1st or 2nd row ($2) or in the 10th row ($2.50) and, said the reporter, "Neither of the men had badges visible" as they were required if they were licensed by the city of New York. At one of the Tyson hotel agencies the best available was in the 13th row ($2) while a Fred Rullman outlet on Broadway offered the 10th row ($2.25). When the reporter suggested at Rullman's that $2.25 was a steep price to pay for a $1.50 ticket, the clerk said he had to pay a speculator $2 to obtain the seat for his agency. At another ticket agency on Broadway (one of those owned by T. J. McBride) the best offer was middle of the house at $2.25; that office also claimed it paid a scalper $2 for the ticket.[31]

An unnamed informant told the reporter the sidewalk speculators were not the real problem; the system was an old one in which most venues used their own outside man and gave him all the best seats to sell in the lobby, either splitting the proceeds with him or paying the man in the lobby a salary. That is, it was all collusion as the speculators (the real independent ones) did not get the best tickets. According to the informant the man in the lobby at the Fourteenth Street Theatre was William Guernsey; at the Fifth Avenue, Ed McDermott; at Wallack's, Gus Hamilton; at the Rankins' new theatre on Third Avenue,

Ward and O'Brien; at Harrigan and Hart's, Ed Harrigan's father, assisted by three or four other men; at the Union Square, George Tyson; and at Niblo's, Brown and Carman. "With the exception of the Academy of Music and the Casino, every theatre in New York is in with outside men, either speculators or men in their own employ..." added the informant.[32]

With respect to the Star Theatre the informant said the lobby man charged 75 to 100 percent over the box office price, hawking seats in the lobby for $2.50 to $3. Some of the venues were said to sell their houses for the season to the man in the lobby — that is, for a certain sum they gave the lobby man first pick of the seats, allowed him to pay for the seats after he had sold them, and allowed him to return all unsold seats. William Hennion, the lobby man at Daly's, reportedly paid 90 percent of his receipts to management, which was the smallest profit margin any lobby man worked under, while a fair price for the season at the Union Square Theatre was $2,000 and 50 percent of the scalping proceeds after the $2,000 was made.[33]

Also angry about the collusion was the *New York Times*, which editorialized, "This is plainly unjust to the public.... Keeping an agent to whom it is necessary to disavow to the customers to whom you refer him is neither an honorable nor a businesslike proceeding." Another point made was that such activity hurt actors and producing companies whose pay was based on a percentage of box office receipts as the extra money theatres made from collusion with scalpers never showed up as box office receipts, keeping that figure lower than it really was. Still, the editor did not object to a theatre charging more for seats when it felt it had a hit, just that it should be done in an open and straightforward manner.[34]

Harry Miner, who managed three theatres in New York City, agreed with the idea that collusion was widespread, "I don't mean to say that it is customary for managers to take out nearly the whole of their orchestra and give it to the speculator in the lobby, but it has been done on several occasions. But as to managers being in with ticket speculators, why, of course we're in with them. Why shouldn't we be?" Miner said it was because theatres could not eliminate scalpers, and many had tried, so the venues had to go in with them or the speculators would get all the extra profits. According to Miner the scalper who had the lobby privilege of a house got as many tickets as he wanted and sold them for $1.75 ($1.50 face), at least that was his understanding with the manager, with the extra 25 cents split equally between them. When he sold a seat for more than $1.75, and Miner admitted that happened, the speculator kept all the extra. Claiming that in the long run a manager lost more than he gained from dealing with speculators, Miner said he was willing to end the whole business "provided every other manager in this City will do the same. I'd be a fool to do it all alone." He added he would support legislation to ban speculators, again provided other managers would do the same. Responding to collusion charges in his venue — the Union Square Theatre — spokesman Sheridan Shook exclaimed tersely there was no collusion with scalpers. Reportedly, there were then 94 licensed ticket speculators in New York City.[35]

Seven letters to the editor on the topic of collusion were published in the *New York Times* on a single day, December 15, 1883. All expressed anger at what theatre managers were allegedly doing, and all seemingly believed the charges. Some advocated boycotting establishments engaged in collusion while others supported the idea of legislation against the practice, and so on. One of those letters was from Daniel Frohman of the Madison Square Theatre, who wondered why the theatrical managers should try to fight the ticket speculators' system when the city licensed them, gave them badges, "and supports them in selling the seats in front of the theatres at any excess price they choose to impose on their customers." Of course Frohman was trying to divert attention away from the managers and shift the blame to the city of New York.[36]

When a reporter visited Harrigan and Hart's Theatre on Broadway on the evening of December 15, 1883, he found eight to 10 scalpers in front of the venue and that they had plenty of good seats and were well patronized by the public. Within the street door of the theatre three other ticket sellers stood intercepting people. They operated within six feet of the box office and each had a diagram in one hand and a bunch of tickets in the other. Those three also had plenty of good seats and sold orchestra seats ($1 face) in the lobby for $1.25, $1.50, $1.75, and even $2 for a few, although most went for $1.50. Balcony seats (50 cents face) were hawked by the lobby men for $1. A policeman was present near the box office but took no action despite the fact that, observed a reporter, "None of the ticket sellers outside or in wore a badge." One speculator (not one of those then working at Harrigan's) remarked, "There are always from three to five men in the lobby there, and they, of course, have the best seats. Speculators have to buy of them, and the public of them or of the speculators."[37]

More letters to the editor flowed in with four published on December 17. They added their own stories about themselves or friends who tried to buy tickets at the box office at various venues but could not obtain any, except for poorly located ones. Three of the four letters gave thanks to or praised the *New York Times* for its coverage of the story and the manner in which they were "going for" the theatre managers. One of the letter writers, "Anti-Lobbyist," observed, "Dan Frohman seems to think that the public wants this speculator hanging around. Do we? I think not. The public avoids him — considers him a pariah." He typified the feelings of many people when he said he had nothing against a hotel agency such as Rullman's and that he often cheerfully paid a 50 cent advance there but it was a different story when he showed up at a venue box office and was told no good seats were available for any performance — a very common experience — then he considered the box office to be a "swindle."[38]

A few days later it was observed that the privilege of selling seats in the lobby of the Fourteenth Street Theatre was controlled by William Guernsey, who usually had two men stationed outside the box office window. Also noted was that Guernsey and his assistants had been missing from their usual spot for several days and the rumor spread that they had been withdrawn by a management that had "grown sick of the swindle on the public and ordered the lobby men to leave." An insider told a reporter the public should consider "that every man who sells tickets inside the street doors of a theatre is in with the house. Whether he sells on one side of the box office window or the other, he is directly or indirectly in the employ of the manager of the theatre." He added, "They should understand that the man in the lobby is simply another box-office, at which the best seats in the house can alone be found. And, finally, they must understand that every cent paid inside the theatre doors for a seat goes to the house." People were advised by this insider to shun the lobby men and if they could not get seats elsewhere to buy from the speculators because, "Better give them the money than the house which is trying to swindle you."[39]

Several weeks later a newspaper editor pondered about the amount of space that had recently been devoted in the papers to theatrical abuses. While he considered it to have been a worthy effort, the editor worried nothing had happened or would happen. "The volley of paper bullets of the brain, aimed at the ticket speculator, has died down to a mere echo. But the speculator is still there." Also regretted was that no theatre manager had come forward with a bill to put before the state legislature, despite a great deal of talk among the showmen that such a thing would be done. If the managers weren't going to draft a law then it was up to others. Proposed the editor, "A few public spirited citizens could probably push through the Legislature a law similar to that of Pennsylvania, which makes the vending of tickets on the streets in front of theatres a misdemeanor. The men in the lobby could be included in the bill, and then the nuisance would end. This would be a sure and swift method."[40]

When an 1893 editorial explained the hotel agency situation and argued those agencies held the bulk of the power and dominated the theatres, it added that sidewalk speculators could be driven away from the venues if the manager saw fit to do so and thus protect his real patrons, the great public. "No speculators are to be found in the neighborhood of Daly's, Palmer's, the Lyceum, or the Star," it declared, "and where they are found it is safe to assume that the money they extract from the pockets of playgoers is shared by the theatre."[41]

Scalping intensified in the period from 1900 until World War I. It became more pronounced and was more noted in sports such as football and baseball. Far more efforts were made to legislate against ticket speculation, while more attempts were made by theatrical managers to eliminate the trade as they continued to wage "war" on the practice. Yet, despite it all, scalping continued.

5

The General Situation, 1900–1917

"Despite vigorous efforts to remove him, the ticket specula-tor continues to be omnipresent.... The public has drifted into the way of accepting the scalper as inevitable, at the same time no doubt, suspecting that the police have also come to assume that attitude."
                                    Christian Science Monitor, 1916

Scalping was common enough and entrenched enough as part of the Amer-ican scene that famed novelist F. Scott Fitzgerald mentioned the practice, albeit briefly, in *The Beautiful and Damned* (1922). The two main male characters were in their mid 20s and were well-to-do members of the upper class. In a part of the novel set in 1913, Anthony Patch and his friend Maury Noble had dinner together and "afterward they visited a ticket speculator and, at a price, obtained seats for a new musical comedy called 'High Jinks.'"[1]

Of all the cities in the world, New York was described by a journalist at the start of 1907 as the one "most infested with theatre ticket speculators." If they existed in, say, London and Paris, he felt that a patron entering a house in one of those cities was still not obliged "to endure what in some cases approaches assault," as he felt they were in New York. He was convinced New York led American cities in the "prevalence of the nuisance." In Boston sidewalk spec-ulation was forbidden by an ordinance said to be strictly enforced, while in Philadelphia speculation in the streets was always to be seen on opera nights, but rarely in front of the venues. A bill to prevent theatre ticket speculation had been introduced at the city council just a few weeks earlier but was promptly killed after a leading scalper obtained the backing of Philadelphia's most promi-nent local politicians. The reporter acknowledged that sidewalk scalping was more common in Chicago than in Philadelphia, yet even in Chicago "it has never attained proportions comparable to the business in Manhattan."[2]

38

Just a year and a half later it was reported that the Theatre Commission of Paris, headed by M. Lepine, Prefect of Police, had drawn up an ordinance, effective September 1, 1908, dealing with ticket speculation. Under the ordinance the price had to be stamped on each ticket and those tickets could not be sold at a higher rate.[3]

Around the same time there was a rush by Berlin opera-goers to obtain tickets for the three Royal Opera performances in Berlin for which Enrico Caruso had been engaged to appear. The entire house was sold out for all three performances soon after the box office windows were opened with the result, "Many would-be seat buyers were turned away to take their chances with the ticket speculators." Best seats cost $6 at the box office with scalpers hawking those at $12 and up. Caruso was said to have received $7,500 for his three appearances.[4]

Two years later Caruso returned to perform in Berlin and what was described as a riot took place on October 25, 1910, outside the Royal Theatre there where Caruso made an appearance in *Aida* in the presence of the Kaiser. For half an hour a throng of patrons engaged in a "melee" with a "gang of professional speculators" who had captured entire rows of the best seats in the house. Negotiations between the two groups became so boisterous that the police were compelled to intervene "with their accustomed roughness." Police drove the crowd into an adjacent park where scalpers resumed negotiations. Scores of people, including several wealthy Americans, were reported to have been victimized by counterfeit tickets that had been sold for as much as $15. When holders of the phony tickets were denied entry at the door, many more angry encounters took place.[5]

To prevent speculation at the Bayreuth Wagner music festival in Germany in the summer of 1912, the management adopted the unusual precaution of compelling ticket buyers to sign an agreement not to dispose of the seats without the written consent of the festival committee. Part of the agreement called on purchasers to pay a fine of $12.50 for each violation of the pledge. Management also stated it would buy back any seats bought in advance provided they were returned at least one month before the performance designated by them. Although the Bayreuth season was still some four months away at the time of this report, there was not a single seat then available.[6]

The People's Institute provided, among other things, theatre tickets at reduced rates for people on low incomes. For several seasons up to 1909 the institute printed slips that, when presented at box offices, entitled the bearer to discounted admission. But in 1909 it was found that many of the admission slips were being sold by scalpers in cigar stores, barber shops, and similar places. To prevent such activity a bill was introduced into the New York State legislature that would have made the unauthorized sales of those slips a misdemeanor. That proposal failed to become law. Charles Sprague Smith, president of the People's Institute, said his group was responsible for 110,000 discounted theatre tickets being sold in the previous year.[7]

A newspaper editor who was fed up with scalping in 1910 applauded a magistrate who had recently fined a speculator brought before him, commenting, "Earnest effort has been made to get rid of this nuisance. But the speculators seem to have a powerful pull. Ordinances against them are either 'hung up' or are found, after adoption, to be defective."[8]

Upon the opening of the second season by the Chicago Grand Opera Company at the Chicago Auditorium in November 1911, a reporter explained that ticket scalping to the extent of over $8,000 "was the indirect cause of the ominous inauguration" of that season. Opening opera *Samson and Delilah*, it was said, did not receive a great reception from the crowd although it deserved one, with the reception blamed on the speculation situation, which, in some unexplained way, led to a crowd that the reporter declared could not be called "brilliant." In some fashion the restrained reception must have been due to a simmering resentment over the scalping situation, surmised the journalist. Florence Couthoui, who scalped 1,200 tickets for $6,000, and H. N. Westfall, 450 seats for $2,500, were listed as the culprits. One of the Opera Company directors, Harold F. McCormick, said he was angered at the speculation situation, explaining the Board of Directors had authorized the sale of 150 seats to hotel ticket agencies for the convenience of out-of-town guests but the situation got out of hand. McCormick confirmed that authorization had been exceeded by 1,500 seats, "The thing is outrageous and if there is anything that I can do to stop it I will."[9]

Whenever a government got involved in the issue it was usually to pass legislation designed to eliminate or control speculators, or to consider such proposals. But on one occasion at least the government itself became a scalper in Chicago. It began in 1911 when the H. N. Westfall Company, a ticket agency, went into receivership and was taken over by the U.S. government, under Receiver McVey. McVey was authorized by Judge Landis of the United States District Court to continue the usual business of the firm until its affairs were wound up; the court considered the matter but saw no reason to not continue the usual trade of the firm as there were then, for example, no state or local laws against it. As a result McVey purchased 800 tickets to Chicago theatres for New Year's Day 1912 performances. According to the report he made a week later to the Federal District Court in connection with the receivership of the firm, McVey declared he scalped those seats for $1,600 in total and made a profit of $300.[10]

And just as oddly, there were a couple of reports of scalping occurring at motion picture cinemas. Speculators were said to have worked a street corner at Broadway and 46th Street in April 1914 where a film was playing. All of the regular theatres were reportedly closed and this cinema box office was sold out. One speculator, familiar to the reporter as a man who regularly worked the Columbia Theatre (a live venue), offered the newsman a 50 cent seat to the film for 75 cents.[11]

Crowds lined up all day on September 20, 1915, at the Forty-fourth Street Theatre where the film *The German Side of the War* was screening. Ads for the film erroneously gave the impression the film was to play for one day only, with the result being that crowds were turned away from each of the eight screenings of the film (all were sell-outs of 1,500 each). Several thousand people had gathered at the cinema before the initial screening at 11 A.M. Speculators bought as many seats as they could and resold them to people in the rear of the crowd at prices ranging from 50 cents to $1 (25 cent face). Others then got the idea of selling soda water checks, obtained from a nearby store, to the most obviously foreign in the crowd, those they believed would not be able to read English. Soda water checks and cinema admission tickets were both pink in color and of the same general appearance. Those were also sold for prices ranging from 50 cents to $1. So great was the crowd around the door that some of those soda water checks were accepted before the fraud was discovered. Sellers of the phony items had all vanished by the afternoon, by the time the fraud was discovered, but scalping of legitimate tickets continued at such a rate that management phoned for the police. Half a dozen policemen arrived, took up positions, and halted the resale of seats. Although many of the scalpers were pointed out to the police, no arrests were made as no one would make a complaint. Finally, said a reporter, "With a policeman for every twenty feet of the line in the evening, the ticket speculators did not attempt to pursue their calling."[12]

A 1915 news report on the scalping situation in Boston observed that one local theatre in its advertising had recently sounded a warning against ticket speculators and that Boston had not been more exempt from the scalper than any other large play-going center. But with respect to premiums paid to agencies that handled theatre tickets, the conditions in Boston were said to differ from those in New York. Whereas in New York the agencies charged, typically, a 50 cent advance, people in Boston paid no advance over the box office price when they bought at any of the five hotel agencies then in operation in Boston. Theater managers were said to see no necessity for changing the system in Boston, claiming the agencies did them a favor and were assets both for the venues and for the hotels.[13]

Still, speculation was considered enough of a problem in Massachusetts that several times efforts had been made at the state legislature to pass bills against ticket speculation, with one argument being that no class of people should be granted special privileges in buying tickets and that any law passed to prohibit street speculation should also prohibit any ticket agencies that sold seats at a premium. John M. Casey, chief of the city of Boston's license division, explained there was then no law against speculation anywhere in Massachusetts but in Boston there was an ordinance that prohibited peddling wares (any goods) on the streets without a license. Police had no authority to arrest a person selling tickets outside the theatre unless the sale took place on the street. To circumvent that measure instances were not uncommon where the scalper, arranging with the owner of a building, had done a thriving business in doorways—because such trade did not occur in the street no arrest was possible. Boston theatre managers also claimed they could not prevent tickets from falling into the hands of scalpers, even in cases where the number of tickets sold to one person was limited, due to speculators using proxies, for example.[14]

Two Boston ticket speculators were arrested and fined there in February 1916. That caused an editor to remark, "Despite vigorous efforts to remove him, the ticket speculator continues to be omnipresent whenever a theatre offers a bill attractive enough to play full houses. The public has drifted into the way of accepting the scalper as inevitable, at the same time no doubt, suspecting that the police have also come to assume that attitude." Over the previous year more than 50 speculators had been arrested by the Boston police, who could still only arrest one of the black market sellers for peddling on the street without a license, occupying a portion of the sidewalk for business purposes without a license, obstructing the sidewalk, sauntering or loitering—all things pertaining to the sidewalk. Therefore the speculator, although he may have accosted his prospect on the sidewalk, usually took him into a nearby doorway or a store and sold him his ticket there. So long as the actual transaction did not take place on the sidewalk, the police claimed they were helpless to interfere.[15]

A Boston reporter spoke to a speculator working only about three feet from the entrance to a Keith house. Normally he got his tickets from the box office a few at a time (actually sending a boy) and sold those seats for $1 (50 cents face). He did not worry about a sign displayed in the Keith lobby that read, "Tickets bought of speculators will be refused at the door," believing that no one would know where a ticket came from and, "Such signs are intended only to frighten the public." In the editor's view the public suffered in the case of the more popular shows not as much from the speculators as from the system by which large blocks of tickets were sent out to the hotel agencies and other brokers. Hearing the words "Nothing better than the fourteenth row" from the box office usually meant, "The best seats have gone to the brokers."[16]

The line up remained a standard method whereby scalpers, and even the large agencies, obtained their tickets. Over time it faded away as a tactic as the street speculator became less important and less dominant and as the agencies came to dominate the field as they got larger and more prevalent. More sophisticated methods were used more often by agencies, such as pre-event deals with venues. As time passed the line up as a tactic was more likely to be used by independent, small time scalpers working alone. Seventy-five American District Telegraph messenger boys and six men lined up some 24 hours in advance in 1900 at New York's Knickerbocker Theatre for the opening of sales for a Maude Adams appearance in the play *L'Aiglon*. Animosity developed between the six men, all speculators, and the man in charge of the boys and the police had to be called to the scene to preserve order. Both the men and the boys were relieved every six hours. The two largest agency owners in New York were Tyson and Rullman, with the former employing 50 of the boys while the latter employed the other 25. Those two operators paid the American District Telegraph Company 30 cents per hour per boy for the use of its employees. Sales for the play were limited to a maximum of four seats per purchaser.[17]

Speculators still sued theatres for one reason or another every so often but failed more than they succeeded in such endeavors. H. J. Charlebois appeared in Justice Young's court in May 1904 trying to get $35 back for unsold tickets he had bought from the Grand Opera House in Los Angeles for seats to a Weber and Fields performance. Charlebois insisted he was no speculator but did admit buying extra seats at times for his friends. According to Charlebois, he went to the venue to Treasurer Wells, who was working the box office, and asked him how many tickets he could obtain for front balcony seats for the Saturday evening show. Because ticket speculation, said a reporter, was "not encouraged by theatre managers" in Los Angeles, Wells told him six would be the limit. But Charlebois said he had urgent need of 25 and begged so hard that Wells finally relented and broke the rule. In court Charlebois declared that it had been agreed by Wells that unused seats could be returned and the money would be refunded. Thus, he took 14 tickets back and asked for a $35 refund. Venue manager Winfield Hogaboom took the stand to explain that no refunds were ever given once seats were sold, to anybody, for one reason, to discourage speculation. Additionally, observed Hogaboom, Wells had disregarded house rules in selling Charlebois more than six seats. No refund was awarded to Charlebois by the court.[18]

An attempt to swindle the Mason Operahouse in Los Angeles was discovered in September 1907 when 40 bogus passes for a play to be presented the following week were tendered for admission tickets. Over 200 bogus passes were thought to have been sold by scalpers to Los Angeles theatre patrons. When the passes were first presented they were routinely exchanged for good seats until a closer inspection of passes revealed they lacked an endorsement on the back by Mr. McKim, the manager of the distribution bureau. Then an investigation was started. McKim kept a pad of blank passes and filled them out for merchants who allowed him the use of their windows for advertising posters of the upcoming play. During his investigation he found his home had been entered in his absence and his pass pad stolen.[19]

As ticket agencies become more prominent more attention was devoted to them. A letter to the editor from "P. M." in January 1907 argued that sidewalk speculators were a nuisance but so were the hotel agencies with their 50 cent advance. Suppression of the sidewalk people, he thought, would not be enough to solve the problem if venues were allowed to place seats with agencies charging a premium. "Why not recognize that sidewalk men and agencies are both parts of a system by which the managers add to the very high price named on the ticket? Make it illegal for any one to ask more than this price," he concluded.[20]

Illustrating the differences in perception and treatment of the sidewalk men (speculators) and agencies was a discount system that had existed between the management of the Metropolitan Opera Company and the hotel agencies that came to an end after the 1909-1910 season. For some years it had been arranged for hotel ticket agencies such as Tyson's and Rullman's to secure tickets at a 20 percent discount and then resell them to customers at the regular price, or more. Later that discount rate was dropped to 15 percent. However, for some time the Board of Directors had been looking to raise opera income. Thought was given to raising the price of tickets to $6 but ultimately it was decided to eliminate the discount. One estimate was that the discount allowed the agencies amounted to a $70,000 income loss to the opera company each year.[21]

On the other hand, the Metropolitan Opera Company held a quite different attitude toward the speculator. Company spokesman Mr. Brown declared, at the same time the discount elimination was announced, that he planned a "war" on speculators. He went a little farther than most of his fellow managers in that he was planning to wage a "war to the death" on the scalper, whom he considered "the greatest enemy of the opera-going public." Brown grumbled, "I have a pigeonhole in my desk full of letters of these men. If I accepted their propositions I might be $20,000 a year richer. Two or three of them have even had the temerity to come and talk with me." He said he was then using every means in his power to put a stop to the sidewalk men and that if the public would assist him he was confident his end would come soon. "I have detectives in the box office corridor all the time to see that any one who has been asked to get tickets for speculators is never sold any," he insisted.[22]

An article in *Variety* in November 1911 remarked that speculating in theatre tickets as it applied to hotels during the course of the past year or so had been undergoing a change. The new way was for the hotel agencies to guarantee the sale of a certain number of tickets each night to a particular theatre, securing those seats from the box office at face value, without paying any premium but also without having any return privileges for the seats. That is, once the agency had bought a ticket it was stuck with it unless it could sell it to a customer. A trio of New York houses (the Knickerbocker, Broadway, and Criterion) were then delivering a total of 300 seats a day to some of the agencies. Immediately after a play opened, or sometimes even before it opened, Tyson & Company agency agreed to pay the box office $600 for 300 seats per performance with the guarantee covering a specified period—for example, Tyson could have agreed to take that number for two weeks, or two months, and so on. Such deals, of course, practically ensured a "run" for any shows that were taken up in that fashion by the agencies. Managers liked the arrangement because through selling the hotels 300 seats, they had their shows hyped among out-of-towners, who asked the ticket stands in the hotel where a good show was. Although the usual 25 cent premium under the old method on a delivery of 30 to 50 seats per day was lost from an agency such as Tyson's, the guaranteed return of $600 per day was more advantageous. Also, under the old method wherein the hotels and theatres divided the 50 cent premium charged, the disadvantage was that the venues had to accept the return of any unsold seats at the last minute. Theatrical managers were said to be leaning more and more to the idea that the big outlet for theatre tickets in New York was the hotel with its thousands of transients.[23]

Such deals, of course, required some ability on the part of the hotel agencies to pick winners from losers from all the plays about to open in New York since they were committing a good deal of money for a fixed period of time. The best of those play judges was reportedly George J. Bascomb, who worked for Tyson & Company. Bascomb would drop in on a new production in its tryout period in the wilds and decide on the spot whether it would do for the big town. Often Bascomb said okay to a production and plunked down a lump sum for a certain number of tickets at the New York theatre to eventually play it. However, there was sometimes a dark side to such financing deals. "There have been instances in the past though where by something akin to 'hold up' methods, the hotel people were compelled to contribute a large amount to one show, in order to have the entre to the box offices of other attractions," explained a newsman. "This was called forth though only in cases of weakly financed productions that seemed to have all the qualities of a hit."[24]

As of the start of 1913, the agency Tyson & Company (controlled then by William M. Erb) supplied 28 New York hotel stands with theatre tickets. It used to be that when one sold out its supply for a specific show it phoned (after receiving a request from a patron) the other 27 offices, one by one, until it could locate a pair. But by 1913 it was a procedure that went through the head office, with greater efficiency. Tyson & Company then carried 7,000 charge customers and rendered monthly statements to every one. Each customer had some particular want, such as, "One fat man must be given aisle seats not behind the fifth row, or else be placed in a box." This agency handled about 25,000 seats per week with the charge being mostly $2.50 per ticket ($2 at the box office was the price then at most venues for orchestra seats). "With the installation of the labor-saving plan and the delivery of tickets by auto and motorcycles, Mr. Erb said the Tyson business had increased," according to a report. A stronger demand for tickets from hotel agencies also arose when New York City finally passed an ordinance that drove scalpers off the streets.[25]

One estimate had it that there were then 14,000 to 16,000 orchestra seats available each day in New York (84,000 to 96,000 per week) that retailed at the box office for $2, which meant Tyson & Company controlled the sale of 25 to 30 percent. Before *The Lady of the Slipper* began its New York run at the Globe Theatre, Erb bought $40,000 worth of seats for that run, covering the first 10 weeks. At 2,000 tickets per week and six performances a week, that worked out to Tyson & Company controlling about 333 orchestra seats for each performance.

It was not likely that the number of orchestra seats exceeded 500 or 600 at the most. Outside of the opera productions, that move by Erb was the largest single investment among New York ticket speculators. "The Tyson Hotels," as the establishments that hosted Tyson & Company ticket stands were called, included Knickerbocker, Astor, St. Regis, Martinique, Savoy, Rector's, Marie Antoinette, Waldorf-Astoria, Belmont, Vanderbilt, Ritz-Carlton, Imperial, Holland House, Breslin, McAlpin, Grand Union, Murray Hill, Netherlands, Great Northern, Wolcott, Biltmore, Prince George, and two branches in office buildings.[26]

By 1915 Tyson & Company was controlled by the Shubert brothers, theatrical entrepreneurs. At this time New York had a single cut-rate ticket agency as well. Joe Leblang ran the Public Service Theatre Ticket Office where tickets could be had for half price, or even less on occasion. Leblang worked on a margin of 10 percent with all the venues that did business with him. Some venues only let him have seats on outright buys at 10 percent below the half price he resold them for; other venues allowed him to return unsold seats. A $2 orchestra seat could be had at Leblang's for $1 (at least for the venues that worked with him, not all did); he obtained it from the venue for 90 cents. One point that theatres liked about this agency was that it kept the cut-rate element away from the box office windows where they flaunted their half-price coupons in the faces of full-price paying customers. And that was something managers did not like to see. Venues had long issued half-price coupons, for example, on their own to various people such as friends, relatives, business associates, sponsors, and the like. When a production was not doing well and not drawing big crowds such coupons were issued even to strangers; sometimes things got so bad the venue issued coupons entitling the bearer to free admission (hence the phrase "papering the house") in an effort to fill more seats in the hope that would eventually somehow result in more paying customers.[27]

Competition from Leblang's agency, as minor as it may have been, did not sit well with Tyson. And a new ticket deal that started on September 6, 1915, saw Tyson & Company become the distributor of most New York theatre tickets and the abolishment of the cut-rate agency. On the same day the new agreement took effect the Shuberts sold Tyson to C. A. Zabriskie. Under the new arrangement Tyson then distributed seats to all the various agencies and brokers (including other hotel agencies) that handled tickets. During the first week of the new regime it was reported that Leblang's office was deserted. Those changed conditions were possible when the two main theatrical producers— the Shuberts and Klaw & Erlanger — reached an agreement to form that ticket alliance. If their combined productions and other shows they controlled through venue rental were all removed at once from New York there would have been little left. As part of the alliance the two producers agreed not to distribute seats for any of their shows in a cut-rate agency and to do all distribution to other hotel agencies and brokers only through Tyson at an advance of 25 cents per ticket over the box office price, with the final reseller restricted to a 50 cents advance over the price stamped on the coupon. Many observers did not understand why the Shuberts had sold Tyson just at the time they were forming the alliance, in view of the fact that in the previous season Tyson had sold at least $1.5 million worth of theatre tickets. Of the amount sold for the Shubert theatres, said a ticket handler, it was felt that about 60 percent of the gross through Tyson went to Shubert shows through the agency clerks pushing those shows for the obvious reason that the Shuberts owned Tyson. One belief among many observers was that outside ticket agencies would not patronize Tyson unless forced to do so, first trying the box office to get good seats for resale, hoping a theatre treasurer would be willing to hold out, say, 20 or 30 seats per night for such an agency.[28]

A week later the ticket compact had weakened considerably. At Leblang's agency the staff was still not selling half price tickets in advance but clerks were telling prospective purchasers seats for certain productions could be obtained any evening just before performance time. While the clerks verbally named the shows that would be available there was no written sign in the office announcing the names of those plays. Those tickets came into Leblang's at the last minute from outside ticket agencies (not Tyson) that had obtained seats one way or another through outright buys (no return privilege) and thus funnelled their unsold seats to the cut-rate shop. Some disgruntled agencies — then forced to do business through the Tyson agency instead of directly with the theatres as in the past — were waging a media campaign with their ads advising the pubic to stay away from the box offices of venues that would rather sell their seats through an agency because of increased revenue. In the ads Tyson was referred to as "The Theatre Ticket Trust." Not long afterward the whole ticket alliance arrangement collapsed entirely.[29]

During this period law makers were more active than ever before in their pursuit of scalpers. But they were no more successful than when they had ignored them.

6

Laws, Arrests, Police, Courts, 1900–1917

"The greatest evil that theatregoers in this city have to contend with is the ticket speculator. Their conduct is outrageous and they should be suppressed. They are practically highwaymen and hold up everybody that goes to a place of amusement."

Magistrate Crane, 1901

"You men who sell tickets in front of theatres often charge $1 or $1.50 more than the tickets cost and if a poor man wants to take his wife and family to a theatre he is compelled to accede to your demands if he cannot obtain suitable tickets from the box office."

Magistrate Herman, 1911

On January 5, 1906, Chicago's Mayor Dunne announced he would at once issue orders to arrest all scalpers of theatre and amusement tickets who operated on the sidewalks or the streets. As well, he added, he would try to have passed a city ordinance that would require a license fee of $500 to be paid by every dealer in theatre tickets.[1]

An anti-speculating ordinance was passed in Chicago because it was reported in March 1907 that city officials had begun a determined fight to enforce that measure. To that end eight theatre managers, including Harry Powers of Powers Theatre and Will J. Davis of the Illinois Theatre, and three speculators were arrested on warrants alleging violations of that ordinance. Twenty-seven more warrants had been issued, still waiting to be served. The managers were charged with violating two sections of the ordinance. One provided that managers would provide diagrams of their houses showing the number and location of every seat in the venue, and that the seats would be checked off as fast as the tickets were sold. Under the other section it was required of managers that they print a notice on every ticket to the effect that it was a revocable license and was not acceptable if the holder had bought it from a speculator.[2]

Several months later 12 Chicago theatre managers and ticket scalpers who had been arrested and charged with violating a state law by selling seats at an advance over the published rate were discharged when their cases were called in Municipal Court. Their dismissal was on the ground that the section of the Illinois law under which they were arrested was unconstitutional.[3]

Appealed to a higher court, the Illinois Supreme Court declared in December 1907 the state law forbidding the sale of theatre tickets for a price higher than that printed on them was unconstitutional. A newspaper editor bemoaned the decision observing, "The law was condemned on the ground that the theatre, not being like a common carrier which operates through a franchise, is under no obligation to sell any tickets at all, and is entitled to charge what it pleases if it chooses to dispose of them." With respect to the public, the court noted if it did not like the price it could refrain from buying "and can do so without injury to health, safety, morals, or general convenience." As far as it went that decision was sensible, thought the editor, but it did not go far enough and ignored that what the public resented, justifiably, was the element of deception and exploitation that it saw or thought it saw in the sale of seats through speculators. "To box office prices no serious objection is ever made, however high they may be," he explained, "but when the management is suspected of announcing one price and selling at another, then the public, whether reasonably or unreasonably ... feels itself robbed as well as deceived, and yearns for laws to stop it."[4]

With the purpose of forcing theatre managers and owners themselves to banish scalpers from Chicago, the city's license committee recommended in November 1910 an ordinance that would close all theatres and places of amusement on Sundays. The committee planned to urge that such an ordinance, if enacted, be enforced until theatres had permanently broken with the scalpers; in other words, the measure was to be used as a club to bring the venues into line.[5]

Managers of nine downtown theatres in Chicago decided in March 1912 to accept the City Council's proposition to reduce their license fee from $1,000 to $500 a year on condition they would not take back from hotel ticket agencies any seats sold to them. Heretofore, it was said, the custom of most agencies had been to take up all the most desirable seats and, if they failed to sell them, return them for credit just before curtain time. A naively optimistic reporter declared, "Without permission to return the tickets, it is thought the purchases of scalpers will be greatly reduced, if not wholly stamped out."[6]

Nothing much worked against the scalpers in Chicago and the situation had reportedly become so aggravating by March 1915 that the issue had once more been raised in the city council as that body pondered taking steps to revoke the licenses of certain theatres. The council's judiciary committee had received an opinion from the corporation counsel that if tangible evidence could be produced showing collusion between scalpers and venues the mayor had the power to revoke the theaters' licenses. The police provided a report, and based on that, the committee delivered the material to the mayor, asking him to revoke licenses. But the mayor declined, arguing if the matter were taken into court and his revocation action was not upheld, he would be personally liable. For the information of the council, Municipal Librarian Rex prepared a report gathered from a list of 125 cities to which he directed inquiries. Twenty of those cities had ordinances regulating or prohibiting scalping, including New York City.[7]

A new anti-scalping ordinance became effective in Chicago on January 1, 1916. But it did not sit well with the venues and as a result most Chicago theaters refused to sign a form wherein it stated the theatres must not participate in ticket scalping on penalty of the automatic revocation of their licenses. City Collector Forsberg had returned 30 checks for the annual license fee to 30 theaters because they had not also returned one of the signed forms with their checks. Thus, as of January 1, every Chicago playhouse, with the exception of the Auditorium and Colonial, was operating without a license. Despite that, Chicago ticket brokers continued to operate and did not seem worried over the prospect of not getting any more tickets for speculation. One broker, Ernie Young, had been running an advertisement in the local papers for several days to the effect that he would continue to furnish choice seats for all Chicago shows.[8]

That Chicago law marked a contest between the venues and the city. Under the new law it was required that the price of the ticket had to be shown plainly on the face of each ticket, that it was to be sold at no other price, and that no ticket was to be offered for sale by anyone but the agent of the theatre at the theatre. After Forsberg had returned all the license fee checks to the venues that had sent them in without enclosing a signed form pledging adherence to the anti-scalping law, he announced he would give them 15 days of grace. If the forms still remained unsigned after that period of time, Forsberg insisted he planned to call on the chief of police to close the recalcitrant playhouses.[9]

Despite the fact that Philadelphia had no law against the trade, arrests of scalpers were made nevertheless early in 1907. Dr. H. G. Molsom and others, patrons of the Academy of Music there, presented a petition to Mr. McKenty, director of that venue, saying they had been annoyed by speculators when they were in the vicinity of the venue. Then the police, acting on the "orders" of McKenty, said a news account, went to arrest ticket speculators if any were found selling opera tickets in the vicinity of the Academy of Music, arrested seven on February 8. Each of the men had a pack of tickets.[10]

Some five years later Philadelphia police conducted a sweep in which 10 men were arrested on January 28, 1912, while attempting to sell theatre seats near the Forrest, Lyric, Adelphi, and Broad Street Theatres. All were charged with disorderly conduct and locked up. Those arrests were called the first results of the effort of the Director of Public Safety to stop theatrical ticket scalping in Philadelphia. Commented a journalist, "and it is understood that the arrests will continue night after night until the streets are freed of speculators and theatre patrons may go direct to the box offices."[11]

In New Haven, Connecticut, the City Board of Aldermen was said to have acted favorably on August 31, 1907, on a new city ordinance that mandated a fine of $100 for every person who sold a ticket to a Yale University athletic contest for more than its face value. Under the provisions of the measure every ticket to any Yale event had to have shown on its face its scheduled price; any person was prohibited from selling such a ticket for more than its specified price; and any Yale student, agent, employee, or representative was prohibited from selling such a ticket to a scalper or to any person who sold it for more than its face value.[12]

By the time New Haven Mayor Studley signed the measure into law in mid–October, the law had been expanded to declare that every ticket to a place of amusement in New Haven had to have printed on it the price at which it was to be sold, and that a fine ranging from $10 to $100 would be levied on anyone selling it at a greater price than its face value. One commentator remarked that the ordinance was the most drastic anti-speculation measure that any city had adopted in New England.[13]

Frank Schweitzer was arrested by the police in Washington, DC, in March 1900 in front of the Grand Opera House in that city, charged by the theatre management with obstructing the street. It was alleged Schweitzer was a scalper who by means of agents managed to secure a large number of seats and then sold them at advanced prices. According to a report, the venue management had made several attempts to thwart the scheme, "but without avail." When he was arrested Schweitzer was offering seats at double the box office price.[14]

When he was brought into Washington Police Court a couple days later charged with obstructing the street in front of the Grand Opera House, Schweitzer was declared guilty and fined $10 by Judge Scott. Venue managers in the city believed that because of that outcome a precedent had been established that would effectively protect them and their patrons from ticket speculation thereafter. Chief of Police Sylvester was a major prosecution witness. He told Scott of the numerous complaints which had been made against the sidewalk men. The arrest of Schweitzer, he said, was the result of a determination to break up the practice. It was explained that speculators had purchased a number of seats and disposed of them at advanced prices on the sidewalk, which caused management to post signs informing the public that tickets bought from speculators would be refused at the door. Mrs. and Mrs. Sylvester had personally gone to the venue on the previous Saturday night where they were directly accosted by Schweitzer. At that point the chief announced his identity and ordered the scalper away from the immediate area of the venue. When Schweitzer refused to comply and after "finding that he was not authorized to sell for the theatre" Sylvester ordered a nearby constable to arrest Schweitzer.[15]

Police in Los Angeles had a state law against scalping in 1905, but they did not know about it. No sooner had they found out about it than it was declared void by the courts. On September 25, 1905, scalpers were busy in Los Angeles buying and selling circus tickets. Then the attention of the police was called to the fact that the last sitting of the California State legislature had passed a law against ticket speculation. It read, "Every person who sells, or offers for sale, any ticket or tickets to any theatre or other public place of amusement, at a price in excess of that charged originally by the management of such theatre or public place of amusement, is guilty of a misdemeanor." Yet it had no effect on the scalpers dealing in circus tickets because, said a reporter, "Hundreds of dollars were squeezed out of honest people by these leeches." Seats costing $1 at the box office were scalped for $2. Los Angeles Police Captain Bradish admitted no arrest of scalpers had been made, adding that the law was "a new one on me."[16]

On March 31, 1906, the business of theatre ticket scalping was pronounced legal by the Supreme Court of California when it declared the state anti-scalping law to be invalid, holding that the practice of ticket speculation was not injurious to the public welfare, the owners of theaters or to the purchaser of tickets. The act was considered by the court to be an unwarrantable interference with the inherent and constitutional rights of individuals and for that reason was void. Further, the statute in question violated the constitutional guarantee securing to every person the right of acquiring, possessing and protecting property. Hope for some type of relief was held out in a suggestion made in the decision to the effect that if the practice of selling tickets by scalpers was objectionable, the managers of theaters had it in their power to make tickets non-transferable by printing conditions on the ticket, and they could restrict the number of tickets sold to any one person.[17]

The Dowling Anti-Theatre Ticket Speculators' bill came up in the New York Senate in March 1902 for final passage and came very close to passing that chamber. Although the final vote was 25 to 16 in favor it failed to receive the constitutional majority necessary for its passage, falling one vote short. Senator Dowling said his measure was designed to prevent "extortion" of the theatre patron. Dowling believed many of the venue managers were in league with the scalpers and mulcted the public with regularity. His bill prohibited the sale of theatre tickets elsewhere at higher rates than were charged at the box offices with any violation being a misdemeanor.[18]

New York State's Legislative Assembly remained quite active when it came to introducing proposed laws against the practice, but less active when it came to adopting such measures. At Albany, Assemblyman Wagner of New York introduced an anti-scalping bill in January 1907. It provided that speculators who sold tickets at prices above the regular price, or persons who purchased such tickets, or persons who established agencies for the sale of seats at advanced rates were guilty of a misdemeanor with the penalty being a fine of not more than $500 or imprisonment for not more than one year, or both.[19]

Two more bills against the practice were introduced in the New York Senate in February 1907 by Senator Saxe of New York. One bill made it a misdemeanor for scalpers to stand around in the streets in the vicinity of theaters and sell seats at a rate in advance of the box office price and also prohibited the theatre managers from cooperating with the speculators in such sales in any way. In the other bill municipalities were forbidden to issue licenses to ticket speculators and were instructed to call in and revoke any such licenses then outstanding.[20]

During debate on the Saxe proposals, Senator Mullaney opposed the bills vigorously arguing 150 men, some of whom had gone through the Civil War, would be put out of business. Also opposed was Senator McCarren who declared the proposals would not cure the evil in any way but, rather, would give the hotel agencies a monopoly. Senator Agnew offered an amendment that would have included the agencies (the bill proposed by Saxe affected only the sidewalk men) such as Tyson's. Agnew argued those brokers were a greater evil than the sidewalk men because they divided profits with the venues. Saxe explained he wanted to end a situation whereby men accompanied by women were often made to appear "small" because of haggling over the price of seats. Senator Foelker of Brooklyn and Senator Owens also came out opposed to the bill to forbid city licensing because of veterans being involved in the business. Finally, both proposals from Saxe were overwhelmingly defeated in the New York Senate in March 1907.[21]

A week later, by a vote of 92 to nine, the New York Assembly passed the Wagner bill, which was aimed at preventing collusion and the division of profits between theaters and scalpers and ticket agencies. Assemblyman Wagner's bill did not prevent ticket speculation but it did prevent what he described as the "illegal sharing of profits" while "honest speculation in theatre tickets is not prevented." Hotel ticket agencies were also not affected unless it could be shown that they were in collusion or in league with the management of a theatre for the "extortion" of advanced prices from the public. The measure aimed to get after "barefaced collusion," elaborated Wagner, "not legitimate ticket speculation."[22]

Supporting Albany legislators in their efforts to ban the sidewalk men was a group calling itself the Association for Public Duty. It made public a letter Oscar Hammerstein wrote to association vice president Willis Dowd saying that because of the sidewalk men venue managers were compelled to place tickets on sale in the hotels. Hammerstein argued that if the sidewalk men were abolished the "equally obnoxious hotel ticket office" would also vanish.[23]

On a March evening in 1911 Senator John Godfrey Saxe of New York attended a play at a theatre in his district and ended up paying $12 for two seats in the fifth row that he bought from a scalper. So irritated was he by that event that he introduced another proposed measure. This one was introduced in Albany on March 20 and provided that any person who in a city street or public thoroughfare sold or offered for sale any ticket of admission to any theatre or other place of amusement shall be deemed thereby to have committed a public nuisance and was guilty of a misdemeanor. "Nearly all the principal theatres are in my district," complained Saxe, "and the best seats are in the hands of scalpers who charge from $3 to $4 for each seat. The Aldermen have tried to meet the situation by passing an ordinance, but this is to be fought. This is a nuisance that affects my district and I hope the bill will be passed."[24]

New York Senator Stilwell introduced a bill in May 1911 that would command the mayor of New York City to grant licenses to sell theatre tickets upon the payment of a $1,000 license fee, to be reduced at the end of the first year to an annual renewal fee of $500. (New York's licensing law had disappeared by this time and been replaced, after a void of a couple of years, by a ban on sidewalk men.) Also required under the proposal was that the speculator be bonded for $5,000 and that he wear a non-transferable badge and that the wearer not sell immediately in front of the venue, nor falsely represent the seats he had to sell, "nor conduct himself in a boisterous or disorderly manner." An editor with the *New York Times* was annoyed because Stilwell's measure would have overridden existing New York City laws. Why not let the city's ordinance stand he wondered, "the public of this city has too long been insulted by the ticket speculators and no longer wants to tolerate their presence on the sidewalk. The city has declared their traffic a nuisance. Senator Stilwell, by his bill, would have the nuisance licensed."[25]

There was no opposition from theatrical managers at a hearing in February 1915 before the Codes Committee of the New York State Assembly on Assemblyman Steinberg's bill aimed at theatre tickets speculators. The measure provided that venue managers print the price on all tickets and that it would be a misdemeanor for anyone to sell the tickets at a price in advance of that printed on them. Steinberg believed that would stop scalping, but several Assemblymen argued there was a loophole in that nothing in the bill prevented managers from stamping a price on the ticket higher than the actual price and then selling it at a reduction from the printed price with the scalper then free to sell for a profit at the printed price.[26]

Meanwhile, New York City continued along with its licensing law, almost two decades old as this period began. A public hearing was held in November 1901 before the Law Committee of the Board of Aldermen on the proposed ordinance to increase the license fee of theatre tickets speculators to $300 for the first year and $150 for annual renewals. Isadore Cohen, a lawyer representing the Ticket Speculators' Association, said the group was in favor of the higher fee "as it would protect the members from the competition of irresponsible outsiders and would also protect the public from imposition." Exactly how the public would be protected by an increased license fee was not stated. Many speakers opposed the proposal, all from theatre management, including speakers representing the Lyceum Theatre, Daly's Theatre, the Sire Brothers, producers, and Daniel Frohman, producer.[27]

At a meeting of the Municipal Council the following month the ordinance to raise the license fee to $300 and $150 was adopted. Under the new measure those licensed sellers also had to wear a badge "half the size of a silver dollar," showing their occupation whenever they were plying their trade. That measure failed to become law.[28]

Isidore Hein and Joseph Bower were convicted and fined $2 each by Magistrate Mayo for scalping tickets for the opening performance of *Miranda of the Balcony* at the Manhattan Theatre on September 24, 1901. Two months later an appeal of this test case was dismissed by Justice Clarke in the New York Supreme Court as the validity of the city ordinance preventing licensed speculators from selling tickets on the sidewalk right in front of the entrance to any place of amusement was upheld. Defendants argued the ordinance was unconstitutional but Clarke held it was the proper exercise of police power to prevent obstruction under such ordinances, and not to permit the sidewalks in front of places of amusement to be obstructed by speculators.[29]

One week later at the Jefferson Market Police Court Samuel Marks was arraigned before Magistrate Crane on the charge of illegally peddling on the sidewalk when he was scalping tickets in front of a theatre. After ordering the prisoner to be held Crane thundered, "The greatest evil that theatregoers in this city have to contend with is the ticket speculator. Their conduct is outrageous and they should be suppressed. They are practically highwaymen and hold up everybody that goes to a place of amusement." Crane added, "A man simply has to fight his way through these speculators when he wants to go to a theatre and it is about time they were suppressed."[30]

And four days after that John M. O'Brien and John B. Lang appeared in the same court, before Magistrate Cornell, charged with peddling on the sidewalk after being arrested in front of the Knickerbocker Theatre a few days earlier where they were scalping tickets. Cornell declared speculators had a right under the law to sell tickets in front of a place of amusement provided they did not stand immediately in front of the venue door and did not obstruct the passage of people into the house. O'Brien was directly in front of the theatre door and was convicted and fined $2. Lang was several feet away from the door and was discharged.[31]

The Committee on Laws and Legislation of the New York Board of Aldermen held a public hearing in February 1902 on the proposed ordinance of Alderman Joseph Oatman to regulate the selling of theatre tickets. Provided under the ordinance was that all tickets had to have the price plainly printed on them and must not be sold above that price. A violation would be a misdemeanor punishable by a fine of $25 or 10 days imprisonment for each offense. It was an ordinance intended to do away with speculation. No one at the hearing expressed opposition to the proposal, while representatives of theatre owners and managers (including those for Charles Frohman, Daniel Frohman, the Sire Brothers, and Oscar Hammerstein) all spoke strongly in favor of the measure.[32]

Thompson and Dundy of the Hippodrome venue continued their fight against scalpers in Yorkville Court in New York in April 1905 when they pressed their complaint against scalper Leon Levy, who had been arrested on the complaint of Mr. Dundy. "We are overrun with speculators," said Dundy in court. "They crowd around the doors, and those holding tickets find trouble in getting in. They pester every one, and we are going to do everything in our power to get rid of them." Levy declared he had a city license and a right to sell tickets. Retorted Dundy, "You have no right to go right up to the entrance. We have started this battle and we will fight you to the end." In court Levy was convicted and fined $2.[33]

Isidore Berbier was arraigned in court in New York in August 1905 charged with creating a disturbance in the lobby of the New York Theatre a few days earlier. Venue employee John W. Nash, who appeared against Berbier, accused him of blocking the entrance to the theatre and refusing to leave when ordered out. Calling his arrest an "outrage," Berbier told the court he sold a ticket at the entrance to the theatre to a purchaser who was then refused admission. Berbier took the ticket himself and attempted entry but was also denied admission. The scalper protested and soon found himself arrested. Berbier claimed it was all discrimination in favor of a speculator by the name of Canary and that after it had been announced at the box office that all the best seats were sold out, Canary appeared on the street with the best seats and sold them for $1.50 ($1 face) with the venue getting 25 cents on each seat sold that way.[34]

A couple of days later Canary appeared in court and denied all the accusations while Marc Klaw (of Klaw and Erlanger), owner of the venue, also appeared in court to refute Berbier's contentions. Magistrate Mayo fined the scalper $5 for creating a disturbance.[35]

On December 6, 1905, the right of a theatre manager to refuse admission to holders of tickets sold to them by a sidewalk speculator was upheld by the New York State Court of Appeals. It was the end of an action brought by scalper William H. Collister against the owners of the Knickerbocker Theatre. Collister sought to recover $4,000 representing a year's income lost, he alleged, through the action of the defendants in preventing him from carrying out his business. In a unanimous opinion written by Judge Vann, it was held the proprietor of a venue had a right to refuse tickets obtained through scalpers in cases where they had been given warning. A theatre ticket, said Vann, was a license that could be revoked for a violation of the conditions of the contract by the holder of the ticket. In short, the court held that a theatre was a private business, which could be opened and closed at the will of the proprietors, who had full power to fix the rate of admission and limit the number admitted and impose regulations as to who would be admitted. With respect to that decision Daniel Frohman, manager of the Lyceum Theatre, remarked, "This decision is certainly a most just one, and will do away with one of the greatest nuisances of the profession. It will put an end to the noisy mob of harpies that hawk their wares on the sidewalk.... It will also do away with the inference that the manager and the speculator are in league...."[36]

When the box office at Madison Square Garden opened on May 19, 1906, for the first day of the sale of tickets for the New York run of the Barnum & Bailey Circus it was marked by a freak snowfall, a rush of scalpers, and a charge of police reserves. A line up had formed by 5 A.M. and contained hundreds in line many hours later as the box office opened, including many speculators. Some of those scalpers got seats but many were recognized and were not sold any tickets. Those men got belligerent and refused to leave the line until they were sold seats, arguing they had as much right to buy tickets as anyone else. With the line thus not moving the police were called and reserves were sent over in a patrol wagon with instructions from Inspector Cortright, said a report, "to dispense the speculators and arrest any who made the slightest resistance." Officers moved into the line swinging their clubs and knocked off a number of hats. Scalpers threw snowballs in retaliation. Arrested were Frank McCrahom and Louis Phillips. Each was fined $2, McCrahom for interfering with police and Phillips for disorderly conduct. Police officers remained in front of the venue box office all day with speculators gathered in groups that watched glumly from a distance. "Every small boy who came along was bribed to go to the box office and purchase a ticket," commented a reporter. "Adults also had many chances to make 25 cents on the side. Through these channels the speculators managed to get a lot of seats."[37]

At the beginning of 1907 New York City Mayor McClellan sent his annual message to the city aldermen. Noting the business of ticket speculation was regulated by an ordinance from those aldermen and that certain restrictions were placed on those engaging in the trade by that ordinance, he declared, "It is a matter of common knowledge that in recent years these restrictions have been ignored in the most outrageous fashion, until sidewalk ticket speculation has become an intolerable nuisance." He added, "No license whatever is given by law to speculators to affront or harass in any way those who decline to purchase their tickets at exorbitant rates. The tactics employed by many of these men are a deplorable blow to the good name of our city, as a very large percentage of our theatregoers are visitors." McClellan pointed out to the councillors that it was within the power of the executive to stop speculation by directing the Chief of the Bureau of Licenses to revoke all existing licenses and to issue no new ones. However, he was not then inclined to go that far, feeling that imposing additional restrictions could be the answer. McClellan explained the city received only $5,000 a year in revenue from license fees paid by the scalpers and urged the aldermen to do something to curb the nuisance.[38]

Perhaps in response to McClellan's urgings, an ordinance was favorably reported two months later, in March 1907, to the Board of Aldermen by its Law Committee. The proposed ordinance did away completely with the sidewalk speculator and prohibited the sale of tickets in hotels or elsewhere at a price above that printed on their face. Coming after several public hearings, the report of the committee found the sidewalk men to be an "intolerable nuisance" and that they frequently disobeyed existing ordinances. Also, it was found the hotel agencies were a convenience to some people but were a detriment to the general public who found the house sold out at the box office only to be angered to find "hundreds of seats on sale at a material advance in hotels."[39]

However, one month later it was clearly indicated at a meeting of the aldermen, said a reporter, that the proposed ordinance would fail. During the debate an exasperated Alderman Brown exclaimed angrily, "This theatrical game beats anything you ever saw at Coney Island. It is the greatest faking game that ever happened." Brown also declared that the only reason speculation existed was because theatre managers wanted to make more money.[40]

After an enormous struggle, many rancorous public hearings, and much soul searching, New York aldermen passed an ordinance on December 1, 1908, which, if signed by the Mayor (it was), would do away entirely with sidewalk ticket speculation 30 days after the measure became law. At the same time the aldermen passed another ordinance supposedly meant to do away with the hotel agencies (and agencies in other locales) "who, it has frequently been shown, have an agreement with the theatre managers," said a journalist. That, too, would go into effect after 30 days. Provisions within the first measure called for the repeal of all ordinances dealing with the licensing of ticket speculators, for the printing of the price of a theatre ticket upon the face of the ticket, the prohibition of the sale of such tickets elsewhere than in the box office of the theatre hosting the event, and the prohibition of the sale of the seat at a price greater than that printed on the face. On the question of the power of the aldermen to regulate the price of a ticket, the Corporation Counsel gave an adverse decision indicating such an ordinance would not stand up in court. Many observers were said to feel the sidewalk ordinance would stand up in court and put them out of business while the ordinance for agencies would not stand up in court and be struck down — something the observers believed many industry insiders wanted to happen.[41]

Along the way the measure to ban agencies fell by the wayside but the law prohibiting sidewalk speculation went into effect at midnight on January 14, 1909. Said a prominent theatre manager, "For the first time in a quarter of a century our patrons will be free from the annoyances of these men. It really seems as if the millennium is here, so annoying has the situation been." Even at that early stage a new scheme to sell tickets within the provisions of the law was in its beginnings. Known as the New York Theatre Ticket Library, it had an office beside the New Amsterdam Theatre and was headed by Leon Levy, one of the best known of the sidewalk men. On January 14 it was said to have seats for more than 30 venues, for weeks in advance. It took mail requests and sent out seats by messenger. Levy explained that when a new show opened his concern had a number of people line up who bought tickets outright (no return privileges). He agreed his firm would be fighting the hotels for business. Of course, there was nothing new about Levy's plan; he had simply opened a regular agency of his own, although he probably had none of the cozy insider deals at the time that usually marked the interaction between venue and agency.[42]

Still, Levy's business, and the need for it, disappeared almost immediately after it got started. On January 15, 1909, Assistant Corporation Counsel Sterling delivered the opinion that the measures adopted on December 1 by the Board of Aldermen and signed by the Mayor did not forbid sidewalk ticket speculation. It was pointed out by Sterling that the aldermen had simply destroyed the old ordinance that mandated licensing scalpers without substituting anything in its place and that while it formerly required a license to sell tickets on the sidewalk, now none was needed. As a result, all over the city that evening, scalpers were out in force. Sterling's opinion was delivered to all police stations and officers were instructed to make no arrests. When he was informed of the opinion Mayor McClellan expressed surprise, but around City Hall there was a reported cynicism with some believing "at least some of the Aldermen knew what was going to happen when they framed their recent edict." One immediate result was said to have been to increase the number of street scalpers since even the old license provision no longer applied.[43]

Showman Marc Klaw was one who seemed to buy into a conspiracy theory since he commented, "It looks mighty funny to me that the speculators seemed to know all about this decision long before it was made public. Speculators for at least three weeks have been buying up all the seats they could get for future engagements, and they must have known that they would not be interfered with." Klaw vowed that no matter what action the city took his firm would fight the scalper to the "bitter end." Maurice Jacobs, of the New York Theatre Ticket Speculators' Association, commented the only way to regulate the trade was to raise the price of licenses. While many proposals had been made over the years to increase that fee, it had remained at $50 for the first year. Jacobs argued the annual license fee should be $500, which would mean that only a few of the "more respectable class" of speculators could engage in the occupation. He declared his lobby group would present just such a proposal to the Mayor and the Board of Aldermen.[44]

Several arrests were made in the afternoon and evening of January 16 in the war that the police, backed by several theatre managers, were waging against scalpers. Hearing that the regular ranks of speculators had been swollen by several hundred men taking advantage of the no-license-necessary condition who had bought seats that day for the purpose of scalping at night, and fearing trouble in front of theaters, Inspector Walsh sent out some 20 plainclothes men with instructions to arrest any scalpers who annoyed pedestrians. During the afternoon the management of Proctor's Fifth Avenue Theatre and several merchants occupying stores adjoining the venue made complaints against speculators, charging them with disorderly conduct. As a result police arrested five men. When the venue opened the management stationed 15 of its own men outside the venue. They mingled with speculators and warned potential buyers that seats obtained from scalpers would not be honored at the door. That led to confrontations in many cases and then to arrests. When one of the arrested was brought before Magistrate House in West Side Court that day House observed, "I am satisfied that when the recent ordinance was adopted, which people thought would wipe out the ticket speculators, some wise Aldermen knew just what would happen. The ordinance is wide open."[45]

One day later ticket speculators held a meeting to discuss their business. It was a gloomy affair despite the fact that Magistrate Finn had that morning discharged all those arrested the previous day in front of Proctor's. A major worry was that with no license then necessary to scalp, the trade would be flooded with new entrants and all would suffer under such intense competition. Coming to no conclusion as to what to do except to declare "conditions were intolerable" they determined to make an appeal to theatrical managers and aldermen to see if something could not be done.[46]

Alderman Redmond came forward on January 18 to explain the by then discredited measure. "Some time ago a New York newspaper sent a reporter to me with a ready-drawn ordinance, repealing an ordinance permitting ticket speculators to ticket-speculate. I introduced it, because the young man from the paper of which I speak seemed anxious to have me do so." It was passed and signed by the Mayor and then, continued Redmond, "the ticket speculators got to work and they found through their counsel that, while this ordinance drawn by this newspaper did repeal the other ordinance, it did not prohibit ticket speculators from ticket-speculating. So they could go on ticket-speculating as before, and the Corporation Counsel, when appealed to, said they were right." Following all that, a certain newspaper did an editorial that severely criticized that person (not using a name but implying it was a city official) who had drawn such a poorly drafted measure, pointing out that 73 aldermen at $2,000 per year in salary, one Mayor at $15,000, and so on, "yet at $193,000 a year, all this talent could not frame a ticket-sellers' ordinance." Redmond added, "The only funny thing about this tragic piece of business is that the newspaper which framed this terrific indictment was also the paper that framed the ordinance I introduced at its request."[47]

Sporadic arrests continued, even though there was little basis for such action. Scalper Albert Bereher was arrested in front of the Liberty Theatre on

January 23 and charged with disorderly conduct. That arrest was made by Sergeant Ketson who had gone to the venue at the request of manager Mayer, who had complained speculators were making a disturbance in front of the theatre, shouting they had seats for sale and drawing a crowd. Ketson spotted Bereher, with a crowd around him on the sidewalk, and ordered the crowds to disperse whereupon, he said, Bereher "became impertinent," telling the officer he had no right to interfere. Ketson then arrested Bereher.[48]

Police launched another raid on scalpers on the afternoon of January 27 when they swooped down on sellers in front of Carnegie Hall, Hammerstein's, the Victoria Theatre, and the American Music Hall and arrested 11 men selling tickets. They were arraigned before Magistrate Cornell in the West Side Court that same afternoon and charged with disorderly conduct, but were promptly discharged. Rumor had it that Police Commissioner Bingham had decided to take the matter into his own hands and arrest all speculators, despite the opinion of the Corporation Counsel that there was no law restraining them from selling seats. George J. Duncan, president of the Theatre Ticket Speculators' Association, informed police that individual suits for false arrests would be brought against the police and that he intended to secure an injunction restraining the police from making any more arrests. Following that a police order went out late in the afternoon that speculators who had licenses were not to be harassed, and that evening they would be found plying their trade without interference. No police official would admit the order came from headquarters. It was said, however, that Bingham had again referred the matter to the Corporation Counsel hoping for a decision or instruction that would clarify his course of action with respect to the many complaints about the speculators that he had received in the past week.[49]

It was known that the arrests a day earlier ordered by Bingham followed the receipt of a letter by him from Marc Klaw. Although Klaw refused to discuss the letter, he was understood to have told the Commissioner that if the scalpers who sold seats in front of his house were not driven away or arrested he would regard it as evidence that the police "stood in with the speculators." Two scalpers, Maurice Blau and David Marks, members of the speculators' lobby group, called on Klaw and proposed a plan whereby they might assist the theatrical managers in drawing up an ordinance for the Board of Aldermen to pass that would limit the issuing of licenses to only a few, each of which would cost $1,000 per year. Klaw said he refused to enter into any such agreement.[50]

Later that year Michael Marks was arrested for "offering to sell tickets for admission to the Victoria Theatre without having procured a license therefore." After he was convicted and fined $5 in May 1909 by Magistrate Kernochan the matter was taken up by the Ticket Speculators' Association, who financed an appeal in this case. Judge Mulqueen in General Sessions Court handed down a decision on October 2 reversing the action of Kernochan in imposing a conviction and fine on Marks and declared the selling of tickets on the street to be lawful. Noting the ordinance of December 1, 1908, passed by the Board of Aldermen, Mulqueen declared, "It requires no further argument, therefore, than a statement of this proposition to indicate that the defendant has been convicted of an offense which did not exist. There was no requirement that any speculators should have a license. The business, being a lawful business, can now be conducted without the permission of the local authorities, and the defendant having been arrested merely for plying his lawful vocation, his arrest and conviction are without justification." He agreed that the city or state could regulate the business and require a license, but in the absence of such ordinances the business could be conducted freely, and those engaged in it should be "protected rather than persecuted." Judge Mulqueen concluded, "For these reasons I believe that the business of a ticket speculator is lawful and that no license is required to carry it on in this city. Hence it follows that the defendant was improperly convicted."[51]

Yet arrests continued. Nine speculators were arraigned before Magistrate Harris on December 12, 1909, after being arrested for selling tickets near Proctor's Theatre at 28th Street and Broadway. Harris discharged them all saying he did not feel he could convict and fine them as the laws governing the activities of speculators were described by him as too confused at present. But he did warn those brought before him to keep away from the theatre entrance.[52]

Apparently unwilling to give up, the New York Board of Aldermen tackled the problem again at the beginning of 1910 with a newly elected and installed city council, thought to be less favorably disposed toward the speculators than had been the previous council. Public hearings were held before the Board on a slew of new proposed ordinances put forward by aldermen. A proposed measure from Alderman Schloss prohibited, under the penalty of a fine and/or imprisonment, the sale of any theatre tickets whatsoever on the streets of the city. If it became operative the sidewalk men would have to go out of business. Theatrical managers were reported to be confident the new city government would go farther to help them than did the old one. Alderman Becker's proposed ordinance was to charge each speculator $200 a year as a license fee and to bar him from operating within 200 feet of a theatre with the penalty being a fine of $25 and/or jail. Yet another ordinance, put forward by Alderman Dowling, mandated a license fee of $500 for the first year and $250 a year for each renewal. Theatrical managers favored the Schloss measure.[53]

When it became known the managers would appear again before the councilmen to launch another fight to abate the nuisance they asked Marc Klaw (he had led the fight by the managers that culminated in the disastrous December 1, 1908, measure) to lead the fight again. But he was not enthusiastic, grumbling, "Our efforts met with such disaster last year that I do not feel like starting into the fight again. Of course, I want to see sidewalk speculators abolished, and I will do everything, in my power to bring about this condition, but what is the use of our interfering if it is only going to make matters worse as it did last year?" Still smarting from the previous measure, he argued it was a good law that would have ended the sidewalk speculator then and there, "but some inconsequential individual in the Corporation Counsel's office took a hand and gave it as his opinion that the ordinance wasn't any good. This, mind you, before a test case could be made, so all our efforts went for nothing."[54]

Klaw added he was opposed to keeping scalpers a certain distance from venue entrances since that only put the nuisance in front of some other place of business. For him the best remedy was to abolish the scalper entirely and the next best thing was to make the license fee so high that only a few people could engage in the business. G. J. Duncan, president of the New York Theatre Ticket Speculators' Association, also favored a scheme to make speculators pay a high license fee. "It is not our fault if a lot of irresponsible persons have made conditions intolerable on the streets. The members of our association are willing to pay a good stiff fee and keep the business on some kind of businesslike basis," he explained. Duncan did not consider it a victory a year earlier when the Corporation Counsel gave the opinion that no ordinance then existed in the trade. "It simply resulted in our business being flooded with young men with a few dollars to invest who brought discredit upon the older and more respectable agents," said Duncan.[55]

Becker's proposal was quickly withdrawn but hearings continued on the other two. One speaker at one meeting was C. F. Guyon, a merchant and member of the public who said he had grown tired of being insulted by speculators. "Last night eleven theatres had sixty speculators in front of them and ten policemen unsuccessfully trying to keep order," he fumed to the council members. "If the managers wish the hotel agencies to sell their tickets let them pay them a commission and not split with them the extra money they make the public pay." Lawyer Michael J. Moran told the hearing, "I believe in licensing any legitimate occupation but this business is an extortion.... Our women should be protected from insults. We can get along without the speculators and without being blackjacked into buying our theatre tickets." Before the hearing was half over Charles Burnham, president of the Theatrical Managers' Association lobby group, left the chamber declaring the aldermen were not sincere and the Schloss proposal had no chance. Outside the council chamber he said to reporters, "The only way to regulate this speculating business is to do away with it altogether. A high license fee won't do it. The theatrical managers are becoming disgusted at the way the Aldermen handle the matter. They never do anything to abate the nuisance."[56]

Speculators who appeared before the council committee to speak on the matter all favored a high license fee (as they always had) — in this case the Dowling measure. Adopting a threatening manner Marc Klaw said unless scalping was abolished altogether he would sell to those sidewalk men all the seats they wanted, at a premium. "If the Aldermen cannot regulate the traffic, then I am in favor of every theatrical manager in the city standing in with the speculators

... that we will sell the tickets to them at a premium. If we don't do it some one else will, as the middleman generally gets the profits."[57]

In February 1910, as it got close to time for the aldermen to vote on the Schloss proposal, Marc Klaw called a special meeting of theatre managers before the vote so he could offer a resolution calling upon all managers to print in bold, black-face type in their theatre programs the names of aldermen who voted against the Schloss ordinance, if it lost. Their names would appear in a prominent place in the program of most of the theaters in the city, some 40 in all since all the managers, with the important exception of the Shuberts, were members of the Theatrical Managers' Association. It was Klaw's idea to display the names in that fashion until the next civic election at which time, he hoped, those who voted against the Schloss measure would be defeated. With respect to that idea Alderman William C. Towen scoffed that it did not matter what Klaw did with his programs because "There is no doubt in my mind that the theatrical managers, or most of them, stand in with the speculators.... They are a nuisance, and I believe if the theatrical managers or the owners of the theatres were on the level they could put them out of business themselves. Somebody is standing in with them, that's certain." The Schloss measure failed to become law.[58]

Later in February 1910, 12 speculators operating at the entrance to the Metropolitan Opera House were arrested in a single evening by several police officers and charged with disorderly conduct in that it was alleged they annoyed patrons of the house, blocked the sidewalk and used offensive language. At Night Court before Magistrate Barlow police testified that when passers-by refused to buy tickets from them the scalpers would use "insulting epithets such as cheap skate" and the like. Management of the Opera House had asked the police to drive the speculators away. It was said the seats held by speculators had come to them from hotel agencies that had not been able to sell them and, having no return privileges, placed them in the hands of the sidewalk men for whatever they would bring. Magistrate Barlow discharged all 12 speculators with a reprimand.[59]

Finally, in February 1911 the Board of Aldermen passed an ordinance that abolished ticket selling of any kind in the streets and public thoroughfares, but it did not prohibit the sale of theatre tickets in offices or in other private premises, such as in hotel agencies, only on the streets. According to an editor with the *New York Times*, "It is so clearly drawn that no loophole can be found in it by the most astute attorney." Regarding the last attempt in 1908 that had no result but to abolish licenses, the editor remarked that due to a lack of licensing the "dubious field of employment" had been opened to a group of men "who could not, in ordinary circumstances, obtain licenses to run pushcarts. The old speculators of the pavement were bad enough. The new ones are an insolent, noisy, mendacious lot of fellows who have added a new pain to theatregoing in New York." Obviously, the editor was delighted with the new bill, which he thought would rid the public of the speculators' importunities and enable playgoers to get tickets at the box office and at the advertised prices. With prices that ranged from 50 cents to $2 he felt the theatre was one of the cheapest forms of popular amusement, "But when one must pay a brigand on the sidewalk an advance of from 100 to 200 per cent on the advertised price, or be crowded out of the theatre, there is ample excuse for indignation."[60]

After being signed into law by the New York Mayor the new ordinance took effect after 30 days — on March 20, 1911. One day earlier 90 members of the New York Ticket Speculators' Association met and voted to make a test case of the new law. John Lang, who had been scalping tickets in front of the Metropolitan Opera House for 15 years, consented to be the "victim." George Duncan, president of the group, continued to insist that the sidewalk men wanted a high license fee as the regulation of their trade, and the only regulation. Still, he was prepared to concede a little. He was prepared to allow a requirement that speculators post a $2,000 bond and if any speculator was twice found guilty of insulting theatregoers his license be revoked. Duncan's group also declared itself willing to have a law passed that no scalper be licensed unless he had lived in New York State for one year and was also a registered voter. Implementing these measures, he declared, would eliminate the "rat" and other disreputable speculators, and it was only that crowd that annoyed, irritated, and harassed the patrons. Also discussed and approved by them was the idea of having a place (a piece of sidewalk) roped off in front of or near the theaters where the speculators could ply their trade. "If this plan could be carried out," said Duncan, "and we were assigned to a stand like the taxicab men, those who want tickets for any theatre and are unable to obtain them at the box offices would know where to go for them." To show that it was acting in good faith the association went so far as to sacrifice a few of its members — it tried, found guilty, and expelled six of its members who had been charged with insulting playgoers.[61]

On the afternoon of March 20, John Lang sold seats in front of the Metropolitan Opera House and was duly arrested. Also that day Police Commissioner Cropsey eased the fears of some managers that the police might not actively enforce the new ordinance when he called together the police captains and ordered them to enforce it. They were told to serve summonses on all ticket speculators found buying or selling seats on the streets and to bring them before the courts. During the evening of March 20 all was reported quiet with no scalpers working the streets. Although many were to be seen hanging around the streets they were not selling.[62]

Quiet, however, reigned in the streets for a very short period of time after it was revealed that police officials, on March 21, gave orders to officers not to make any more arrests of speculators until the constitutionality of the law had been determined by the test case. Because of that a renewed batch of complaints were made of annoyance from the sidewalk men. That evening at the

New Amsterdam Theatre some 15 to 20 scalpers, described as "loud-mouthed and pushy" were to be found "jostling and annoying patrons." Management called upon Thomas Stouter, "the house policeman," to clear the sidewalks but Stouter no longer had a badge and could make no arrests. (Until a month or two earlier venues had been able to have some of their private employees invested, apparently, with certain police powers, including the power of arrest. Thus, those private individuals became quasi-policemen of a sort. That power had been stripped recently from private firms as part of an overall reorganization of policing.) Scalpers at the venue taunted Stouter by pointing to two big holes in his overcoat where his police badges had been and laughed merrily. When Stouter's efforts failed venue manager Murray phoned in for regular police, but when they arrived they informed him about the no-arrest policy. Klaw & Erlanger wrote a letter to Police Commissioner Cropsey protesting the removal of powers from the "special" police. After that produced no satisfaction they wrote a letter with the same request to Mayor William Gaynor, enclosing a copy of Cropsey's letter of refusal to reconsider. Gaynor replied, "The action of the Police Commissioner was particularly at my request and meets with my full approval. I do not propose to have policemen any longer at the beck and call of private individuals. You must run your theatre with your own hired help."[63]

New York Supreme Court Justice Newburger denied a writ of habeas corpus by John Lang on March 28, 1911, remanding the man to the custody of the police for trial; he had already been fined $10 by Magistrate Krotel. Newburger's decision was based on a long line of legal opinions upholding the right of the Board of Aldermen to pass ordinances dealing with the regulation of the public streets and sidewalks. "Nor does the ordinance deprive any citizen of the right of earning his livelihood in a lawful manner, as is contested by petitioner," he held. "It simply prohibits the party from selling tickets on the streets in front of any licensed theatre or place of amusement. He may sell his tickets in any store, office, and to any person, but not on the streets in front of a licensed theatre."[64]

Two days later the police were out in force on Broadway with orders to warn scalpers that selling tickets on the street was illegal. Police were given orders to first warn the sidewalk men to stop selling and then to arrest those who refused to obey the warning. Within 30 minutes the men were said to have all stopped working and to have disappeared except one, John Hardy, who was arrested in front of the Knickerbocker Theatre for refusing to heed the warning. Managers of venues expressed surprise at the unexpected crackdown by the police as they expected them to wait until the Court of Appeals had passed on the law. Later that day at Night Court Magistrate Krotel discharged Hardy saying the police had no right to interfere with him until a decision on the law had been delivered from the high court.[65]

The Appellate Division of the New York Supreme Court affirmed the decision of Justice Newburger, on April 13, 1911, upholding the city ordinance, in a unanimous decision. In a comment on that decision a newspaper editor said, "Yet so persistent have been these pests of the pavements, and so successfully have they plied their obnoxious trade, in spite of many futile attempts to suppress them, that nobody believes they have yet been persuaded that they must go out of business." He also argued that law or no law, scalpers would only be suppressed if people refused to buy from them "or it will persist, and in time the new law will be a dead letter, and all the old annoyances of ticket hawking will be renewed."[66]

Abe Adler was arrested in June 1911 by a policeman who testified he saw Adler approach several people and offer to take them to a place where they could obtain theatre tickets. Arraigned before Magistrate Herman in Night Court for violating the ticket ordinance he was found guilty and fined $3. Said Herman to Adler, "You men who sell tickets in front of theatres often charge $1 or $1.50 more than the tickets really cost and if a poor man wants to take his wife and family to a theatre he is compelled to accede to your demands if he cannot obtain suitable tickets from the box office." Magistrate Herman continued, "I am opposed to this and I think it is an imposition on the part of you men.... I am going to watch these cases closely, and others who come before me on a similar charge will probably be sent to the workhouse instead of being fined."[67]

Arrested on June 10, 1911, for violating the ticket ordinance was Edward Aarons, a speculator, who said he had an office in the Hotel Normandie and a temporary office at 1404 Broadway (it consisted of the doorway). Policeman John Bennett was passing 1404 Broadway (a millinery shop) and saw Aarons standing in the doorway shouting, "This is the place to get your theatre tickets." Bennett then arrested Aarons even though the latter protested he was not violating the law because he was not selling on the street. He added that he paid a weekly rental for the privilege of using the doorway and was not soliciting trade, but only announcing that he had tickets for sale. Represented by a lawyer in Night Court, Aarons produced rent receipts for his doorway usage at 1404 Broadway. Magistrate Breen said that in view of the fact Aarons paid a rental he was entitled to the privilege of selling seats there, and discharged him. When the location of the place was explained to Breen the magistrate commented, "Oh yes, I have bought tickets there myself."[68]

Leon Curley was arrested near the Palace Theatre at Broadway and 47th Street on May 12, 1913, on a charge of being a ticket speculator. The complaint was made by William C. Crane, who alleged Curley abused him when he refused to buy tickets. Arraigned before Magistrate Kernochan in Night Court Curley was convicted and sent to the workhouse for five days. In imposing a jail sentence Kernochan declared, "Speculators in this city are becoming a nuisance again. Unfortunately the law only allows the Magistrate to impose a fine of $10, but in this case it has been shown that you, Curley, were disorderly and insulting.

That is a flagrant breach of conduct, and therefore I am able to send you to the workhouse."[69]

Five speculators working the crowd at the Metropolitan Opera House were arrested on the night of March 27, 1916, as the result of the work of four plain-clothes officers, including Isabella Goodwin, a rare female cop. Metropolitan management had asked the police to curb the activity of the scalpers and the plainclothes officers, "well dressed and looking like opera enthusiasts," went to the venue. All five were arraigned before Magistrate Ten Eyck in Night Court where all pled not guilty. All were convicted and fined $5 each.[70]

One of the more unusual lawsuits from this period shed a different light on the scalping issue. It was a 1915 suit brought by author Roi Cooper Megrue, author of the play *Under Cover*. The object of the suit was to compel theatrical managers to include the premiums received from the sale of seats through the agencies in their statement of gross receipts in order that authors could share in that additional revenue over the face value of the tickets. A favorable decision in the case, of course, would have opened the way for lots of lawsuits against producers and managers by authors, and other creative talent, who had contracts giving them a percentage of a play's gross receipts. Show producers maintained the author was only entitled to royalties on tickets sold at their face value. However, it was a poor argument that did not stand up since anytime a producer sold cut-rate, discount tickets to a production, that lower rate for the ticket was included in the gross box office receipts, not the face value. On occasion the amount of premiums generated by agency sales could be high. Reportedly, musical comedy successes that had played New York had, at times, produced premiums that exceeded $2,000 in a single week. Also, sometimes the producer and the show did not get any of the premium money with the house management retaining it all. (When a producer rented a venue for his production it was not uncommon for him to leave ticket distribution and sales entirely in the hands of the house.) More usually, though, the producing manager had an understanding with the house management before contracting for an engagement, whereby he received his share of any premiums. The Megrue suit failed.[71]

Sometime before 1917, perhaps a year or two, U. S. Senator Charles Thomas of Colorado visited New York, stayed at the Vanderbilt Hotel and ordered tickets for a hit show at the ticket agency in the lobby. To his surprise and indignation he was required to pay a premium in addition to the regular price of $2. Over time the unhappy memory stayed with him and in 1917, after U.S. entry into World War I, the U. S. Congress was looking for new sources of revenue and proposed an excise tax on live theatre, then the major medium of American entertainment. Senator Thomas, an influential figure on the Finance Committee, was instrumental in bringing about the final outcome, which saw a 10 percent admission tax imposed on the theatre, a tax that remained for decades. A year later, in 1918, hearings were held by the Senate Finance Committee on the burdens of the recently imposed 10 percent tax on admissions. At the hearing Thomas needled Marc Klaw, complaining in 1918, as he had in 1917, about the premium charged on theatre tickets at the hotel agencies. Klaw declared, "There are no ticket scalpers any more. They have been legislated out of existence."[72]

Well, maybe they weren't completely gone. Although one could be forgiven for thinking they must have been gone after all the legislative efforts against them. And if that wasn't enough to eradicate them there were always those never-ending wars that management undertook on their own to abate the nuisance. Or was that collusion?

7

War on Scalpers, or Collusion, 1900–1917

*"I myself would not go there, or to any other theatre that
allows speculators to sell its tickets. There should be a bill
passed by the Legislature prohibiting the sale of theatre tickets by speculators."*
Magistrate Crane, 1902

*"Ticket speculation leads to the dishonesty of employees....
No device can frustrate the sidewalk men. The only recourse
is a law which prevents the continuance of this nuisance."*
Oscar Hammerstein, 1908

*"...I will give five thousand dollars ($5,000) to any one who
can prove that any such arrangement with [scalper] Marks
or any other living individual existed whereby they could
secure a single ticket for speculative purposes."*
William M. Gray, New York Giants baseball club, 1911

Theatrical entrepreneurs the Sire Brothers, lessees of the New York Theatre, opened their war on the scalper in August 1900. When they made a statement to that effect to the press four speculators went to police Inspector
Thompson later in the same day and complained that Constable Lawrence,
then detailed to the venue, was interfering with them in the pursuit of their
business. Thompson promptly transferred Lawrence. When night came the
speculators, about 10 in number, took their usual positions on the sidewalk.
All along the walls of the theatre were posters on which were warnings against
the purchase of street tickets. Scattered around in front of the door were half
a dozen or so Sire employees, stationed there to spot all who disregarded the
warnings. After scalper Lang's potential sale fell through because of a Sire
employee named Muller, Lang appealed to Police Captain Brennan, who had
arrived on the scene with a squad of officers. Muller was then arrested on Lang's

demand, but at the station Muller was dismissed and Lang was told his complaint (that Muller had interfered with his business) was one for a civil action. David Marks, speculator, was then arrested on a complaint from venue treasurer Barnes. He was charged with disorderly conduct, which was later described as having been "loud talking." In total, eight patrons bought seats from street scalpers and were refused entry at the door. During all that activity a crowd of 500 passers-by (not theatregoers) stopped to watch the action, and caused a real jam on the sidewalk that the police then had to clear.[1]

One night later not a single speculator tried to sell seats in front of the New York Theatre over the entire evening. A man stood some distance away for a few minutes and sold two seats. Those buyers were spotted by the Sire watchdogs and so the door staff turned them away.[2]

Just a month later the Sire Brothers learned that about 200 choice seats for the opening night of their next attraction at the New York Theatre, *A Million Dollars*, had been purchased by scalpers. To block them from making sales, besides the posters that remained all over the place, they planned to place 20 private security men around their venue to work as spotters and, said a reporter, "the management will have about twenty policemen in uniform stationed about the theatre to keep order." A. I. Sire, of the firm and a lawyer, was working on a bill that he intended to have introduced at the next session of the state legislature and that he believed would put an end to ticket speculation if it became law. According to a journalist, "Mr. Sire says he is doing this without the help of other Broadway managers, to whom he has appealed in vain to join him in his crusade, some saying that they prefer to fight the speculators in their own way and independently, and others holding that ticket speculating is no longer an important issue in the theatrical business."[3]

Despite the war, just nine months later, in May 1901, complaints were made by the public that one could not get good tickets for any performance date at the Sire Brother's New York Theatre yet scalpers seemed to be there with seats for any performance for $1 to $2.50 per seat (50 cents face). An unidentified scalper told a reporter that speculators were getting their seats from a number of men who seemed to be the only ones able to get them. Those men, it was said, paid for their tickets at the rate of $1 and the speculators then had to buy them at a price greater than $1 and, in turn, resell them to the public for an even higher price. Angrily denying that allegation was one of the brothers, H. B. Sire, who exclaimed, "There is not truth in it. If we wanted to get $1 for our seats, we would simply put the price up to that figure. We do not sell our tickets to speculators...." Ending his piece by observing he could not get any good seats at the box office, the reporter described the scene at the venue on the previous evening, "The crowd of speculators about the New York Theatre has grown to such proportions that six policemen are detailed at the theatre to keep order. At night the blockade established by the speculators is complete. Persons passing in either direction, whether they show any disposition to enter the theatre or not, are grabbed, offered all sorts of bargains, and diagrams of the house are thrust before them."[4]

Fist fights remained a not uncommon outcome of clashes between managers and scalpers in the course of the former waging their wars upon the latter. William Keough, proprietor of the Star Theatre at Lexington Avenue and 107th Street in New York, had been waging war on speculators for some time. When he arrived at his venue on the evening of February 8, 1902, he found half a dozen scalpers around his entrance preparing to do business. In response to a Keough demand to move on, they refused and an encounter ensued in the course of which Keough was set upon by three of the speculators and punched in the face by at least one of them. Police arrested the three on charges of assault and disorderly conduct.[5]

One day later Magistrate Crane, sitting in Harlem Police Court, took occasion when the three scalpers were arraigned before him for their attack on Keough to denounce ticket speculation in general, and the collusion between the scalpers and theatre managers in general. Before him were Leopold Spear, Sigmund Kurtz, and Louis Loeb. "I have something to say in regard to these ticket speculators," Crane began. "I have sat in these cases and I know the game well. Now, the half of the theatres in this city, I really believe, stand in with the speculators, and divide the spoils." Lashing out, he continued, "It is a disgrace that a person cannot buy a decent seat at the box office, but must go to the speculators on the sidewalk and pay double the price. Some theatres sent their best seats to hotels, and there get prices for them far beyond their value." Declaring he planned to stand by every honest theatre proprietor, as few of them as there were, he added, "Neither you nor I want our wives and mothers insulted and jostled by speculators when they go to the theatres." On the matter of collusion, he fumed, "Why, I understand that at one theatre a relative of the owners is employed as a speculator, and you cannot get a decent seat at the box office, but must go to this man and pay double the price. I do not say this is so, but I have been told so. If it is true, the manager should be punished criminally. I myself would not go there, or to any other theatre that allows speculators to sell its tickets. There should be a bill passed by the Legislature prohibiting the sale of theatre tickets by speculators."[6]

When Magistrate Crane stopped for a moment to catch his breath, Keough stood up to say he could prove speculators were in league with the proprietors. According to him he had been offered thousands of dollars to go into combination with them. Crane listened attentively and then complimented Keough on his "manly stand" in refusing to yield to them, and for the good he was doing in his Harlem neighborhood by managing his venue along "honorable and upright" lines. Crane fined each of the three scalpers before him $10 on the charge of disorderly conduct.[7]

Hugh McGarry, a Pinkerton security guard, was attacked in front of the Criterion Theatre (at Broadway and 44th Street) on February 15, 1902, by a dozen ticket speculators who punched and kicked him into unconsciousness. From that initial encounter the fight snowballed to the point where a hundred or more men and boys were involved, striking people at random and tussling with men whom they thought were scalpers. So troublesome had been the speculation in front of the Criterion that manager Charles Frohman had for some time employed a number of Pinkerton detectives to stop the sidewalk sales and also to warn patrons that if they bought seats from the sidewalk men they would find themselves denied entry to the venue. Trouble started that evening when scalper Jacob Marks accosted a couple to buy seats to see Mrs. Leslie Carter in *Du Barry*. McGarry appeared and told the couple not to buy from Marks. That so enraged the latter that he punched McGarry in the face and knocked him down. When he got up the pair started to scuffle again but a dozen scalpers quickly rushed to the aid of Marks. Bystanders then joined in to assist the vastly outnumbered security man. Police arrested Marks and charged him with assault. An hour or so later when things had settled down a policeman passed the Criterion and noticed a number of speculators in a heated debate. He heard Mimon Coriat denouncing the scalpers for allowing Marks to be arrested. After hearing that the policeman arrested Coriat on a charge of disorderly conduct.[8]

Later that month the Criterion was in the news again when Justice Scott in the New York Supreme Court rendered a decision that denied the injunction asked for by scalper William H. Collister (his action was against the Criterion) to prevent theatre managers from putting out signs and verbally warning patrons not to buy from the sidewalk men. On the evening of the day Scott delivered his ruling a dozen or more speculators worked the street in front of the venue, as a symbol of defiance, vowing they would appeal the ruling. Those dozen persisted with the usual scalper cry of "tickets — best seats in the house" despite the fact there were two Pinkerton security men on duty at the venue and a "special policeman" to warn off patrons. Still, some tickets were sold by the speculators, and some of those trades were seen by the spotters with the purchasers being denied entry. It was said to be known that the scalpers had a good many seats for *Du Barry* for all performances up to almost three weeks into the future. Some of the sidewalk men tried to circumvent the spotters by directing their customers away from the venue to the inside of nearby stores where they hoped to carry out the transaction without the purchaser being identified by one of the watchers.[9]

On a daily basis the Criterion kept two or three employees out in the street to perform the function of spotter. At the same time the Broadway Theatre employed a dozen watchers — a tactic that did make it almost impossible for the sidewalk men to do any business. Meanwhile, at the New York Theatre, a man with a megaphone warned would-be purchasers about the perils of street buys.[10]

Litigious speculator William Collister lost again when, on April 25, 1902, the refusal by the New York Supreme Court to grant him an injunction restraining Albert Hayman and others, proprietors of the Knickerbocker Theatre, from interfering with him in his business of selling tickets in front of that venue was upheld by the Appellate Division. Collister had relied heavily in his case on having a license from the city. Speaking for the court Justice Patterson held, "The privilege accorded by the city authorities cannot change the inherent nature of a theatre ticket. If that ticket is something that may be bought and sold by any one ... then there would be a good ground to support the plaintiff's contention." But, continued Patterson, the weight of authority was to the effect that a theatre ticket was only a license given by the proprietor to the buyer of that ticket to enter the premises to witness a performance, "and that in its nature it is a revocable license."[11]

Despite that decision, scalpers continued to work the street in front of the Criterion. Managers were, obviously, pleased with the decision that a ticket was a revocable license. Oscar Hammerstein commented that he had not been bothered much lately by the sidewalk men but, nevertheless, "this decision by the courts, it seems to me, puts the matter up to the Board of aldermen. They issue the licenses, and it is now for them to act." According to this article the sidewalk men were only working at the Criterion and not at any other house.[12]

George M. Betts, a representative of the Theatre Ticket Sellers' Association, responded to the suggestion that scalpers were then only working the Criterion by hotly denying it. He argued there were "several other theatres who not only allowed us to conduct our business but endorsed it." Among them were said to be the Dewey, the Academy of Music, the Grand Opera House, the Third Avenue, the Metropolis, and Madison Square Garden. Betts claimed there were men standing in front of every one of those houses selling seats to all performances and the sole cause of trouble was that Charles and Daniel Frohman and the Sire Brothers "control the interests of the majority of Upper Broadway Theatres and have arbitrarily decided that we are grafters, whereas we can produce evidence that we undersell every hotel and other outside ticket stands."[13]

When the Knickerbocker Theatre opened for its new season on September 1, 1902, it had on hand eight New York policemen and several private security employees to prevent operations by the sidewalk men. Through their efforts about 60 people who bought seats on the street were refused admission at the door. By that time the street business had dried up for the night. None of the scalpers was arrested.[14]

Three days later speculator David Marks was arrested in front of the Knickerbocker after venue manager Alfred Hayman made a formal complaint against him. Marks was charged with disorderly conduct, a technical charge that arose from allegedly blockading the sidewalk. Hayman was described by a reporter as "one of the bitterest enemies" of the scalper. A few days later Marks was fined $2 in the Yorkville Court.[15]

At Madison Square Garden on March 30, 1903, the managers of the Barnum & Bailey Circus declared — what else — "war" on speculators. Employees of the circus were sent out to mingle with the sidewalk men and to warn the public against buying any seats from the sidewalk vendors. Some did anyway and more than a dozen people were denied entry to the circus. They went back to the scalpers and demanded their money back. Then the speculators insisted the police arrest circus employee Oliver Lester who, they said, was guilty of interfering with their business. Oddly enough, the police did take Lester into custody and down to the station. However, once he arrived there a sergeant immediately released him. After holding a brief meeting the scalpers declared they would bring a civil action against the circus management.[16]

Barnum & Bailey introduced new tactics in their war a few days later when management announced that starting on April 13 all tickets sold at the box office would be put in envelopes and sealed at the box office. Door staff would be instructed to refuse tickets not presented in those envelopes with the seal intact. Behind that scheme was the idea that people would not be willing to buy seats "blind" on the sidewalk and thus the problem of the speculator nuisance would be ended.[17]

Heinrich Conreid, director of the Metropolitan Opera Company, said, in February 1904, that he would "wage war" against speculators in the next season and that he had a new plan to thwart them, but he would not reveal it to the press. Of late, complaints about the sidewalk men around the doors of his venue had become, he said, "fast and furious." Numbers of people had asserted that Opera House management were in league with the scalpers, for the usual reason that no seats could be obtained from the box office but the scalpers always had good seats for every performance. Conreid had been personally criticized a great deal over the issue and was still smarting from it. He said the Opera House refused to sell to any speculator or known agent of any speculator but the sidewalk men just had too many proxies on the go. "I want to say that I am ready at any time to receive any suggestion from anyone who thinks he knows a method by which the speculators can be thwarted," pleaded Conreid. "I have tried every means I could think of. I have not been able to stop it. The assertion that we are in league with the curbstone men is absurd. Statements that we allot a certain number of tickets to the speculators before every performance are unworthy of answer."[18]

Shortly before the curtain went up on September 26, 1904, at the Colonial Theatre in Bridgeport, Connecticut, the manager Edward C. Smith got into an altercation with scalper Robert Franz, in which the latter received a black eye. According to a reporter, "It was Bridgeport's first experience with theatrical ticket speculators. Franz was summarily dealt with and unable to realize on a single ticket of the many he had purchased for the opening of the road tour of *Paris by Night*."[19]

As of August 1905 a "war" on speculators had been going on at the New York Theatre (Klaw & Erlanger) and had been led by the venue manager, Mr. Werba. But then A. L. Erlanger showed up personally, on the evening of August

29, to lead at least one of the battles. Across the front door was a huge sign that said tickets bought from scalpers would be rejected at the door. Reinforced by 15 private security guards and a dozen police officers sent over from the nearest station, Erlanger addressed the 20 or 30 sidewalk men who were mingling on the street with the playgoers and passers-by. "I want to tell you," said Erlanger, "that I own this theatre from the sidewalk to the roof. It is a dollar house, and is going to remain a dollar house." Manager Werba exclaimed the war would continue, regardless of the expense to the theatre, until the ranks of speculators were abolished. A reporter pointed out the venue sent seats to the hotel agencies to be sold at anything more than a dollar that the buyer was willing to pay and, "If this fight is to maintain the dollar rate, why aren't the hotel tickets sold under a guarantee that only $1 will be charged for them." Werba refused to discuss the matter.[20]

At the meeting of the Theatrical Managers' Association held later in 1905 a committee was appointed to lobby the New York Board of Aldermen to see if something could be done to eliminate the sidewalk men. Theatrical showman F. F. Proctor said, in a letter about scalpers, "As the speculators are licensed by the city we are powerless in our efforts to drive them away from the front of the house. We have no way of telling whether the purchaser of the ticket is a speculator or a bona-fide theatregoer. They do not purchase the tickets in blocks, but send men, women, and children, while they also use the telephone to reserve the seats. The problem is up to the theatre-going public to solve."[21]

Then there was the "war" waged by the police against the sidewalk vendors in front of New York's Hippodrome on December 29, 1906. Trouble began the day before when famed theatrical entrepreneur Lee Shubert himself was so bothered by the men that he made a complaint to the police — and that brought them out in force on the following day. Several scalpers who showed up to work the street in front of the venue were arrested.[22]

Two schemes somewhat different from the usual run of tactics were tried briefly, but unsuccessfully, in this period. One was tried by venue owner Augustin Daly who sold not seats in advance, but coupons. Information on the coupon stated the number of seats, location of the seats, and the day of performance. Admission tickets were issued to the coupon holder when he arrived at the box office at the time of the performance; he then had to pass directly into the venue with his ticket. A similar scheme had been used a few years earlier, but for one night only, at the Victoria Theatre. Coupons given out were even more enigmatic, with a changeable code printed on them. They also had to be presented on the night of the performance. Problems with those schemes were that there were too complicated, necessitated much more staff time to process, caused delays and jams at the box office, and so on. With regard to the more usual tactics a reporter commented in 1907 that the continued prosecution of individual scalpers had proved ineffective and, "Signs warning people not to buy tickets from speculators have caused much amusement as they seem generally to be found where speculators are thickest. However this sign gives the manager the right to refuse admission when he has an inclination to do something."[23]

Following a January 1907 conference between Shubert management and artists that included E. H. Sothern, Julia Marlowe, and Lee Shubert, it was officially announced that under no circumstances would any seats for the Sothern-Marlowe engagement at the Shubert Brothers Lyric Theatre be laid aside for the use of hotel agencies or sidewalk speculators. All tickets would be sold from the Lyric box office only. Secretary Allison of the Shubert concern visited Mayor McClellan at City Hall and assured him of full cooperation from the Shuberts in his efforts to suppress ticket speculation. Regarding the action taken with respect to the Sothern-Marlowe engagement Allison declared it was only the beginning of a new policy that would eventually eliminate scalpers from all the New York theatres under the Shubert management.[24]

Klaw & Erlanger reportedly opened not a war, but a "vigorous campaign" against the speculators at the New Amsterdam Theatre on October 21, 1907, which they proposed to continue during the run of The Merry Widow. They placed a dozen Pinkerton men in the lobby and whenever a scalper approached perspective customers of the box office he was ordered to move on. Perceiving the security men intended to keep the area around the entrance door clear the sidewalk men moved over to a candy store and a cigar store adjacent to the venue. From there they urged playgoers to go into the stores to buy seats. Supposedly they did a thriving business for 20 minutes or so even though the scalpers only offered balcony and gallery seats (not good locations). Erlanger's representative said he was pleased to learn that no good seats were available from the scalpers, owing to the precautions (not reported) taken at the box office during the preceding week.[25]

At a meeting of the Theatrical Managers' Association, still in 1907, the members were addressed by New York State Senator Saxe who asked their cooperation in assisting him in an endeavor to pass a bill at Albany that would do away with ticket speculation. On a motion made by Marc Klaw, the lobby group resolved that a committee be appointed to confer with the Merchants' Association, the City Club, the People's Institute, the West End Association, the Citizens' Union, and similar bodies for the purpose of cooperation in "abolishing the nuisance of ticket speculation."[26]

Cooperation as a tactic in this period reached a peak in the latter part of 1908. It began when the Theatre Managers' Association, representing 55 local theatres, announced it was to hold a special meeting on September 11 to try to devise some plan to eliminate ticket speculation. Marc Klaw was a major leader in this drive to develop a cooperative plan. He said the Klaw & Erlanger experience with scalpers had been an exceedingly hard one recently and during the run of The Merry Widow in the previous season, "We were overrun with ticket speculators, who used every conceivable method to secure tickets to sell in

front of the theatre." He stated the managers had studied every method of eliminating them and determined to make a strong fight before the Board of Aldermen to have them stop issuing licenses to speculators and to revoke existing
ones. Asked about the charge of collusion Klaw replied that was another reason the managers and theatre owners were anxious to do away with the sidewalk men. "So far as I know, there is no basis for such belief," asserted the
showman. "We tried any number of schemes at the New Amsterdam Theatre,
but somehow the speculators managed to get a number of good seats for each
performance."[27]

As he prepared for the meeting manager Harrison Grey Fiske commented,
"It is an outrage that the city in return for a trifling income, should license an
obvious imposition on the public. I have always opposed the nuisance..."
A. R. Erlanger added, "Certain it is that the public deserves every protection
and it appears to be up to the Aldermen to grant it. We have tried by every
means in our power to prevent tickets from getting into the hands of the speculators but have never been entirely successful." Mr. Harris, of Cohan & Harris, expressed his belief that the sidewalk men should indeed be eliminated but
"why then not abolish the ticket agencies in the hotels and elsewhere. There is
no reason in my opinion why any class of ticket speculator should be favored....
If all ticket speculating can be abolished, I am in favor of it, not otherwise."
Such sentiments marked a difference among the managers, although those
believing as Harris did were in the minority.[28]

After that much publicized meeting the managers emerged having
appointed a committee consisting of Daniel Frohman, Marc Klaw, Charles
Burnham, and E. F. Albee. It was charged with lobbying the Board of Aldermen to abolish sidewalk ticket speculation (agencies at hotels and other sites
were to be left alone). Confidently Klaw declared after the meeting, "The ticket
speculator will soon be a thing of the past. There is no doubt that this nuisance
will be abolished and the entire theatrical profession will stir public opinion
to such a degree that the Aldermen will not dare dissent from the general verdict." After defending hotel agencies as providing a needed service and a convenience, for which they were entitled to a fee, Daniel Frohman continued,
"the ticket speculator does nothing but harass the box office and prosper on
the toil of other men.... The managers cannot prevent tickets from falling into
the hands of speculators. Even with the employment of detectives it has been
impossible to defeat the sidewalk men."[29]

As a counterattack a group of scalpers came forward to charge that certain theatre managers had speculators who worked for them at their venues and
who tried to keep the truly independent sidewalk men away from their theatres. According to the sidewalk men the scalpers in the direct employ of those
venues got as many seats as they wanted from the box office, could return any
unsold seats and split the profits evenly with the house. Mentioned as managers who engaged in such practices were the very four from the meeting who

were appointed to the lobbying committee — all denied the accusations. Some of the sidewalk men admitted they bought tickets on occasion for $2.50 ($2 face) from the hotel agencies and then sold them for higher prices in front of the venues.[30]

William Brady was one manager who did not belong to the Manager's Association. "It is impossible to suppress the speculators ... I would be a curious bird to join this hue and cry against the speculator. I look with great pride on ticket speculation as the cornerstone of my financial structure. Years ago, in San Francisco, I bought $5 tickets for an Edwin Booth engagement and sold them for $8 and $9." Commenting further, he added, "I have no patience with the tendency of the Americans to nag at the petty thieves, to wage a relentless warfare against small offenders, while highwaymen with millions hold up their heads in the community and enjoy respect."[31]

An editor with the New York Times wondered about the manager's campaign against the scalper since the managers seemingly suffered no direct financial loss. If the reasons for the campaign were the ones put forward by the managers— to save the play going public from annoyance and extortion — why do it after not taking that action for years, he cynically mused. Not that the editor had answers to his wonderings. He mentioned the charges made by the speculators, but observed they were not the best of witnesses. Mentioned also was that the degree of opposition to the scalper was unclear and that "almost everyone" now and then was reluctantly glad to get an evening's entertainment thanks to a speculator. Also noted was the fact the public could end ticket speculation if it wished by not buying from the sidewalk men, but it had never done so. "To protect the public from something from which it is perfectly able to protect itself without help, and from something which it seems on the whole to like, even though it much dislikes those who supply it, is— well, just a bit amusing," concluded the editor.[32]

Marc Klaw challenged cynics like Brady and insisted scalpers could be eradicated. Oscar Hammerstein agreed and observed, "Ticket speculation leads to the dishonesty of employees. The men in the box office must withstand untold temptations— bribes from the speculators. They must have a hard time being honest when large sums are offered for their friendly intervention. No business which requires underhanded and unseemly methods should be tolerated.... No device can frustrate the sidewalk men. The only recourse is a law which prevents the continuance of this nuisance."[33]

Later in September at a public meeting before the Laws and Legislation Committee of the Board of Aldermen Marc Klaw said the men he represented in the Theatrical Managers' Association had spent $10,000 in one year trying to do away with the sidewalk men and had nothing to show for it except half a dozen lawsuits and a case of assault. Another speaker was John T. Brush of the New York Giants National League baseball club who told the committee the scalpers had to be done away with if the proper regulation of ticket sales was to be effected. He said as many as 16 speculators had been thrown out of his ball park in one day, that they were a nuisance and his club was "extremely anxious" to get rid of them.[34]

Hearings continued into October and November of 1908. Scalper David Neuberger declared Brush, despite his previous testimony, had hired speculators himself to sell tickets outside the gates to his ball park. Several other members of the trade maintained there was not a theatre in the city where all the tickets were on sale when the box office was first opened, meaning the hotel agencies got the first choice of seats. Klaw reiterated he would be willing to see laws go into effect that would abolish all speculation, both sidewalk and agency.[35]

After much debate the Law and Legislation Committee came up with a proposed ordinance that prohibited the sale of seats at any place other than the theatre hosting the event, required the price to be printed on every ticket, and made it unlawful to sell or offer for sale any such ticket for a sum in excess of that printed on the ticket. It applied to all locations, sidewalk and agencies. Violators were subject to a fine of not less than $10 and not more than $50, and/or up to 10 days in jail. Alderman Redmond, chairman of the committee, observed, "The hearings demonstrated beyond any doubt that there has been an arrangement in existence between theatre owners and the hotel agencies. It seemed to us that to do away with the speculators without doing away with the agencies as well could be farcical." Marc Klaw said, of the measure, "It means a great deal to the theatregoers of the city and will mark the end of a fight at the City Hall and Albany that has lasted for fifteen years." In his view it also meant "the abolishing of many incentives to dishonesty on the part of theatre employees for it is well known that men employed in theatres have at times been in league with speculators with consequent loss both to theatre owners and the public." But more debate and compromise took place and by the time the Board of Aldermen passed the ordinance on December 1, 1908, it applied only to the sidewalk men, repealing the old licensing ordinance and prohibiting all sidewalk speculation. Or at least that was what the Aldermen thought they had done, or pretended to think they had done. Legal opinion almost immediately declared the ordinance had effectively repealed the old licensing measure but had not prohibited the activity or regulated it in any way.[36]

Theater manager William Morris set out to work on the problem himself in 1910 when he employed a standard tactic whereby he engaged a number of people as watchers to follow the people who bought tickets from scalpers to the doors of his American Music Hall and point them out to the door staff— who refused them entry. Supposedly it resulted in driving the speculators plying their trade in front of his venue out of business within one week. Edward L. Bloom, a spokesman for Morris, explained, "Any theatrical manager who is on the level can stop the speculator nuisance without any more laws or ordinances. We have worked out the scheme here to perfection. Last Saturday night there were so many speculators in front of the American Music Hall that our patrons could hardly squeeze through. The nuisance got so bad that we determined to take matters into our own hands..." Bloom boasted, "Any manager who says that he cannot keep the speculators from doing business in front of his theatre is standing in with the speculators. It can be done, and we are showing how."[37]

Manager Charles Frohman tried another method, also in 1910. Slips of paper containing a special notice were added to the programs at all Frohman venues that said, "Orchestra seats for this theatre are sold at Tyson's and other hotel agencies for $2 each, with the agreement that purchasers will not be charged more than $2.50 a ticket. The management of this theatre will consider it a favor if patrons will report any overcharge." Frohman saw the notice as a general warning to protect the public against the possibility of being overcharged by any hotel agency.[38]

Later in 1910 scalper Harry Cohen entered the lobby of the American Music Hall and tried to sell seats. Venue employee Frank Shanley, a "special policeman," ordered him out. Cohen became abusive with the result there was a "pretty little mix-up" for a few minutes until police arrived and arrested Cohen. At the station he was found to have about 200 tickets for the American Music Hall on him. In Night Court Magistrate Hermann fined him $3 and told him he was a nuisance and that he would not get off so easily the next time.[39]

On the occasion of the seventh annual banquet of the Theatrical Managers' Association in 1911, president Charles Burnham announced that a general convention of theatre managers would be called in New York in a few months to consider the curbing of scalping. Describing the scalper as an "intolerable nuisance" and slamming the lack of progress that had been made in eliminating his activities, Burnham expressed a sincere wish that he would be eliminated.[40]

A 1905 letter to the editor from "Theatregoer" showed the persistence of the collusion idea. The letter declared, "Notwithstanding the noisy protest of the managers that they are not in league with the ticket vampire, and in the face of their specious declaration that 'tickets bought from speculators will be refused,' the best seats are handed over to the ticket offices and speculators. In fact, both classes pre-empt seven-eighths of the house for the entire run of a successful production."[41]

So many letters arrived at the newspapers criticizing the Metropolitan Opera House, and in some cases also its director Heinrich Conreid, of operating in collusion with the sidewalk men, because nothing was ever available at the box office yet scalpers had seats every night on the street, that Conreid publicly addressed the issue. "To any one who can produce evidence that the management of the Metropolitan Opera House, any employee, official, or agent connected with the theatre, is in collusion with the speculators, I will cheerfully pay $500," he declared.[42]

When New York Mayor McClellan urged his aldermen to take measures to curb the speculator in 1907, a reporter was moved to remark, "It cannot reasonably be doubted that some of the house managers are in league with the speculators and share their profits; the men whom they arrest are the men who are not in the pool and who are interfering with the trade of other [house] speculators."[43]

When Mayor McClellan took his public stand the *New York Times* printed many letters from people hoping the Mayor would be successful. But an editor remarked they had received even more letters manifesting "a deep-rooted belief that the relation between the speculators and the theatre managers is much closer than the latter do or ever did admit. Indeed, that belief has ever been an almost universal conviction, and managerial denials, no matter how solemn or passionate may be their terms, seem to shake it in no slightest degree." In his view, the public would not believe the denials on the part of management until managers put an end to the operations of the speculators themselves, or when it was accomplished by the passing of a city ordinance.[44]

Around the same time McClellan took his stand, New York State Senator Saxe was trying unsuccessfully to get anti-speculation legislation passed at Albany. Saxe explained that he had received many letters from New York, which, in his opinion, contained proof that in many cases theatre managers were the employers of speculators and divided the receipts with them. Just a few days earlier he had a personal experience that he felt tended to confirm such sentiment. He and a friend bought seats from a street scalper and got admitted easily to the venue despite the fact "This was a theatre where flaring signs are placed conspicuously at the door to tell the public that the tickets bought on the sidewalk would not be accepted."[45]

Promoter Lee Shubert was publicly accused of being in collusion with speculators who, said a news account, "throng the entrance of the playhouse at every performance and offer to sell the regular $2 tickets for several dollars in advance of that price." It all took place in the lobby of the Shubert-controlled Herald Square Theatre in October 1907. Speaking to friends and reporters Shubert angrily denied such allegations, explaining he was satisfied to have the theatre filled at the regular seat rates and that he would not willingly have the public deceived by making people believe that the house was all sold out for weeks in advance when such was not the case. "I have ordered the entire staff of the Herald Square to be vigilant and to drive away all persons from the lobby who have tickets to sell," Shubert insisted. "If there is a remedy to prevent speculators from obtaining their stock of tickets I should like to know it." However, the showman did add he was pleased to hear his currently running play "was complimented by Reginald Vanderbilt and his friend Thomas Clarke last Friday, when they paid $25 each for two seats in the orchestra. It was a good advertisement for the merits of the show, but I assure you the theatre only realized the regular price of $2 each for those seats." When the reporter asked at the box office he was told the play was sold out for the next six weeks, with the exception of a few seats left in the last two rows. But as the reporter left he was offered two seats in the 2nd row for that night. Asked for two seats for the coming Saturday night performance, the scalper said he could supply them, for $5 each. Describing the scene in front of the Herald Square Theatre in the evening the reporter wrote, "Dozens of ticket speculators blocked the theatre entrance last night, making it difficult for patrons to enter the theatre. These salesmen were very active and fairly opposed persons who tried to get into line to buy seats."[46]

A 1908 letter to the editor from "Grandpa" outlined how he went to Madison Square Garden to buy five tickets for the circus on the coming Saturday. While the box office told him they were all sold out for that performance Grandpa was annoyed to find a scalper "at his elbow" as he spoke to the box office clerk. He bought five $1 tickets from the speculator for a total of $7.50. Although he had not wanted to pay a premium to a speculator he did so in the end because he did not want to disappoint his grandchildren, whom he was treating to the circus. What annoyed him most of all was that he sensed collusion, "The speculator was check by jowl with the management, for he stood well into the lobby, only a few feet from the box office," he explained. "I suppose this condition of affairs will endure as long as fools continue to buy tickets from speculators, but there should be some pretense of protection for people like me, who can't help themselves."[47]

As people crowded into the Keith & Proctor vaudeville show at the Fifth Avenue Theatre on the evening of November 28, 1908, some bought seats at a 50 cent advance over the box office price from three speculators on the steps (part of the venue property) while outside on the pavement (the street proper) stood nine speculators with a grievance. According to the group of nine the three selling on the steps were not bothered by the police while the nine were constantly harassed by the police. About a week earlier, the three had appeared, supplied with "wads" of tickets and every night since it had been the same story, the nine told a reporter. They were allowed to stand on the steps with no interference while the police drove the nine away every time they tried to stand on the stairs. One said he was anxious to be arrested so he could make a test case but the police reportedly told him they had instructions not to arrest them but to keep them away from the house. When the reporter asked the police why they drove the nine away and allowed the three on the stairs to remain unmolested, they explained the three were on private property and could not be touched without instructions from the theatre management. Said one cop, "Besides, I understand they have the privilege of standing there." Venue manager Irving, when an explanation was sought from him, claimed he knew nothing about the matter.[48]

As the World Series between the New York Giants (National League) and the Philadelphia Athletics (American League) got underway in New York on October 14, 1911, there was much confusion over the ordering and receiving of tickets. Thousands of people who sent in mail orders and money never received seats, yet speculators all over the city reportedly all had piles of tickets. Police detailed men to prevent scalping at a few places in the city but, remarked a reporter, "In many other places about town, however, tickets were for sale in any quantity desired. Only the price differed from that which the club had advertised. Three-dollar seats commanded $5 to $10 with the prospect that these prices would advance again today." So much mail was "lost" from people who had mailed in orders that the Post Office announced it would conduct an investigation. William M. Gray, Secretary of the Giants, was compelled to issue a statement, "A newspaper reporter told me to-day it had been stated to him that a ticket speculator named Marks had arranged with certain New York Club officials which enabled him to secure one thousand tickets to the world's series at 50 cents advance per ticket. I brand unqualifiedly as a malicious, malignant lie, and I will give five thousand dollars ($5,000) to any one who can prove that any such arrangement with Marks or any other living individual existed whereby they could secure a single ticket for speculative purposes." According to the reporter every hotel agency and other agency had tickets for sale and "the army of scalpers who secretly ply their trade on the streets and escort their prospective purchaser into some near-by store to complete the transaction had hundreds more." Seats could be obtained in any section of the park desired and whole blocks of seats could be had, if desired. "The speculators have been so successful and the average fan had failed so miserably in getting tickets that open charges of collusion between club officials and speculators were often heard," he concluded.[49]

Testimony under oath given before a referee in bankruptcy in Chicago in January 1912 by H. N. Westfall of that city with reference to his relations as the owner of a ticket agency, with theatre managers, said a newspaper editor, "sheds a rather unpleasant light on managerial methods." Westfall, in a sworn statement, said he had been scalping under agreement with every leading theatre in Chicago. Some of the contracts he had were more favorable that others; that is, some allowed him to return all unsold tickets. At the end of each week he settled accounts with each venue, "splitting the premium above the regular price" equally. This editor worried that such collusion was eroding the public's faith in theatrical managers and that disgust over scalping may have even been causing a decline in theatre attendance.[50]

In a strongly worded 1917 editorial a Boston newspaper man accused theatre managers of collusion with scalpers and condemned the practice, contending that scalping would not be possible without the consent of the managers. "There was a time when the self-respecting managers of respectable theatres were ashamed of the imposition. Then they took the trouble to assert, at least, that it was carried on without their approval, frequently without their knowledge," he declared. "They do not appear to be ashamed by it any longer. On the contrary, they defend it as a business necessity, claiming that unless the brokers and scalpers helped them to obtain more than the stipulated price for seats they could not present costly attractions without loss."[51]

More attention seemed to have been paid by the media to scalping in sports in this period, or perhaps more of it was happening. Baseball came to the fore as the sport most often associated with ticket speculation.

8

Sports, 1900–1917

"it might be well to have it understood that a student who sells tickets to a speculator is doing something unworthy of himself, detrimental to the university, and unfair to the management and the general public."
The Spectator, Columbia University, 1903

"every effort will be exerted to foil the speculators ..."
Ban Johnson,
President of baseball's American League, 1910

"The ticket speculating evil has become the biggest question in baseball."
Barney Dreyfuss,
President of the Pittsburgh baseball club, 1912

On the night of November 20, 1902, on the Yale University campus at New Haven, Connecticut, a group of five Yale students forcibly took away from Sidney Troeder, a scalper, his tickets for the upcoming Yale-Harvard football game. On December 12 they were arraigned in City Court in New Haven on charges of breach of the peace (assault) preferred by Troeder. William Barnum, Harold P. Sawyer, and William R. Orthwein were fined $100 each while Bradford Ellsworth was fined $200. In the case against John Moorhead the State decided not to proceed with a prosecution.[1]

A year later, in November 1903, Columbia University's undergrad newspaper, *The Spectator*, took exception to the actions of undergrads who had sold tickets for the Yale-Columbia football game to speculators in an editorial that said, in part, "Those men who sold their tickets to the Yale football game as a speculation should realize that they violated a well-understood principle of college morals. It is not desirable that intercollegiate athletics should became a field of profit for a lot of ticket speculators who fleece the public and there was a good deal of just criticism last Saturday because outsiders were offering large blocks of tickets for sale at an advance in price, while none could be

86

procured at the box office." The editor argued the "evil" would have been a good deal less if a large number of seats had not been obtained by the scalpers from students and "it might be well to have it understood that a student who sells tickets to a speculator is doing something unworthy of himself, detrimental to the university, and unfair to the management and the general public."[2]

New Haven adopted an anti-scalping law in the fall of 1907 that mandated the price be stamped on every ticket and that it was unlawful to sell a ticket for a price greater than that which was stamped on its face. It was adopted by the city just before a couple of big football games were scheduled for Yale. A reporter commented that speculators "reap a rich harvest on tickets for the Yale-Harvard and Yale-Princeton football games, which they sell for $10 to $12 apiece, buying them for their face value of $2. Their harvest will vanish with the strict application of the new ordinance, and they have engaged clever lawyers to try to break the law. They will be aided by the theatrical trust, which will be also hard hit by the ordinance." He claimed the local theatres increased their prices two and three times the face value of their seats whenever there was an intercollegiate event scheduled, and the venue managers "have been accused of working in conjunction with the sidewalk speculators in allowing the best seats to be put at the disposal of the speculators."[3]

A 1908 account observed that in spite of efforts at Yale to suppress speculators the latter did a "thriving business" during the fall football games that year. A score of special policemen and detectives were scattered throughout the area but trade was still conducted. On the evening of November 21 four scalpers were arrested and fined $10 each. But as game days neared speculators became bolder and openly plied their trade on the streets near the stadium and in the vicinity of the railroad station. Many of the scalpers disposed of their seats for the Yale-Columbia game at Grand Central Station in New York and on the trains between New York and New Haven. Seats in the best location reportedly sold for as much as $50. Speculators that year often did their selling through a second or third party owing to the instruction from Judge Tyner, who ordered the police to arrest all men found shouting "buy or sell" around the city, and not wait for proof that they had tickets in their possession.[4]

In November 1909, in the days before the Yale-Harvard football game at Cambridge, Massachusetts, scalpers sold seats on the 30-yard line for as high as $35 while, on the other hand, they never paid more than $12 to buy a ticket, presumably from the students. A reporter believed "It is the first time on record — and the records for speculation on Yale-Harvard game tickets are voluminous — that the speculators have agreed and then stuck so tenaciously together on the amount they would give for a seat."[5]

U. S. Navy officers announced in November 1910, from Philadelphia, that they would investigate the sale of Army-Navy football tickets by some cadets to speculators. "Ticket scalping in connection with the Army-Navy football contest has been one of the features of the annual game which officers of both institutions have been trying to prevent for years. In spite of all precautions, however, the ticket scalper has always been on the ground ..." said the statement. Seats were scalped for $12 to $15 mostly, but sometimes they went for as high as $20 a seat. Hundreds of University of Pennsylvania (site of the contest) students who were entitled to two seats each immediately sold them to scalpers, receiving from $5 to $8 per ticket.[6]

One year later the Army-Navy game took place at the same location and scalpers were again at work. This time, though, students at the University of Pennsylvania could not be solely blamed because tickets allotted to the university had not yet been received by the school. Seats then being scalped were those from sections reserved for Army and Navy officials. Those tickets were available from various agencies in Philadelphia and at the corner of Broad and Chestnut Streets. One scalper, of several working that corner, was Louis Gloucester who had come in from his home town of Boston for a short time to work the game. He told a reporter that he got his supply of seats from Navy and Army officials and officers. Price per ticket ranged from $10 to $15. A reporter observed, "In former years the presence of speculators on the streets or in hotel corridors has been laid at the door of the university students, but no student of the university has yet received a ticket and consequently could not speculate."[7]

A day or two before the annual Pennsylvania-Cornell Thanksgiving football game, in 1916 in Philadelphia, a group of University of Pennsylvania students were so incensed because speculators had gotten hold of so many tickets that they made prisoners of a dozen of the scalpers and took the tickets away from them. Many of the scalpers resisted but were overcome and marched into the Athletic Association Building where they were "thoroughly searched and the pasteboards taken away. Cash (face) value was paid in every instance, however," according to a journalist. Students who took part were said to be among those who were unable to get any of the 2,000 tickets that went on sale at that building in the morning. When those seats were gone the disgruntled students were angered at the sight of scalpers offering some of those seats for sale and decided to take matters into their own hands.[8]

The National Baseball Commission, the supreme court of the sport, announced in December 1908 its decision in the scalping case in connection with the playing of the World Series the previous October between the Chicago and Detroit clubs. Telling of inadequate arrangements for handling the tickets in Chicago the report went on to declare the Chicago club was deserving of the "severest criticism and censure" for the manner in which they handled the sale of the tickets. No direct charge was made by the report nor was any proof offered that any one connected with the Chicago club as an employee was in collusion with the scalpers, "yet the Chicago Club admitted that it sold 630 tickets to one person," observed a reporter. In conclusion the National Baseball Commission stated it believed it would be a very hard matter to prevent World Series tickets reaching the hands of scalpers, even without collusion on the part of any one connected with the clubs, "unless the city authorities themselves pass proper laws and ordinances to prevent scalping of tickets, and for that reason the commission recommends that an effort be made by every major league club to secure the necessary legislation in their respective cities for this purpose."[9]

President Charles H. Ebbets of the Brooklyn baseball club announced early in the 1909 baseball season that he planned to eliminate scalpers from his ball park and the immediate area around it. When his team returned from its current road trip Ebbets claimed he was prepared to protect patrons from the ticket speculators, although he would not tell reporters any specific details of his plan.[10]

A lack of seats at the box office was reported from Pittsburgh in October 1909 for upcoming World Series games between Pittsburgh and Detroit at Forbes Field. But it was also reported that sections of the grandstand had "been bought in bulk by several ticket syndicates and the tickets placed on sale at prominent cafes and downtown cigar stores." Officials of the ball club promised they would investigate.[11]

At an October 3, 1910, meeting of the National Baseball Commission it was announced the 1910 World Series between the Philadelphia Athletics and the Chicago Cubs would open on October 17. Bearing in mind the trouble with ticket speculators in past World Series, the Baseball Commission added the following warning to its announcement, "The public is cautioned against paying any higher price for tickets than those fixed in the official schedules. Every effort will be made to prevent ticket scalping and the licenses granted to the ticket sellers will be revoked if they are found in the hands of scalpers. The commission reports the co-operation of the public to bring about proper results and has the assurance that the various municipal authorities will assist them in their work."[12]

Lending support to the stance of the National Baseball Commission was Ban Johnson, president of the American League, who said, "every effort will be exerted to foil the speculators.... The officials in charge of the ticket sale have been warned in particular to be on their guard against all kinds of trickery in the disposition of tickets, and the interest of the public will be protected."[13]

During the World Series of 1911 at the Polo Grounds between the New York Giants and the Philadelphia Athletics, Police Commissioner Waldo sent a special squad of 40 officers to the ball park on October 11 to arrest all people found selling tickets on the streets and sidewalks. A total of 12 were arrested with nine of those being fined $10 each. No more than six tickets were found on any one of the arrested men. According to police, there were central stations from which the speculators plied their trade, each coming back for a new supply when all his seats were sold. The three men not convicted had offered to take the plainclothes police (posing as buyers) to a place where seats might be obtained and Magistrate Krotel held this evidence was insufficient for a conviction.[14]

After the Series switched to Philadelphia a couple of days later, and stirred by reports of scalping in downtown Philadelphia and in the vicinity of the ball park, Assistant Superintendent of Police O'Leary sent 50 men in plainclothes on October 16 through the business section of the city to pick up all persons who had seats to sell. Seven men were arrested downtown while five more were taken into custody in the grounds of the ball park.[15]

One of those arrested at Shibe Park was an unnamed man who had on his person 100 $1 tickets that had gone on sale that same morning at the Shibe Park box office. Although not more than two tickets were supposed to be sold to any one purchaser he claimed he had bought his seats through an arrangement with one of the box office employees. Other speculators who were caught hawking their wares on downtown streets in Philadelphia were each fined $7.50 on charges of disorderly conduct.[16]

After the Series ended the National Baseball Commission announced it would meet in Cincinnati on November 14 to begin an investigation into alleged scalping in connection with the Series. Prior to the meeting Ban Johnson (also a member of the Commission besides being American League President) wrote to John T. Brush, President of the New York Giants of the National League, in answer to a communication demanding an investigation of rumors of collusion between the Giants and the scalpers. Johnson wrote that when he arrived in New York the day before the opening game of the Series he had no information there had been any trouble over the sale of seats. "In the few succeeding days, from information brought me, I was firmly led to believe that the leading ticket brokers of New York were abundantly provided with tickets and in consecutive sectional numbers. It seemed to me that this condition could not have happened unless there was collusion between some one in your office and these scalpers," declared Johnson's letter. Each of the two men — Johnson and Brush — condemned the other and insisted the other should conduct an investigation. In the exchange between the two men it was alleged that someone in the Giants organization handed out to scalpers 8,000 or 9,000 tickets at an advance of $1 each.[17]

A month later August Herrmann (from the Cincinnati club), chairman of the National Baseball Commission, declared the Commission had spent $1,500 on detectives during its investigation to try and determine the facts. While the Commission acknowledged tickets were in the hands of speculators in both New York and Philadelphia and that exorbitant prices were asked for seats, the Commission claimed it still had no idea if any collusion was involved. Herrmann appealed for anyone with information to come forward. Reporters expressed surprise there was no rebuke or action taken against the Giants because Johnson was widely believed to have strong evidence at his fingertips to show that collusion had occurred.[18]

Just one day later at the annual meeting of the American League it was announced that the league would not allow its champion team to take part in any more World Series unless it was allowed full charge of the sale of tickets to the games on American League grounds. Ban Johnson was said to have been incensed because the two other members of the National Baseball Commission — President Thomas Lynch of the National League and Chairman Herrmann — did not show enough interest in the ticket inquiry. Apparently they refused further investigation of points Johnson wanted to follow up. When Johnson was questioned about what happened at the investigation he admitted that in the evidence collected by detectives employed by the Commission the names of several New York theatre ticket men were involved and that it also appeared that one man had received an allotment of 6,000 seats. But the evidence was said to be not convincing enough to warrant making it public.[19]

And just two days after that the National League held its annual convention but it largely ignored the slap from the American League, choosing not to fight. With respect to the American League resolve not to participate in any more World Series contests, National League President Lynch declared, "I can't see that it means anything." One resolution the league did adopt was as follows, "Whereas, The present laws regulating the sale of tickets of admission to places of amusement are inadequate to protect the rights of the public; and Whereas The National League of Professional Baseball Clubs stands opposed to that imposition known as ticket scalping; therefore, be it Resolved, That the National League and the individual members thereof urge the states of Massachusetts, New York, Pennsylvania, Ohio, Illinois, and Missouri, and the cities of Boston, New York, Brooklyn, Philadelphia, Pittsburgh, Cincinnati, Chicago, and St. Louis to enact legislation that will make speculation in amusement tickets an offense punishable by fine and imprisonment."[20]

At the start of 1912 the National Baseball Commission issued a final report that completely exonerated the Giants and the Athletics of any blame for the widespread scalping that had occurred during the previous World Series. Emphatically the Commission declared there was no evidence, even by intimation, that any officials of the Giants or the Athletics had been in collusion with the ticket speculators but, on the contrary, every reasonable precaution was taken by both clubs to protect the public. It was admitted that lots of seats had been sold by scalpers and at exorbitant prices but that it all just happened despite the teams' best efforts to stop such activity. Capturing a sentiment held by many journalists toward that report was one newsman who referred to the document as "The whitewash report of the commission was given out yesterday...."[21]

On his return to Pittsburgh from a National Baseball Commission meeting, and in the wake of its final report, Pittsburgh Baseball Club President Barney Dreyfuss said, of the work of the Commission, "The ticket speculating evil has become the biggest question in baseball. I believe the club owners and managers finally have come to realize it. I am satisfied all city governments in the two big league cities will act on this question now that the National Commission has adopted my suggestion about asking the cities and states for laws against ticket scalping." He argued the team owners had tried hard to prevent the evil in every World Series that had been played but in the absence of any laws prohibiting the practice they had not accomplished much. "I believe that if the amusement loving public will take enough interest in the matter to insist upon having proper laws, strictly enforced, that speculation in baseball and theatrical tickets can be stopped," concluded Dreyfuss. "Some cities are so accustomed to this form of robbery that they cannot be aroused easily."[22]

When a reporter with the *Los Angeles Times* reviewed the furor over the 1911 World Series, in early 1912, he felt it was an example about how baseball rumors got out of hand and were embellished with the result that people were led to believe that scalping conditions in New York the previous fall were worse than ever before when they were actually better. Describing the ticket scandal in New York as another far-fetched story, he added, "Ticket scalping has been going on in New York 365 days a year for many years, and is still unchecked there. In fact, John T. Brush, who employed a well-known detective agency to help him protect the public, is the only amusement promoter in New York who ever attempted to break up the bad practice."[23]

In the period shortly before the October 1912 start of the World Series between the New York Giants and the Boston Red Sox, draconian measures were announced in an effort to eliminate scalping. The sale of seats in both cities was to be under the direct supervision of the National Baseball Commission instead of the clubs involved, as a result of past fiascos, especially that of 1911. To thwart efforts by scalpers to get tickets for games at the Polo Grounds in New York no seats were sold by mail. The entire lower section of the stadium — 15,400 seats not reserved — was sold at the Polo Grounds only on the day of a game at $2 each. Applicants had to queue in line, could only buy one seat each, and had to go directly into the stadium as soon as a ticket was bought. That arrangement was also in use for the sale of unreserved bleacher seats at $1 each. John Brush, President of the Giants, considered this method to be the fairest way to deal with fans after the experience of a year earlier.[24]

The only reserved seats at the Polo Grounds were the 8,500 in the upper tier of the grandstand, sold for $3 at the box office. Before they were put on sale, though, the priority list (as designated by the Commission) had to first be satisfied. First on that list was 75 tickets for each member of the Commission; two seats each for eligible members of each of the contending teams; next came the seats to fill the requests of all officials of all minor leagues approved by the Commission; next came applications from, in the words of a reporter, "parties of prominence, which may or may not include a lot of people"; then came requests from the press of New York and Boston (a number to be determined); then came the requests of the press of other cities; then came applications from the season box holders at the Polo Grounds; then came applications from officials of the other major league clubs. After all those requests were filled, then reserved sales were made available to the public. Such sales had to be made in person and were limited to a maximum of two seats per person. Sales of seats for the games in Boston were conducted differently because it was said the Boston club knew all its patrons and was thus able to deal with them individually. Mail orders were accepted, and if "found satisfactory" the applicants were notified and the order filled. An immense amount of clerical work was involved, which the Boston Red Sox were willing to undertake. It was all done under the supervision of the Commission.[25]

After the first game had been played the precautions taken for the Giants and Red Sox World Series were declared to have been effective, at least to the extent that fewer tickets found their way into the hands of scalpers, although that put the price up. Three-dollar seats were scalped on game day for $40 to $60 in a few cases but a more usual price was $12.50. A year earlier $6.25 had been the most usual price obtained by speculators. When the tickets were first distributed it was said that a number of baseball players were seen disposing of seats to scalpers at an average price of $7, which gave the player a $4 profit over the $3 face the seat had cost the players, and netted the scalper $5.50 per seat. One baseball executive, described only as being connected with one of the Western clubs, was said to have sold 75 tickets in two batches to one New York scalper for a total of $300. For the first time in the history of the World Series, Wall Street itself was invaded by speculators. About a dozen men with seats to sell visited, separately, the New York Stock Exchange and the Curb Exchange and disposed of many tickets at $15 and at the major hotels, the scalpers did a "brisk business" realizing in a few cases as much as $15 and $20 per seat. That first game on October 8 had a paid attendance of 35,730 with official box office receipts of $75,127. One reporter declared, "Scalpers cleaned up about $50,000."[26]

Prior to the start of the 1913 World Series between the Philadelphia Athletics and the New York Giants a news account remarked the "usual" World Series scalping scandal had already appeared in Philadelphia. Even before the sale of tickets to the public commenced numerous speculators already had "liberal" supplies of seats that they were hawking for about three times the face value. Where the tickets came from "nobody knows" but the management of the Athletics was willing to make a guess. To that time the only seats distributed had gone to "leading politicians" and to the local newspapers. It was estimated that seats to the value of $19,000 were sold to the local papers, and of that amount, less than $4,000 worth went to the people employed in the newspaper offices and to large advertisers. Allotment of tickets to newspapers in New York was conducted differently with each paper being limited to a purchase of 50 seats for members of its staff.[27]

At the close of that 1913 World Series the National Baseball Commission announced it would make no investigation of scalping in either city. Chairman

Herrmann declared that although a "large number" of tickets had been secured from scalpers the whole situation was exaggerated and, in any case, it could not be stopped. Leslie Constans of the Pittsburgh club, who represented the Commission in supervising the sale of World Series seats, voiced the sentiment of the Commission when he asserted that scalping was the result of the laws, or lack thereof, rather than the fault of the contesting clubs. He said, after dealing with the ticket problem for five years, if a law was in force "making it illegal to sell a ticket above its face value, there would be no speculating. In New York the only offense is loitering, and any speculator is allowed to sell at any price within doors. The problem belongs to the city and State authorities and until they step in the practice cannot be stopped." With respect to the World Series and scalping Constans concluded, "Every series has shown the same conditions and the same dissatisfaction by the fans."[28]

During the 1916 World Series between Brooklyn and Boston seven men charged with speculating in tickets were fined $5 each by Magistrate Steers in Flatbush Court. All were arrested in the neighborhood of Ebbets Field in Brooklyn.[29]

Yet another new drive was launched against World Series ticket speculation in September 1917 by Charles Comiskey, president of the Chicago American League club. He established a special department at the White Sox ball park, had telephones installed, and issued an appeal requesting the public to communicate any information regarding people trying to obtain mail order seats with the intention of having them resold at "fabulous prices" by the speculators. Said Comiskey, "I am earnestly endeavoring to eliminate the scalping of tickets and I am seeking the cooperation of the public in this. It is an unnecessary evil and should be done away with. Any information regarding scalping will be acted on immediately." Despite that stand scalpers were said to be defiant even though U. S. Attorney Maclay Hoyne had threatened to prosecute them on charges of conspiracy to extort. Speculators insisted they would be able to fill any reasonable order for seats and declared there was no legal way to stop them.[30]

Chicago Police Chief Schuettler threw his support behind Comiskey and announced that for the opening game of the Series he would station several hundred policemen around Comiskey Park to prevent ticket speculation. Any one caught selling seats in the vicinity of the park would be arrested, he warned.[31]

Prior to an October 1908 boxing card at McCarey's Pavilion in Los Angeles, the Pacific Athletic Club, card promoter, announced it had "decided to stop the scalping of gallery tickets which has become a nuisance since the crowds are being attracted to the shows." But its plans to end speculating were limited to building a small extension to the box office booth and adding two extra ticket sellers to their staff.[32]

When a sell-out crowd turned out on March 25, 1916, at Madison Square Garden for the Moran-Willard boxing match it was a crowd described as running the gamut from average to rich and very rich. With plenty of seats to sell the speculators "ran rampant among the spectators" and did a roaring business. For the most part they avoided the planted plainclothes policemen in the crowd looking for them as only three arrests were made. "A golden harvest was reaped by speculators who had opened offices in various establishments in Twenty-eighth Street and in Madison Avenue," exclaimed a reporter. "These scalpers were beyond the power of the police, and to their heart's content they bellowed the fact to passers by that they had plenty of tickets for sale and at fancy prices, too." Box office prices for the seats were $3, $5, and $25.[33]

In the following period, 1918–1949, governments at all levels remained active in attempting to legislate the practice with about the same amount of success they had in the past. Additional activity by the government involved the conducting of official "probes" into scalping. The practice became even more prevalent in the world of sports. Agencies increased their dominant financial position in the trade but the sidewalk men often drew the bulk of the anger, criticism, and legislative action. Although they were relatively minor players in the trade they were more readily visible and they were easier targets.

9

The General Situation, 1918–1949

"It is the curse of New York. It is impossible in that city to get a ticket for a popular show at the rate advertised in the newspapers."

Los Angeles Times, 1924

"Everywhere the practice is looked upon with disfavour by the general public, and yet it exists and thrives with varying success in every large city in the United States."

Morrow Mayo, 1925

"There is, also, some curious thrill in getting tickets from a speculator. The purchaser takes a pride in being charged heavily."

Heywood Broun, 1929

"What is there to be done about it? Nothing. How is the problem to be solved? It can't be...."

Paul Gallico, 1934

Noel Coward's play *Bitter Sweet* opened November 5, 1929, in New York at the Ziegfeld Theatre after it had enjoyed a successful run in Boston. Perhaps illustrating the ambivalence that sometimes existed toward ticket speculation was a print ad for the play that stated, "Nearly every ticket speculator has been to Boston and they are already renting stores near the Ziegfeld Theatre and are digging for tickets at the box office through confederates. They've seen the show."[1]

So well known was scalping in America that it was even featured in at least one Hollywood film. *Saturday's Heroes* (1937, RKO) had lead actor Van Heflin portraying Val, a college football hero who was expelled from school for ticket scalping. Val cleared all that up by selling to a rival college the suggestion that college football players should be openly financially subsidized by their schools so they would not have to spend a lot of time and energy on working up a lot of devious underground schemes in order to get some money. Then Val went on to win the big game over his former alma mater and, of course, he won the girl.[2]

In its year-end edition for 1920 an editor for *Variety* repeated the slogan of a large ticket agency, "Tickets on Sale for All Theatres— 50 Cents Advance!" only to add, "What a joke that little slogan of the theatre ticket agencies has turned out to be, providing you are not willing to sit somewhere back of the 12th or 15th row." Noting that for carrying an account with an agency there was a $12 per year fee and to have the tickets delivered to your door there was a 50 cent additional messenger fee he added, "If you are one of the theatregoers who care to sit somewhere within the first ten rows of the stage, you will find there is no such animal as a '50-cent premium' on the seats. You are lucky if you manage to sit anywhere between the fifth and the tenth rows by the payment of a $2 advance for any of the hits and in the first five rows the premium is apt to be anywhere between a deuce ($2) and a fin ($5)."[3]

Less than two years later the *Variety* editor returned to state, "The legitimate theatre managers of New York and Chicago (and they interlock to a considerable extent) are dead up against the ticket speculating thing. Its past bodes ill for its future. The managers have finally reached that conclusion. But they don't seem to know what to do." For this editor any plan that allowed ticket agencies to handle seats was dangerous unless the theatrical managers had some degree of supervision over those agencies with the power to order an investigation if necessary. *Variety* argued here the best method was to set up a single central box office to be used by all theatres, and under their control to some extent.[4]

A Los Angeles reporter was moved to write in 1924 that the practice of scalping there was growing "at a very rapid rate." From there he moved on to comment on the New York situation by stating, "It is the curse of New York. It is impossible in that city to get a ticket for a popular show at the rate advertised in the newspapers." A ticket buyer, he said, had to pay a bonus anywhere from a 50 cent advance to two or three times over face, and "A new show in New York is usually underwritten by ticket speculators." On the other hand, he thought, the managers looked to the cut-rate outlets to save a dying show because, "Without loss of prestige the managers could not cut prices themselves."[5]

At about the same time manager S. Masters of the Hollywood, California, American Legion stadium announced in Los Angeles that he was declaring "war" on the scalpers who had been operating there during the previous few weeks. One tactic used by the speculators, explained Masters, was to call the venue and reserve blocks of seats under fictitious names asking the seats be held at the box office until just before show time. When prospective patrons came up the window on the evening of the performance only to be told the place was sold out (often due to the tickets held by fictitious reservations that would never be picked up) they thus became possible customers for the speculators. As a first step in his war Masters issued an order that reservations made by persons unknown to the management would be held only until 1 P.M. on performance days, instead of until 8 P.M.[6]

Journalist Morrow Mayo produced a general article on the practice in America, in 1925, and started by saying, "Everywhere the practice is looked upon with disfavor by the general public, and yet it exists and thrives with varying success in every large city in the United States." While he mentioned that ticket speculators sometimes underwrote a show in New York he said as far as he knew it had never been done in Los Angeles. Mayo went on to explain how the practice worked in Los Angeles and, by implication, most other big American cities, outside of New York City. When a new show came to town the ticket broker ordered what he wanted several weeks in advance from the theatre, something like this: Monday 150 seats, Tuesday 100, Wednesday 50, Thursday 75, Friday 125, Saturday 200 or all that could be had, matinees 100. That block of seats the broker ordered was the pick of the orchestra seats and was received by the agency before the advance was opened to the public, even, perhaps, before mail orders were filled. Seats were usually obtained on credit with settlement made at the end of each week. Each evening about 7:30 P.M. (or 30 minutes before show time) the broker returned any unsold seats he still had for that night to the theatre box office and received credit for them. Thus, said Mayo, by such a move "the theatre automatically decreased its seating capacity at advertised prices."[7]

Generally, continued Mayo, the broker charged a 50 cent advance over the box office prices, selling a $2 seat for $2.50, for example. "The theatre and the broker usually make a sixty-forty split of the excess profit," said the reporter. Because of the admissions tax a $2 seat at the box office cost $2.20. A ticket broker bought that seat for $2.40 and in turn sold it for $2.75 (there was five cents tax on the extra 50 cents). Under that arrangement, which Mayo believed to be the usual one in most large cities, the theatre made an extra profit of 20 cents on each seat while the ticket speculator made a gross of 30 cents. Due to that system, argued Mayo, it was obvious that the theatre not only approved of prices higher than those that it advertised but received its share of the extra 50 cents. By passing out blocks of choice seats to 10 or 15 brokers the venue automatically created 10 or 15 box offices selling seats at advance prices instead of one box office and one price. "Under the system of speculation which is found in most large cities the theatres sometimes give as many as half their orchestra seats to the brokers." As far as Mayo was concerned the entire onus for the system had to be placed on the managers. "The moment they decide to do business directly with the public ticket speculation automatically ceases," he concluded, and, "If it is to be stopped in Los Angeles is no different from any other city. The first move must be made by the theaters."[8]

At a June 1926 testimonial luncheon in New York for Will Hays, who had a few years earlier been named to head the major Hollywood film producers lobby group, Hugh Frayne, national organizer of the American Federation of Labor, announced that members of the AF of L would refuse to appear in productions under managers who tolerated ticket scalping. Referring to the practice, Frayne declared, "If we can find no other way to stop it, we will enforce our objections by having our people refuse to work in theaters where practices of that sort are countenanced." He explained that very often the public was turned away from a box office where they were told the venue was sold out, only to find a scalper next door selling seats at advanced prices.[9]

A few years later at a meeting of the council of the Actors' Equity Association — a union much closer to the problem — it was declared the actors would do their utmost to stand by the managers who were seeking to abolish the ticket agency custom of buying blocks of seats months in advance. That support, it was understood, would go to the extent of boycotting productions by withdrawing players whenever managers failed to support the plan to eliminate the ticket speculation "evil." Equity was even thinking of placing recalcitrant managers on the unfair list — an established trade union tactic. It was a theatre managers' committee that had first approached Equity to solicit its support. Said the Equity statement, "We believe that it is to the best interest of our people that the 'gyp' should go and that the theatre which supports the 'gyp' should be closed." Equity's council also suggested to the managers' committee that it would be desirable to obtain support for the plan to curb speculation from prominent people and groups such as U.S. Attorney Charles H. Tuttle, Rabbi Stephen S. Wise, the Drama League of America, and the Federation of Women's Clubs.[10]

Scalping in foreign locales was mentioned in the media in this period, but very infrequently. A central plaza location in Moscow — said to be the equivalent to New York's Times Square — reportedly had a speculator problem in 1935. Early that year two men who had hawked theatre tickets in the area were sentenced to hard labor in prison and the people from whom they had illegitimately bought seats were discharged from their jobs. A drive against speculators had been underway for some days after a quiet police check of the area had revealed the presence of "numerous" scalpers. Among the sources of tickets for scalpers were workers who received them free as a bonus for faithful work and, it was reported, "Several representatives of factories who received such tickets will be tried for selling them instead of distributing them to the rightful owners."[11]

Much later, in September 1948, a People's Court in Moscow sentenced three ticket scalpers to jail terms ranging from five to six years after they were convicted of having speculated in football (soccer) tickets. The trio, who worked together, specialized in scalping seats to the famous Moscow Dynamo football stadium.[12]

Police in Mexico City announced in April 1945 they had arrested and convicted 300 ticket speculators with some of them fined as much as $100 and others sentenced to jail for as much as 15 days. Enforcement of the laws against ticket scalping was revived that week after some high government officials were dismayed when they found they could not get tickets to a bullfight except by paying double the face value to the street vendors.[13]

When the 4th International Film Festival closed in August 1949 at Marienske Lazne, Czechoslovakia, it was noted that although Russian films won the major prizes, the scalpers did their best business from hawking seats for such American entries as *Johnny Belinda* and *Treasure of the Sierra Madre*. During the two-week festival 50-crown ($1) tickets for *Johnny Belinda* were sold on the black market for 1,500 crowns ($30) and the cinema was sold out for every performance.[14]

Sentiments that blamed the public for the evil of scalping, or even favored the practice, or argued, in the end, nothing could be done, began to appear more frequently. L. Lawrence Weber, a producer and Secretary of the Managers' Protective Association, issued a statement in 1929 defending the managers in connection with "the supposed evil of ticket speculation." It was a favorite topic for those who enjoyed taking pot shots at managers, he believed. "Why the managers are blamed is beyond my comprehension," he grumbled. "The ticket speculator is supported by the theatregoer who is willing to pay for the comfort of obtaining theatre tickets with ease." As to the advance in price paid, why, argued Weber, it was "frequently regulated by the well-known and oft-quoted economic law of supply and demand. The man who cannot afford to live at a first-class hotel and whose financial means compel him to live in a furnished room is not riled at the hotel." In any case, concluded Weber, "there comes a time in every play's life when tickets can be purchased at the box office at box office prices."[15]

Responding to Weber's defense of scalping was a letter to the editor from Norman C. Levy, who pointed out the common sentiment that most people did not patronize the agencies through choice but through necessity because there were no good seats available at the box office for virtually any show if you tried to buy for a performance within a few days. "I maintain that the public do not patronize the ticket brokers because they want to, but because the managers of the theatres are compelling them to by not keeping an adequate supply of tickets on hand for that portion of the public that either does not desire, or refuses, to patronize ticket brokers."[16]

Famed theater critic Heywood Broun weighed in on the speculation issue in a late 1929 piece wherein he argued every producer with a hit on his hands allowed thousands of dollars to slip through his fingers every week because he stepped aside "and lets a fellow called a speculator reap golden profit in a field where he has sown not a single seed. The poor manager is the dupe of the speculator or broker. I am not moved at all by the pleas of theatregoers that ticket

speculation is an evil thing which should be eradicated." With respect to existing laws that limited the amount of premium an agency could charge for a seat,
Broun declared "this flies so squarely in the face of sound economic theory that
the super-charges continue and even mount to undreamed-of heights." Broun
argued that when a patron found no seats were to be had at the box office even
though he was willing to buy eight weeks in advance it meant the price set on
the tickets was out of line, that is, it was too low. "The seats have gone to the
speculator because the manager was selling them too cheap."[17]

As far as Broun was concerned the box office of the average theater was
the worst of all possible places at which to buy seats. If the show was a success
all the best seats were elsewhere but if, on the other hand, the play was not a
hit, tickets could be obtained more cheaply at a cut-rate agency. He felt there
was not much sincerity in most of the criticism of ticket speculators because
if any great portion of the public wanted to get along without the agencies then
those brokers could not long survive. Considerable numbers of patrons did
not wish to get tickets eight weeks ahead even if they were available at box
office prices; many preferred to make a decision at the last minute, he maintained, "and it is no more than just that they should pay extra for this coming
at the eleventh hour and receiving good accommodations. There is, also, some
curious thrill in getting tickets from a speculator. The purchaser takes a pride
in being charged heavily. He will have something to talk about when he gets
home."[18]

Brock Pemberton was a well-known New York theatrical producer who
wrote a long piece in 1933 outlining some of the background of agencies
involved in ticket speculation and some of his own experiences. Years earlier,
he said, box office men were the custodians of tickets and agencies started to
get involved by making the odd gift, in order to secure seats to sell. From voluntary gifts it was just a step to "regular tribute" with the theaters flourishing
during World War I and the boom years that followed. And as more and more
brokers bid for the best tickets the price they had to pay to the box office treasurers soared. Producers were not ignorant of that traffic, "some of them shared
the spoils." Until the stock market crash of 1929, continued Pemberton, the
owner of the theater was usually the one to profit since the standard contract
between venue owner and play producer stipulated the venue would have sole
handling and distribution of tickets. Some producers, though, were powerful
enough to demand the ticket privilege for themselves. The tribute exacted from
brokers could be so large that the producer, if he received it instead of the venue
owner, "may receive more from this source than from his share of the play's
profits. A conservative broker is authority for the statement that the amount
collected by a producer thus situated from premiums on a hit of several years
ago totaled $70,000."[19]

When Pemberton booked the play *Strictly Dishonorable* into the Avon Theatre four years earlier his contract gave the venue owner disposition of tickets.

The play was a hit and ran from September 18, 1929, to January 1, 1931. Later legal action over the owner's estate revealed extra deposits of $25,000 had been made to one bank over a three-month period by that individual during the run of the play. According to Pemberton, during the play's run all 462 orchestra seats and a few dozen balcony seats were turned over to the brokers. "Five hundred seats for eight performances are 4,000 and for thirty weeks are 120,000," explained Pemberton. "Multiply that by any figure you choose to think of as a premium — however modest — and it's a nice income, especially if you've done nothing to create it. This covered less than half the run."[20]

Years earlier when brokers first became involved, continued Pemberton, the method of distributing seats was to allocate certain blocks to an accepted group of brokers. The tickets were given on consignment to be sold, or returned just before performance time if unsold. Under the next development, when plays became hits the brokers expressed their willingness to purchase tickets outright (no return privilege). That led to the "buy," something Pemberton thought was "one of the roots of the evils of the ticket business." Once the seats were bought brokers maintained the tickets belonged to them and they could charge whatever premiums they desired. As years passed buys were frequently made in advance of the New York showing; often the brokers formed a pool and financed a production. Outright buys meant that brokers sometimes got stuck with blocks of seats on their hands they could not sell, if the play was a flop. To cover those losses the agencies charged even higher premiums for the tickets they could sell. Buys were not evenly spread about the theatrical industry; some managements were favored over others. Any producer who issued tickets on consignment to a broker, and allowed full return privileges, found himself at the mercy of the broker who was loaded up with tickets obtained for other plays through outright buys — he obviously tried to steer his customers toward buying those seats. Producers had a weapon or club they sometimes used. Explained Pemberton, "The club was a hit show already established, with which the manager belabored the poor broker to force him to load up with pasteboards for a flop under threat of cutting off his supply of hit tickets. Many times the public has paid to save the pride and investment of some management that owned both the success and an unwanted show." As recently as one year earlier, when the Depression had brought the New York theater to its lowest ebb, he added, "First-line producers kept plays on the boards that were complete failures by means of buys, and the brokers passed the loss on to the public in higher premiums for hits."[21]

Some idea of the toll the public had paid could be seen in the many bankruptcies of theaters and theatrical firms during the Depression but none among brokers, maintained Pemberton. In his view a conservative estimate of the amount paid by the public, above the box office price, to see *Strictly Dishonorable* was between $500,000 and $1 million (using $750,000 and a 63-week run would have meant $12,000 extra per week; with 500 seats for each of eight shows at brokers it worked out to $3 extra for each of those tickets, seemingly high, but perhaps possible). "Not a dollar of this reached the producer, who would have been enabled to produce more plays if it had," concluded Pemberton. He argued that one of the reasons for the current bad situation was that of the individual nature of the business — that is, the producer with a hit was an autocrat. "If all managers had been willing to sacrifice the dubious advantages of side-money, reforms could have been made at any time, but always someone had a hit."[22]

Author Paul Gallico was motivated to write a column on scalping in March 1934 after a personal experience at the just finished New York Golden Gloves amateur boxing tournament at Madison Square Garden for which he could not obtain tickets, except from a scalper. "I use the Golden Gloves tourney merely as a spring board from which to take off, because the ticket speculator problem confronts every promoter of attractions from here to the West Coast and from Maine to Florida," he asserted. However, he had no solution, remarking, "What is there to be done about it? Nothing. How is the problem to be solved? It can't be, as long as the laws of supply and demand are valid just so long will there be ticket speculators and just so long will they continue to gouge the public." Gallico believed all scalpers got their tickets from "digging." That term was then coming into use to describe the practice of the speculator — or more usually his proxies — of standing in line, waiting his turn, and then buying two or four seats, or whatever the limit was, and returning over and over to repeat the process. While that has always happened, and still does to this day, the vast majority of tickets that reach speculators do so from bulk buys before sales to the public are even opened and/or through various collusive deals with box office personnel, and so on. Street scalpers regularly were forced to get their seats direct from the agencies at times, the bulk buyers. Sometimes the sidewalk men had their own deals with brokers. Gallico's belief that scalpers got all their seats from digging was very naïve.[23]

Gallico returned to the subject almost exactly one year later, again just after a Golden Gloves tournament. Declaring the speculator to be "king" he asserted that was so "Because, brethren, we aren't men, but mice. We've let him get a foothold here; we encourage him; we stand for him, and we patronize him." He admitted that he never bought tickets at the box office for anything, merely calling up his broker, telling him what he wanted to see and where he wanted to sit, and paying $1 or $2 for that service.[24]

Warren P. Munsell, Jr., who had been a company manager for several well-known theater producers, penned an op ed style piece in 1948 in which he also blamed the public for the existence of the evil. Noting that an informal agreement under which the theatrical industry operated — the Theatre Ticket Code — permitted brokers and agencies to handle up to 75 percent of a venue's tickets, Munsell argued, "but in actual practice broker allotments are nearer to fifty percent. Though this figure seems high (in an average 1100-seat Broadway

theatre it means 550 seats), agency sales justify such a division." What Munsell neglected to mention, assuming his numbers were accurate, was that the
agency took the best 550 seats in the house; they were not scattered randomly
throughout the venue. Many theatregoers and national firms, said Munsell,
maintained standing orders at their brokers for entertaining out-of-town buyers or executives, and "refuse to buy at box offices. Their continued patronage
of the theatre depends on special, short-order service." Nonsensically he added,
"Furthermore, without brokers to 'push' the high priced tickets (almost all the
balcony seats are retained by the box-office for direct sale) even the biggest hits
would soon be playing to half-filled orchestras." Concluded Munsell, "Though
the average customer regards the premium-charging agency as an evil, its existence after all depends not upon the profession which supplies it but upon that
part of the public which patronizes it." He declared it was a misconception to
suppose that only the brokers had decent seat locations because despite the 550
seats in the hands of agencies "and another thirty to forty set aside nightly for
press, producer or star, there are still more than 550 available at the box-office
for the general public."[25]

And it was in this period that the power of the agencies and brokers was
more fully revealed and explored, as their position of dominance over the sidewalk men became more apparent.

10

Agencies, 1918–1949

"[Ticket agency brokers] want to save and promote a legitimate business. They are not and have not been out to gouge anybody. These calumnies and slanders to that effect are all untrue.... The sidewalk theatre ticket speculator must be driven out of business. It is he who has caused the business to fall into disrepute, and we intend to go after him just as hard as the authorities would."

Nathan Lieberman, Theatre Ticket Brokers'
Association of Greater New York, 1925

Legendary showman Florenz (Flo) Ziegfeld announced on June 16, 1918, that he would wage not a war but a "general fight" against ticket profiteering, and that every means would be employed to prevent seats from falling into the hands of brokers, with respect to his forthcoming show, *Follies* (the 1918 version). One of those means was to state that all seats for that show would only be available at the box office. Ziegfeld's statement was in reply to charges from the brokers that the manager's decision to sell tickets directly to the public had been reached only after seats had been offered to the agencies at certain prices and refused. Flo admitted he had agreed to sell tickets to the brokers on condition that they filed a bond binding them not to resell them at an advance of more than 50 cents a ticket.[1]

At the close of the first week's run of the 1918 *Follies* Ziegfeld maintained the initial phase of his offensive against the scalper had met with success. "So far as the *Follies* are concerned, at least," he said, "we have proved that you can sell every seat in the house at the box office and still sell out every performance. We have done that so far, including the matinees, at which every seat was sold at the regular price, running from 50 cents to $2."[2]

Ziegfeld added he had accomplished that with 36 ticket agencies working against him instead of for him. Agreeing that hotel ticket agencies served a very useful purpose he argued that some of them had been charging such exorbitant prices that it had done great harm to the theatrical business. "An advance of 50 cents on the regular price gives any hotel agency a fair profit, but some of them have been charging $5 or $6. I sell tables at the *Midnight Frolic* for $12; the speculator, in many cases which have come to my notice, sells them for $22. I give the show; what does he give?" he explained. In previous years Ziegfeld had sold the first 18 rows in the house for the earlier editions of the *Follies* for the entire 14 weeks of the run. Because Flo believed the hotel agencies performed a certain service, one worth about 50 cents a seat, he had told the brokers that he stood ready to renew that arrangement, as long as the agency was prepared to post a $100,000 bond — to be contributed to the Red Cross if a seat was sold for more than a 50 cents advance but, remarked Ziegfeld, "None of them has taken it. I don't know what contracts the hotels have with the agencies, but I do know that the speculators are doing a lot of harm to the theatres; so this year we are selling everything at the box office, selling four weeks ahead, first come first served; and we are selling out!"[3]

In order to achieve success in curbing scalpers Ziegfeld observed he had to have reliable men in the box office. Also, he had two men watching the box office lines all the time, watching for known speculators and their proxies. They also checked up on mail order requests to make sure they were legitimate. One came from a girl in a Pennsylvania school requesting five seats. When the application was checked it was discovered there was no such person and the name of the school had been used with no authority. Because speculators got next to no seats for the 1918 *Follies*, said Flo, "They are working against us, instead of for us. Because they can't get seats they knock the show, but we seem to be beating them just the same." Concluded Ziegfeld, "Now that the ice is broken, I see no reason why a good many other managers shouldn't be able to do the same thing ... there is no excuse for the extortion which has been practiced and I believe the *Follies* has shown how to beat it."[4]

A report in the *Washington Post* related the story of Flo's success and applauded the stance he took over the *Follies* at the New Amsterdam Theatre, declaring "the public loved it" — good seats at the box office at the poster prices. Other managers were said to have also loved his plan, with those men being unanimous in endorsing Ziegfeld's actions.[5]

The showman continued to maintain he had the speculators beaten when he announced after 19 days of the run of the *Follies* every seat had been sold out at box office prices with not a single ticket placed in the hands of the agencies. Ziegfeld also told reporters that on the previous Saturday he turned down an offer of a long-term buy of 475 seats a night, from an unnamed party that he said would have netted him $1,700 a week above the box office income for the same seats. "I am no philanthropist but I honestly believe that ticket profiteering, if continued, means death to the theatre."[6]

During the influenza epidemic in the fall of 1918 in America, the New York theatre industry was one of many areas to suffer, in this case a major decline in attendance. Hotel ticket agencies suffered heavy losses in the first two weeks of October on the outright buy contracts then in force. Twelve agencies were then recognized as the leaders in that field and, according to a report in *Variety,* lost at least $1,000 a night in total in that period. At the Central Theatre there was a nightly buy in play of 120 seats, which producer William A. Brady was said to have "forced" on the brokers, who were left each night with 50 percent unsold. *Under Orders* at the Eltinge Theatre had a "forced" buy in play of 250 seats nightly (with no return privilege) and of those about 150 found their way each day to Joseph Leblang to be sold at his cut-rate discount agency, if possible. The Cyril Maude show, *The Saving Grace,* at the Empire Theatre had a forced outright buy of 200 seats a night and during the week the report was written even the Leblang agency would not take them. *Information Please,* with Jane Cowl at the Selwyn, had a buy of 500 a night in place although in this case brokers had a return privilege that ranged from 20 percent to 30 percent. The Winter Garden venue had a buy in effect of 250 seats a night with a right of return of one-third. Nightly losses of those agencies were estimated to be as follows: McBride, $100; Tyson Company, $150; Tyson & Brother, $75; Tyson & Company, $100; Broadway, $150; United, $75; Leo Newman, $75; Louis Cohn, $75; the Library, $50; Alexander, $50; J. L. Marks, $25; and a similar amount for a downtown broker. After the initial run, Ziegfeld brought the 1918 *Follies* back to New York in October for a run at the Globe. However, this time he did business with four agencies, despite his earlier position. No reason was given for Ziegfeld's change of mind.[7]

When *Variety* looked at agencies in general in New York at the end of 1918 it said those brokers then handled in total about 4,500 seats a night, 30,000 seats a week, and with a season of 40 weeks it meant about 1.2 million tickets handled in a year by the agencies at a gross of $3.5 million to $4 million. The largest agency was Tyson Company (it had stands in 19 of the most important hotels and handled about 750 seats a night); next were McBride (five locations, 750 tickets), United Theater Ticket Company (500), Tyson & Brother (500), Tyson & Company (500), Bascom Inc. (500), Leo Newman (300), Broadway Agency (300), Louis Cohn (200), Alexander (200), the Library (100), and J. L. Marks (100); then were three smaller agencies (150 seats in total). Tyson Company also handled newspapers, magazines, books and other commodities at its hotel stands for which it paid rentals ranging as high as $20,000 a year to the hotels. All the others were just ticket agencies, except Bascom, which handled other items similar to those found at Tyson Company locations.[8]

At the time *Variety* compiled its report New York City had just adopted an ordinance whereby an agency was limited to charging no more than a 50 cents premium per ticket over the box office price. That caused the reporter to muse the new measure would bring to an end the practice whereby agencies often bid against each other to get all the good seats for a particular show for a specific period, forcing other agencies who lost out in the bidding contest to buy its tickets—whenever it got requests for that show—from the winning broker, thereby pushing the price to the public up even more. But under the new law there was no profit possible for the second agency since no second premium could be added. This reporter argued agencies could be broken down into two types, the legitimate broker, which was good for the transient hotel guests, and the "gyp" agency, which gouged as much as it could get from the public. "There is no doubt that the agencies to a great extent managed to get anywhere from $1 to $2 advance for the majority of the seats that they passed over their counters, and they could still have continued to do so had they stopped the boys that were grabbing off anywhere up to $8 over the regular price," he explained, blaming the so-called gyp agencies as being the cause of the law that limited the advance to 50 cents for all brokers and for all tickets.[9]

Joseph Leblang remained the "king" of cut-rate discount ticket brokers in New York, in the words of *Variety*, at least at the very end of 1918. He was said to have been the reason the majority of smaller cigar store stands that did business with passes in the olden days no longer did so. Also, Joe made it possible for a show to hang on when the going was rocky over the first couple of weeks of a run, by filling more seats with people prepared to pay half price to see a play, and hopefully build a better business through word of mouth, and so on.[10]

According to the *Variety* account the cut-rate discount ticket was an outgrowth of the old lithograph ticket days when every barber shop, saloon, and store that would hang a half sheet (advertising poster) in the window would receive a couple of tickets for the advertising privilege. A barber shop that accepted six to eight half sheets to display got six to eight pairs of seats that it usually sold off at the rate of two for one. In later years, in New York there appeared a number of small cigar stores that trafficked in passes for tickets. Those places existed on tickets furnished them by either pass grafters or by the dump of a block of seats for a house that was papering—that is, deep discount or free coupons were floated to get bodies into seats, create talk about a play, and so on. Joe's Theatre Ticket Office, as Leblang's business was known, systematized the process. Instead of waiting for the casual pass grafter to drop in or for an advertising dump to come along, Leblang went to the theatre managers and started to make deals with them for seats in advance—to be sold by his agency for, usually, half price. At the beginning Joe sold 200 to 300 seats a night but by the end of 1918 business had grown to the point that he sold as many as 2,000 discount seats per night.[11]

At the time Leblang started his business there was a scheme in place for disposing of tickets at half price through the People's Institute. As mentioned earlier an Institute member took his half price coupon to the box office and exchanged it for an actual seat. Box office staff and venue managers were said to have come to dislike the scheme because a person would come to the box office, select the seats he wanted from the diagram, receive his tickets, and then without prior notice hand over half the money requested and the coupon. Since only certain rows of the venue were available to People's Institute coupons it left the box office staff often having difficulty in retrieving tickets they had given out for an unavailable row.[12]

Buys on the part of agencies continued to be a prominent part of the theatre scene in New York in 1919, with the buys being made before the production opened in New York. *Variety* reported that in the first week of October that year of the six new shows that opened that week, ticket speculators had bought about $250,000 worth of tickets in total. That brought the number of buys then active to 25 and with the average buy being for about $1,000 a night to each theatre it meant the brokers turned over around $25,000 a night to the managers. The largest new buy was for the Charles Dillingham production *Apple Blossoms* at the Globe. Brokers took 460 seats a night for eight weeks and with the price scale being $3 to $3.50 at the box office it meant the buy was worth something over $90,000 total over its life. For the production of *Hitchy-Koo* (Raymond Hitchcock) at the Liberty agencies took 400 seats a night for four weeks and with tickets ranging from $2.50 to $3 it was a buy that was worth about $30,000.[13]

Chicago was home to one of the best known and most publicized of America's ticket scalpers, and probably the only woman member of the trade at the time (around World War I)— Mrs. Florence Couthoui. A record deal for Chicago was done in August 1919 between the Klaw & Erlanger theaters and Couthoui, or as the press dubbed her, "queen of the ticket scalpers," for seats at the Blackstone, Powers, Colonial, and Illinois theaters. After weeks of negotiations, the deal gave her agency the absolute option through the season on all seats in all venues up to and including the 10th row on the main floors for any and all attractions. It meant she need not take more than she wanted at any time but could take all the stipulated seats whenever she wanted. However, once she had taken up a ticket she had no right of return. "The deal places all other scalpers at Mrs. Couthoui's mercy for these houses have to get their tickets through her," observed a newsman. Smaller deals of a similar nature had been struck by Couthoui with producers Comstock & Gest at the La Salle venue, and with A. H. Woods at the Woods Theatre. At the latter, though, she only had an option on the first three rows instead of the first 10. Klaw & Erlanger houses, when they concluded their deal with Florence, followed the precedent of the Shubert venues in Chicago. Reportedly, the Shuberts had the same deal in place with Couthoui for the previous two years.[14]

Another report just six weeks later indicated Chicago had become the highest priced theater town "in the world" because of its ticket scalping system. "Almost every house in town (all K. & E. and Shubert theatres and some of the independents) is selling at $2.50, $3 and $3.50, depending on the attraction and the choice of nights, so that Mrs. Florence Couthoui, who has a virtual monopoly of the desirable seats, can stay within the law and still get plenty of gravy by charging printed prices," remarked an observer. Rival scalpers had to buy from her if they wanted anything inside the first 10 rows and she charged them a 25 cent premium above her price. In turn they charged 50 cents to their customers and with the added war tax it meant that a Saturday night seat for a hit musical bought from an outside broker cost $3.50 plus 35 cents war tax, plus 25 cent premium to Couthoui plus a 50 cent premium to the second scalper plus eight cents war tax on the premiums, "or a total of $4.68, an unheard of rate. The house gets $3.25 out of the mess."[15]

According to this account Couthoui did have a return privilege, contradicting the earlier story. Still, she insisted that no returned seat be sold to any other broker at box office prices, even if she could not use it, demanding that if any rival broker wanted the seat it had to apply to her and she would retrieve the seat she once had and returned, and would sell it to her rival with her markup added. Couthoui's profits were estimated here to be in excess of $5,000 per week. Klaw & Erlanger houses, which for a year had advertised heavily, "Seats at our box office only," modified their ads to read, "Seats at our box office or at offices of our sales agent, Mrs. Couthoui."[16]

For the first time in a long time, said a 1919 account, a ticket scalper had taken advertising space in the Chicago daily papers. Florence Couthoui "who has a practical monopoly of the ticket-agent business in Chicago" put an ad in the local papers on a Saturday announcing the following theaters had established branch offices with F. Couthoui & Company: Blackstone, Cohan's, Grand, Colonial, Garrick, Illinois, La Salle, Princess, Powers, Studebaker and Woods. Reportedly, the only two legitimate houses in the Loop who were not dealing with Couthoui were the Olympia and Cort. Florence had ticket stands in the following hotels; Auditorium, Blackstone, Congress, La Salle, Morrison, Sherman, and in numerous clubs and office buildings. Her ad also included the following, "The price printed on the ticket is the price you pay."[17]

Two years later an article argued the "Queen of the Scalpers" had so much power she could sometimes set the admission price for coming shows. "Mrs. Couthoui has been handling the first ten rows for all shows for the first six weeks of their run," went the story, with the box offices left to handle what she had left over. In that way the public was educated to the fact that choice seats could only be obtained from the Couthoui agencies and that the cost was the same as at the box offices (in New York brokers bought from venues at face and added on their premium; Couthoui bought from the venues below face, added her premium and charged the customer face). Thus Florence was able to entrench herself solidly with the theatregoing public and held that leverage over the managers' heads. When the arrangements for the price scaling of tickets for the Chicago run of *Tip Top* (Fred Stone) were underway producer Charles Dillingham's representatives were prepared to ask for a $3 top. However, Couthoui said she could get $3.50 for the seats and so it was done. Top priced tickets at the box office went for $3.50. They were sold to Florence for $3.25, and resold to the public by her agency for $3.50.[18]

When showman J. J. Shubert was in Chicago in the summer of 1921 to oversee the opening of his newest theater, the Great Northern, he met Couthoui and she managed to get him to order a repricing and reprinting of the tickets for the opening of *Midnight Rounders* (Eddie Cantor) at that venue, scaling the house at $3 top instead of $2.50. When a show was scaled without input from Florence at, say $2.50 top, Couthoui got all the seats she wanted but had to take them at face and when her 25 cent premium was added on she thus charged her customers more than the box office did. However, when she dictated the price at, say $3.50 top, she also got all the tickets she wanted but at $3.25, which she resold for $3.50, as did the venue box office. Because she had better seat locations to offer than did the show's own box office it meant all the more business for her. That fostered a customer loyalty to her business and in turn gave her more influence to dictate terms, including the pricing of tickets.[19]

Chicago's legitimate theaters reportedly had over 30,000 seats, as of the end of 1921, with each venue giving on average nine performances a week. Fifteen percent of these seats were given over to Florence. Described only as being "past middle age," she entered the business in a small way years earlier when she ran a cigar stand in the Congress Hotel with her business at the time limited to cigars, periodicals and newspapers. She received numerous requests off and on for theater tickets from guests of the hotel and that gave her an idea. She went to Frank Scott (her husband at the time) who ran a railroad ticket office in the same hotel and asked him to call at theaters and see if he could make some arrangements whereby tickets could be supplied to her. Scott did so and was able to induce a number to do business with his wife, giving her tickets at box office prices. She charged whatever premium she could get away with, depending on demand. With that business developing into a lucrative one she began to expand. Florence leased other stands in hotels until, by the end of 1921, she had an outlet in every first class hotel in Chicago. At first, newspapers, periodicals, cigars, and so on, were her main source of income but by 1921 they were incidental items.[20]

Seeing the success Couthoui enjoyed led to other brokers starting up agencies and going to theater managers with various propositions and competing against each other, offering to pay the venues a premium of from 25 cents to $1.25 per seat (Couthoui was one of the competitors), with the result that profits for brokers began to decline. At that point, according to Couthoui, she had her lawyers draw up an ordinance that mandated no theater could do any business with scalpers in providing them with seats at a premium and if a venue accepted greater than face for a ticket it would lose its license. The ordinance was introduced and passed into law by the Chicago City Council in a rush. Couthoui then approached theaters and promised to take around $200 worth of tickets per night per show and sell them at box office prices, but she had to make a profit and that profit would have to come from the theaters and not the patrons. The managers agreed. Couthoui did not want the shows scaled at $2.50 top in

Chicago because the producers tended to insist on getting their full $2.50 per ticket, but scaled at $3 or $3.50 top they could afford to give her a commission on each seat. She claimed she sold about half of her seat allotments to outside brokers at the box office price plus 25 cents, giving her a 50 cent total profit on the seats, 25 cents from the venue and the same from the other brokers. According to the reporter who provided the story Couthoui used bribes, and so forth, to buy theater managers and treasurers, gave them gifts and made special loans to them, and engaged in other shady practices to get control of the business in Chicago.[21]

One year later trouble began to strike the Couthoui ticket empire. The Harris-Powers theater chain in Chicago notified the Couthoui agency it would no longer be considered as a branch office of the Colonial, Powers, Illinois, and Blackstone theaters. In other words, there would be no seats for attractions playing those four houses available at any of the Couthoui outlets. Rumor had it that Florence's diggers would be called out and again be employed — to stand in line and buy, or dig out, as many seats as they could — as they had several years earlier, when the Powers houses had imposed a similar, but short-lived prohibition on her. Blowing its own horn, *Variety* delivered the following analysis, "This latest move results from a constant local newspaper campaign, derived from the inside facts *Variety* has been carrying for the past six months about agency ticket handling." It was forecast the new order would help hold down the price of tickets and would mean that a show would survive, or fail, or its merits since flops would not be carried from advance buys made by agencies.[22]

Despite the statements about no seats for Couthoui from the Harris-Powers houses less than three months later, in March 1923, it was reported the Couthoui agency had made an outright buy of 200 seats a night for the upcoming George White *Scandals* at the Illinois Theatre. When playgoers lined up at the Illinois to buy tickets they realized, commented a reporter, "The Powers offices were fooling them when it was stated the tickets would only be sold at the box office at the box office prices."[23]

Chicago staff of the Shubert chain cut off the supply of tickets to the Couthoui agency in August 1927. Out of a total of 14 legitimate houses operating within the Loop, nine were operated by the Shuberts. Reportedly, the order to stop the seat supply came from J. J. Shubert. Couthoui then controlled 26 ticket stand outlets in the Loop. Officially, the reason given for the action was that the Couthoui stands favored George White's *Scandals* (running at the Palace, an Erlanger house) over *Gay Paree* (then running at a Shubert venue). It was said to be a fact that the gross of *Gay Paree* fell off by thousands of dollars per week when *Scandals* opened. A conservative estimate was that 65 percent of all orchestra seats for legitimate houses were nightly sold by Couthoui outlets. Besides her stands, Florence supplied the most important social clubs in the city with their ticket requirements. When she heard of the action taken by the Shubert chain, Florence was said to have immediately issued an order to all her outlets to inform all patrons for any seat for a Shubert house attraction that they were sold out, and to hype the other shows. During the theatrical season Couthoui nightly handled 3,500 to 5,000 seats by this time. It was a regular occurrence for her outlets to sell 400 orchestra seats for one night for a hit, as her stands were then doing for *Scandals*. Financial arrangements had apparently changed somewhat by this time. It was reported that for the usual show her premium was 50 cents, for a hit it was $1, and for a ticket to a hit, billed to a charge account, there was a $2 premium per seat. Prior to the cut off she bought her tickets from Shubert at the box office price and then remitted 20 cents to the Shubert organization for each seat sold. Some observers felt the real reason for the cut off was that the Shuberts were trying to get more money out of Florence for each ticket sold.[24]

Defending the institution of ticket agencies was a New York newspaper editor who stated in 1920 that they performed a genuine service for a fee that was not exorbitant. "If they did not do this, people would soon cease to patronize them. The majority of theatregoers simply will not stand in line at the box office for tickets, or plan their amusements far enough ahead to make the box office a feasible means of distribution," he reasoned. Tickets for a successful play commanded a scarcity value, he concluded, "and the attempt to regulate their price by law is an attempt to check the forces of demand and supply. Many years of agitation and much well intended legislation have failed to accomplish that."[25]

At the same time the editor was praising the agencies, William H. Edwards, Collector of Internal Revenue for the U. S. government, announced he had begun an investigation to determine how far the tax laws had been observed by ticket brokers. Under the tax law the 10 percent admission war tax extended to any premium charged for a seat, up to a 50 cent premium. But if the premium charged was greater than 50 cents then the tax law required 50 percent of the excess over 50 cents be paid as a tax. It was true, said a reporter, that not many brokers observed the latter part of the law. Edwards' investigation was fueled by many stories about big premiums being imposed on tickets for many hit shows by the brokers, up to a $5 to $10 premium. John McBride, of the McBride agency, was said to have given many examples to the government of overcharging that had come to his attention, believing the federal government had been defrauded of about $200,000 to that date by reason of the failure of speculators to report their sales in accordance with the law.[26]

During one of the periods of increased efforts by the theatrical managers to reduce the "menace" of the speculator, producer Henry Savage announced in New York in 1922 that he had arranged to limit the number of seats turned over to the brokers for *The Clinging Vine*, which was about to open at the Knickerbocker. "The complaint hitherto, in the case of a successful attraction, has been that all seats in the first ten or more rows have been sold through the brokers at premiums and that orders far in advance for those locations would not be accepted at the box office," explained Savage. When all the good seats were taken by brokers—and they were for most shows—it was always for a specified period of time, say, six weeks, or eight weeks. Theoretically, a patron at the box office who was willing to take a good seat for far in advance, say three months, should have been able to buy it. However, the box office would still refuse even though no firm demand was then on the ticket because the deals with brokers could be and were extended, depending on how the play went.[27]

District Attorney Banton in New York began a secret drive in 1925 for evidence against ticket agencies believed to be charging more than the legally allowed premium of 50 cents per seat. State law provided for enforcement through the comptroller with whom bonds were filed by brokers. Agents of Banton were secretly buying tickets at suspect broker outlets. One hotel stand was said to have been known to have flagrantly violated the 50 cent maximum, charging $6 each for $3.30 (face) seats. "Perhaps the most offensive practice of this hotel is copping more than its allotment by digging tickets from a strict 50-cent premium agency and reselling for 100 percent more than paid the legitimate broker," said a spokesman for Banton. That state law also required each ticket acquired by a broker to be stamped with the broker's name and the price paid. A violation of the law could lead to the forfeit of an agency's $1,000 bond and the revocation of its state-issued license to sell but more was at stake because the federal government had a tax claim for half of any premium charged that was in excess of the 50 cents.[28]

As the criticism and denouncing of ticket agencies increased, members of the profession asserted they had been "kicked" and "slandered" all their lives with no one to tell the truth in their defense. Because of that, 30 of the 57 licensed theater ticket brokers in New York City met on the day before Christmas in 1925 at the Hotel Astor. They organized the Theatre Ticket Brokers' Association of Greater New York to promote their interests, largely through agitation for legislation to eliminate the statute that limited premiums to 50 cents, or at least modifying it in some way. As an alternative to the elimination of the maximum premium of 50 cents, they proposed legislation that allowed them to charge 50 cents and also a "reasonable fee for service"; they were prepared to leave the setting of that fee to the judgment of the State Controller. As well, the fledgling group hoped to drive the sidewalk speculator out of business and to prove the licensed agency broker was a necessity. Said Nathan Lieberman, general counsel of the group, "These men want to save and promote a legitimate business. They are not and have not been out to gouge anybody. These calumnies and slanders to that effect are all untrue. They can't live if their profits are limited to 50 cents on a ticket." Lieberman said in conclusion, "The theatre ticket broker aids New York to keep up its reputation for hospitality. The sidewalk theatre ticket speculator must be driven out of business. It is he who has caused the business to fall into disrepute, and we intend to go after him just as hard as the authorities would."[29]

New Year's Eve 1926 was a financial bonanza for New York's theatrical producers as practically all of them had raised the prices of their attractions for that festive occasion. It was also a time that promised rich rewards for the scalpers. Inquiries by a reporter at agencies revealed their premiums for hit shows ranged from $2 to $6 above the figure printed on the ticket. One agency quoted a price of $16.50 for a seat to George White's *Scandals*, or $5.50 over the face value of $11. Those same two figures held for a production called *Broadway*. Another broker in the same block charged a premium of $2.50 on a *Scandals* ticket ($13.50 total) while a third agency asked $9.90 for a ticket to *The Captive* (its New Year's Eve box office price was $6.60). Those last two figures held for tickets to *The Constant Wife* (Ethel Barrymore).[30]

Years later, in 1946, the U. S. Bureau of Internal Revenue seized the books of the Jacobs Ticket Agency of 225 West 49th Street, New York City, which was operated by a nephew of fight promoter Mike Jacobs, immediately after the indefinite suspension of the licenses of the agency and two of its employees on the ground of illegal overcharges for tickets to the Louis-Conn fight. New York City License Commissioner Benjamin Fielding was then involved in an investigation of ticket gouging. At the arraignment of the accused the police revealed the ticket broker quoted prices ranging from $150 to $175 for $100 seats and from $65 up for $50 tickets to the Louis-Conn bout. The legal charge then allowed by state law was a maximum premium of 75 cents (plus 20 percent tax, that is, 90 cents in all) over face value. On a similar charge, Fielding suspended the agency license of William Trosty who operated from a stand in the Hotel President. Police said they purchased two $50 tickets from him for $90 each, causing them to make the arrest. Trosty said he had paid $60 each for the seats from the Jacobs Ticket Agency. Representatives of the Bureau of Internal Revenue were called in by Fielding to see if any conspiracies or tax evasions were going on. Other overcharges then being investigated by Fielding (involving other brokers) that were not then completed included the sale of four $12 seats for the Louis-Conn match for $90 (legal maximum was $51.60), five $4.80 tickets for *State of the Union* for $44 ($28.50), and four seats for *Annie Get Your Gun* being sold for $58 instead of the legal $30.[31]

Incidents such as the above that popped up from time to time, and the resultant publicity that attended such revelations, helped to create pressure to curb the abuse. One result was that local and state authorities put as much effort into considering legislation and/or passing legislation in this time period as they had in the past. Whereas in the past such legislation and failed attempts had usually targeted the sidewalk men, sometimes with agencies being specifically exempted from the measures, during this time most such attempts targeted the agencies. It was in recognition of their growing dominance and importance. Sidewalk men usually came under these new measures also, but the brokers were the real targets.

11

Laws, Arrest, Police, Courts, 1918–1949

> *"The business of ticket speculator is parasitic in its very nature."*
> New York District Attorney Swann, 1918
>
> *"The evils of ticket speculating are undisputed."*
> Justice Francis Martin, 1923
>
> *"The existence of extortion due to present unregulated conditions in the business of reselling tickets of admission to places of public amusement is widely recognized."*
> Judge Irving Lehman, 1924
>
> *"The people of the city should not be compelled to pay exorbitant prices for theatrical performances in the city."*
> New York City Mayor Fiorello La Guardia, 1940

Chicago city officials determined to clamp down on speculation in 1918 by adopting some type of legislation. One measure involved the annual amusement license for $500, which theaters had to hold and required renewing venues to give them a promise they would have no traffic with ticket scalpers. Many venues held out taking out the annual license, complaining the city was seeking to hinder legitimate box office sales. However, after several months as holdouts, seven theaters capitulated in July by filing their license applications, sensing the city meant to implement something in the way of a measure.[1]

Later that year Chicago had an anti-scalping ordinance on the books and Levy Mayer, attorney for the city of Chicago, advised theatrical managers that in order to protect themselves they should prevent any seats being sold for their houses at any locations other than at the box office. Mayer also pointed out the practice of printing the price of $2.50 on a $2 ticket as a subterfuge was illegal. Venues had run that scam by printing two full sets of tickets for their houses, one stamped $2 and one stamped $2.50. Those $2.50 seats were given to scalpers as "agents" of the theater to sell on a 10 percent commission; it meant the scalper got 25 cents for each seat sold and remitted $2.25 to the house. Seats unsold were returned to the box office. All patrons at the venue box office paid $2 for a ticket, with the first set of $2 tickets being the ones used.[2]

Illinois Governor Small signed into law on July 11, 1923, a statute calling for a fine of $500 or imprisonment for one year for any ticket scalper caught selling theater tickets for more than the price printed on the ticket. A reporter remarked how easy it would be for two groups to circumvent the new law simply by printing a price on the ticket in accordance with the premium arrangements the group had agreed to. "Insiders claim that the new law got its birth primarily because those who handled its creation are determined to break down the close relationship between the theatres and the ticket scalpers," explained the journalist. Those same insiders asserted the practice of outright buys was what hurried the new law. Patrons going to the theater and asking for seats down front found out that 200 and 300 of the best seats were in the hands of speculators. When curtain time came empty seats were to be found, because the brokers had not hawked all of their allotment and could not return the unsold seats, "and the hostile feeling of the patrons, who were forced into back rows or the balcony because they refused to pay the scalpers' prices, manifested itself."[3]

San Francisco tried to deal with scalpers in 1920 by passing an ordinance that charged speculators a license fee of $300 a month each to ply their trade. Surprisingly, five scalpers paid the fees, under protest, to a total for the group of $4,500 before court action derailed the measure. A judge first declared the ordinance to be invalid as a police measure and the only question to be decided was whether or not the measure could be sustained as a lawful exercise of the taxing powers of the municipality. When the District Court of Appeal handed down its verdict on March 31 it held the law to be constitutionally invalid. Seeing the writing on the wall the San Francisco city officials had been considering a new ordinance as they awaited the legal verdict on the ordinance. That substitute measure under consideration would have required all theaters to have printed on their tickets a notice to the effect that the tickets were not transferable. Reportedly, city authorities believed that measure might stop scalping. It did not become law.[4]

Police officials in Washington, DC, announced in June 1923 that little or no trouble was being caused by ticket speculators due to the "untiring" work of the District and the Internal Revenue Bureau. Because of those efforts, remarked a reporter, "virtually all the scalpers have discontinued operations." A day earlier only one man had been arrested for selling tickets at an exorbitant price; he was fined $50.[5]

Three separate bills, each designed to stop speculation in theater tickets, came up in the Massachusetts Legislature in March 1924 for final disposition.

Those three proposed laws each had received unfavorable reports from the joint legislative committee on legal affairs, which held public hearings on each and later in executive session decided to report the measures unfavorably. A majority on the committee believed any of the bills, if enacted into law, would be declared unconstitutional by the Massachusetts Supreme Court. Several times within the previous few years when bills proposing to outlaw ticket speculation had been introduced in the Legislature the cry of unconstitutionality had been raised there. Proponents of the measures that would do away with theater ticket speculating were said to be depending in 1924, more than ever, upon public sentiment, which had been growing steadily against the practice as seats for popular attractions were sometimes quoted at excessive prices and scalpers sometimes were known to "corner the market." Public sentiment was understood to be behind any bill that would make it possible for all ticket buyers to enjoy "fair play."[6]

Anticipating possible constitutional problems, Massachusetts legislators submitted questions to the high court, seeking an advisory opinion in advance. On April 23, 1924, the Supreme Court of Massachusetts, in answer to those questions, held the Legislature had a right to regulate ticket brokers. That opinion said that if the Massachusetts Legislature found legislation necessary for the purpose of safeguarding the public against exorbitant rates of admission to theaters and other places of amusement it could constitutionally enact such legislation. It could also enact legislation subjecting scalpers to reasonable regulation and impose a reasonable limit on the resale price of tickets.[7]

With the way cleared for action the Massachusetts Legislature enacted a measure and the control of the resale of tickets in that state passed into the hands of the Department of Public Safety, as of September 4, 1924. The measure had been passed during the closing hours of the last session of the Legislature with 90 days having to elapse before it became effective. Under the new law nobody could resell theater tickets or tickets for other amusement attractions without first obtaining a license from the Commissioner of Public Safety, and he had the power to make rules and regulations for the operation of that business. When that bill had first been introduced by Representative Richard D. Crockwell of Medford, it made it unlawful for a speculator to charge more than a 50 cent premium per seat, a bill modeled after the one in New York, which had already been declared constitutional by that state's Supreme Court. Still, in its final form the measure did not provide for a limit on the premium in the resale of a seat but it gave the Commissioner of Public Safety broad powers to regulate and control, albeit unspecified. A further provision of that law provided that licenses had to be taken out annually at a fee of $100 per year.[8]

The Los Angeles City Council voted in an ordinance on May 26, 1941, that prohibited the hawking of tickets within 250 feet of the entrances of such structures as the Hollywood Bowl, the Coliseum, and baseball parks.[9]

Judge Joseph Sherbow ruled invalid, on October 28, 1948, an ordinance that had been hastily drafted by city authorities in Baltimore against football ticket scalpers. Sherbow declared the facts showed that measure had been passed especially on account of a game upcoming in just days between Navy and Notre Dame. It should be possible to frame a valid ordinance against scalping, Sherbow ruled, but the last-minute job rigged up by the City Council on a Monday night in anticipation of a game on the following Saturday had holes in it. For one thing it dealt only with speculation in football tickets. Also, noted the Judge, it was within the power of the U.S. Naval Academy to correct the situation that had arisen with respect to the game, for which 60,000 people were expected. Sherbow pointed out the Navy Athletic Association sold midshipmen as many seats as they wanted and it was understandable that some of them "might succumb to temptation as some have in the past."[10]

Late in World War I the federal Work-or-Fight Order and the New York State anti-loafing law both went into effect on July 1, 1918. Apparently under those laws one not only had to show he was employed but also that he was useful and lawfully employed, or there were consequences. New York District Attorney Swann was then still in the process of defining occupations under the law. An occupation had to be "lawful," "recognized," and "useful" thought Swann. The purpose of the measures was to change the status of people who "were of no benefit to society." A crush of 10,000 men applied for work at the State Industrial Commission on that first day. Swann did announce that falling within the "useless" or "injurious" occupation category was that of ticket speculator. Said Swann, "The business of ticket speculators is parasitic in its very nature. The ticket speculator buys up tickets and deprives the theatre-going public of them unless they will stand and deliver." He added, "This is equally true of the man on the street and the man in the ticket speculator's office. They will all have to get out of this business. They will be given a chance to find other occupations, but in due course they will have to shut down or be prosecuted, provided they are between eighteen and fifty years of age. I don't think anybody is clever enough to find anything useful in holding up the theatre-going public."[11]

A few days later as the New York State roundup of "slackers and loafers" continued, Assistant District Attorney James Smith had served many subpoenas on men who could not give a satisfactory account of themselves—in terms of their occupation and/or draft status. Those subpoenaed were summoned for an examination. Among places and areas raided by the police as they conducted fishing expeditions were pool halls, saloons, and theatrical districts. Five subpoenas were served on ticket speculators in the theatrical districts.[12]

Near the end of September that year Swann announced he had decided to put an end to the theater ticket speculation business in Manhattan. He ordered subpoenas served on all scalpers along Broadway and also upon managers and owners of ticket agencies in the theater districts, requiring them to appear at his office and show cause why their occupation should not be declared non-essential during the war. Swann explained he had reached the conclusion that the public interest required the suppression of ticket speculation because of the situation he had found in his probe of excessive profits made by scalpers in the recent presentation of a military play for war charity. After those summoned were questioned, continued Swann, "we shall order them to engage in more essential occupations. Those of the speculators capable of doing military service will be compelled to go into the army."[13]

A few days later 15 of the 80 speculators who had been summoned to Swann's office to show cause why their business should not be abolished as non-essential had been questioned by Swann. Especially annoying to the District Attorney was the practice of the sidewalk men to use doorways of stores (or actually going into retail outlets) to make their transactions in order to avoid the city ordinance against hawking seats on the street. On the other hand he found next to no collusion, explaining he had learned the theater managers had investigated the ticket speculating operations and found that no more than one venue manager was profiting by collusion with the scalpers.[14]

New York State returned to the battle to end scalping in the early to mid 1920s as a variety of bills were considered. A 1921 effort that passed both houses in Albany would have made it unlawful to sell seats for more than 50 cents above face value but was vetoed by governor Miller as he believed it was unconstitutional — that is, it was beyond the powers of a state to set the price of a commodity.[15]

More bills to curb speculation were introduced in the New York State legislature in 1922. The Walton-Smith bill would license all people reselling tickets, at a fee of $100 annually, and would prohibit them from charging more than 50 cents above the box office price for a seat. The Smith bill would permit theater owners to have printed on the tickets a contract that the ticket should not be sold for in excess of 50 cents over face value. Playwright Augustus Thomas, who supported both bills and represented the Society of American Dramatists, the Actors' Equity Association, and the Actors' Fidelity Society, told the politicians that one of the "most hurtful and pernicious" faults of the theater was the speculation in tickets. "Ticket speculation is an abuse which authors are powerless to correct and actors equally so. The managers come more in immediate contact with the difficulty, but are hardly more able to combat it than is actor or author," said Thomas. "For its correction we have come to the Legislature. It is our only resort." The Walton-Smith bill became law in 1922.[16]

Later in 1922 Reuben Weller was arrested for violating that New York State law and the case began to make its way through the court system as its constitutionality was tested. During one of those proceedings in 1923 the prosecutor, Assistant District Attorney Robert D. Petty, said, in court, "I have been informed that about fifteen men control all the choice seats in the theatres of this city. The common people cannot afford to pay the price asked by the ticket speculators. You have to be a man of wealth to sit in the front row of the theatres."

He added, "I cannot afford to sit there at the prices that are charged. If the business of the theatre so affects public interest that a license is required the State has the right to fix the rate of admission.... Discrimination of this kind against the common people is causing the discontent of today."[17]

Finding that theatrical managers and ticket speculators had combined, tending to a monopoly that prevented the public from seeing performances at a reasonable price, the New York Appellate Division upheld, on November 30, 1923, the constitutionality of the speculation law passed in Albany in 1922. It found the Legislature acted wholly within its rights in requiring ticket speculators to take out state licenses and in limiting their charge to no more than 50 cents above box office prices. Those findings were made in affirming the conviction in the Court of Special Sessions the previous February of Reuben Weller, a scalper arrested in front of the Palace Theatre on the charge of selling a $2.20 seat for $3.30 without a license. District Attorney Banton, who had caused the arrest of Weller in October 1922, issued a statement in the wake of the decision calling on theatrical patrons who were overcharged to file complaints with him. At the same time the Appellate Division also upheld the right of the New York City Board of Aldermen to pass the municipal ordinance against speculation, which prohibited a premium in excess of 50 cents. Judge Rosalsky in General Sessions had declared the ordinance invalid. Decisions upholding the constitutionality of these measures were in all cases done so by a vote of three to two.[18]

Justice Francis Martin wrote the decision in which he said patrons had to rely on the honesty of scalpers but "The overwhelming evidence shows an abuse. It is the duty, therefore, of governmental agencies to meet the conditions and find a remedy. It is idle to say that the State and city are powerless to prevent fraud and extortion in the resale of theatre tickets. The evils of ticket speculating are undisputed. The street speculator in particular has become a nuisance. His purpose is to prey on the people by selling his tickets at an extortionate price." Unaccepted by Martin was the idea that the sole remedy had to come from the managers of the venues because to concede there was no cure for the "evil" except through a remedy initiated by the managers would have meant the State "is without power to promote the general welfare of the people by legislating to meet the evil, to accomplish a plain governmental purpose."[19]

In his decision Martin relied heavily on the testimony of David Marks, who had been a ticket broker and seller for some 30 years. Marks painted a picture in which the agencies were compelled by the producers to finance shows in advance by buying huge blocks of seats in advance, and paying a hefty premium on those seats as well. In short, it was a very one-sided picture in which the managers were portrayed as guilty of all the negative aspects of the business and were all powerful in imposing their will on the helpless and hapless agencies. Martin added in his decision, "This combination of theatre owner or manager with speculator or broker by which the attraction is financed or underwritten by the ticket broker or speculator tends to a monopoly which prevents the public from seeing the performance on any reasonable terms. Under the circumstances disclosed the regulation of the business of reselling tickets would seem not only a necessary but also a proper means of meeting the evils sought to be remedied."[20]

Just a few days after that decision upholding both state and city laws limiting seat premiums to a maximum of 50 cents was released, District Attorney Banton began a campaign against speculation. One of the first people who came forward in answer to Banton's call to report overcharges was Elliott Norton, who complained he was forced to pay $13.20 for two tickets (each was stamped $3.30) for the previous Saturday's performance of *The Nervous Wreck* at the Harris Theatre. An investigation was launched by Banton's office. Norton paid the amount asked on Saturday under protest, after demanding only a 50 cent advance based on what he had read in the papers about the law. When that request was denied he complained to the District Attorney's office on the Monday. One of the proprietors of the selling agency, the Arrow Theatre Ticket Company, when contacted by a reporter, said it was all a misunderstanding and they had to send to another ticket agency to fill Norton's request. It was the other broker who overcharged, explained Arrow, who then marked the seat up by only 50 cents more before reselling it and all of that had been related to Norton. However, Norton denied he had ever been told such a story.[21]

Two weeks later Banton continued to insist that ticket brokers who overcharged and/or operated without a license would be prosecuted and that a small percentage of speculators in New York City were continuing to ignore the law. "This bunch of buzzards are not going to get away with it any longer," thundered Banton. Complaints from the public were still wanted and rumor had it that Assistant District Attorney Miles O'Brien had compiled a list of 57 ticket speculators suspected of violating the law and that all would be hauled into court within the coming few weeks.[22]

Surprise raids on theater ticket agencies in Manhattan were begun on December 20, 1923, by 50 detectives, process servers, and other representatives of Banton, resulting in the arrest of eight persons charged with selling tickets without a State license. The drive against the unlicensed agencies was launched at the request of the State Controller's office. James W. Fleming, State Controller, explained that he had received many complaints of gouging on theater tickets. A belief that many of the ticket agencies were warned of the impeding raids was expressed by the District Attorney's men after they had visited 27 places but made only eight arrests.[23]

On February 19, 1924, the Court of Appeals upheld the validity of the New York State 50 cent law and affirmed the conviction of Reuben Weller. Judge Irving Lehman held the statute prohibited brokers from charging more than a fixed and presumably reasonable profit, "and thereby it reasonably tends to end the extortion which the Legislature could properly find exists and constitutes an abuse which is so general and of such importance as to call for legislative remedy." Lehman concluded in his decision, "The existence of extortion due to present unregulated conditions in the business of reselling tickets of admission to places of public amusement is widely recognized. The abuse is due to acts of the ticket brokers alone or in conjunction with producers, and these acts are calculated to injure large numbers of the public in connection with a business which is at least to some degree, affected with a public interest."[24]

Members of the Grand Jurors' Association of Bronx County were addressed at their annual dinner in February 1924 by Justice Francis Martin of the Appellate Division of the New York State Supreme Court (he wrote the decision sustaining the 50 cent law). He remarked that profiteering by theater ticket speculators seemed to be unchecked and that no apparent effort was made to enforce that 50 cent law. "I cite this example of the theatre ticket law as one of the many opportunities that may be mentioned where Grand Jurors have the authority for upholding law enforcement," said Martin. "Although the theatre ticket law has been on the statute books, and has now been affirmed by the Court of Appeals, there has been no general enforcement of it."[25]

One day after Martin's address New York State's 50 cent law was held to be unconstitutional in a five-to-four decision delivered on February 28, 1927, by the United States Supreme Court. Held by the court was that a theater was a private enterprise and was not to be compared, for purposes of governmental regulation, with corporations that had a clearly defined legal relationship with commerce. The decision was rendered in a case involving the Tyson agency against District Attorney Banton. Also held by the court was that the right of an owner to fix a price at which his property could be sold or used was an inherent attribute of the property itself. That is, the state could not engage in price fixing in this instance. Therefore the State, through the law, was held to have deprived persons of property without due process of the law.[26]

Within the decision the justices observed there were about 60 first-class theatres in the borough of Manhattan. Brokers annually sold about three million seats, principally for admission to these theaters. Tyson sold about 300,000 seats yearly. The practice of the brokers as revealed by the record, continued the decision, was to subscribe in advance of the production of the play and frequently before the cast was chosen for tickets covering a period of eight weeks. "The subscriptions (buys) must be paid for two weeks in advance and about 25 percent of the tickets unsold may be returned. A virtual monopoly of the best seats, usually the first 15 rows, is thus acquired and the brokers enabled to demand extortionate prices of theatregoers." Producers and venue owners were eager to make those advance sales because, for one thing, they were an effective insurance against loss arising from unsuccessful productions. "The brokers are in a position to prevent the direct sales of tickets to the desirable seats and to exact from the patrons of the successful productions a price sufficient to pay for the loss of those which are unsuccessful, plus an excessive profit to the broker," continued the decision.[27]

In the wake of the U. S. Supreme Court decision David Lawrence wrote, in a Consolidated Press dispatch from Washington, DC, "Few decisions of the Court have attracted so much attention among legislators as this five-to-four ruling." Although the court declared the theater was a private business that could be regulated so as to ensure good order and protect public morals, it added the theater was not so "charged with public interest" as to warrant control of the prices at which its tickets could be sold. Justices voting in the majority were Sutherland, Taft, McReynolds, Vandevanter, and Butler. Dissenters were Holmes, Stone, Sanford, and Brandeis. Lawrence stated, "The majority contended that a theater performance or an athletic contest for that matter is not a business 'affected with the public interest,' and hence the prices charged are a matter entirely between the buyer and seller." Minority justices pointed out brokers bought all the good seats and constituted a virtual monopoly. Majority justices answered that point by arguing that while some brokers may have practiced fraud or charged extortionate prices, if brokers deceived the public they could be reached through the usual laws governing fraud or misrepresentation and that it was a wrong policy to put out a dragnet bringing in the innocent with the guilty. Many newspapers delivered editorial opinions on the decision; some were happy with it, some were not. In the opinion of the Chicago *Daily News* the controversy was not likely to be settled in the near future. Meanwhile, "it is plain that the abuses of ticket scalping and willful disregard of the public interest by greedy or stupid managers of theaters will have to be combated by public sentiment and voluntary organization, rather than by statutory regulation," observed the editor.[28]

Disappointment with the Supreme Court decision was also expressed in the pages of the *New Republic*, where a writer lamented that over half the orchestra seats for New York City theaters were in the hands of speculators and until the passage of the 1922 measure no limit had been placed upon the "greed" of the scalper. This writer chided the court, concluding, "Has the Supreme Court forgotten its own preachment that it must be remembered that legislatures are ultimate guardians of the liberty and welfare of the people in quite as great a degree as the courts?"[29]

Unimpressed with the whole business was the editor of the *Saturday Evening Post* who tended to blame the public, observing that even the government "cannot put a sense of financial values into the heads of citizens who lack it either all the time or when engaged in their regular New York theater orgy." Although newspapers and public officials railed against scalpers, the editor believed "the public which pays ten dollars for a three-dollar seat rather enjoys the experience. Indeed, there are those who brag of being overcharged and who seem to like being treated as suckers. The truth is that being charged outrageous prices is considered a sign that they know how to live in a metropolis. It signifies their smartness." Scalpers would disappear immediately, he argued, if the public refused to patronize them. "After all, the Government has more worthwhile things to do than to protect people from the consequences of the last word in gilded indolence. Besides, there is just a little question whether even the Government can repeal the law of supply and demand."[30]

Within days of the Supreme Court decision New York State Senator Thomas I. Sheridan and Assemblyman Peter J. Hamill made a joint move on agencies. Their newly submitted proposal would regulate agencies and speculators by requiring detailed records of transactions and by imposing a tax of 50 percent on the difference between the agencies' price and the price as stamped on the ticket. "It is an attempt to meet the new situation," explained Sheridan. "There must be some sort of regulation to protect the public. If the agencies are going to try to scalp people they will have to pay for the attempt." Two other bills were introduced around the same time by New York City Assemblymen. One from Edward M. Fay would have abolished all reselling of boxing tickets and would mandate fight tickets only be sold from the box office. Assemblyman Joseph A. Gavagan's proposal embodied a scheme to continue in effect the 50 cent law. On the back of the ticket was to be printed an agreement that the ticket was not to be sold for more than 50 cents above the original price. The proposed law would have declared such wording to be a contract and any aggrieved person would be entitled to collect the penalty.[31]

A year after that New York State Assemblyman Maurice Bloch introduced a proposal into the Legislature. At the suggestion of United States Attorney Charles Tuttle, Bloch amended his bill aimed at theater ticket scalpers so as to put more teeth in it. One of the new provisions provided that no theater ticket was to be sold other than at the place of a licensed broker. Also done away with under the measure were the ticket offices to be found in drug stores, candy shops, and other retail outlets where seat sales were only an ancillary business. Provision was also made that no commission or bonus be given to a theater employee by a broker in connection with the resale of tickets.[32]

After a few more changes the Bloch proposal was passed by the New York State Senate in March 1928. Under its provisions, agencies were required to post the face price of the ticket prominently alongside their demanded price and to keep a detailed account of purchases and sales that were to be open for inspection. License fees for an agency were to increase to $200 annually from $100 for the main office and a new yearly tax of $50 was to be imposed on each branch office.[33]

Nothing happened with the above measures as none were enacted into law. Yet the politicians kept trying. On April 21, 1940, New York Governor Lehman signed the Mitchell bill into law. It prohibited the reselling of tickets for more than 75 cents above the original price and required that the maximum price at which a ticket could be resold had to be printed on the ticket. As well, it transferred from the Secretary of State to the local licensing authorities the regulation and licensing of those engaged in the business of reselling theater tickets, and provided for a bond as indemnity against damages caused by misstatement, deceit or fraud. Sponsored by Assemblyman MacNeil Mitchell (R., New York) the bill amended the General Business Law.[34]

Back in the fall of 1918 when New York District Attorney Swann was in the midst of his campaign against scalpers as part of his roundup of loafers and those engaged in "useless" occupations, he had New York City Alderman Williams put before the Board of Aldermen a proposed ordinance that would limit the premium charged by speculators to a maximum of 50 cents over face value on each ticket. Swann said he received many letters from people commending his proposed ordinance. One was from Flo Ziegfeld, which said, "Sincerely trust you will succeed in having proposed ordinance passed, but doubt it. I fought them tooth and nail. Alderman Quinn proposed an ordinance that would have wiped speculators out entirely, but like all ordinances against the speculators, it is the last you hear of them and speculators go on their merry way."[35]

Ziegfeld added that a distinction needed to be made between a speculator, or profiteer, and the "legit" ticket agencies such as Tyson, and McBride who, said the showman, favored the Williams ordinance. "It is to be regretted that New York is the only city in America where ticket speculation is openly permitted," moaned Ziegfeld, "where there are hundreds of thousands of strangers who come to the metropolis for amusement and who cannot be protected because the profiteering in tickets has grown to such enormous proportions that the influence of the speculators is too great to permit of an ordinance being passed."[36]

Despite Flo's pessimism, the Board of Aldermen adopted the ordinance regulating ticket speculation on December 17, 1918, by a vote of 58 to five. That came after a number of public hearings on the measure and after a favorable recommendation from the Aldermen's Committee on General Welfare.[37]

The five who voted against the measure were the Socialists who wanted the license fee set at $25 (instead of $250) and the premium limited to 25 cents per seat. A theater could lose its license should the manager sell any of his seats at any advance over face value. One speculator estimated the amount of business done nightly in the New York agencies was between 4,500 and 5,000 tickets and the measure meant an annual loss to agencies of about $1 million. Reportedly, the New York *World* newspaper was crediting itself with having successfully promoted the bill to final passage, through articles in its pages concerning the business. *Variety* thought Flo Ziegfeld was more responsible for getting the bill passed after he started to agitate for some such measure in the summer of 1918. It seemed he wanted to secure two tables to his own production, *Frolic* ($12 for a table, at the box office), at the last minute for friends from out of town who asked him to get them tickets. However, the box office was sold out and Ziegfeld was only able to get his two tables by paying a scalper a total of $46. Ziegfeld was furious that a scalper was making more money out of *Frolic* than he was and was not going to stand for speculators who would sell tickets for double the face value and reap the corresponding profit, without having made the investment of anything beyond the amount of their original purchases.[38]

During that time speculators also managed to attract some unwanted attention when one of them reportedly complained to the District Attorney of the attitude assumed by producer A. H. Woods toward tickets for his shows *Friendly Enemies* and *Under Orders*. Woods decreed that if speculators bought tickets for *Friendly Enemies*, which was in great demand and brought a large premium, then seats for *Under Orders* must also be bought. Because of that stand, grumbled the scalper, ticket men were obliged to take in weekly $2,400 worth of tickets for *Under Orders* with no return privilege. Also, Joe Leblang sold $1,500 worth of cut-rate seats for *Under Orders* each week giving Woods a guaranteed gross from the agencies of $3,900 weekly for that play. Other managers did not blame Woods for his action, considering it to be good business and those who knew how much the speculators were "overcharging" for the *Friendly Enemies* seats gave them no sympathy.[39]

Mayor Hylan of New York signed the measure on December 28, causing it to become law immediately. Under the ordinance the regular or established price of each ticket had to be printed conspicuously on its face and the theater or other amusement place issuing it was prohibited from exacting or receiving any amount greater than its face value. Brokers and speculators were limited to a price no more than 50 cents over face value and were required to take out a municipal license, for a yearly fee of $250. Upon a conviction for violating the measure a person could be imprisoned for up to six months and/or fined up to $500. In addition, the city had the right to bring a civil action against a violator for the recovery of a penalty of $250 and the scalper's license could be revoked. The old ordinance that prohibited speculators from doing business on streets and public thoroughfares remained in force. Penalties in the bill also applied to theater managers and employees who violated the law. Assistant District Attorney A. J. Talley said, "It is the most practical remedy that has yet been provided to reach this long-standing form of profiteering against the millions of amusement seekers here."[40]

Over the course of a week at the end of February 1919, 12 men were arraigned before Magistrate Thomas Nolan in New York on the charge of operating a ticket agency without a license. Four of them were discharged — two because they were merely employees of an agency — and eight were convicted. Those convicted were all fined $10 but had the fines suspended and were given 10 days grace to obtain a license. Assistant District Attorney Kilroe promised that if the eight convicted men failed to secure licenses they would be arrested again if they tried to sell tickets after the grace period expired.[41]

Later in 1919 raids by agents of the Bureau of Internal Revenue resulted in the arrest of five scalpers. Prisoners were taken to the Federal Building and charged with defrauding the government by failing to pay the war tax on theater tickets. Raiders had a list of 42 speculators who were alleged to have failed to pay the war tax but after the first part of the raid all the others on the list closed up shop and disappeared, obviously tipped off. Revenue agents said one arrested broker received $17.60 for two orchestra seats for a musical comedy. The price should have been $7.60 maximum, which meant a $10 profit for the broker and, under the law, the federal government was entitled to $5, 50 percent.[42]

Policewoman Mary Sullivan toured the Times Square district on a November evening in 1919 and arrested three scalpers for overcharging. Two were sidewalk men. Sidney Hill sold Sullivan two tickets for the play *Clarence* at the Hudson Theatre for $9.20 each ($2.75 was printed on the ticket); Barney Warfield sold her two seats for Ziegfeld's *Follies* at the New Amsterdam Theatre for $4.40 each ($3.85). Lew Newman was arrested at his agency store by Sullivan after he sold her two tickets for *The Gold Diggers* for $5 each ($2.75).[43]

A day later an expression of dissatisfaction with regard to the scalping situation was made by William A. Brady. A statement made on behalf of the Theatrical Producing Managers' Association was to the effect that the "intolerable situation of illegal ticket speculation had resulted from the failure of the District Attorney to enforce the anti-speculating ordinance." Swann lashed back that it was the managers themselves who were largely responsible for the lack of enforcement. "The regulation of ticket speculation is up to the managers. If the producers and theatre managers would use due diligence tickets would not find their way into the hands of speculators." He also remarked he had drafted and caused the ordinance to be enacted by New York City Aldermen only after due consultation with the managers and their approval of it obtained. Brady complained several prominent managers had written to Swann making specific charges of violations of the law but no action had been taken; Swann's office claimed those complaints had never been received.[44]

Such clashes prompted the theater managers to hold a conference with Swann and others, on November 13, 1919, to discuss ways to protect the public from overcharges by scalpers. Managers promised to bar every profiteering agency from the ticket-purchasing list. Said William Brady, "I state authoritatively for the producing managers that the managers will take off their list any speculator convicted or even arrested for violating the ordinance. We will forever keep him off the list. The stronger the ordinance is made the better we will like it." Also discussed were ways of revoking an offending agency's license in a less cumbersome and timelier fashion. Brady argued again, "Ticket speculators are an absolute necessity and every large city has them, but in most places the speculators are better regulated than in New York." Assistant District Attorney Talley pointed out, "Tickets for a successful play have been sold en bloc to speculators, only on condition that they buy another block for a failure." To which Brady replied, "That exists to a very limited extent. The managers will take care of that. The members of the association are five to one against it."[45]

In discussing the problem Marc Klaw contended that lack of sincerity, in one or another quarter, had always been at the bottom of failures to end the scalping evil. Arguments by some agencies and managers that the public would not go to the box office were not founded on fact, he said, and that it was only because they had learned that seats were not to be found there that they went to scalpers and agencies. As an example, Klaw cited the long lines at the ticket windows at cinemas as evidence that even the "prosperous persons" were willing to stand in line for tickets if they knew they would be served fairly and in turn.[46]

Surveying the situation from a distance was an editor with the *New York Times* who remarked that at least a dozen times in recent years more or less sincere efforts had been made by city officials and theater managers to curb scalping yet in spite of their attempts, "This method of exploiting the public's interest in the stage has gone on and on, with no real change, and the situation, or rather the extortion, is now worse, if anything, than it has ever been before." He had no faith that the most recent law, and the joint efforts of politicians and managers, would have any effect either because of "the sad truth that, as long as somebody has something to sell at a price somebody else is willing to pay, the transfer will take place, law or no law."[47]

For the few scalpers arrested around this time, sentences got a little harsher. In Jefferson Market Court on November 17, 1919, Magistrate John McGeehan imposed the toughest sentence said to have ever been imposed on a scalper in New York State. He gave John Smith (the name the arrested man gave) a choice of paying a $100 fine or going to the workhouse for 10 days. "The next speculator to appear before me," said McGeehan while imposing the sentence, "is going to be sent to the workhouse for six months. It is just about time that the city were rid of these nuisances, and I intend doing my part in scouring New York of the pests." Smith had been arrested after he had been seen selling tickets in the lobby of the Metropolitan Opera House where he was charging $5 for balcony seats ($3 face). He was also observed distributing his business cards to chauffeurs standing outside the opera house by their vehicles. Smith pled guilty. Most magistrates in most such cases were then fining speculators $5 to $10 although, in one case around that time, Ernest Gross, arrested in the street for scalping, was sentenced to three days in the workhouse when he appeared before Magistrate William A. Sweetzer in Night Court.[48]

Sydney J. Hill, an employee of an agency, was fined $200 on November 29, 1919, in Jefferson Market Court by Magistrate W. Bruce Cobb, following his conviction for scalping. He sold two tickets for a total of $9.90 even though they were marked as $2.75 each.[49]

On January 5, 1919, New York City's 50 cent law was declared unconstitutional by judge Otto A. Rosalsky in the Court of General Sessions. It had been under fire since it had been passed and the decision left brokers jubilant and theatrical managers gloomy. Pending an appeal of the decision all price restrictions on the price of a ticket were removed. Speaking for the Producing Managers'

Association, president Sam H. Harris remarked, "The managers will have to evolve some plan by which to prevent overcharging or otherwise the theatre business in New York simply will be killed. When a man pays a speculator $10 for a theatre ticket it is impossible to make him believe that the manager is not in on the deal." In his decision Rosalsky commented both scalpers and theaters thrived because the public was willing to pay any excessive price that may be asked. "There is no doubt that the evil flowing from this business should be corrected, but the relief, unfortunately, cannot come through the courts, for the courts are merely the interpreters of the law," he held. "In California and Illinois the people have sought to remedy a similar situation, but the legislation was declared unconstitutional." Rosalsky thought a remedy could come from the managers of the theaters through the medium of a contract entered into between the managers and the agencies to sell seats at a reasonable price. He thought such an arrangement could be effective if the parties acted in good faith.[50]

In the wake of that decision New York City officials said they would appeal but in the meantime, however, there would be no action taken against scalpers charging whatever prices they wanted, but those officials insisted the law against the street sale of seats would be strictly enforced. Agency spokesmen said they would operate on the same basis as they had during the time the law was in effect, "That is, taking 50 cents advance for the general run of attractions where the demand was not strong and jacking up the price to whatever the traffic would stand on such shows that the public really wanted and were willing to pay for." When he declared the law unconstitutional, Rosalsky also declared, "Inasmuch as the business of a theatre is not a public enterprise affected with the public interest then it must necessarily follow that the business of its offshoot — the ticket speculator or broker — cannot came within that category."[51]

New York Supreme Court Justice Greenbaum upheld Rosalsky's ruling in declaring New York City's 50 cent ordinance to be invalid on January 27, 1920. He said, tersely, "It seems clear that the municipality lacks power to enact the ordinance."[52]

Police Commissioner Whalen of New York launched a "war" in February 1929 against scalpers who hawked tickets on the sidewalk, a practice still illegal. It started a couple of nights earlier when police officers, acting on complaints from Flo Ziegfeld, rounded up 13 alleged scalpers. Continuing the campaign the next night a squad of plainclothes officers went to Madison Square Garden where a hockey game was scheduled. Ten alleged speculators were arrested there, charged with disorderly conduct and interfering with pedestrians. Said Whalen, firmly, "Scalpers will not be permitted on the sidewalks. Ticket speculators will have to keep fully within the limit of the law."[53]

Two days later five of the 10 men arrested in front of Madison Square Garden were sentenced to five days each in the workhouse by Magistrate Bushel in Night Court on charges of disorderly conduct and annoying pedestrians. Bushel said he was making an example of them; all five had previous arrests for ticket selling activities.[54]

A police drive against scalpers working circus patrons in the vicinity of Madison Square Garden during the Easter Week school holidays in 1934 resulted in the arrest of 16 speculators' "steerers" and 27 scalpers. Arraigned before Magistrate Aurelio in West Side Court on disorderly conduct charges, the steerers were fined $2 each and the peddlers received suspended sentences. All were warned against future offenses. According to the police, the steerers stood near the box office after the house had been sold out and "accosted" mothers with their disappointed children who had been turned away. Scalpers charged as much as $4 over face value.[55]

Mayor Fiorello La Guardia of New York attended a George Gershwin memorial concert on August 9, 1937. Earlier in the day he took action to block profiteering by scalpers in the tickets for that event. He phoned Police Commissioner Valentine and informed him he wanted police officers assigned to the vicinity of the stadium to keep speculators away. La Guardia explained he took that action because he had been told that speculators, in some instances, were demanding as much as $20 for a seat. Prices for the memorial concert were purposely made low, he said, in order that everyone who wished to do so could attend and on that account the boosting of prices by speculators was especially undesirable.[56]

A few months after New York Governor Lehman signed the Mitchell bill that transferred licensing authority over ticket sellers from the State to city authorities, Mayor La Guardia announced a new set of regulations covering the sale of theater tickets. The city's Department of Licenses was to have the assistance of the police department in imposing better control over seat sales. License Commissioner Paul Moss issued the new regulations, effective July 3, 1940, which called for the fingerprinting of every licensed broker and of every employee of every broker. To get rid of sidewalk speculators, added Moss, "No licensee shall sell or permit any person in his employ to sell any tickets of admission in any place in the City of New York, other than the premises approved and licensed to be used for such purpose by such licensee." Regulations also prohibited any licensee from purchasing tickets for resale from persons other than the owners of places of amusement. All tickets were to have the box office price plainly marked on them, with the maximum premium being 75 cents per seat. La Guardia observed that operators of theaters, ball parks, Madison Square Garden, and the Metropolitan Opera House had often complained about having speculators in front of their buildings. "The people of the city should not be compelled to pay exorbitant prices for theatrical performances in the city," added the Mayor. "The decline in theatre patronage during the past years may in part be attributed to the prices that have to be paid for tickets, which often so disgust patrons that they do not go anywhere."[57]

At the end of 1943 License Commissioner Paul Moss told a meeting of theater managers and producers that around the beginning of 1944 he would start holding a hearing on each application he received to renew a ticket broker's license, instead of the usual routine, no-questions-asked renewal. Moss explained he had called the meeting "to find some way to correct a condition that must eventually hurt the industry." Reports were said to have come to him that ticket brokers were compelled to pay more for seats than the price printed on the tickets. Calling the situation very serious he warned that "all managers and producers must be on their guard, as it may be that I might be compelled to suspend or revoke a license of a theatre that houses a great hit, which of course could be very disastrous." Moss urged the group to police their property and "see that the practices complained of are stopped."[58]

As 1945 began Moss imposed a draconian measure on the city's theatre industry when he ordered that all tickets to seven popular shows were to be sold only through the box office or by mail on a first-come, first-served basis— that is, none through a broker. That measure brought the wrath of not only the brokers but also that of the producers and theatre owners down on Moss. In the face of that united protest, Moss gave ground. He settled with the trade on a program on industry self-regulation, under which the League of New York Theaters agreed to aid in a rigid enforcement of a maximum premium of 75 cents per ticket. Solemnly, the venue owners promised Moss they would withdraw all seats from a broker against whom there was any evidence of overcharging rather than wait for the License Commission to get its more cumbersome legal machinery into action. Although Moss expressed his skepticism about self-regulation and threatened more drastic action should it fail, he had been defeated by the unified protest from the industry.[59]

Over this time the Bureau of Internal Revenue kept up its own battle to collect taxes from the scalpers. IRS agents conducted a raid on speculators working near Ebbets Field in Brooklyn on a Sunday afternoon in May 1927 just prior to a game between the Dodgers and Philadelphia. Summonses were issued to eight scalpers to appear at the office of the bureau. John E. Brady of the IRS said the ticket men had not been complying with government regulations requiring reports be kept on how many seats were sold. Brady made it plain the raid had nothing to do with the payment of income tax nor was the agency concerned about the price of tickets. "There is nothing wrong about ticket speculation as far as we are concerned, but we wish to see the books of these people to find out if the Government is getting what is coming to it," he declared. The federal government remained entitled to five percent of any ticket premium that was 50 cents or less, and 50 percent of any excess premium above the 50 cents.[60]

Almost a decade later, near the end of 1936, the IRS issued amended regulations intended to prevent amusement (as the war tax had come to be called) tax evasion by scalpers on the premiums they collected. Mostly those new regulations had to do with even greater detail in the records that had to be kept by brokers and by theaters or others who sold tickets for resale to brokers—a double check. Action to tighten up the regulations followed an investigation by IRS agents in New York City that showed an "apparent evasion of taxes on the resale of amusement tickets."[61]

A new development in this period was the holding of government investigations into the business of ticket scalping. These probes appeared to have no specific end in mind — such as the drafting of a law — but were conducted simply to expose the evil of ticket speculation, and possibly function as springboards to some type of specific action.

12

Government Probes, 1918–1949

"In all New York's legit theatres there are not over a dozen managers or producers who are on the level either with themselves, the brokers or the public on the ticket thing."
Variety, 1927

"the great majority of brokers are scalpers and should be eliminated."
John Murtagh, New York City
Investigation Commissioner, 1949

Even the U.S. Congress almost held its own investigation. Congressman Bloom (D., New York) introduced a measure in Congress in 1924 calling upon the House to appoint a committee of five members to investigate the selling and distribution of theatre tickets by theatrical managers and owners of theatres, baseball clubs and amusement places of all kinds to the ticket speculator and brokers of New York and other cities throughout the country. According to the Bloom resolution, methods then used to distribute and sell seats "have gouged the interstate traveling public and have resulted in scandalous price fixing and unfair trade competition." Impetus for the action of Bloom was said to link back to producer William A. Brady, who had been very vocal in his condemnation of scalpers over the previous few weeks. Brady's charge that three Broadway managers had received bonuses totalling $225,000 yearly from speculators was a prime motivator for Bloom's resolution. William Brady steadfastly refused to name the managers unless he was placed under oath. Nothing came of the Bloom resolution.[1]

One government probe that did take place was conducted in 1927 by United States Attorney Charles H. Tuttle, who investigated Broadway's theatre ticket situation. Testimony of witnesses was given before United States Commissioner Cotter. Joseph Newman, manager of the Broadway Theatre Ticket Company, told Tuttle of the exorbitant demands of box office men. He cited the case of Leon Errol's *Yours Truly*, saying George Buck, the box office man at the venue, had demanded a $2 "commission" on each ticket sold to the agencies and that his firm, after paying the commission for two weeks, had refused to do so any longer because it thought the fee exorbitant. After that, he said, the firm was unable to get tickets at the box office. *Yours Truly* was not the success its producers had hoped for and Newman felt the excessive demands by the theater treasurer helped cause that. He added that on other occasions box office men had "killed their own hits" because of such excess "commissions" that usually were 25 cents, 50 cents, and $1 a seat for the big hits.[2]

Under questioning by Tuttle, Newman admitted his agency sold tickets for the Maloney-Delaney fight at Madison Square Garden in February 1927 at a price of $90 for each of nine seats while the box office price was $22 each. Newman said those nine seats had cost his agency a total of $765, leaving a profit of only $45. He had been unable to obtain seats for the fight from the Garden box office and had been forced to buy them from individuals who hawked seats among the brokers. As well, Newman testified his agency sold two sets of tickets to *Rio Rita* at the Ziegfeld Theatre — one set of five seats for $125 ($27.50 face) and the other a group of eight tickets for $104 ($44 face).[3]

Leonard E. Bergman, general manager of the A. L. Erlanger Amusement Enterprises, testified that box office men at theaters were paid poorly, only $1,500 a year by their employers, and in his opinion that was not a living wage. And that left those employees vulnerable to temptation to graft. Bergman said that when he was treasurer of the New Amsterdam Theatre in 1925 his "graft" netted him in the neighborhood of $12,000 to $15,000 a year from the extra he charged speculators for tickets. When Tuttle was asked if the theater management got any of that money he replied, "not a single penny in any way, shape or manner," but he admitted that management saved considerable money by employing the treasurers at $1,500 a year and permitting them to take graft. And that was why they did it. Answering questions from Tuttle, Bergman said that percentages of a production's gross receipts went to the owner of the theater in which it was staged, dramatic and musical authors of the piece, and others. "In other words," said Tuttle, "the whole plan is not only a plan to gyp the Government, but also to gyp the author, the music writer, the theatre owner and anybody else who has a percentage in the gross profits?" To which the witness replied, "Yes, sir."[4]

As the probe continued, W. J. L. Banham, president of the New York Board of Trade and Transportation, sent Tuttle a letter congratulating him on his work and declared, "The charges that have been intermittently made of the holding out of desirable theatre and sports tickets, followed by an abnormal increase in the stated face value of the ticket, have reached such proportions as to shock the sensibilities of the citizens of New York, and no doubt to make us New Yorkers appear in a very poor light to our fellow-citizens in this country."

He hoped that Tuttle, whose only mandate was to contemplate the infraction of Federal law (as in speculators defrauding the government out of taxes due on sales), would, nevertheless, provide New York with suggestions for remedial legislation.[5]

Another witness was Arthur Hammerstein, producer and manager, who described the theater ticket business as having sunk deep into corruption and graft, not through any fault of the public, but because it was "in the hands of gougers and ticket brokers and if you don't cater to them I dare you to have even half a house, for they have taught the public not to buy at the box office." He said box office men were willing to accept such positions without salary, knowing they could get large sums from the ticket brokers. George Buck testified that when he had the ticket privilege for his brother Gene's show *Yours Truly* he had charged ticket brokers an extra $1.50 a ticket, instead of $1 each. Hammerstein had earlier testified that George Buck's actions had caused him to be known derisively on Broadway as "Buck and a half." Theaters in New York, asserted Hammerstein, "are controlled by the ticket brokers. If you do not get along with them you can't get along with your show, no matter what you have to offer." He also said he had heard some years earlier that Leonard Bergman, manager of the Erlanger theatrical enterprises and formerly treasurer of the New Amsterdam Theatre, had received $1 a ticket as a bonus from the agencies and had paid the money to "Mr. Ziegfeld and Mr. Erlanger." Both men denied that allegation. Ziegfeld maintained that a $1 a seat premium for 500 tickets each night for *Rio Rita* had been offered to him and he had refused to accept.[6]

While George Buck was mentioned several times in testimony because of direct premium payments of $1 to $1.50 per ticket, he was said to be not the only manager or showman who had done likewise during the previous theatrical season. Buck said he collected $1.50 a seat from some agencies, others paid him 75 cents, and so on down to as little as 15 cents a ticket. Such seats were all within the first nine rows, said Buck. He estimated he had collected $5,000 to $6,000 in that manner. An accounting slip from McBride's agency showed that broker alone had paid him $1,000. According to Buck he said he was not on salary and did not divide the money with his brother Gene or anybody else. It was reported that when Gene Buck booked *Yours Truly* into the Shubert Theatre he was to have complete say about ticket distribution. For that reason the Shuberts were not in on the collections made by George. Arthur Hammerstein, when he declared that Leonard Bergman got a bonus of $1 a seat for the hits at the New Amsterdam, meaning about $800 nightly, said he got that information from Louis Cohn, a ticket broker who died about a year earlier. Bergman, while admitting to a take of $12,000 to $15,000 a year, maintained he never got over 12.5 cents a seat for himself when he was treasurer of the New Amsterdam, a fact said to be confirmed by other brokers.[7]

In his testimony Ziegfeld agreed box office men received bonuses from the agencies but he insisted that was not the real reason the public was gouged, but rather the burden imposed on agencies to buy tickets for failures in order to get seats for hits was the real problem. Flo thought that all box office men received gratuities from the brokers. Producer George White (*Scandals*) admitted his organization had gotten money that way but said he was unable to estimate the amount. "It might be $10 and it might be $60,000 or $70,000," he said. Tuttle called his attention to statements by agencies that they did business with him directly on the bonuses, to which he answered, "I say they lie." White claimed his treasurer George Morely made all the deals with the agencies. He also announced he would pay the government half the money received from the brokers, and it was understood he was advised to do so promptly by his lawyer, who was there with him at the Tuttle hearing. According to White two-thirds of the seats for the floor of his attractions went to the agencies that made a buy for at least 20 weeks.[8]

Julius Schleifstein, treasurer of the Liberty Theatre, announced he had made an amended return for his personal income tax on the advice of his counsel. He told Tuttle that box office men did take tickets back from agencies and kept down agency losses, in return for which gratuities were given. Schleifstein testified that every box office in the city accepted such gifts from the agencies, except the Metropolitan Opera House. At one time Tuttle believed perhaps as much as $750,000 was paid annually to the box office men as graft but later revised that figure down to $250,000 a year. Julius told the inquiry he received $4,700 in 1925 and $3,500 in 1926 but the amount paid to his box office was actually twice that amount with the other half of the bonuses paid out to Schleifstein's assistants.[9]

The *Nation* magazine was disgusted at the revelations from the Tuttle probe showing that not only did the agencies graft off the public, but the agencies in turn were grafted upon by the box office men who were able to, in some cases, equal or exceed their salaries as box office managers or treasurers from the graft. A Brooklyn newspaper, the *Eagle*, referred to those box office grafters as "pasteboard plutocrats." Tuttle's hearing came about from the successful prosecution of the Alexander ticket agency and its two proprietors. It started with the discovery by Federal officials that the agencies (the Alexander firm was selected as a test case from the 13 initially involved) were not making proper returns to the Internal Revenue Service. As the research developed it appeared there was a complicated system of collusion between the theaters and the agencies in holding out large blocks of choice seats for sale to the public at higher prices than face value. Said the Washington *Star*, "This is a pernicious practice." Admitting there was a certain convenience in being able to buy theater seats in hotel lobbies and for that service a reasonable commission above the box office price was justifiable, the editor added, "But the wholesale vending of large blocks of seats through agencies that are no more nor less than box-office extensions, with the theater employees not the theater owners themselves profiting, is nothing less than a graft upon the theater-going public." The Alexander agency and its two officers were found guilty by a jury on July 13, 1927, and convicted on all 14 counts; each count represented a month between March 1926 and April 1927, when the firm failed to make proper income tax returns to the government on amounts received for theater tickets in excess of 50 cents over the established price.[10]

In the fall of 1927, after the Tuttle probe had concluded, an outraged editorial in *Variety* damned the theater managers for blaming the ticket agencies for the mess and for the "outrageous conditions" uncovered by the Tuttle investigation. A statement to that effect was signed on behalf of managers of 59 of the 70 legitimate Broadway theaters. "In all New York's legit theatres there are not over a dozen managers or producers who are on the level either with themselves, the brokers or the public on the ticket thing," said the editor. "The stand-in managers are the gougers; they are the ones who have forced ticket agencies to give up to them. They didn't care what other brokers did to the public or with their theatre tickets, and they don't care now. They want that easy money; side money, and they don't care, the brokers don't care and very few of the public care." Pessimistically, the editor concluded, "Ticket speculators in New York cannot be regulated or suppressed.... In New York City are over 20,000 men who would tell the district attorney, the managers, the brokers or anyone else to mind their own business if attempting to instruct them where and how they shall purchase and pay for their entertainment."[11]

Jack Levy, owner and manager of the Premier Theatre Ticket Company at 1539 Broadway, was sentenced on October 11, 1927, by Federal Judge Henry W. Goddard to eight months in the penitentiary and fined $5,000 for violations of the Ticket Tax law for which he pled guilty in July. Sentence, which had been deferred, was imposed because Levy violated an agreement with United States Attorney Tuttle and the Court that he would not again sell any ticket for more than 50 cents above the price printed on it. But he went on to sell several $5.50 World Series tickets for $15 each. Tuttle, in asking sentence be imposed, told Goddard that Levy had done "what is now all too common along Broadway" in stamping his tickets, as required by law, but with a stamp that was illegible and disclosed neither the price demanded nor the name of the agent who sold the tickets. The U. S. Attorney also told Goddard that Levy had defrauded the U. S. Government out of more than $6,300 during the 14 month period covered by the indictment.[12]

The conviction of Edward and Oscar Alexander and the Alexander Theatre Ticket Corporation for evading payment of the 50 percent tax on ticket premiums above 50 cents was unanimously affirmed by the U. S. Circuit Court of Appeals in December 1927. Edward and Oscar had each been sentenced to six months in jail and fined $5,000 while their company had been fined $1,000. It was a test case on the constitutionality of the ticket tax law.[13]

In the wake of the Tuttle hearing it was reported that an "agreement" was struck between Tuttle and most of the brokers not to charge a premium over 50 cents above the printed price. It was, though, an informal and voluntary agreement and a few agencies declined to be part of it. Additionally, a few more brokers opened for the first time and by October 1927 *Variety* reported high premiums, in excess of 50 cents, were "back strong." Apparently, though, the new ones were making proper tax reports and paying the 50 percent levy to the government. Good seats for the hit shows on Broadway were then being scalped by brokers at twice the face value and sometimes more, although box office men were said to be receiving no gratuities.[14]

United States Attorney Tuttle, in a January 1, 1929, statement issued by him in response to criticism directed against him for not enforcing the law against ticket speculators, denied jurisdiction and placed the responsibility at the door of the theater managers. He noted that producer William Brady had criticized him for not enforcing the New York State law "which I had passed at the last session of the State Legislature." Enforcement, he insisted, was a matter for the State and not the federal authorities, "and, no doubt, these officials will act whenever the theatrical managers manifest a sufficiently real desire to check ticket gouging by submitting the evidence." As far as Tuttle was concerned, "The managers know the agencies who are doing the gouging, and, indeed, they have a record of it because existing law requires each ticket agency to write its name and resale price on the back of the portion of the ticket taken up by the management."[15]

Some 20 years later New York City conducted a probe of its own into the practice. Financial records of the city's major ticket brokers were subpoenaed on May 3, 1949, by the city's Investigation Commissioner John M. Murtagh. It marked the beginning of an investigation into exorbitant ticket prices for Broadway hit shows and was ordered by Mayor O'Dwyer after he had heard reports that tickets for such shows as *South Pacific*; *Kiss Me, Kate*; and *Death of a Salesman* were being sold by brokers for eight times the box office price. Murtagh exclaimed that if necessary he would use other methods to end the practice of scalping and that he would look into reports those box office personnel and some producers were in collusion in selling seats to unscrupulous brokers. Rumors that some theater owners did not check carefully on the activities of box office employees were also to be scrutinized. While he agreed the Ticket Code Authority existed — a vague and voluntary code of conduct which the owners and producers had generated — he pointed out the code authority had not taken punitive action against a broker in two years. Even though the city then had in place an ordinance that limited the ticket premium to a maximum of 75 cents per seat (plus 15 cents tax, 90 cents total), a reporter commented, "The city has investigated ticket scalping in the theatre repeatedly in recent years without appreciably reducing the number of complaints." Brokers were then estimated to control 50 percent or more of the orchestra seats for hit shows, on the basis of advance buys. To increase their share to an even higher level some brokers used diggers and, with or without cooperation from the box office personnel, made frequent purchases from the box office in person or by mail. Around that time, also, some producers tried to curtail the brokers' share of the seats to hit shows by imposing a black out week on a regular basis. Thus, brokers received no seats at all every fifth week for *Death of a Salesman*. For *South Pacific* producers were said to have cut the allotment to brokers in half for the first eight weeks of the run. Murtagh acknowledged he expected considerable difficulty in getting at the facts and asked for public cooperation in unearthing examples of scalping. Working with the Commissioner in the probe were the New York City Department of Licenses and the Police Department.[16]

It was standing room only every night at the Majestic Theatre in May 1949, where the musical *South Pacific* packed them in. Yet Christian Christopherson had 18 choice seats in the orchestra when he was arrested at his office (he ran a company that offered various business and stenographic services) charged with conducting a ticket brokerage business without a license. He pled guilty before Magistrate Frederick Strong and explained he charged a would-be purchaser $2 an hour for his services in obtaining the ticket, beyond the box office price, that is, a fee to cover the time involved in getting the seat. He had been discovered after the License Department had received a tip. Warning him he would go to jail if he repeated the offense, Strong fined him $100 and suspended a 15-day term in the workhouse.[17]

Still in May, it was announced by the city administration that a plan was under consideration for strict regulation of the ticket brokers and the theatrical industry. Said Murtagh, "I was naïve enough to think that the threat of an investigation would hurt the black market in tickets to hit shows. I know better now." That change of heart came about after Murtagh saw what a "mess" most of the books were in and the impossibility of figuring out if scalping existed, from those records. He had subpoenaed the books of 32 brokers but came away "disgusted" from the lack of vital information continued therein.[18]

On May 18 Murtagh announced he would seek to revoke the license of the Majestic Theatre where the hit musical *South Pacific* was running because Jack Pearl, the venue's box office treasurer, would not cooperate in the inquiry. Pearl had been asked to appear at Murtagh's office for questioning and while he did appear he gave only his name and address, refusing to answer any other questions. For example, when he was asked what his position was at the Majestic he refused to answer. Therefore, said Murtagh, he would ask Edward T. McCaffrey, License Commissioner, to revoke the venue's license and he would also turn the complaint over to District Attorney Frank Hogan for possible prosecution on a criminal basis. As a result of Pearl's refusal to cooperate, Lee Shubert (president of the Magoro Corporation, which owned the Majestic) announced he had suspended Pearl as box office treasurer. Earlier Shubert had said he would do all in his power to get his employee to talk. *South Pacific* (a sell-out for each performance since it opened on April 7) had been grossing

$56,000 weekly. Richard Rodgers, Oscar Hammerstein II, Leland Howard, and Joshua Logan (producers of the show) made the following statement, "The producers of *South Pacific* welcome Commissioner Murtagh's investigation and offer him all possible cooperation in bringing relief to a sadly abused public. We ourselves are as much victimized as the public. We are merely tenants of the Majestic theatre. We do not employ the box office staff and we have no control over the disposition of tickets."[19]

Lee Shubert was himself subpoenaed by Murtagh, on May 20, along with all the records of the Magoro concern. Meanwhile, he said he would not seek to close the Majestic (245 West 44th Street) when two of the show's producers, Rodgers and Howard, went voluntarily to his office and promised their support for his drive to break up the ticket monopoly. Murtagh explained that because of the position of the producers, along with the suspension of Pearl, he did not expect any further barriers to his investigation of seat distribution at the Majestic. Rodgers told the Commissioner he was very upset about scalping since if a speculator hawked a seat for $50 *South Pacific* received only $6, "and $44 has been taken away from the theatre as a whole and the less successful shows suffer. Some one who contributes nothing to the theatre business makes the other $44. That is why we are so upset about this. We would like to see some other show get this $44. That would make for healthy business in the industry." He added, "Nobody gets anything out of this graft but the fellow with his office in his hat and we don't like him." The main reason for the investigation, explained Murtagh, was not to relieve playgoers who were paying exorbitant prices, "but to make more tickets available to those who cannot afford to pay black market prices. People with fat expense accounts don't need our help, but deprive the average New Yorker and visitor to the city of an opportunity to see our shows."[20]

A couple of days later, Murtagh announced he had recommended to Mayor O'Dwyer and to License Commissioner Edward McCaffrey that the broker license of the John Ahearn Agency be revoked for failure to keep proper records of purchases and sales of tickets. When Ahearn had been questioned he was said to have been unable to explain satisfactorily the disposition of his tickets for *South Pacific* and for other shows. After two weeks of looking into the matter Murtagh declared, "Ticket scalping is much more widespread than was at first believed." To that point, he conceded, he had uncovered nothing to prove that producers were working in collusion with brokers in the scalping activities.[21]

On May 25 the Commissioner announced he had moved for the revocation of a second license — that of the Phil Rosen Theatre Ticket Service — also for a failure to keep adequate records as to its purchase of *South Pacific* tickets. As this agency was not on the allotment list for that production it was understood the Rosen agency employed diggers to obtain seats and from April 1 to May 16 it had sold 24 seats to that show. The Rosen agency was not on the allotment list for any theater, which indicated it was not among the major brokers in the city.[22]

Because of Murtagh's probe a meeting was held near the end of May, called by the major ticket brokers but also including theater owners and producers and an official from Actors Equity. After conferring with them the brokers announced they planned to organize into a group that would drive from the business those brokers who had been charging exorbitant prices for seats to shows. Raised at the meeting was the subject of "ice." Ice was an industry term that referred to a gratuity (read bribe) paid by "unscrupulous" brokers to box office personnel or others to get tickets to hit shows. Brokers had contended, said a reporter, that if they refused to bribe those who distributed tickets, unlicensed brokers would. Just before that meeting, members of the League of New York Theaters and the newly formed Committee of Theatrical Producers discussed the advisability of reducing the maximum number of seats that could be allotted to ticket agencies. Under the current code — set voluntarily by the theater industry — 75 percent of the seats to a show could be turned over to brokers.[23]

Jack Pearl was subpoenaed again by Murtagh. When he appeared on June 1 he again refused to answer virtually all questions. He remained under suspension from his job (from May 18) but he refused to say if his boss Lee Shubert was paying him; his salary had been $110 a week. In the wake of Pearl's second stonewalling Murtagh declared he would bring back Shubert for more questioning.[24]

A day later Shubert was questioned and denied he was still paying Pearl but did admit the man's salary of $110 a week was held in escrow because Pearl's membership in a union protected him against dismissal except for dishonesty or habitual drunkenness.[25]

At the time of the probe, on the face of every theater ticket sold in New York was printed the following warning, "Maximum re-sale premium on orchestra or box-seat ticket, $.75; other locations, $.50 plus 20 percent tax. Retain stub to support any claim for overcharge." Venues hosting the three biggest hits of the time (*South Pacific*; *Kiss Me, Kate*; and *Death of a Salesman*) had a total of 4,276 seats, 2,241 of them on the orchestra floor. On any given night demand was very high. Reporter Richard Maney said a Hollywood big shot had recently boasted he had paid $200 for two seats to *South Pacific* (about $6 face, each). The Theatre Ticket Code, supported by the League of New York Theatres and Actors' Equity, allowed roughly 65 percent of the orchestra seats for those shows, and others, to be allotted to the favored agencies— that is, the approved agencies. Seats thus allotted to brokers fell into two categories; in one category returns of unsold seats were permitted as late as 7 P.M. on a performance day, in the other category were outright buys (no returns allowed). Besides that method, brokers obtained extra seats in other ways such as through the use of diggers lining up at box offices, by mail order, and by bribing box office personnel. Also, about 40 to 60 house seats were set aside each night at each theater for disposal at the discretion of the producer to friends, relatives, stars in the shows, and so on. It was not uncommon for some of those to find their way to brokers. After all such allocations of seats were made prior to the fact, there were a lot less available for the public to buy than most people realized.[26]

The license of the John Ahearn Ticket Agency was revoked on June 7 after two hearings on the charges it violated the statute requiring the firm to keep detailed records of seat purchases and sales. It was the first revocation as a result of the probe. Murtagh also sought the revocation of a third license, that of the Louis Cohn Theatre Ticket Office, which was alleged to have overcharged as much as 100 percent over the box office price. Examination of the Cohn records showed overcharges for seats for *South Pacific*; *Kiss Me, Kate*; *Death of a Salesman*; and *Detective Story* ranged from $3.88 to $7.40 per seat, and extended to more than 1,000 tickets.[27]

Meanwhile the city's licensed brokers held a stormy session at the Astor Hotel that ended with shouting and yelling but with nothing resolved. Before they began discussions they listened to short speeches from producers Hayward, Rodgers, Kermit Bloomgarden, and Max Gordon (all four representing the Committee of Theatrical Producers) and producer Brock Pemberton (head of the New York Theatre League). Representatives from those two groups stressed that if the brokers failed to clean house themselves the city might do the job for them. They urged the brokers to develop some kind of plan to clean up the industry and warned against considering the Murtagh inquiry as just another probe that would be forgotten after election day. Pemberton admitted producers were "even more culpable" than brokers for the current seat situation because they had "set up a system that may occasionally make it advisable for a broker to pay gratuities for tickets." However, when the brokers met alone it only led to sharp disagreement and angry shouts.[28]

One day later, on June 9, just before its hearing was due to start, the Phil Rosen Ticket Service surrendered its license to McCaffrey. In its surrender letter the agency said the hearing would be a waste of time and that theater ticket distribution in New York City was controlled by "a tight monopoly." Rosen was not a favored broker and, for example, "could do no business with the Shubert theatrical interests." Murtagh agreed with Rosen's criticisms and remarked, "The distribution of tickets is at present in the hands of the theatre owners rather than in the hands of producers where it belongs. My investigation is directed principally at a complete reform of the present method of distribution."[29]

At one of its regular meetings the Committee of Theatrical Producers announced its concerted drive to wipe out scalping. The Committee was attempting to have house seats (the tickets set aside by producers and venue owners for themselves, authors, stars, directors, friends, relatives, and so on) marked so they could be traced in case the tickets fell into the wrong hands.[30]

Expanding the scope of his probe, Murtagh subpoenaed the records of 23 hotels wherein tickets were sold from kiosks, along with newspapers, candy, and so forth. "The more we investigate, the more we realize that the business of distributing theatre tickets needs a complete overhauling," said Murtagh. "The business practices in this field are not calculated to serve the best interest of the public. It is becoming every day clearer that drastic reform is imperative."[31]

In a preliminary report to Mayor O'Dwyer on June 18, Murtagh recommended the abolition of ticket agencies and suggested the current system be replaced by a central ticket agency operated by theatrical producers. He also asked for the revocation of the licenses of three more agencies, bringing the total to seven brokers who had licenses revoked or who were awaiting revocation hearings. As well he asked McCaffrey to order concessionaires in 11 hotels to cease selling seats because they lacked licenses. In his report to the Mayor he asserted, "Nothing short of widespread reform will make tickets available to the public at fair prices. It is up to the producers on behalf of themselves and those of the theatre profession to bring about this reform. I am more than half convinced that ticket brokerage as a whole must go. A central distribution system controlled directly by the producers would seem to be a solution."[32]

Near the end of June Murtagh widened his inquiry again, to include every ticket broker in town. Thus, he subpoenaed the records of 34 additional brokers (over the initial 32). He was then seeking, or had obtained, the revocation of 20 broker licenses on the grounds of faulty record keeping and/or overcharges. Latest to lose their license was the Louis Cohn Theatre Ticket Office. One of the operators of that firm, Joseph A. Deutsch, testified he had charged steady customers $35 for two seats to *South Pacific* and $30 for a pair to *Kiss Me, Kate*. Under questioning he admitted he made gifts of $100 to $200 to box office treasurers but he maintained his office would not overcharge transient customers because he did not know them and "they'd yell their heads off." By this point the brokers were said to be ready to do anything to get rid of Murtagh.[33]

National attention to the Murtagh probe came when journalist Robert Sylvester did a piece on the situation in *Colliers*. Like so many observers Sylvester was cynical and felt this investigation would be no more successful in rectifying the problem than any of the past efforts. He argued ticket gouging was not peculiar to New York City but existed also in each of the three other cities in America where live theater was an important part of the population's nightly entertainment — Boston, Chicago, and Philadelphia. According to Sylvester, scalping had been connected with the theater for over 200 years with the practice originated by a London flute maker named Keith, who cornered most of the good tickets for the Italian opera and did so well "that he threw away his flute tools." McBride's agency in New York (it resold 1.4 million theater seats in a year) was founded by Tom McBride around 1873. Concluded

Sylvester, "The general theory in show business is that the ticket thieves will automatically disappear the minute people stop paying their prices. The time seems a long way off."[34]

During the investigation of the Alexander Ticket Office at 218 West 49th Street it was revealed that over the six months ending June 26 that agency, said Murtagh, had sold 3,291 tickets at a profit of $12,693, or about $4 a ticket.[35]

Ticket brokers, in a resolution adopted unanimously on July 19, 1949, asked that Murtagh be replaced in his inquiry by an "impartial" commission to be appointed by Governor Dewey or Mayor O'Dwyer. In the words of the resolution, Murtagh "has disqualified himself as a fit person to conduct such an investigation." It was a resolution based on two points. First, claimed the agents, Murtagh had demonstrated prejudice "by his intemperate utterances and vituperation directed at those in the ticket business in calling them riffraff and other names." Second, the Commissioner of Investigation "exceeded the bounds of authority, good taste and good administration by naming two individual ticket brokers with whom he believes sports promoters, theatre owners and the public should do business to the exclusion of other brokers." Murtagh reiterated his criticism of most brokers. Two months of investigation had led him to the conclusion "that the great majority of brokers are scalpers and should be eliminated." He said he favored no particular brokers and the cause of that grievance was the selection by the New York Yankees of two brokers with whom they would do business. Murtagh said he had not influenced the choices made by the baseball club.[36]

Supreme Court Justice Thomas A. Aurelio upheld, on July 20, the right of License Commissioner McCaffrey to revoke the license of the Louis Cohn agency for failing to keep proper records and for overcharging — that is, going over the 75 cent maximum premium allowed by the city ordinance. It was a test case and Aurelio found nothing unconstitutional about the city's 1940 measure in this, the first time it had gone to a higher court.[37]

License Commissioner McCaffrey announced on October 7, 1949, the revocation of two more brokers' licenses, bringing to 30 the total number forfeited as a result of the Murtagh probe. However, a month earlier the pressure applied by the brokers against Murtagh finally had an effect as Mayor O'Dwyer took steps unofficially and indirectly to rein in Murtagh.[38]

On September 1, O'Dwyer promised the cooperation of every city agency with the new theatrical committee organized to improve conditions along Broadway. He said the municipal government had an important part to play in eliminating the ticket scalping evil and for those reasons he had invited representatives of all phases of show business to his official residence, Gracie Mansion, a couple of days earlier to organize a committee and formulate a plan. O'Dwyer emphatically denied the purpose of the new group was to impede the inquiry of his Investigation Commissioner. "I want to stop ticket scalping, but I want to do it in such a way as not to damage an important industry," he explained.[39]

Ten days after that a reporter commented that the ticket brokers could
then discontinue their Tuesday afternoon war councils at the Astor Hotel
because Murtagh, at the request of O'Dwyer, had entered what he described as
the "constructive phase" of his four-month old inquiry, which to that point had
taken away over one-third of the licenses of the city's 66 ticket brokers through
revocation or surrender. The first step of the new group organized at the request
of the Mayor, said O'Dwyer, was to incorporate the code of the League of New
York Theatres into the regulations of the Department of Licenses. That, he
added, would enable McCaffrey to administer a code that was established originally by show people to restrain chicanery in the sale and distribution of tickets. It was a sound code, declared the Mayor, but unfortunately it was generally
ignored. Murtagh's probe had shown that very few brokers paid any attention
to that code.[40]

Ten months after O'Dwyer ordered an investigation of scalping, he made
public a covenant, in March 1950, between brokers, venue owners, producers,
and city authorities that he insisted gave the public a better deal. A week earlier the Theatre Ticket Code had been incorporated into the Department of
Licenses by-laws. Reporter Murray Schumach declared, "There is little in the
code that has not already been promulgated by the League of New York Theatres.... Nevertheless, the new code has the advantage of an enforcement provision. The old set-up placed punitive power in the hands of people, some of
whom might have profited by looking the other way. Now these rules are city
regulations to be checked and enforced by the city."[41]

Under those rules the premium was limited to a maximum of 75 cents per
seat, the back of the ticket had to be stamped with all the details of the broker
and price so it could be traced, and the allotment of seats to unlicensed brokers was forbidden. Brokers were forbidden to pay gratuities for choice tickets or to accept premiums for hawking seats to failing shows. Tickets set aside
for box office sale to playgoers had to be stamped accordingly and were not to
be resold to brokers. Finally, theater owners had to keep weekly records showing details of how their tickets were dispensed. Murtagh observed, "The new
rules will substantially facilitate and make more effective the investigation of
ticket scalping." Skeptics noted there was nothing in the rules about the dis-
enfranchised brokers who had mostly not gone out of business at all but simply moved the short distance to New Jersey wherein they carried on a lucrative
business by phone from their newly adopted state. Also, there was nothing in
the rules to stop, or deal with, diggers. One provision declared that no theater
owner was to be liable for the acts of any employee who violated any of the
rules, unless that owner gave consent, or connived, and so on. "This, argue some
brokers, guarantees immunity to theatre owners who have an understanding
with brokers that is executed by worldly box-office treasurers."[42]

By this time producers and owners were less and less involved in launch-
ing "wars" on scalpers as part of their tactics to curb the evil. It still happened

on occasion but much less often as no one's efforts in the past, well-intentioned or not, had been effective. The most significant effort along those lines in this period was the development of the New York Theatre League and the development of a voluntary code of conduct. Of course, that also did not work, but it at least allowed the owners and producers to present themselves to the public as doing something, or at least trying. One reason that no effort to curb the evil taken by producers and owners had worked was because so much collusion existed between them and the brokers.

13

War on Scalpers, or Collusion, 1918–1949

"I have been the uncompromising foe of the ticket grafter all my life. Help me to protect the public from these human sharks."

Showman David Belasco, 1921

"Most producers are working hand in hand with the ticket speculators...."

Eddie Cantor, 1929

In New York in November 1919 the Producing Managers' Association called a special meeting for the purpose of seeking a remedy for the theatre ticket "speculating evil." Appointed to the committee to work out a solution were Arthur Hopkins, Henry W. Savage, and William A. Brady. Evidence was considered that showed some brokers were charging $10 each for seats with a face value not over $3. It was known that as high as $14 a ticket had been charged for two seats to the Empire Theatre for the previous Saturday and front row tables at the *Midnight Frolic* accommodating four people and priced at the box office at $20 had been scalped for as high as $50 and even $60 in one case. All that took place despite the New York City ordinance that prohibited a premium in excess of 50 cents. Managers grumbled they were blamed by the public for the "gyp" methods of certain speculators and, "The facts appear to be that a certain class of patrons insist on getting choice seats and are willing to come across regardless of price, then later complain against the managers." One idea discussed by the managers was the setting up of a single, central box office to sell seats for all of them and to be controlled by them. Another idea was for them to lobby for a State regulatory law, since the city ordinance was considered by them as "apparently ineffective."[1]

One year later, at another Producing Managers' Association meeting to deal with speculation, the group announced it had given up any idea of opening its own centralized ticket office as being impracticable. Reportedly the Producing Managers' Association covered all of the leading producers and theatres in New York, with a couple of exceptions.[2]

One of those who did launch that steadily decreasing item, a "war" on speculators, was showman David Belasco, who started his campaign in February 1921. Results from the first day of that war included six arrests of five men. One of the first of those arrested was quickly released on bail. He returned to the venue and just as quickly was arrested for the second time that night. All those men were working on the street near the Belasco Theatre. Police cracked down following complaints made by Belasco to them that the sidewalk men were annoying his patrons.[3]

Belasco had his attention drawn to the situation a few days earlier when he left his theater and started walking west on 44th Street toward Broadway. He came across a speculator trying to sell a couple of $1 seats to his venue for $3. Incensed, Belasco tried to grab the man who turned and ran. The showman and several playgoers all took off in pursuit but soon lost the man in the crowd. Further incensed by the escape, Belasco returned to his venue lobby, by then filled with theatregoers, and made a speech in which he asked the crowd to aid him in eradicating the evil of ticket speculation by reporting their presence whenever discovered. Reportedly, he was applauded long and loud. Thus encouraged, Belasco moved outside to the sidewalk and continued with his speech, "I have been the uncompromising foe of the ticket grafter all my life. Help me to protect the public from these human sharks. They not only steal your money but are abusive to women and children. From tonight on there will be two plainclothes men in front of this theatre at every performance." Belasco was again applauded and did indeed station two private security people at his venue each night.[4]

Two years after saying they would have no centralized box office, the Producing Managers' Association said, in December 1922, that they would indeed establish a central ticket outlet to replace their individual box offices. Still, there were detractors. One was Flo Ziegfeld, who was out of town at the time of the announcement but opposed it publicly as soon as he got back, calling it "not only thoroughly impractical, but a positive menace to the successful operation of high-class New York playhouses. Without doubt there is a joker in the scheme, whereby particular parties may benefit at the expense of others." He added that if the new idea became a reality, "I think it will largely augment the number of unscrupulous sidewalk ticket speculators." In his opinion the public found it convenient to go to the hotel agencies and other brokers and they could not be forced to go to a central ticket agency any more than to the theater box office.[5]

Although the plan to establish a central ticket agency was formally adopted by the Producing Managers' Association in December 1922 it was held in abeyance for some time because of objections. Finally, in April 1923, it was announced the plan would be put into effect on the coming July 1. One modification was that a premium of 10 percent of the cost of each ticket would be charged instead of a 10 cent premium on each ticket as had originally been slated. That was the charge to operate the central bureau and was not added to the box office price of the ticket. It was said the new outlet was not expected to eliminate established firms, the hotel agencies, and so on, and that it would remain possible to speculate in tickets in a small way by using diggers at the central outlet, but not enough seats could be generated by that method to support the larger speculators. When the central agency plan was adopted the previous December it had the support of Lee Shubert, president of the Producing Managers' Association, who controlled more venues in New York city than anyone else. Thirty of the 53 members of the group were at the meeting in December when the plan was adopted, and only two of them voted against it. Yet dissension and opposition remained and in the end no central ticket outlet was established.[6]

B. F. Keith's Palace Theatre in New York started its own drive in April 1923 against the sidewalk men who worked the streets in its vicinity. Doormen began to refuse to admit people who had bought their seats from the sidewalk hawkers.[7]

Flo Ziegfeld, in an effort to keep tickets for the opening night of his soon to debut *Follies* at the New Amsterdam Theatre away from speculators, announced in June 1924 his staff would only sell seats directly from his personal office, and not from the box office. Sales would only be made to applicants personally known to himself and his staff as "bona-fide purchasers." There were 600 orchestra seats available for that opening night performance but many were already spoken for; 80 went to newspaper people for reviews, 150 seats were set aside for "habitual first-nighters, who have been on the first-night list of most theatres for many years," and some were put aside for prominent people, 60 seats in this case for Bernard Baruch, for example. Thus, there were left only about 150 orchestra seats for sale to Flo's bona-fide purchasers. With additional flourish, Ziegfeld announced he would present a gold watch, suitably engraved, to any person proving to Flo that he had purchased tickets for the opening night from a speculator. As further evidence of good faith Ziegfeld announced that a complete list of all people to whom orchestra seats for the first night of the *Follies* had been sold would be released to the press for publication.[8]

Out on the West Coast, an announcement was made in Los Angeles in March 1925 that in the future the Playhouse and Mason Operahouse there would sell seats only from the venue box offices. Boosting of the price of seats far above the box office price by brokers was given as the reason for the new policy by Louis Macloon, owner of the Playhouse and one of the lessees of the Operahouse. According to Macloon, ticket agencies in Los Angeles, instead of aiding the public in purchasing good theater tickets, had been pursuing a policy of constant increases in price. One example he gave was a recent show at the Playhouse where $1 seats were sold by brokers for $3 each. "The public is entitled to buy theater tickets at the box office scale," said Macloon. He added, "The ticket agency in theory aids the purchaser of a ticket in getting a good seat but in practice extorts from him sums which have been growing larger and larger from week to week. The result has been that prices have become so high that the public has been discouraged from attempting to buy tickets for the better productions which are presented here."[9]

Macloon explained he adopted the new policy upon becoming convinced the public was being cheated. He said a recent production in Los Angeles of *Seventh Heaven* failed in that city because the scalpers reserved large blocks of seats, applicants at the box office had to be turned away and then, 30 minutes before curtain time, many of the reserved seats in the best sections of the theater were turned back, the speculators having failed to sell them at the high prices they demanded. By refusing to sell blocks to the agencies Macloon said he expected a return to the "first come first served" idea at the box office. Also, he publicly invited other Los Angeles theatres to "join with us in stamping out the practice of scalping which is a menace to the theatrical business and to the general public that likes to see good shows at reasonable prices."[10]

Lillian Albertson, a Los Angeles producer of stage attractions, announced in May 1930 her own "war" on scalpers in her hometown. She declared the service charge made by agencies was driving business away. Said the Albertson statement, "Starting today my Majestic Theater will declare war on the ticket scalpers. This parasitic evil has grown out of all proportions to the demand for high premium seats and with the rise in price from the old established 50-cent service charge to 60 cents and more my records show it has actually driven patrons away from the legitimate theater." She added that she had asked the brokers to reduce their fee back to 50 cents per ticket but they had refused. Albertson declared no seats for any of her shows would be available at agencies, hotels, and so on, and that she had set up 40 branch offices in metro Los Angeles to service patrons with, of course, no service charges added to the box office price of a seat.[11]

According to Secretary Kelley of the Theater Managers' Association (Los Angeles), ticket scalping, as it was known in other cities, was practically a stranger to Los Angeles theatregoers. He thought that was because there was no crushing demand for seats at any of the city's legitimate theatres and business was not so good that scalpers found patrons willing to pay a high service charge. The usual service charge had been in effect for years, he explained, "and we have no serious ticket scalping problem." For Los Angeles theater patrons the 60-cent fee per ticket (up from 50 cents) had been in effect since December 31, 1929, and, reportedly, was levied by all brokers and agencies selling theater tickets.[12]

Former New York State Governor Alfred E. Smith asked the public on April 16, 1930, to cooperate with the newly organized New York Theatre League (NYTL), which proposed to keep the premium charged on theater tickets to a maximum of 75 cents per seat, after June 1. As a member of the group's board of governors representing the people, he asked theatergoers not to pay more. He explained the new plan of "collective discipline" agreed upon by managers and ticket brokers had been laid before him because "the theatre interest considered that the public had the greatest confidence in me." Smith accepted membership on the board of governors only when he was convinced "that these men are in earnest and they have set up a plan that will work." Within the New York Theatre League were venue owners and lessees, producers, brokers, the Dramatists' Guild, and Actors' Equity Association. Famed producer George White was one who was opposed to the plan. He described the plan as an attempt to cure with patent medicine an evil that could only be cured by surgery. Questioning the managers' right to subscribe openly to a plan that compelled the public to pay 75 cents extra on each seat, he challenged all producers to sign an agreement with him to dispose of their tickets only through their box offices. White pointed out that under the League's plan he would have to place seats to his shows on consignment with speculators who had a perfect right under the new plan to return any or all seats one hour before curtain time. "There is only one way to handle the situation honestly and sincerely — get rid of the speculator. This can be done overnight," said White. "Let the managers get together and decide that henceforth they will keep every seat in their box office and that not a seat will go to speculators. I guarantee that this plan will wipe out speculation over night."[13]

Defending the NYTL was Richard W. Krakeur, general manager for producer Edgar Selwyn. "It is a strange thing that George White, who spends a great deal of his time in the box office thrilling the public by selling seats himself, hasn't done something about the digger," complained Krakeur. "These parasites are even worse than ticket speculators because they have absolutely no standing whatever and no limit to their fees. They dig into the box office tickets, buy them for weeks in advance, open a shop near the scene of the hit and then solicit trade and charge exorbitant prices."[14]

A week after Smith made his announcement seven theatrical producers, or their representatives, met in the office of George White and went on record as being opposed to the NYTL plan. In their statement they said the new method "is advocating a plan for the curbing of ticket speculation which we deem as not only impractical and unworkable, but not an honest and sincere effort to control ticket speculation." They said the only way to deal with the problem was to sell all seats from the box office and thereby eliminate all premiums and also all the cut-rate discount agencies selling seats for, usually, half price. Apparently that was the real reason for their attack on the NYTL plan because, in reference to the cut-rate agency, their statement demanded the NYTL "eliminate this cancer of show business which destroys value."[15]

Ziegfeld came out in June 1930 and publicly attacked the NYTL plan as one that would not work and also as one that would not "deal with the cut-rate problem." Earl Carroll, then producing a new revue set to open in New York City in 10 days, also came out against the plan. Flo argued that choice seats for hit shows, under the NYTL plan, would be bootlegged by the very ticket brokers with whom the League was ready to do business, "they will bootleg these seats over the telephone or at private sales. It stands to reason that the sixteen or more ticket speculators which the New York Theatre League is going to recognize, dividing the desirable seats for a few hit shows each season, cannot possibly exist on a 75-cent premium, and I charge every sane member of the New York Theatre League with being familiar with this situation."[16]

In an abrupt change of direction the NYTL took a new name, the League of New York Theatres and, working in cooperation with the Postal Telegraph Company, announced on November 10, 1930, that it had emerged successful in the first test of its revised plan to sell seats to the public at 50 cents above the box office price to curb gouging. Some 23 theaters were said to be in the pool and selling seats through the 162 branch offices of the Postal Telegraph Company. Patrons received postal money orders in exchange for their cash, which they took to the venue box office to exchange for actual tickets. Since patron names were on the money orders it was believed speculators had difficulty persuading diggers to use false names. And the last minute exchange of money orders for tickets left little time for speculators, it was reasoned, to try and resell seats.[17]

However, that plan had a short life as the League announced on January 15, 1931, that it was abandoning its plan to control the theater ticket situation and would liquidate its indebtedness as soon as possible. All of its lawsuits were to be dropped, including one against producer David Belasco, who had signed on to the plan at first but quickly dropped out.[18]

But the League of New York Theatres managed to survive as an organization even if their plan had failed, and in July 1938 the League and Actors Equity Association announced what one reporter called the "most drastic code" in stage history to outlaw speculation in the sale of theater tickets. Slated to take effect on September 1 that year to coincide with the start of the new theater season it was a code under which actors would refuse to work for a producer who countenanced gouging of the public. Both groups expressed confidence it would spell the end of the persistent practice of charging theatregoers "as much as the traffic will bear." Supposedly, the significance of the new ticket code lay in the fact that it was the first one to contain any practical means of enforcement. Under the code at least 25 percent of all tickets in all venues would be available at the box office at box office prices; authorized brokers were limited to a price advance of 75 cents maximum for orchestra seats and 50 cents maximum for balcony seats. Brokers were expected to pay the League five cents for each seat sold at a premium with that money to be used by the League to police the code. Also, brokers were prohibited by the code from giving any gratuity to a producer in connection with the sale of tickets. Authorized ticket brokers were forbidden to deal with unauthorized ones. A specific clause provided that the use of diggers posing as legitimate customers constituted a code violation.[19]

Late in 1939, the code between the League and Equity was extended for another year, with some minor changes. For example, whereas before only the League reviewed code violation charges, under the extension both the League and Equity would do it, with equal numbers on the review board.[20]

Meanwhile, in other activity, a lawsuit was decided in favor of the venues. The lawsuit was launched by a ticket speculator against the Martin Beck Theatre in New York after the venue refused to accept tickets sold by him. After operettas at the venue became popular an unlicensed speculator set up a ticket office in a store a few feet from the venue, from where he scalped seats. Martin Beck had a sign posted to the effect that tickets bought from speculators would be refused at his house and with the aid of employees patrolling the sidewalk warned prospective patrons to buy only from the box office. In his lawsuit the speculator asked the theater be restrained from refusing to accept resold tickets without refunding the money to the customers or to the plaintiff and to enjoin Beck "from interfering with the plaintiff in the pursuit of his business as a ticket broker." However the court held for the theater noting that a theater ticket was a license that could be revoked at any time and "The proprietor has the right to decide who shall be admitted to witness performances and who shall be excluded. The absolute control he exercises over his house and the audience is unquestioned." It was a vindication of an often-used management tactic to curb the evil.[21]

New York's Metropolitan Opera Association began an intensive campaign in March 1937 to rid itself of the sidewalk men who plied their trade in front of the house. Management had hired a special security guard to drive away the scalpers and had also appealed to city authorities for assistance. The following notice was prominently posted in the lobbies of the venue and near the box office window, "Warning: The management reserves the right to refuse admission on any tickets that are purchased on the solicitation of sidewalk ticket speculators." Over the years management had tried off and on to eliminate the sidewalk men but in the past had only succeeded in doing so for short periods of time. What prompted another campaign was that, reportedly, the Metropolitan Opera House had received more complaints that year from outraged patrons than ever before. Earle R. Lewis, box office treasurer for more than 25 years there, said the Metropolitan had tried every possible method to prevent speculators from obtaining tickets but nothing had worked. Subscription lists were scrutinized and purchasers of seats for single performances were not permitted to buy blocks of seats unless they were bona fide patrons.[22]

Noted theater critic George Jean Nathan offered his own solution to the problem, in the summer of 1939, when he suggested the industry "kick out" the existing ticket brokers and establish a central, cooperative agency. He felt that would quickly eliminate the existing 75-cent premiums brokers were allowed to charge. "To charge 75 cents over the price of a ticket is a rank, unjustifiable, and properly resentable swindle; the 25 cent charge outlined for a central agency is fair enough in view of public convenience and the covering of operating expenses." However, he added, "employ a squad of sleuths from a reputable detective agency to hang around the central ticket agency, when and if it is established, to watch the employees and to see to it that they don't work in cahoots with diggers."[23]

One idea that was sometimes raised when collusion was mentioned was that the problem was a rogue box office staff that connived with the brokers, unbeknownst to the producer and/or owner of the venue. Of course, sometimes that was true; sometimes, though, it was a convenient way for producers and owners to shift the focus away from the real problem, themselves. After a series of surprise raids were conducted on several of the box offices of the Shubert-managed venues in December 1919, the Shubert organization instituted a new rule whereby box office count up and reconciliation would be conducted the morning after the performance at the Shubert headquarters office (instead of at the venue as in the past) when the box would be first unlocked (having been brought in the night before from the field by headquarters staff). That new rule prompted the resignation of about half a dozen Shubert house managers, mostly in New York City but some in other locales — one in Buffalo. A surface reason for the resignations was that the new rule was an affront to their honesty. Also, the Shubert organization announced it had decided to again place women in the treasurer post in all its venues and in all ticket-selling positions in some six Shubert houses. "During the war, women generally were used in the box offices of the legit houses, but it was then said that the experiment was not a success," added a reporter.[24]

Executive E. F. Albee of the Keith circuit ordered, in April 1920, the box office staff at three Keith venues — Palace, Riverside, and Bushwick — to be completely changed. It came because he found three ticket agencies near the Palace were charging excessive prices for the Palace shows. With an evening weekday top price at the box office of $2 a seat, those agencies were charging $3 and $3.50 and for Sunday nights when top price at the box office was $2.50 the scalpers were demanding $4 and $5. Blame was placed on the box office staff when one of the Keith employees was able to purchase 16 tickets numbered consecutively.[25]

When Charles Bray, western Orpheum circuit manager in San Francisco, opened a "war" on scalpers around the Orpheum in that city he cleaned out the entire box office staff. During his investigation Bray discovered speculators were securing an average of 3,500 tickets weekly out of the Orpheum. After putting on an entirely new staff Bray said he believed he had reduced that figure to 200.[26]

Usually, though, charges of collusion were laid at the feet of the producers and owners. When the Producing Managers' Association made noises near the end of 1920 about curbing the evil, an editorial in *Variety* declared managers did not really want to curb speculation but only pretended they wanted to because they were sharing in the scalpers' profits. "A theatre manager is not going to allow a ticket speculator to obtain $7 for a $3 ticket if he can prevent it. That is more profit for the spec than the manager is making," reasoned the editor. "Nor will the manager stand for a one-dollar, two-dollar or more profit per ticket if he can prevent it. Why doesn't he prevent it? There must be a reason. It is either in the manager's or treasurer's office."[27]

Declaring New York City "a city of boobs," producer William A. Brady charged in January 1924 that $225,000 had been turned over to three theatrical managers as a bonus for allocating tickets to speculators who subsequently gouged the public. Speaking before a large audience at City Hall Brady declared he stood ready to name names, but if and only if he was before an official city body of inquiry and to testify in detail under oath. Brady spoke under the auspices of the city board of education on the topic, "the Theatre and its Duty to the Public." Visitors and residents alike were being gouged to the extent of $6 and $10 for a seat, "They are being robbed to this extent because of the combine of thieves, highbinders and robbers which operates as ticket speculators in the neighborhood of forty-second Street." He grumbled the city administration did nothing about the problem.[28]

In a court decision unrelated to Brady, it was revealed that the Apollo Theatre Corporation admitted the collection in 1926–1927 of $52,000 in excess of ticket face value during a year's run of George White's *Scandals*, which had a top box office price of $5 a seat. That excess money was split 75 percent to the theater owner and 25 percent to the box office treasurer; apparently no one else shared in the money.[29]

Sunday shows on Broadway, a managers' proposal to Actors Equity Association in view of competition from talking movies, were turned down by the actors' union in December 1929. The actors, though, offered to compromise if the managers would abolish ticket speculation. Reporter F. P. Dunn observed, "In effect, this resolution implied that the managers, while pretending to abhor the speculators, whose exorbitant charges are supposed to have injured the theater immeasurably, are in league with these surreptitious gentlemen and, in fact are sharing in the money the speculators make." In the speeches that preceded the actors' vote on the proposal, the charges were put plainly by some of the speakers. None was more outspoken than Eddie Cantor, star of *Whoopee*, then running on Broadway. After theater executive Arch Selwyn called Cantor's allegations "baseless and generally untrue" an angry Cantor replied, "Most producers are working hand in hand with the ticket speculators by forcing them to buy seats for plays that are failures, and the same speculators must charge fabulous prices for the seats for successes. And if producers are not friendly with speculators, why do some of them borrow money in large sums from these speculators?"[30]

Even the New York Police were actively involved, at least once. In a 1930 inquiry on police graft and misbehavior in general, it was revealed police took graft from speculators who hawked their wares outside theaters and such places as Yankee Stadium. Revelations of ticket graft followed the examination of broker Oscar Alexander and representatives of Adelphi Ticket Agency, who all appeared under subpoena. Investigators were told how scalpers were forced to pay $5 a day to the patrolman of the beat in which they operated in exchange for not being harassed by him. Occasionally, though, the scalpers were arrested and their tickets confiscated. Ostensibly those tickets were sent to the property clerk at police headquarters but reportedly they rarely were. It was estimated there were about 200 speculators in New York then and from that it was extrapolated that the amount of money paid to patrolmen to let them operate unmolested was about $365,000 a year.[31]

During this period of time, as in the past, football and baseball were the sports that were most often associated with the practice of ticket speculation.

14

Sports, 1918–1949

"The ticket speculators are the bane of my existence...."
Charles Ebbets, Brooklyn Dodgers, 1920

"Scalpers are bringing the university into bad repute in the eyes of the general public as well as of alumni and faculty."
W. P. Fuller, Stanford University, 1929

"I propose to see that the baseball public is protected against speculators who charge excessive prices."
Walter Corwin, Collector,
Bureau of Internal Revenue, 1930

At Urbana, Illinois, in November 1920, Director Huff of the University of Illinois Board of Athletic Control launched a special campaign against ticket speculation, and gambling, in connection with the upcoming Illinois-Ohio State football game and future Illinois contests. Huff requested the university Council of Administration expel any student found guilty of speculating.[1]

About a year later at New Haven, Connecticut, Harold Woodcock, Yale University graduate athlete manager said 12 Yale men had been blacklisted after speculating in tickets for Yale football games. Those guilty Yale men would not be allowed to obtain tickets for any future football games. Harvard manager Fred Moore added that no more than 50 people were found by the Harvard management to have been speculators, a number said to be smaller that year than in the past.[2]

According to George R. Murray, Graduate Treasurer of the Princeton University Athletic Association, stringent measures were being considered at Princeton in November 1922 to combat "the growing evil of scalping." Under consideration was a plan to keep a careful check on all tickets and that anyone found to be scalping would be barred from attendance at all athletic events at the university in the future. Popular indignation against speculation was reported to be high among the students and an editorial in *The Daily Princeton* stated, "Applying for tickets, every undergraduate assumes the obligation of seeing that his tickets do not revert to unresponsible persons." All undergrads were required to sign a pledge that they would not speculate at the time they applied for tickets to an event and "Unscrupulous distribution of tickets for the legal price is as much of a breach as out and out profiteering."[3]

With the 1923 Army-Navy football game at New York's Polo Grounds only a week away, a canvas of Times Square ticket agencies by a newsman disclosed there was a plentiful supply of seats at the agencies with the asking prices ranging up to $43 and $50 per seat. Most of those seats available from the brokers came from the allotments made to the two service colleges. In the original distribution of the tickets each school received 20,000 while the New York Giants baseball club (owner of the Polo Grounds) retained 7,000. Tickets for the game were printed in one of three colors: West Point received pink tickets; Navy's were orange; Giants' seats were green. Most of the seats for sale at brokers along Broadway, the newsman discovered, were pink with orange ones here and there; almost no green ones were found.[4]

In the early part of November 1926 Commander Jonas H. Ingram, director of athletics at the U. S. Naval Academy at Annapolis, Maryland, received reports that two scalpers staying at a local hotel had been trying to buy tickets from midshipmen for the Army-Navy game slated for Chicago later that month. On the night of November 18 he sent a midshipman to the pair with two tickets that were sold for $40 each to the scalpers, though the original price was only $3.50. After the midshipman took the money he reported to Ingram. Next morning Ingram called on the two men at the hotel, returned their money, retrieved the tickets and warned them that under a provision of the Annapolis city code they were liable to fine and imprisonment for corrupting the morals of midshipmen. He then ordered them to be out of town by 6 P.M. that evening or he would have them arrested. Reportedly, they agreed to leave town.[5]

Stanford University in California appointed a three-man committee in November 1929 to investigate the open scalping of tickets to Stanford football games and, if necessary, recommend a remedy for "the evil." Appointment of the committee came after two hours of stormy argument on the question as to whether students should be deprived of the privilege of receiving the two extra seats that they were then allowed. Some argued that if the students persisted in scalping their tickets they should be allotted to alumni who were then unable to get good seats. Committee chair W. P. Fuller remarked, "Students must realize the seriousness of this business. Scalpers are bringing the university into bad repute in the eyes of the general public as well as of alumni and faculty." Meanwhile, said a journalist, tickets were being sold on campus for from $10 to $40 each.[6]

With the Notre Dame–University of Southern California football game in progress on December 10, 1932, in Memorial Coliseum in Los Angeles, a squad of police conducted raids on the grounds of Exposition Park (surrounding the

Coliseum). Arrests made that day brought the total number of scalpers arrested over the space of a few days to 50. Those men were arrested on charges of violating a city ordinance that prohibited the sale of tickets in Exposition Park without the written consent of the Board of Park Commissioners.[7]

The 37th annual Army-Navy football game took place on November 28, 1936, in Philadelphia at Municipal Stadium before a sold out crowd of 102,000. Best seats went for $6.60 and $4.40 with the crowd paying over $500,000 at the gate. Despite the fact the game drew 22,000 more people than had ever seen a football game in the East and was sold out many days in advance, there were said to be no tickets in the hands of speculators leading up to the game. According to reporter Allison Danzig, "For the first time in memory the ticket scalpers appear to be licked on an Army-Navy game.... Even the licensed ticket brokers have been frozen out of the game." Reportedly it was due to the policy of rejecting at the gate any ticket that bore the government stamp required on all tickets sold at a price in excess of face value. Said the newswoman, "Since no ticket is honored at the gate which is sold for more than the established price as evidenced by the government stamp, legitimate agencies and scalpers alike are frozen out of this invalidation unless the latter run the risk of making surreptitious sales without stamping the pasteboards." Still, some 300 government men were said to have been sent to Philadelphia to monitor and check the situation. Also, to prevent fly-by-night licensed brokers from setting up shop temporarily, anyone who applied for a ticket agency license had to show a year's lease on the property they had rented and from which they planned to conduct their brokerage business.[8]

Delegate Bertram L. Boone II (D., Baltimore Fifth) said on December 3, 1944, he would introduce a bill outlawing ticket scalping such as had flourished in Baltimore the previous weekend — at the next session of the Maryland General Assembly. Boone asserted that seats for the Army-Navy football game had sold for prices as high as $100 each (with a range of from $15 to $100) and added that every top flight sporting event in Baltimore was "plagued by the premium-price boys." For the past several years the need for a strong scalpers' law in the State of Maryland had been apparent, he argued. "The recent disgraceful demonstration by ticket scalpers in conjunction with the Army-Navy football game clearly indicated that effective legislation should be enacted at the next session of the General Assembly," thundered Boone.[9]

The 1945 Army-Navy football game was held in Philadelphia on December 1. In Washington, DC, on November 1, Senator William Langer (R., No. Dak.) alleged that game tickets were falling into the hands of speculators while service men were unable to buy them and promised an investigation into those allegations. Langer remarked that the last time he attended an Army-Navy game in Philadelphia "scalpers had signs up selling tickets for $25." He added, "They now tell me that scalpers have tickets for $25 to $50 to this year's game. I'm going to find out about this situation. There's something screwy somewhere."

Agreeing that something odd was going on, at least, Colonel Lawrence Jones of West Point observed that seats could hardly then be in the hands of scalpers because tickets were not yet back from the printers.[10]

Colonel Jones, graduate manager of athletics at West Point, admitted to Senator Edwin C. Johnson (D., Colo.) on November 18 that scalpers were "undoubtedly" soliciting orders for tickets for the game, even though they still were not back from the printers. Anyway, he told the Senator, "eradicating scalpers is well nigh impossible." Senator Johnson, acting chairman of the Senate Military Affairs Committee, released a letter from Jones written in response to a letter from Johnson following a Senate speech by Langer. Jones explained that 98,593 tickets were being printed for the game, with 7,000 of them allotted to members of Congress, Cabinet members, general officers, the press, athletic coaches, and directors of civilian colleges. Then the remainder were split equally and sent to the Navy Athletic Association and the Army Athletic Association. The latter consisted of 10,000 West Point graduates, 2,300 cadets, 1,200 non-graduate officers of the regular Army, and 1,800 civilian members. All seats were sold by mail. Members of the Army Athletic Association were permitted, that year, to apply for not more than four "personal-use" tickets and six "non-personal" use seats, for a total of 10 each. Jones told Johnson that West Point did all it could to prevent tickets from falling into the hands of scalpers. Members of the Army Athletic Association, he said, were blacklisted if sales to scalpers were discovered.[11]

One year later, in advance of the 1946 Army-Navy game, a service publication, the Army and Navy *Bulletin*, demanded editorially that the game "be returned to its clean, sportsmanlike traditions unfettered by the ugly commercialism of recent years." The piece charged the Army-Navy game had become "surrounded and engulfed by the most aggressive form of commercialism," which, the *Bulletin* declared, involved ticket speculators and gamblers in Philadelphia who "profit from a tax-supported competition between our nation's finest manhood." Proposed by the editor was that the Army and Navy should bar from the game forever anyone whose tickets found their way into the hands of speculators.[12]

Thirteen men were arrested on November 23, 1947, near the Coliseum in Los Angeles in the hour before the USC-UCLA football game. They were all arrested after undercover vice police officers had purchased game seats from them at prices ranging from $15 to $25 per pair. Two days later they were fined $25 each and reprimanded by municipal Judge Louis Kaufman after they pled guilty. Kaufman told the 13, "It is people like you who keep honest sports lovers from seeing many events. This is the last time I shall merely fine such as you. Any ticket scalpers pleading guilty in this court in the future will be given jail sentences."[13]

A Baltimore court was told at the end of October 1948 that scalpers had "connived" with some midshipmen from the U. S. Naval Academy to obtain "large numbers" of seats for the Navy-Notre Dame football game at Baltimore's Municipal Stadium. That testimony was offered by an attorney for the Naval Academy Athletic Association (NAAA), who sought in vain to secure court endorsement of a city ordinance forbidding the sale of football tickets for more than face value. Municipal Judge Joseph Sherbow had issued an injunction forbidding enforcement of the ordinance rushed through the City Council on the Monday night prior to the Saturday match. The injunction had been sought by Max Cohen of East Orange, New Jersey, who opened a Baltimore ticket agency a few weeks in advance of the game specifically to deal in seats for that game. Simon Sobeloff, attorney for the NAAA, urged the court to leave the anti-scalping ordinance in effect, claiming the scalping situation had created a very serious disciplinary problem for Naval Academy authorities.[14]

Just before the public sale of 6,000 tickets to the January 2, 1950, Rose Bowl football game in Pasadena, California, began on December 23, Greg Englehard, assistant athletic director of the host, University of California, said a new plan of selling the seats would be inaugurated. Upon the start of the public sale the turnstile at the Rose Bowl would be opened and those waiting outside in line would be allowed through one by one. As each person entered he received a numbered stub. When 3,000 were inside, the turnstile gate was to be closed with the sale to start inside the fence. Each person holding a stub would be permitted to buy two tickets at $5.50 each. In previous years problems had arisen when scalpers managed, by using many proxies in the line, to get a fair number of seats. While the new scheme was not advanced as a cure-all, Englehard believed it would curb scalpers' activities at least to some extent and force them to use even more proxies than they had in the past.[15]

Even professional football was a draw for scalpers in this early period. For a December 1940 game between the Washington Redskins and the Chicago Bears at Griffith Stadium in Washington, DC, police mounted a huge force to watch for, and prevent, scalping. Police had on hand around the stadium 46 plainclothes men, 150 local uniformed officers and an additional 20 from out of town — said to be the largest police detail ever assigned to a District of Columbia sports event. Yet, only eight were arrested in total for scalping; four of them were fined $5 each for unlicensed vending and the other four were fined $10 each for selling in prohibited areas. Anyone trying to sell a seat at face value, or less, was not bothered by the authorities.[16]

Three years later one person was fined $50 and two others received suspended sentences for ticket scalping at another Redskins-Bears game at the same venue. Each suspended sentence was for a $25 fine or 30 days in jail. In court it was revealed those two men were each selling only a few seats and therefore could not be considered "professional scalpers." Hence the leniency of a suspended sentence.[17]

Even high school football games could have their seats scalped. Ticket speculators invaded the realm of high school athletics in November 1928 in the vicinity of Levisohn Stadium in New York, where the game between the High School of Commerce and De Witt Clinton was played. Several young men were observed accosting passers-by and offering choice seats for the game at "small advances."[18]

In no sport, though, were scalpers more active than they were in baseball. For the games held at Comiskey Park in Chicago during the 1919 World Series there were as many seats in the hands of speculators as, said a reporter, there were "in past World Series." Scalpers got as much as $100 for a set of box-seat tickets for the three games at Chicago ($16.50 face) while grandstand seats for the trio of games went for as high as $60 ($9.90 face).[19]

On one day during those games in Chicago for the 1919 Series 12 men were arrested in downtown hotel lobbies and in the vicinity of Comiskey Park, accused of selling seats at a profit as high as 800 percent. The arrests were made by U. S. Bureau of Internal Revenue agents and their deputies. One arrested speculator was said to have disposed of a block of tickets that cost him $49.50 for a profit of $380. During the day of the arrests scalpers were said to have "thronged" the hotel lobbies selling the three game $16.50 box packages for from $40 to $75 each. Specific charges leading to the arrests were that the men had failed to register as ticket brokers, necessary to pay the war tax to the federal government — 50 percent of any ticket premium that exceeded 50 cents per seat.[20]

President Charles Ebbets of the Brooklyn Dodges announced, on the eve of the 1920 World Series between the Dodgers and Cleveland Indians, "The ticket speculators are the bane of my existence and I understand that they are now trying to corral all the seats possible for the world's series. I want to protect the public against them and for that reason I have decided to employ the system in vogue at many colleges." Each ticket leaving his box office would be registered in the name of a buyer and "If a person buys a ticket from a speculator he has simply to bring it to me, let me know what he paid for it, and I will be ready to expose the original purchaser and turn over the evidence for action by Federal authorities."[21]

Meanwhile, the Cleveland Indians said they were also taking vigorous action to eliminate speculation, while a reporter observed there were no scalpers around the ball park but there was "considerable selling" of seats in downtown cigar stores and hotel lobbies. Team business manager Barnard said the club was making every effort to find traces of scalping by either amateurs or professionals. "I have had twenty men out today trying to buy tickets to discover whether the tickets have been bought as an investment," he explained.[22]

A reporter who looked at the situation declared that if little speculation took place at Ebbets Field it was prevalent elsewhere. "In hotel lobbies, barber shops, cigar stores, bootblack stands all over the central portion of the city either the precious reserved seat slips or the knowledge of where they could be obtained was procurable." Seats with a face value of $5.50 were sold by scalpers for $15 to $30.[23]

Rube Marquard, one of Brooklyn's pitchers, was arrested on October 9, 1920, in Cleveland on the charge of ticket scalping. It was alleged that Marquand tried to sell six box seats for the game in Cleveland for $350 ($52.80 original cost). The arresting officer overheard him in the hotel lobby. On that day six other men were arrested for speculating.[24]

Marquard was found guilty of ticket scalping in Cleveland on October 12 when he appeared before City Judge Silbert, who fined him $1 and costs. Silbert fined him only $1 because he felt with all the bad publicity surrounding the event the player had been punished enough. Just as soon as Brooklyn club president Ebbets heard the result of the case he announced Marquand would never pitch for his team again. Said Ebbets, "I am through with him absolutely. He hasn't been released, however, and if any one else wants him he can have him. But Marquand will never again put on a Brooklyn uniform." President Heydler of the National Baseball League said he would take no further action but he did not believe Rube would be in the National League in the next year. "Baseball doesn't want men of his caliber," he added. Ban Johnson, president of the American League and member of the National Baseball Commission, a governing body of professional baseball, said, "I expected action would be taken but Mr. Heydler declared it would not [be] necessary, saying 'Marquand will be railroaded out of the National league. The National league can clean its own house without help from the Commission.'" When asked if he thought Marquand would be signed by an American League club Johnson replied, "Absolutely not." Rube played for Cincinnati in 1921 and then with the Boston Braves from 1922 to 1925.[25]

Scalpers were driven from Griffith Stadium in Washington, DC, on September 30, 1925, when they were discovered scalping seats for a World Series game for prices ranging from $10 to $30. Clark Griffith, president of the Washington club, ordered the speculators off the grounds of the stadium but they simply continued their operations in the streets around the venue.[26]

Twenty men were arrested in Pittsburgh on October 4, 1927, for scalping World Series seats for the games between the Pirates and the New York Yankees. Yet when two of them appeared before Police Magistrate John W. Orie two days later, he ordered the discharge of the pair, after condemning the method of ticket distribution by the Pirates. "If it is all right for Barney Dreyfuss (owner of the Pirates) to charge five times the regular price for baseball tickets (World Series prices over the regular season price), why shouldn't scalpers be allowed to double their money." Orie remarked that if the others charged with scalping appeared before him he would also discharge them.[27]

More than 100 people holding tickets were turned away from Philadelphia's Shibe Park on October 11, 1929, after they showed up for a World Series game between the Athletics and the Chicago Cubs. Entrance was refused because their tickets had passed through the hands of speculators. It was a situation that resulted because the tickets carried a stamp mark that government agents had compelled speculators to affix showing the original and resale price so that the tax could be collected by the IRS and because the Shibe brothers made good on an earlier promise they would not honor scalpers' tickets. Because of that policy many heated discussions between fans and gatekeepers took place. For example, J. A. Norwood came all the way from Texas to see the games in Philadelphia, paid $20 for a $5.50 seat at a Broad Street agency, and was turned away, complaining bitterly but in vain.[28]

Summonses were issued for 11 ticket speculators operating outside Ebbets Field in May 1930 by United States Internal Revenue agents as a capacity crowd arrived to see Brooklyn play Pittsburgh. It was a drive on scalpers started after the government received many complaints against the scalpers and had been informed that some of them were failing to make proper returns to the IRS. Twenty-two agents under John E. Brady, chief field deputy for the First New York District, mixed with the crowd of 30,000 fans arriving at the ballpark and made purchases from the sidewalk men. In some cases, they said, they paid as much as $4 for a $2 ticket. Agents also found that some of the scalpers were failing to stamp the resale price on the back of the ticket, which was required by law in order to assist the authorities in collecting the tax of 50 percent of the surcharge in excess of 75 cents. Brady said he believed the campaign against the speculators would not only increase the government's revenue but would serve to bring down the prices demanded by the scalpers on days when the demand was heavy.[29]

Walter E. Corwin, Collector of Internal Revenue in Brooklyn, questioned the 11 arrested near Ebbets Field; he exonerated eight and issued arrest warrants for three. "I intend to station deputy collectors in the neighborhood of the baseball park at all games in the future to see that speculators comply with the law," said Corwin. "I propose to see that the baseball public is protected against speculators who charge excessive prices."[30]

Federal agents and Philadelphia police, working in concert, arrested 18 scalpers in the vicinity of Shibe Park in Philadelphia shortly before the start of game 2 of the World Series in October 1930. Seats were hawked by speculators at $25 a pair until about 10 A.M. on game day, but then the price dropped rapidly until just before game time in the afternoon when they were offered at $4 each, $1.50 below the box office price.[31]

In Chicago in October 1935, scalpers of World Series seats were getting around $35 for the grandstand and $50 for the box seats for the three games expected to be played at Wrigley Field. Reportedly, the speculators obtained large blocks of seats at the public sale by hiring proxies to line up for them. In one block in Chicago's Loop district eight signs on as many stores advertising the sale, exchange, or purchase of World Series seats were counted. An investigation into that public seat sale by Commissioner of Police James P. Allman brought the suspension of six policemen assigned to patrol the waiting line at Wrigley Field. A number of customers complained that preferred places in the

line were given to certain individuals. The Commissioner ordered the police
to enforce the anti-scalping law passed the previous summer by the Illinois
Legislature. It prohibited the selling of amusement tickets at prices higher than
the amounts printed on them.[32]

Twelve scalpers in the vicinity of Ebbets Field were arrested on May 30,
1940, as a result of the efforts of Brooklyn Dodgers President Larry MacPhail
to stamp out the practice. The raid that led to the arrests came from a special
squad of police and was reportedly conducted on the order of New York Mayor
Fiorello La Guardia.[33]

Perhaps a typical story of a small-time speculator — representative of many
of the sidewalk men of the time — was the tale of Brooklyn's David Lauer. He
was a 25-year-old shipping clerk who decided to do some speculating on September 7, 1941. Arriving early at Ebbets Field that day he bought 11 $1.10 gen-
eral admission seats for the Dodgers versus the New York Giants game. He had
sold seven for $1.50 each when he was arrested by the police for disorderly con-
duct. Unable to sell his last four tickets he ended the day with a $1.60 deficit.
Then, in Brooklyn-Queens Night Court, Magistrate Peter Horn imposed a $25
fine. Out $26.60 in total, Lauer decided to stick to clerking.[34]

After Kenesaw M. Landis, Commissioner of Baseball, learned of complaints that large numbers of seats for the 1942 World Series games in St. Louis
were in the hands of scalpers, he declared the next time the 16 major league
club owners got together to discuss World Series arrangements he would urge
them to adopt some plan to eliminate ticket scalping. Executives with the St.
Louis Cardinals said every precaution was taken to prevent such an occurrence.
However, in a letter to Landis, H. W. Riehl, general manager of the Better Business Bureau of St. Louis, asked for an investigation of the situation "to allay
suspicion" of irregularity in the distribution of seats. Riehl said the good reputation of baseball had been threatened by the activity of the scalpers.[35]

During the 1947 World Series between the Dodgers and the Yankees, on
one day, 15 scalpers were arraigned before Magistrate John Masterson in Flat-
bush Court. He indicated his displeasure by imposing unusually high bail
amounts on the 15, up to $2,500. Masterson did it, he said, because "faithful
Brooklyn fans have been unable to purchase tickets, while out-of-town ticket
speculators are selling them at high prices." Of those 15, two gave a home
address as Dunham, Kentucky, one as Jenkins, Kentucky, and one at Hartford,
Connecticut.[36]

Eugene Finn appeared in court in Boston in September 1948 charged with
scalping. Police said he had 28 bleacher seats for the Red Sox versus Yankees
game even though some 25,000 fans were turned away. Presiding Judge Fran-
kland Miles was one of those disappointed fans that could not get a ticket for
the game. Miles expressed his disappointment from the bench. "How you get
'em, I don't know," he told Finn, "but in my opinion this is a lowdown business and not fair play to the baseball fans of Boston." Finn was fined the

unusually high amount of $520. Testimony revealed the prevailing price for seats from speculators ranged from $2 to $3 for a 60-cent bleacher seat to as high as $15 for a $1.80 grandstand seat.[37]

Boxing, too, drew a lot of attention from speculators. Aroused over the activities of scalpers at important boxing matches held in Madison Square Garden, promoter Tex Rickard, the Boxing Commissioner, the IRS, and police authorities planned a campaign to curtail the evil and eventually eliminate it completely. The campaign was to start with the upcoming Jack Dempsey versus Bill Brennan bout in December 1920. Seats were priced at $5, $10, $15, and $25 and were to be on sale only at the Garden box office and three agencies — McBride's, Tyson's, and Bascom's — all of which had agreed to a maximum premium of 50 cents per ticket. Why such a plan was expected to work was left unreported.[38]

With the September 1923 Dempsey-Firpo fight in New York only a day or two away one enterprising scalper walked through Rector, Wall, and Broad Streets offering tickets for sale to every passer-by. He was selling $5.50 seats for $8.80 and $11 tickets for $16. So many complaints were made about scalpers charging exorbitant prices for seats to this bout that District Attorney Banton announced he would investigate. One complaint said a speculator was selling the top-priced seats ($27.50 face value) for as much as $77.50, another was charging $60 and $70, while yet another was asking $100 or more for those $27.50 tickets. Said the fight promoter, Tex Rickard, "The speculators are getting some fine prices for their seats and I am unable to remedy a matter of this kind where there is such a big event which the public wants to see and so many ways by which tickets can be obtained. We have tried to stop it, but it is not possible." Rickard said he personally knew of one man who had paid $300 for two ringside seats.[39]

The entire block of the cheapest seats (3,500 at $3.30 each) for the Dempsey-Firpo match did not go on sale until the afternoon of the fight. A gigantic crowd swarmed the box office and those seats rapidly disappeared, leaving thousands of disappointed fans, some of which turned their attention to the scalpers. A reporter observed, "Thereafter baiting ticket speculators became the popular sport of those who couldn't get tickets, and several vendors who wanted exorbitant prices had to do marathons in order to get away. The vendors were left with cuts and bruises." Police arrested 12 men for scalping that day.[40]

Several months after that fight charges that Rickard turned over a block of seats worth $135,000 to that match to a ticket speculator named Mike Jacobs were made by Tom O'Rourke, also a fight promoter, at a hearing in Albany, New York, before the State Assembly's Ways and Means Committee. At a time when almost no tickets were available at Madison Square Garden and the Polo Grounds (the two box office selling points) Jacobs drove up 135th Street and Eighth Avenue with a wagon, claimed O'Rourke, "and was selling tickets there with police protection," for prices as high as $75. Assemblyman Lord said, in general, fight tickets were turned over to speculators by promoters and "It is a well-known fact that certain promoters of prize fighting in New York City, not satisfied with the outrageous fee exacted at the box office, have been and are guilty of placing the tickets for the best seats in the hands of their agents, who dispose of them for two, three and in some instances four times their face value." Lord went on to add, "These agents are generally what is commonly known as speculators, but in this instance there is no speculation. Far from it, for the agents receive the tickets, dispose of them for rates agreed on and presumably are paid on a commission basis for their services." Rickard denied all the charges.[41]

One man who wanted tickets for the Dempsey-Firpo fight was movie star Warner Baxter. From Hollywood he had wired East for ringside seats but learned there was nothing available closer than the last row. Walking along Hollywood Boulevard a disappointed Baxter ran into his director Ernst Lubitsch and grumbled to him about not getting any tickets. A passer-by overheard the gist of the conversation and immediately offered to sell Baxter a "perfect" set of tickets. Warner "dug deep" and bought them; they turned out to be counterfeit.[42]

Still another "war" against scalpers was declared. This one was announced in April 1936 by the Los Angeles Police Department after they learned counterfeit tickets were in circulation by speculators for the upcoming match between Charley Coates and Frank Rowsey, slated for the Olympic arena in Los Angeles. Said Ray Kleinberger, chairman of the Board of Police Commissioners, "If the crooked speculators think they can get away with it, they'll find out that they're mighty mistaken." Matchmaker Joe Waterman declared, "Don't buy tickets from speculators. I have been battling them for months without success and can't stamp them out without the whole-hearted co-operation of the boxing public. Every ticket sold at the Olympic and from recognized ticket brokers must bear my signature to be valid." Scalpers were said to be operating in ever-increasing numbers in flagrant defiance of the law at the Olympic and Hollywood arenas. The sidewalk men were legally permitted to sell seats as long as they were at least 300 feet from the arenas. However, said a reporter, the scalpers, "the greedy leeches of any prosperous sporting enterprise, are operating outside the very doors of the local stadiums."[43]

Four employees of the Jacobs Ticket Agency — one of New York's largest brokerage firms dealing in seats for sports events — were arrested in June 1946 on charges of demanding excessive prices for tickets to the Louis-Conn boxing match. Police said $150 to $175 were being asked for $100 ringside seats and $65 for $50 tickets. Harry Markson, a publicity man for Mike Jacobs (promoter of the fight), said his boss had no interest in the ticket agency bearing his name and "he hasn't been in the place for 10 years."[44]

When Mike Jacobs retired in 1949 he did so as a boxing promoter — and the dominant promoter in the sport — having moved on from ticket brokerage.

Journalist Arthur Daley observed that Jacobs got started in the fight game, in a circuitous manner, as a young newsboy. He got two free tickets to a fight given to him by a customer. When he got to the arena someone offered to buy the seats from him at double the face value. Amazed by that turn of events he sold them and soon was a ticket speculator, who was introduced to boxing promoter Tex Rickard (the dominant matchmaker before Jacobs) by chance. Thus began a partnership and a gradual takeover of the promoter business by Jacobs. When Tex promoted the Dempsey-Carpentier fight he offered guarantees of $500,000, a very high and unprecedented sum. Rickard involved Jacobs in selling the seats and, remarked Daley, "Jacobs soon got wealthy peddling pasteboards for all future Rickard presentations."[45]

From other areas of sport came other stories. Sheldon Fairbanks, general manager of the new Boston Garden, declared war on scalpers at his venue in December 1928 when he announced he would pay a $5 reward to every policeman who apprehended and convicted a speculator. Reportedly the reward was posted with the approval of Police Commissioner Herbert A. Wilson.[46]

Two ticket speculators who were trying to buy seats for a basketball game between Columbia University and Yale University in February 1930 were roughed up by two football players on the Columbia campus. Scalpers had been approaching students as they left the box office window in John Jay Hall and offering them up to $3 each for the $2 seats. A group of football players standing in the lobby of the building watched them and apparently were annoyed. Two of the players left the group, grabbed the scalpers, and roughed them up. After a few minutes of being pummeled the speculators broke free and ran off.[47]

Lou Daro promoted wrestling matches at the Philharmonic Auditorium in Los Angeles. In September 1924 he said he had been offered $3,000 for the entire block of stage seats for the upcoming Lewis-Zbyszko match but he had refused. All the seats would be sold from the box office at the regular price of $5, he maintained. Daro added he had been approached at a different time by speculators who had offered him big money for blocks of seats in the best parts of the house, but he said such offers were always declined.[48]

Five scalpers, arrested in February 1937 at the Vines-Perry tennis match at the Pan-Pacific Auditorium in Los Angeles, were each sentenced to 10 days in jail when each was unable to pay a $100 fine. Arraigned before Justice of the Peace Holland in Beverly Hills Court, all pled guilty to charges of vagrancy. They were arrested by members of a squad of 10 deputy sheriffs who patrolled the grounds on the watch for speculators. During their court appearance one of the five, Phillip Davis, made a comment about being "railroaded in a kangaroo court" and suffered an additional sentence of $200 or 100 days in jail. Davis went to jail for 110 days.[49]

Eleven men were arrested for scalping tickets to a basketball game at Madison Square Garden in February 1945. They were selling seats at amounts ranging up to $3 over face value. When they were arraigned in Night Court Magistrate Raphael Murphy imposed sentences of $10 or three days in jail on each of the 11 men.[50]

John Murtagh, the New York City Investigation Commissioner, started a March 1946 drive against the black market sales of seats for college sports events in the lobby of Madison Square Garden. One of the first speculators arrested in that drive was Theodore Horoshak, who was fined $25.[51]

In the modern era the enactment of laws against the practice became less prevalent while government probes became somewhat more prevalent. The scalping of sports tickets continued to be a common practice and was joined by something new, the scalping of tickets to music events, especially rock concerts.

15

The General Situation, 1950–2005

"Ticket scalping on Broadway, although it is not practiced openly, is still practiced with impunity."
                                                            John Corry, 1980

"The scalpers and their profits serve no one but the scalpers. Those monies belong to the people who created the show, pure and simple."
            Rocco Landesman, producer, *The Producers*, 2001

So well known and so institutionalized had the practice become by this time that *Good Housekeeping* published a consumer guide to the ins and outs of the custom in its October 1956 issue. Noting the difficulty everyone — out-of-towners and New Yorkers alike — had in getting seats for Broadway shows the piece presented advice for the consumer in how to obtain such items. The best bet was to start early and to order through the mail, but not to be overly fussy in location request. While it was said to be okay to ask for "two orchestra seats in the center section or on the center aisle, no farther back than the twelfth row" it was not alright to ask for "third row center." But being too vague was as bad as being too specific because one was "asking for trouble" if one requested "any seats for any performance." Admitting it was next to impossible to get tickets at the box office for the same night's performance, the publication advised a trip to a ticket broker (they could then legally charge a premium of $1 per seat at a time when the box office price for a dramatic play ranged from $1.75 to $5.75 and seats to musicals ran from $2 to $8.05).[1]

If none of the above worked then *Good Housekeeping* advised its readers to go to the ticket scalpers. Their premiums ranged from $5 to $50 per ticket and "their telephone numbers can be obtained at practically any first-class restaurant, hotel or ticket agency in New York." Although if you had reached that point, commented the piece, "you will be involved in the racket side of the business." Among the "chiselers" were said to be crooked box office treasurers who sold choice seats to favored customers for premiums of $10 or more. While the account tried to separate brokers from scalpers as though they were two independent groups it did comment, "And even among the licensed ticket brokers, there are some who evade the legal restriction on what they are allowed to charge by adding a service fee to the monthly bills of favored customers." Still, the piece argued, "the biggest loot goes to the scalpers, who get quantities of tickets by undercover devices." Those devices included bombarding the box office with mail requests, bribing box office clerks, bribing clerks in licensed agencies, and employing diggers to stand in box office lines.[2]

John S. McBride died on November 29, 1961, at the age of 84, five years after he retired as chairman of McBride's Theatre Ticket Offices. His office had been in the Paramount Theatre Building in Manhattan and had been ever since the structure was built in the 1920s. Thomas J. McBride, his father, had a newsstand in the old Union Square Hotel during the latter part of the 19th century. After being educated at Fordham University, John joined the family in developing a new sideline — that of selling theater tickets. So well did he succeed that the ticket agency soon became the company's chief business. John's first office was at 71 Broadway, then in Times Square where it was first in the Cadillac Hotel and later in the Putnam Building, predecessor of the Paramount on Broadway and West 43rd Street. In his early years in the business he fought against the unscrupulous people in his profession and tried to educate the public to their methods. "Unless the gypping stops, the whole amusement business will be in a bad way," he said in an early post World War I interview. At one time he sponsored a bill that made it illegal to charge more than 50 cents above face value for a ticket. During that time he also joined forces with showman Flo Ziegfeld in opposing a plan for a central ticket agency. By 1939, though, John McBride had joined the other side and opposed any measures that would limit a ticket broker's surcharge.[3]

Scalpers always had a low and somewhat sleazy image, as typified in the example of Jack Ruby. In November 1963 after Lee Harvey Oswald had assassinated President John F. Kennedy and after Ruby had assassinated Oswald, Ruby was recalled in his native Chicago as Jack Rubenstein, "a fancy dresser, ticket scalper and cautious chiseler." Acquaintances recalled he scalped tickets to sporting events and theatres and sometimes he worked the bars in South Bend, Indiana, hawking seats to Notre Dame football games.[4]

More and more opinions were expressed that enacting laws against the practice was hopeless, efforts that were doomed to failure. John F. Wharton was a theatrical attorney and a former officer of the Playwright Company. In 1962 Wharton saw nothing morally wrong in ticket speculation. One of his arguments was that theatregoers had a naïve notion that they should be able to buy seats at the printed price, for the latest hit, on short notice, and the ending of that notion would be the beginning of wisdom and reform. In the case of a big hit demand was so great some people had to wait. The people who would not wait, in some cases, were wealthy enough and willing enough to buy at a high price. Furthermore, that should not cause resentment. When demand for Van Gogh's paintings sprang up, he mused, did anyone resent the fact that only the rich could buy them? Or seek laws limiting the resale price of the speculative art dealer? Laws to end it would not work, reasoned Wharton, just as Prohibition laws did not work, because the buyer saw no moral wrong in what he was doing. "But nothing will be done until everyone realistically faces the fact that it is not dishonesty on the part of anybody that creates high ticket prices, but the fact that thousands of buyers will pay such prices. So long as they will, someone will supply them," concluded Wharton. "And the attempts of naïve reformers to change this by laws aimed at the suppliers will not reduce the prices. They will only succeed in making ice."[5]

Scalping of seats for the Bolshoi and other leading Moscow theaters was reported to be a lucrative business there, according to the newspaper *Sovetskaya Rossiya*. Seats for the Bolshoi and other theaters such as the Satire, Taganka, and the Mayakovsky generally sold for $3 and $4.50 while scalpers got as much as three or four times face value for them. Only about 10 percent of seats to most plays and performances were sold in advance with the rest sold the day of the performance. Customers wanting to avoid scalpers often waited in line for five or six hours. People with the Hero of the Soviet Union medal or veterans of World War II could go to the front of the line. As a result, scalpers had become an accepted way of getting a seat.[6]

Journalist John Corry discussed the situation in New York in 1980. Many ticket brokers, he observed, frequently ignored the law that allowed them to mark up a theater ticket by only $2 (over time the legally allowable maximum premium charged by brokers was increased from its initial 50 cents) and charged double or triple the box office price instead. *Evita* seats that cost $25 or $30 at the box office, for example, were scalped for $50 to $85, while seats to lesser hits were scalped for $50 or $60. "In the small and sometimes tortuous world of Broadway, scalping is passively tolerated, even if it is not condoned. Skimming is different; it is the theater's equivalent of stealing, and is generally abhorred," he wrote. "Ticket scalping on Broadway, although it is not practiced openly, is still practiced with impunity."[7]

Corry called 12 ticket brokers, all selected at random from the phone book; only three were willing to quote legitimate prices over the phone. The others either showed no interest in making a sale by phone, or else insisted that the caller visit the ticket agency. A call to one agency, the Manhattan Theater Ticket Service, asking if it were possible to buy house seats to any "good musical" elicited the following response, "There is no such thing as house seats. They don't exist. Don't even bother coming in." Then he hung up. Of course, remarked Corry, all Broadway shows had house seats; while the number for each show varied, a musical would have at least 100 house seats for each performance. When house seats were not taken up by people connected with the production, they were put on sale at the box office, sometimes on the day of a performance and sometimes the day before. Then Corry made calls to 12 high-ranking corporation executives, asking them if they or their firms used ticket brokers. Two of the executives who said yes identified two of the brokers Corry had selected from the phone book — both had declined to sell seats or to discuss prices on the first phone calls. Consequently Corry's newspaper called them again, this time using the names of the corporations as recommendations. One of them then said he had seats to *Evita* for $65 and tickets for *A Day in Hollywood/A Night in the Ukraine* for $50. The other was still wary of phone conversations but politely asked the caller to visit his office.[8]

Apart from collusion with theater personnel (through the payment of ice), explained Corry, brokers secured seats through their allotment from theater owners or producers. Allotments were not fixed; they could vary from week to week for the same show. Brokers did charge excessive premiums, at least at times, on those allotment seats. For example, said Corry, on November 4, 1980, a theatergoer purchased two tickets to the November 5 performance of *Evita*. The broker who sold them charged $55 each ($23.50 at the box office). They were part of the allotment of *Evita* tickets the brokers had received.[9]

Some Broadway sources told Corry that Ticketron outlets furnished brokers with tickets. For example, on a single day, September 25, 1980, the *New York Times* learned the Ticketron window at Madison Square Garden sold 1,192 tickets to *42nd Street* (then the hottest ticket on Broadway) in about two hours. Ticketron was allotted 196 to sell for each performance of the musical and in theory they could be sold at any of the 400 Ticketron outlets east of Chicago. The seats sold at the Garden outlet on September 25, all for performances between January 5 and January 31, 1981, apparently moved into the Ticketron system on September 22. On the day 1,192 seats were sold from the sole Ticketron terminal in the Garden, the terminals in all the other 399 locations sold a total of 142 tickets from the same batch. Moreover, the seats sold from the Garden were chosen from the choicest seats in the allotment. One day after the big sale a Garden box office executive, unnamed, explained what happened by saying that "hordes" of buyers had shown up. Shortly afterward, David Merrick, producer of *42nd Street*, withdrew the remaining tickets from Ticketron. Also, he canceled all ticket brokers' allotment for his production. Meanwhile, Garden president Michael Burke, embarrassed by the situation, called William A. Shea (a prominent lawyer for whom New York's Shea Stadium was named) for advice. Shea suggested an "independent investigation" be made and offered the service of David Cutner (a lawyer with his own firm) to conduct the probe. It was an offer that was accepted.[10]

On October 27, 1980, Cutner filed his report, which said in part, "We find no evidence of improper conduct by any Garden employee." Asked to comment,

Shea remarked, "Our people at the Garden aren't aware of theater. They aren't up to date on the shows. If the guy who owns *42nd Street*— Merrick — doesn't want to sell tickets, he should tell us. There was only the ordinary number of people on line at the Garden that day. Maybe there were some scalpers among them." All of the 1,192 seats were the expensive ones. All the sales were for cash, without a single credit card being used, for a total cash sale of $41,720 for seats that had a scalping value on the street of perhaps $100,000. Such cash sales could, of course, never be traced. "Among theater people, ticket scalping is resented not necessarily on moral grounds, but because the brokers, who have neither an artistic nor a financial connection with a show, are making money from the labors of others," observed Corry. Because theater people had taken all the artistic and financial risks, they felt the money belonged to them. Corry thought the ice, or bribes, paid to theater personnel by speculators for seats was less rampant at the start of the 1980s than it had been in the 1950s and 1960s. Some, though, thought there was more skimming in more recent times. Skimming took place when someone connected with a show sold a ticket while making it appear the ticket was never sold. Thus, those involved in a production lost directly because gross box office receipts were reduced from face value, unlike for regular scalping. An example of skimming would be a ticket listed on the books as given away (perhaps to a reviewer) or a free pass, but actually sold.[11]

As 1988 began *Phantom of the Opera* was the hottest show on Broadway. It was a time, said reporter Jeremy Gerard, when scalping was worse than ever before. "More people are paying more money to more different middlemen, whether they are charities selling high-priced tickets to raise money, scalpers working the street, ticket agents operating outside the city, or well-connected people with access to the large number of house seats available to the producer, the theater owner and certain members of the company." Before *Phantom* played its first preview at the Majestic Theatre on January 9, it had sold a record $16,583,417 worth of tickets. "Most of those tickets will be resold for much more than their face value," said Gerard. More than half that advance sale had been to theater parties, usually charities that resold seats at a premium to raise funds for their organizations. On the day the Majestic box office opened in November 1987 (after several months of mail and group sales) people lined up overnight, including scalpers offering cash to anyone who would buy four pairs of seats to two performances— the limit set by the Shubert organization, which owned the Majestic.[12]

Under the law, New York State Arts and Cultural Affairs limited the surcharge on the resale of tickets to $2 over face value. But according to Gary Walker, spokesman for New York City's Consumer Affairs Department, which licensed all agents, excluded from the law were businesses that provided a service with the tickets, such as accepting credit cards or offering a delivery service. Of course, that left a huge loophole for those wanting to charge higher premiums. Seats for *Phantom* were then being scalped for $175 and $200 ($50 face) while seats for three weeks down the road were readily available for $100 to $150 from any number of Connecticut and New Jersey brokers. New York State and City regulations did not control the resale of theater tickets outside their jurisdictions. Therefore, to avoid the law, as weak as it was, many brokers set up shop in a state bordering New York. Many of the best seats for *Phantom*— 64 for each performance — were house seats, plus 12 more seats controlled by the Shubert concern.

On nights the house was not taken up with a theater party, the number of house seats increased to 124 to the company and 38 to the theater owner. Those 162 seats represented 10 percent of the venue's 1,609 seats. And, of course, those 162 were pulled from the choicest group. According to the show's general manager, Alan Wasser, house seats were closely watched. "Virtually every contract we sign with members of the team includes a line that it is illegal to resell house seats," explained Wasser. "Beyond that warning it's up to the individual's conscience. But we insist they keep records of where every pair of tickets goes, and those records are available to us and to the Attorney General's office." Gary Walker noted in all of 1987 his Department of Consumer Affairs registered only one complaint about ticket scalping.[13]

Declaring in October 2001 they wanted to cut into the lucrative market of the scalpers, the producers of *The Producers* announced they would, beginning in November, set aside at least 50 seats every performance and charge the unheard of amount of $480 per seat. That was almost five times the cost then of their most expensive seat, $100, itself a high for Broadway. Since the show had opened to rave reviews the previous April seats had been almost impossible to obtain. Reporter Jesse McKinley observed the move marked the first time in Broadway history that producers withheld and aggressively marked up some of the best seats for those willing to pay for assured access, a practice then employed in luxury suites for sports teams like the New York Knicks and the New York Yankees, as well as in boxes for events like the U. S. Open and in special seating at rock concerts.[14]

Producers of the show said the decision was made after months of watching scalpers buy seats for the show and then quickly resell them at "an enormous profit." Said Rocco Landesman, one of the play's producers and president of Jujamcyn Theaters, which owned the St. James Theater (where *The Producers* was running), "The scalpers and their profits serve no one but the scalpers. Those monies belong to the people who created the show, pure and simple." Scalpers regularly got hundreds of dollars above face for *The Producers* tickets outside the St. James, with less open but no less profitable sales going through hotel concierge desks and through ticket brokers. Also booming was the online market. Sites on the Internet a day earlier offered four orchestra seats for a couple of days hence at $742.50 each, $642.50 above face. "We're trying to get that part of the market," said Tom Viertel, another of the musical's producers. Target customer base for the $480 seat was described in the announcement as "large corporations, first-class tourists and individuals seeking prime locations, frequently on short notice." No special extras or amenities came with the $480 seat; no area roped off from the $100 seats, no champagne, and no food. Said Viertel, "We're not selling incidentals. We're selling access."[15]

Earlier writers who spoke in favor of the practice usually included morality in their discussion. However, when journalist John Tierney discussed the issue at the end of 1992 he did so only from an economic perspective; it was a rant against regulation of any kind and in favor of deregulation. Tierney declared that economists argued that restrictions inconvenienced the public, reduced the audience for sports events, wasted the time of the police, deprived New York City of tens of millions of dollars of tax revenue, and drove up the cost of many tickets. No evidence was offered to support any of those points. William J. Baumol, director of the C. V. Starr Center for Applied Economics at New York University, said, "It is always good politics to pose as the defender of the poor by declaring high prices illegal ... but when you outlaw high prices you create real problems." Richard Thaler, an economist at Cornell University, asserted, "Some people think it's fair to make everyone stand in the line, but that forces everyone to engage in a totally unproductive activity, and it's discrimination in favor of people who have the most free time. Scalping gives other people a chance, too."[16]

Tierney said the more interesting questions, according to economists, was why scalping was considered so abhorrent because, "Other business can resell products for whatever the market will bear. Airline executives do not get arrested for charging hefty premiums to customers who buy tickets at the last minute. Brokers in New York could then legally charge a premium on each seat of $5, or 10 percent of face value, whichever was greater." Robert Shiller, an economist at Yale University, commented, "Economists know that speculators prevent shortages, and we don't see why the government should regulate ticket sales. I'd like to see more scalping."[17]

Perhaps one of the more unusual places for scalping to thrive was in Washington, DC, at the White House. Tom Peyton, a U. S. Park Service official who helped manage White House tours, explained in 1997 that for years sidewalk men had made money by standing in line for White House tour passes (free), then hawking them for as little as $5 and as much as $50. But the custom had become so common by 1997 that the U. S. Park Police began a crackdown in July of that year. Plainclothes officers arrested three men on one day and one on the following day, after all had been found scalping passes outside the Visitor Center in the 1400 block of Pennsylvania Avenue. Those arrested were charged with illegal vending, a misdemeanor. Thousands of the free tickets were given away at the center on a first-come, first-served basis Tuesday through Saturday from 7:30 A.M. until the day's supply ran out. People got in line as early as 5 A.M. and by 6:30 A.M. the line was often a block long. Anyone in line was entitled to receive four tickets. After the center's supply ran out the scalpers hawked the tickets to tourists downtown, often on street corners and in front of hotels.[18]

Overall, legislative activity in this period lessened. While it lessened especially in New York State and New York City it was a little more noticeable in other parts of America.

16

Laws, Arrests, Police, Courts, 1950–2005

"A judge is not going to take it seriously. They are probably as serious about ticket scalping as they are about prostitution. That is, not very serious."
Frank Antico, City of Philadelphia, 1994

"You can't make scalping go away by legislating against it any more than you can prostitution."
John Scher, concert promoter, 1996

In December 1958, Los Angeles Police Chief Parker called off his officers from making further arrests of ticket scalpers. He did so after reading a decision of the Appellate Division of the Superior Court upholding a person's right to rid himself of excess amusement tickets—for profit or loss.[1]

A bill designed to curb the operations of ticket speculators in California was introduced in the Legislature at Sacramento in February 1961 by Assemblyman Jesse Unruh (D., Los Angeles). He said he did so because for years scalpers had "bilked" the public by charging exorbitant prices for seats to events in the Coliseum and in the Sports Arena — both of which happened to be in his district. Unruh's bill would amend the state agricultural code to make it a misdemeanor for anyone who had not secured a written permit to sell tickets at prices higher than the standard rate while they were on property controlled by a state district agricultural association. Both the Coliseum and the Sports Arena were located on land owned by the 6th District Agricultural Association. No other venue in California was affected except the Cow Palace in San Francisco. "I have had many complaints from people who were anxious to see events at the Coliseum and Sports Arena and wound up paying ticket scalpers two and three times the regular price for their seats," Unruh explained in introducing his bill. "Officials of the 6th District Agricultural Association also have told me that suspicious underworld elements may be behind most of the scalping operations. In addition, shady ticket peddlers have created a terrific nuisance for people caught up in the crowds preceding each event."[2]

Los Angeles City Council approved of the Unruh proposal and gave their unanimous support to the bill, adopting a resolution urging the State Legislature to pass the measure.[3]

As agitation grew in favor of the legislation, Bill Nicholas, manager of both the Coliseum and the Sports Arena, argued forcefully for the measure. However, he admitted, "We have pretty positive evidence that some box office employees work with the scalpers—for a kickback, of course. But, don't forget that the public is also party to this situation. There are always those people who are willing to pay a little more for something better." Legitimate licensed brokers in Los Angeles like Gittelson Bros. (in business since 1916) then charged a basic service charge of $1.25 or $1.50 for most events. But for a big event such as a fight with $25 ringside seats a flat fee was levied of 10 to 15 percent. Of course, nothing prevented them from charging as much of a premium as they liked.[4]

On May 24, 1961, California Governor Brown signed Unruh's bill into law after it had passed in the Legislative Assembly by a vote of 76 to 0 in March. The bill carried an urgency clause to make it effective immediately—Unruh inserted that clause because the baseball season was underway.[5]

A few months after that, in September 1961, Los Angeles City Council ordered City Attorney Roger Arnebergh to prepare an ordinance prohibiting the sale of tickets at prices higher than those charged at the box offices for any "place of public assemblage."[6]

In the middle of November that year Los Angeles Mayor Sam Yorty chose to let a City Council ordinance on ticket scalping become law by default rather than give it his approval by signing it. He said he did not veto the law because the council had favored it so strongly. If the mayor neither signed nor vetoed an ordinance within 10 days after council passage, it automatically became law. Yorty explained the Police Commissioner and Police Chief Parker feared that the law could be difficult to enforce. Yorty added that it might also be a hardship on people trying to sell seats they had purchased but later found they could not use. "My concern is that any completely harmless sale of a surplus ticket ... if it occurs in a public place, renders the seller liable under the ordinance," he said. Under the new law, it was illegal to resell a ticket for more or less than its face value in a public place with anyone convicted of such an offense subject to a $500 fine and/or up to six months in jail.[7]

A bill introduced in the Kentucky Legislature early in 1966 would have subjected scalpers—those who sold seats for more than face value—to a fine of $50 to $100. The bill was confined to the resale of tickets to athletic events and was sought by the University of Kentucky, with the nation's top-ranked college basketball team, along with several other state schools. But in the Senate the measure was forced back into committee — effectively killed — after Senator Vernon McGinty (D., Louisville) wondered if the bill might not be in restraint of free enterprise and after Senator Thomas Brizendine (D., Franklin) admitted he preferred buying tickets from a scalper to standing in a long box office line. Then they and the other Senators forced the proposal back into committee.[8]

Even though the New Jersey Legislature made ticket scalping illegal in 1983, by the next year many brokers were circumventing the law by charging exorbitant "consultant" fees. Although the new state measure did not forbid the resale of seats, resale prices could not exceed 20 percent over the original cost. Said Paramus Chief of Police Joseph Delaney, "Ticket brokers are abiding by the law in that respect but they're tagging on an additional consultant fee per ticket that brings the price right back up again." As an example, he noted that a $15 seat bought before the new regulations went into effect could be resold by a broker for $50. Now, though, while the same ticket could not be resold for more than $18, it was not unusual for a broker to add an additional fee of $32, bringing the price back up to $50. Anyone convicted of scalping a ticket under the New Jersey measure faced a maximum fine of $1,000 and six months in jail on the first conviction and up to $7,500 in fines and 18 months in jail for a second offense.[9]

Scalping in New Jersey became legal again in 1995. For 12 years there had been a law against it, then in October 1995, after an intense lobbying effort by brokers, Governor Christie Todd Whitman approved legislation that temporarily repealed the anti-scalping law (it was an 18-month trial period to supposedly determine if the repeal would free up more tickets). Whitman contended the move would make more tickets available to the public, thus lowering prices. John Scher, president of Metropolitan Entertainment, a New Jersey concert promoter and a critic of lobbying efforts to repeal anti-scalping legislation, observed, "You can't make scalping go away by legislating against it any more than you can prostitution. However, New Jersey had a law that helped keep prices under control and they killed it. This is a black eye on the State of New Jersey." Journalist Brett Pulley said that when the New Jersey law was first enacted in 1983 the limit on profit encouraged illicit street-corner seat sales. In turn, the street market encouraged a growing market in counterfeit tickets. When the legal brokers found they could make little profit, brokers in nearby states with no scalping laws cashed in on events at New Jersey venues. In response, New Jersey brokers joined together in 1995, forming a lobby group that ultimately got the law repealed. Sponsor of the 1983 law, State Senator Richard J. Codey remarked that without the price limits "these guys can make a mint. You get Barbra Streisand at the Meadowlands and these brokers don't have to work again for a year."[10]

Illinois State Senator William Marovitz (D., Chicago) was joined in June 1990 by representatives of the sports and entertainment industries in urging the General Assembly to pass a bill that would increase the penalty for ticket scalping to a maximum of a year in prison. At a news conference, Marovitz said scalpers should be put out of business because they gouged the average fan by charging more than the face value of seats. "We think this is a very good law, a get tough law which, in fact, will make more tickets available to the average ticket-buying fan," said Marovitz. Joe Mudd, a former state representative from Peoria who then lobbied in Springfield on behalf of ticket brokers, argued the whole thing was a move by sporting teams, theaters, promoters, and major ticket agencies Ticketmaster and Ticketron to control the market. Mudd called on the legislature to repeal the 1935 law prohibiting the selling of seats for more than face value. He noted scalping was permitted in most states, including neighboring Indiana. Marovitz's bill would add a maximum of one year in jail to the existing maximum fine of $5,000 for those convicted of scalping. He argued the threat of prison time and civil suits (also added under the measure) were needed to beef up what he called the "totally ineffective" current law that was only occasionally enforced such as on game days outside stadiums or at rock concerts.[11]

One of those who attended Marovitz's press conference was reporter Rob Karwath. He remarked that the Chicago Yellow Pages showed several dozen ticket brokers in business, some of whom had placed large display ads hyping their ability to obtain even the rarest of items, such as seats to the Super Bowl. An employee at one of the agencies said his firm got many of its baseball tickets from season seat holders who could not make it to every game. "You can sell an automobile above the manufacturer's retail price," he added. "If that is legal, this should be." Representatives of the city's professional sports teams— Bears, Cubs, and White Sox — who attended the news conference all said they would not renew seats for any season subscriber caught scalping or selling his seats to scalpers. Cubs President Don Grenesko said his organization had sent out workers to buy tickets from brokers and was "tracing those tickets back, trying to see if they are [from] season ticketholders." Mudd said brokers would remain in demand as long as sports teams, theaters, and so on continued to set aside some of the best seats at events for them, denying them to the general public. "For them to say that they want to make tickets available to the little guy is a joke," he stated. "By the time the tickets get to the ticket office, all the good ones are skimmed off."[12]

Broadway producers and managers in New York were greatly upset in April 1957 when the city's License Department began enforcement of a regulation that prohibited the sale of more than 10 tickets to unlicensed purchasers. Especially hard hit by the curb were package-tour agencies and groups bussed in to see plays, particularly in the summer. The ban was part of the city's campaign to wipe out the black market in tickets. Under existing regulations, theatre box offices were obliged to make a daily report of tickets sold to brokers and of instances where 10 or more seats were sold to an individual.[13]

Just two weeks later the License Department announced it had temporarily suspended its regulation banning the sale to unlicensed purchasers of more than 10 seats. Partly that was in response to legal efforts by groups opposed to the rules to obtain a restraining order, pressure from producers and theatrical managers who lobbied hard, and to a realization by city officials that the regulations might not be a good idea.[14]

A plan that supposedly would let the law of supply and demand drive out Broadway's black market in tickets was revealed on February 8, 1962, by Robert W. Dowling, Mayor Wagner's Cultural Executive. According to Dowling, "free market" prices, as high as the traffic would bear, for the first eight rows of a hit would be set by the producer. The actual prices would be stamped on the tickets and the resulting profits would go to the producer's gross, rather than a profiteering middleman. Those high-priced seats would be sold at the box office and through licensed brokers. As well, his plan called for a city investigation to determine how widespread was the practice of scalping and the establishment of a central ticket agency with a telephone service to inform playgoers up to just before curtain time which shows had seats available and which brokers still had tickets on hand. Dowling also wanted an education drive to persuade the public to "have more self-restraint" and to stop dealing with the "gyp" and the unlicensed brokers. When asked about other abuses such as the use of diggers, bribes to clerical employees, ice to box office treasurers, and so forth, Dowling said, "At this moment we have no direct evidence of illegal ticket practices. But we do have cold shivers that practices involving ice do exist."[15]

Theatrical people on Broadway were reportedly only lukewarm to Dowling's proposed plan, and cynical. A consensus, according to one unnamed producer was, "Sure, we're in favor of the plan.... But in view of previous suggestions that got nowhere, let's see what is done about this one."[16]

Ten days later Dowling declared himself shocked to learn about a ticket speculator clause in the standard contract between Broadway dramatists and producers. The clause, which provided for the distribution of money received by producers from speculators, was brought to Dowling's attention by a reporter. When asked for comment Alan Jay Lerner, president of the Dramatists Guild, said he was surprised to learn of the clause's existence in the 70-page contract and said he did not remember it. Lerner added, though, that since he had now become aware of the clause he was quite certain it would come out of the contract, which was then being modernized and improved. He thought the clause was likely put into the contract in the 1920s, when speculation was not illegal. The clause in the contract used by all Broadway dramatists and producers was contained in Article 3, Section 9, of the "Schedule of Additional Production Terms." Under the heading of "Compensation, Deductions and Expenses, Basis of Computation," the clause read: "where percentage weekly compensation is based upon gross weekly box-office receipts, the percentage shall be computed upon receipts from all sources whatsoever, including any and all sums over and above regular box-office prices of tickets received by the Producer, or by anyone in his employ, from speculators, ticket agencies, ticket brokers or other persons, and any other additional sums whatsoever received from the production of the play." Describing the clause as "pointless," Lerner (he wrote the book and lyrics for *My Fair Lady* and *Camelot*) stressed it did not mean in any way that the Dramatists Guild condoned ice. "The Guild bitterly opposes ice.... There has never been an instance that I know where a producer has declared income from ice and where the author has shared in it," he stated.[17]

Sidney Kingsley, a Pulitzer Prize–winning playwright, strongly opposed the elimination of the speculator clause in the standard contract. He contended the clause was a weapon the dramatist could hold over the heads of producers who dealt with speculators. By demanding an accounting of profits from scalpers, Kingsley explained, the producer would be discouraged from illegal practices. He said it had been particularly useful in stopping speculation on his hit play *Dead End*, produced in 1935. Then, he said, speculators operated openly. Kingsley also argued that Dowling should be shocked by the "evil" and not by the clause, declaring, "The evil lies in the box office, where the control of tickets is. Mr. Dowling has for many years been an extensive theatre owner. He should know where the evil lies and where it should be corrected. As long as this evil exists, some such clause in the contract is necessary to give us the right to question it."[18]

While Dowling did hold a number of meetings with Broadway producers and theatre owners and appointed a committee of six of their number to combat scalping, nothing happened and the Dowling proposal faded from sight.[19]

Arrests still took place, but apparently not as often as in the past. Betty Schack, operator of the Manhattan Ticket Service in New York, who pled guilty to two charges of ticket scalping, was sentenced in December 1964 in Criminal Court to pay a $500 fine or to serve 60 days in jail. An additional 30-day jail sentence was suspended. Judge J. Howard Rossbach said he felt the fines that could be imposed by law on ticket speculators were too low and should be increased by the Legislature.[20]

Two months later a father and son who pled guilty in New York to scalping paid fines totalling $1,250 in Criminal Court. Judge William E. Ringel fined Leon Cohen $1,000 or 240 days in jail on four counts of overcharging for seats to Broadway theaters and a New York Mets baseball game. He owned and operated the Capitol Ticket Service. Philip Cohen, his son, was fined $250 or 60 days in jail on one count.[21]

In May 1969, the New York State Court of Appeals held the city's Department of Licenses could not prevent the resale of theatre tickets to unlicensed agencies beyond the city boundaries. Department regulations had been challenged by a licensed broker who had been selling tickets to a Washington, DC, agency; there was no ticket broker licensing law in the District. In a unanimous decision, the court said the city's exercise of power in this case had exceeded its authority. The court opinion declared, "A statute, the sole object of which is to assure that licensed ticket brokers do not resell tickets at amounts in excess of a specified price, does not authorize a city official to completely prohibit trade in such tickets with agencies located outside the City of New York." Conceding there might be some scalping involving out-of-state brokers and New York City residents, the court suggested "a narrowly drawn regulation to deal with that problem." The decision reversed a lower court ruling and canceled the License Commissioner's action.[22]

Richard Weisberg was sentenced to 30 days in jail and fined $250 for scalping in June 1972. At the time of his arrest at Madison Square Garden he had over 50 tickets — mostly for Garden sports events — in his possession. Judge Shirley Levittan in Criminal Court told him if he did not pay the fine he would serve an additional 30 days in jail.[23]

The popularity of Barney — the purple dinosaur character who was a favorite with children — caused an outcry over scalping in New York City in 1993. In December of that year tickets to 11 *Barney — Live at Radio City* concert shows went on sale. Although performances were not scheduled until March 1994, every seat for every show sold out within two hours of the box office opening. Yet, the city's 67 licensed brokers seemed to have plenty of Barney seats. Some of them were charging more than five times face value — one asked $200 for a $30 seat. Of course, all such excess premiums were illegal as New York State featured a maximum surcharge of $5 or 10 percent over face value, whichever was higher. Many disappointed parents were so angry they flooded the complaint lines at the city's Consumer Affairs Department. Forced to action, the city launched an investigation and in the end issued more than a dozen citations for overcharging. Ten brokers were busted for operating without a license and the city agency reached a settlement with the offending sellers. Still, within two months of Barney's last show, local hockey and basketball fans were paying as much as 10 times face value for seats to the Rangers and Knicks playoff games. Said reporter Charles Mahtesian, "The public, however much it may resent being gouged, is not entirely sure it wants to give up the option of buying tickets from scalpers."[24]

Mahtesian argued that even where laws were on the books, they were routinely ignored and that scalpers at arenas did not get caught very often and even when they were any resultant fines were not much more than a day's profit. "Rarely does any sports fan, theater buff or concertgoer protest to the authorities about an individual on-site scalper," he said. "The complaints that tend to come in are about brokers." He regarded a broker as a scalper with a license and a mailing address. "Some operate from outside a state in order to evade its laws. By reselling tickets to Philadelphia or New York City events from a New Jersey address, for example, Jersey brokers are not covered by the laws of the jurisdiction where the event is held," he explained. "Nor are they covered by New Jersey law, since it only pertains to New Jersey events."[25]

Some jurisdictions put more effort than others into keeping the individual scalper under control, thought Mahtesian. In Philadelphia, where only licensed brokers were permitted to resell tickets, the city's Licenses and Inspections Department often sent a detail to baseball and football games in order to thwart scalping. Using spotters armed with binoculars and stationed on Veterans Stadium ramps, investigators monitored the parking lots for any signs of illicit deals. "Scalpers are not a major problem at the stadium," said city spokesman Frank Antico. "The complaints we receive are more from people buying from agencies." Baltimore also reportedly kept close tabs on scalping activity and City Council had stiffened its regulations in response to the popularity of Camden Yards, the new home of baseball's Orioles. The legislation came at the behest of Orioles' owner Peter Angelos, who noticed more and more scalpers positioned outside the ticket gates as the summer of 1994 progressed. Often, though, any effort by civic authorities was wasted because the courts did not always take the offense seriously. Antico explained that the main problem with the law was in taking it before a judge because "A judge is not going to take it seriously. They are probably as serious about ticket scalping as they are about prostitution. That is, not very serious."[26]

New York State Governor Mario Cuomo signed a new anti-scalping measure into law in August 1991. Insiders believed the new law would help remove the sidewalk men from the vicinity of venues but that it would not significantly restrain the thriving illegal resale of tickets. Earlier that week, for example, New York Theater Tickets, in Union City, New Jersey, offered good seats for *Miss Saigon* for $175 each ($60 face) and for *Phantom of the Opera* for $150 each. The new law replaced Article 25 of the Arts and Cultural Affairs Law 60 days after Cuomo signed the measure. Under the new law fines for scalping were increased by $100 per violation and could thus go as high as $1,100 and/or one year in jail. To convict a scalper police only needed to show the violator participated in an illegal transaction, an easier standard than existed under the old law. The resale of tickets for events at major arenas was not permitted within 1,000 feet of the facility. However, companies like Ticketmaster, the national concern that purchased Ticketron in 1990, were not covered by the anti-scalping law because state legislatures had accepted their contention that they did not resell tickets but rather acted as agents of the venues. Their service charges ranged from less than $1 to $7. Testifying before the State Legislature some six months earlier when hearings on the new measure took place, Gerald Schoenfeld, on behalf of the League of American Theaters and Producers, said, "Scalping corrupts employees, gouges the public, undermines our price structure and tarnishes our image." One legislative staff member remarked, "The real problem is that many people don't think that scalping is a problem. They think people who have the money ought to be able to buy whatever they want. It's hard to convince them otherwise."[27]

By the mid 1990s New York State had joined New Jersey in a push to repeal anti-scalping laws. Assemblyman Joseph Pillittere of New York (D., Niagara County), who had sponsored a bill to lift the restrictions, said, "My concern is that we have driven ticket brokers out of the state. We have given up a lot of tax revenue, and I believe that we will have to do something to get the brokers back." Brokers across the region were running well-financed campaigns arguing that a free market would bring prices down through competition.[28]

That New York State law expired in June 1997 because state legislators were deeply divided over whether to allow brokers to set their own prices for the resale of seats. Republicans in the State Senate had been pushing to deregulate the resale of seats but the Democrats, who controlled the Assembly, blocked the Senate's plan, contending an unregulated ticket market would cause prices to soar. The Assembly had been under pressure by consumer advocates and members of the state's entertainment industry. Ticket brokers had lobbied hard in the Senate. In the end the Senate relented and passed an extension of the old law — the law that had been in effect six years earlier and limited price mark-ups to no more than $5 or 10 percent of the face value of a seat, whichever was greater. Despite the old law being regarded as ineffective and impossible to enforce Governor George Pataki signed it into law on September 23, 1997.[29]

That law expired in June 1999 and once again efforts were made to repeal it or to strengthen it. Once again, though, a deadlock ensued and led to the same old compromise whereby the current law — the $5 or 10 percent premium — was extended for another two years.[30]

New York State Attorney Eliot Spitzer said in an April 2001 interview, as expiry time for the law approached, that it had become almost futile to enforce the state's anti-scalping law but as long as such a law remained on the books his office would enforce it, but instead of focusing on street sales he would shift his efforts to large groups that obtained seats illegally and resold them. Spitzer said he backed the elimination of the state law as it was unreasonable to attempt to put artificial controls on scalping if consumers were willing to pay higher prices for events. "Consumers will be better off if we deregulate scalping, let the market function and get rid of the corruption in the box office," he explained. "You have people who are being paid bribes to secrete tickets out without the general public ever getting a chance to buy them. What we need to do is focus on this theft. That is where the fraud is." Also, he said it was increasingly difficult to prosecute scalping of seats to events in New York with brokers out of state and on the Internet.[31]

On June 1, 2001, the New York State Legislature passed a new anti-scalping bill that made it a felony to bribe box office employees to divert tickets and raised the premium maximum to 20 percent of the face value of a ticket instead of the old 10 percent. The new bill, which was to run for two years, imposed a fine of either $1,000 or twice the scalper's profit as well as a prison term of up to four years. Spitzer had argued the cap should be lifted and penalties should be stiffened for bribing venue employees, producers, performers, and venue owners. Additionally, the bill made it a felony to offer or to receive a bribe of more than $1,000 to divert tickets.[32]

By the early 1960s the 50 percent tax on excess premiums over a stipulated amount that speculators were required to pay to the IRS had been reduced. After a long battle between the brokers and the tax collector the tax was reduced to 10 percent, which made it virtually an extension of the 10 percent admissions tax that was levied on the box office price of tickets. However, under Section 4231 of the tax code, subdivision 5, the owner, manager or employee of a theater still had to pay a 50 percent tax on any amount he received in excess of the established price. In recent years the amount collected under that part of the tax code was described by reporter Howard Taubman as "laughable"; 1961, $104,000; 1962, $183,000; 1963, $127,000. Such amounts represented around .000001 percent of the total tax revenues.[33]

State and local officials conducted several probes into the practice of ticket speculation and while many dramatic revelations were made public, the practice continued along, seemingly unaffected.

17

Government Probes, 1950–2005

*"I am amazed at the callous attitude of people involved in
the ticket distribution area of the theater who continue to
engage in these practices."*
New York State Attorney General Louis Lefkowitz, 1965

*"This conspiracy has led not only to the unjust enrichment
of certain brokers and persons who control the original source
of tickets but to a dual system of distribution — one for persons with wealth and access...."*
New York State Attorney General G. Oliver Koppell,
1994

Charles H. Tenney, New York City Commissioner of Investigation, disclosed on May 1, 1956, that he had been checking on reports of ticket scalping
on Broadway hit shows. Rumor had it, he explained, that scalpers were getting
as much as $75 a seat for the musical *My Fair Lady* ($7.50 face). Tenney's probe
had started some two weeks earlier. Licensed brokers were then allowed by law
to charge no more than a $1 premium over the box office price for a ticket.[1]

A few weeks later Tenney confirmed he was checking into alleged irregu-
larities in the mail-order sale of seats to plays. Reports received by Tenney contended that thousands of tickets to stage attractions were being diverted by
unlicensed brokers to black-market operators. People employed to obtain seats
by mail all resided in the metro area and reportedly were paid $3 to $6 for every
seat they obtained.[2]

While nothing came of the short-lived Tenney probe, it did prompt a
reporter to chronicle the story of *My Fair Lady* tickets. Having opened at the
Hellinger Theatre on March 15, 1956, the hit was in its second year when Murray Schumach did his survey. When he went to the box office in the first half
of April 1957 he was told that no seats were available at the box office through

the end of August, except for some seats for Wednesday matinees in August. For those who tried to purchase seats by mail there was nothing available for any Friday or Saturday evening for the remainder of 1957. Every day except Sunday between 2,000 and 3,000 mail requests were received at the box office.[3]

The Hellinger Theatre had 1,551 seats and of the 900 orchestra tickets for each show, about 450 were allocated among 80 licensed brokers in the city. However, every fifth week the brokers got no allotment (supposedly to give the public a better chance at getting a seat). Among brokers that was known as a "black" week. Another demand on availability was house seats; 16 people or groups got 70 tickets, at box office prices, for each performance. Stars Rex Harrison, Julie Andrews, and Stanley Holloway got two tickets each, director Moss Hart four, producer Herman Levin 12, Columbia Broadcasting System (CBS — which provided the show's entire capital of $400,000) 16, and so on. Thus, except for a black week, 520 of the orchestra seats were not available to the ordinary playgoer at the box office.[4]

Schumach interviewed people in line, with tickets, waiting to get in for a Saturday matinee performance. He found the vast majority of those questioned had written for tickets between six and eight months earlier. The second largest group said they had bought seats from a broker for the box office price plus the legal premium of $1. For those people the wait from date of purchase to show time had ranged from a day to a few months. Then there was a group who said they had bought either from scalpers or brokers but who had all paid around $20 over the box office price of $8.05 for an orchestra seat. All those seats had been obtained on less than two days notice. Tenney maintained speculation for tickets to *My Fair Lady* was "under control." He believed "most irregularities are carried on by small operators, generally unlicensed ones." At least six such agents were said to be operating out of Newark, Jersey City, and Union City, in order to avoid New York State regulations.[5]

The New York State Attorney General's office announced at the start of December 1963 that it would disclose at public hearings in the following week the existence of a Broadway black market in theater tickets involving millions of dollars annually. It was understood Attorney General Louis Lefkowitz had information that scalping was widespread with one source involved in the investigation saying, "We've been told that the take on ice in one recent musical was over a million dollars a year." In the previous spring Lefkowitz began an investigation of theatrical financing that was later broadened to include the practices involved in the distribution and sale of tickets.[6]

Commenting on the upcoming Lefkowitz hearing, Broadway producer David Merrick said, "I'm delighted there is a possibility that an official position may be taken that might lead to legislation to correct the abuses of ticket scalping. I think that it has been a blight on the theater for a very long time. I'm all for this investigation." City License Commissioner Bernard J. O'Connell declared his office would take punitive action against any theater operator found guilty of "shaking down theatregoers" for more than the ticket prices established by law.[7]

At the hearing a state accountant testified that a black market in theater tickets netted about $10 million annually. Witnesses testified that all brokers paid ice for blocks of seats and could not stay in business unless they made those payments; ice ranged from 50 cents to $7 a ticket. Leading companies in the New York metropolitan area, including nine major banks, regularly bought tickets from brokers at exorbitant prices for their clients. CBS — the sole financial backer of *My Fair Lady*—paid scalpers up to $100 for a pair of seats for CBS clients. Two witnesses, one a prominent producer, said they believed the $10 million figure was conservative. Edward F. Reuter, the accountant, and senior accountant in the State Law Department said he examined 1,219 ticket transactions, obtained from companies, and found 962 of those transactions had been overcharges and overcharges had been involved with seats to every production running on Broadway at the time. Reuter said banks paid up to $25 a ticket to a number of shows ($9.60 was the highest box office price at the time) including *Barefoot in the Park, How to Succeed in Business Without Really Trying, Oliver!, Never Too Late, Jennie,* and *A Funny Thing Happened on the Way to the Forum.* Most of those purchases, said Reuter, were made through brokers in New York City, although in some cases an agency in Union City, New Jersey, had been used. He estimated the amount of ice paid out annually could be as high as $10 million.[8]

Melvin D. Hecht testified he had been employed as a runner or messenger and later as a seller for a midtown ticket agency from 1957 to 1962. (During the hearing Lefkowitz did not allow the release of broker names "as a matter of fairness" but promised the names could become public if other proceedings, such as criminal ones, resulted from his hearing.) Hecht said on Monday mornings he would deliver payoffs from his employer to box office treasurers at every theater that had a show running. One envelope contained a check for the regular box office price of the tickets sold, he continued, and another envelope contained cash. Marion Branch, a coordinator for CBS, testified that for some time she had purchased from brokers four or five pairs of seats each week to *My Fair Lady* at up to $50 a ticket, for CBS clients. Branch explained the brokers had been paid in cash and that it had cost CBS about $400 a week for the seats.[9]

One broker testified, "Every broker pays to the box office. The practice is universal." Another broker maintained, "It's a regular custom to pay ice. Prices depend on how hot the show is. The broker is forced to pay ice and forced to pass this on to the public. Otherwise a broker could not stay in business." A box office treasurer, described as working for one of the hottest hits on Broadway, told the hearing, "Brokers pay up to $7 a ticket over the box office price. The money is sometimes spread to persons connected with management and production of the show." Lefkowitz observed that so long as theater employees and others reported ice on their income tax returns they were violating no statutes in accepting ice. Producer Leland Hayward argued for more stringent legislation because "We've driven away the professional theater lover because of this gouging. David Merrick, a producer who then had six shows running on Broadway, also said legislation was needed. He said that a theater owner, through an intermediary, had offered him all the ice if Merrick brought his show to his venue; Merrick declined. Alvin Cooperman, executive director of the Shubert theatrical interests, said any employee who was found to be accepting ice would be "summarily dismissed."[10]

Another revelation from the Lefkowitz hearing was that one actress sold her two nightly house seats to a broker for $10,000 for one year. As a general rule, it was said in this account, a theater owner was entitled to the same number of house seats per performance as the total allocated to all the company members.[11]

When *Newsweek* reviewed the hearing it said, with respect to perhaps $10 million annually going to the black market, "What this means for the average — that is, no expense account — theatregoers is exclusion from the hit shows. What it means to the theater is far more serious. Last year, a period of gloom in which investors lost more than $5 million, somebody, not connected creatively with the theater, made almost twice that."[12]

Later in December the New York District Attorney's office disclosed it had started an investigation aimed at possible criminal indictments around the alleged black market in Broadway tickets. Assistant District Attorney Jerome Kidder, who headed the Frauds Bureau, said the State Attorney General's office had turned over "documentary evidence" to him recently. Lefkowitz's office had then subpoenaed and/or questioned some 90 people, mostly box office personnel. But it was admitted that most of those summoned had refused to answer any of the questions; they had taken the Fifth Amendment.[13]

At the December 23 session in Lefkowitz's office to question box office employees, 28 witnesses appeared under subpoena and 25 refused to testify — citing the Fifth. Sources close to the probe revealed that 72 people had appeared for questioning to that date and 50 had refused to answer queries, invoking the constitutional amendment against self-incrimination.[14]

Beginning late in January 1964, the long line of customers at the box office for the hit musical *Hello, Dolly!* was under constant surveillance by state investigators. Armed with miniature cameras and subpoena forms, and using a signal system prearranged with box office employees, the investigators were on the lookout for scalpers and, in particular, the members of an alleged scalping ring based in New Jersey. The men doing the surveillance worked for Lefkowitz. Sources said that five or six people were served with subpoenas that were in the line, during the first couple of days of watching, at the St. James Theater at 246 West 44th Street. What prompted the stakeout was a phone call from producer David Merrick to David Clurman, the special Assistant Attorney

General in charge of the probe. Merrick told Clurman that his box office people had spotted several apparent diggers at work. Before *Dolly* opened on January 16 Merrick departed from Broadway custom and announced he would not give brokers any ticket allotments, but when demand slackened he would include the brokers. Three investigators had been working the line, which at times had numbered as many as 200 people. When a box office employee spotted a constant repeater in the line he signaled an investigator, who moved in and asked the person for identification. If he was considered suspicious, his picture was taken and he was served a subpoena. Some of the alleged diggers were reported to have been using a nearby hotel room to change clothes to confuse the ticket sellers.[15]

On January 31, 1964, New Jersey announced it had joined the New York drive to end scalping and the payment of ice. Arthur J. Sills, state Attorney General, said he would immediately open a full investigation into the activities of New Jersey ticket brokers. Sills made his announcement after a meeting with Lefkowitz in New York wherein the latter turned over to Sills several leads on New Jersey brokers engaged in scalping. The first target, it was learned, would be an unlicensed broker in Union City described as a "tiny store on a corner in a very unlikely neighborhood for a ticket broker" with the neighborhood being mostly residential with no theatres or large businesses. It was said to be a boiler-room operation with several men working telephones taking ticket orders. The shop was not set up to sell seats over the counter and there were no tickets immediately on hand. Lefkowitz said the New Jersey brokers got their tickets both from diggers and by delivery in New Jersey, apparently by persons connected with box offices, and it was there that ice reportedly entered the picture. Sills remarked that from the information he had received, many brokers were going to New Jersey to avoid the Lefkowitz probe.[16]

William Weiss, 62, died in February 1964, in a plunge from a midtown hotel window, listed as an "apparent suicide." His body was found almost at the exact hour he had agreed to appear at the office of District Attorney Frank Hogan for questioning about scalping. He was known as the man who "could get any ticket for a price" and was believed in the industry to be New York's biggest unlicensed ticket broker. Keeping no books or records he was described as a man who "worked out of his hat." Among bellhops, brokers, and box office employees, Weiss had a reputation as one who could come up with any hard-to-get ticket. Hotel employees in midtown Manhattan were said to have known how and where to reach Weiss at any time. Some old-timers in the theater district called him a "legend."[17]

Later in 1964 a plan to channel to the theaters the money going to speculators was recommended by the State Attorney General's office. Lefkowitz proposed the creation of a "premium ticket" for Broadway hit shows— perhaps 100 choice orchestra seats a performance, to be sold by brokers at $25 each (top price at the most expensive Broadway show was then $9.90; most were several dollars less). He felt such a plan would add more than $400,000 a year to the gross receipts of a production. Such tickets would be available within 48 hours of a performance to theatergoers who "want to buy at the last minute and don't object to paying a high price." While similar ideas had been put forward by producers and others in the past this was the first time such a plan had been proposed by a high state official. Under the plan the broker would add the standard $1.50 fee to the seat and thus sell it for $26.50 with $20 going to the theater and the broker getting $6.50. Lefkowitz suggested those premium seats should not be made available until 48 hours before a performance as that kept the seats from being circulated a long time prior to the show date and out of the ice channels. Similar plans had been advocated in the past by John Wharton, a prominent theatrical lawyer, and Robert Dowling. None of those plans, of course, was ever implemented, although premium tickets did arrive much later, to a limited extent.[18]

Not long after Lefkowitz made his proposal Broadway theaters, restaurants, bars and street corners came under surveillance by state investigators looking for scalpers. Investigators were equipped with motion picture cameras and miniature cameras that could take pictures from a block away. It was another investigation conducted by Lefkowitz. A source involved in the probe said "Although scalping has been reduced, it is still substantial." A pair of seats to Hello, Dolly! were sold for $125, for example. Employees and officials of 50 leading private clubs had been subpoenaed by Lefkowitz. "We have information that people who work at these clubs have been middlemen in getting tickets at high prices for club members," explained an insider. The surveillance was understood to be aimed at diggers, brokers and some theater employees. As well, it was reported there was concern in the Lefkowitz office over the recent increase in the number of house seats to hit shows.[19]

On November 9, 1964, using information from the Lefkowitz probe, District Attorney Frank Hogan announced two brokers, a former broker, and six salesmen employed by five ticket agencies were arrested on charges of ticket scalping. Six separate criminal informations were returned by the grand jury that had been investigating the situation. In addition to the defendants, three ticket agencies were named in the informations as co-defendants and charged with violations of the General Business Law. Included in examples of overcharging given by Hogan were tickets for 1963 performances of Rigoletto, Faust, and Aida that should have been sold for $12.65 top, but went for $17.50 and $18.50 each; $15 and $16 charged for a 1963 New York Giants football game ($7.65 legal maximum); $35 for seats to Yankees baseball games during the 1963 World Series ($12). Hogan pointed to overcharges of as much as $20.40 for seats to How to Succeed in Business Without Really Trying; $16.52 overcharges for Funny Girl and Hello, Dolly!; $7.72 excess charge for New York Mets baseball seats ($5.15); and $5.63 for tickets to Radio City Music Hall that had a legal sale price of $2.85. Among those who purchased seats at excessive prices were First National City Bank, the Chemical Bank New York Trust, United States Steel Company, American Telephone and Telegraph Company, Haines Hosiery Company, and the ad agency Kenyon & Eckhardt.[20]

Lefkowitz issued a statement in May 1965 declaring that ice and scalping "still exists in New York theater despite the prosecutions that have taken place in the last year," adding, "I am amazed at the callous attitude of people involved in the ticket distribution area of the theater who continue to engage in these practices." As a result of Lefkowitz's 1963 hearing, two bills recommended by the Attorney General that tightened the regulations against scalping and imposed more detailed record keeping on producers were passed by the State Legislature.[21]

Then, in March 1966, Lefkowitz announced he had started a grand jury investigation into reports of ticket scalping and ice on Broadway. Reports had been received that seats to some of the hit shows had been selling for $28 to $30 each. Several brokers and box office employees had already been subpoenaed.[22]

Almost three decades later New York State Attorney General G. Oliver Koppell began filing suits in April 1994 (he was up for re-election that fall) against out-of-state brokers who scalped seats for Madison Square Garden events. After receiving praise for that action, Koppell had extended his probe to include Broadway's ticket distribution system. Reporter Frank Hill observed, cynically, that Koppell knew a similar probe had kept one of his predecessors, Lefkowitz, on the front pages of the newspapers for months. Hill herein said the word "ice" in a scalping context was derived from an old machine politician's acronym for incidental campaign expenses. One producer commented, "Shows are hosts surrounded by parasites." He believed one theater employee collected up to $15,000 in tax-free ice from one hit show.[23]

Called the most sweeping probe in three decades, Koppell conducted his investigation jointly with the New York City Department of Consumer Affairs. There were then 67 licensed brokers in New York; 34 had been served with subpoenas a week or two into the probe.[24]

Journalist John Tierney attacked Koppell's probe as a waste of time, money, and so on. After vilifying the investigation Tierney rehashed the arguments of economists in favor of free market pricing and deregulation. No earlier probes had generated such a level of opposition, and the fact that this one did perhaps indicated the increasing stranglehold the capitalist hegemony held over the media.[25]

A concierge at a Manhattan hotel was charged in August 1994 with scalping and prosecutors were investigating possible scalping by concierges at three other hotels. All those concierges had been subpoenaed by Koppell. Rene Madrigal, a concierge at the Four Seasons Hotel, sold $65 seats for *Beauty and the Beast* to undercover investigators for $165, said Koppell. That part of the probe stemmed from undercover videotapes made by ABC's *Prime Time Live* television program showing concierges scalping seats.[26]

A week later Koppell declared the probe by his office had found a "perva-sive problem" of tickets for plays, concerts, and sporting events being illegally sold at huge mark-ups. He said the American Express Company, through its Platinum Card service, played a role in a system in which huge ticket price mark-ups had become commonplace. According to the Attorney General, the company was offering to sell choice seats to the most popular Broadway plays within two days of a performance, and charging as much as $175 for tickets with a face value of $65. American Express said it had suspended the Platinum Card sales of such tickets in New York pending results of the probe but that, in any case, it was not selling tickets and was only a "paying vehicle" that matched up customers with brokers, mainly out-of-state ones. The probe showed only 55 percent of the seats for Barbra Streisand's Madison Square Gar-den concerts ($125 seats sold for as much as $350) were sold to individuals with the rest sold to groups or large buyers, and many of those ended up being resold by brokers. A sample of people who had attended the Streisand concerts were interviewed and 70 percent obtained their seats through brokers or sidewalk men. New York City Commissioner of Consumer Affairs, Alfred C. Cerullo III, said the most serious problem in enforcing existing laws was that New Jersey and Connecticut, though they had anti-scalping regulations of their own, had no reciprocity with New York State. "No enforcement scheme is effective when brokers can simply cross state borders. What law we get should be enacted in unison with New York and New Jersey," said Cerullo.[27]

At the end of December 1994, American Express and a ticketing service called US Assist agreed to pay a total of $75,000 to settle allegations of scalp-ing — through the Platinum Card service — the New York State Attorney Gen-eral announced.[28]

Also at the end of 1994 the Koppell probe issued a draft report wrapping up some eight months of investigation and concluding that "a massive, com-plex network" existed that illegally sold seats for huge profits. A Republican successor to Koppell was scheduled to take over from Koppell in the following January. Within his report Koppell described a conspiracy involving the sys-tematic siphoning of large blocks of tickets to illegal brokers by corrupt box office employees and concert promoters, managers and agents, among others. Although there had been some arrests and a few small fines levied, no major indictments were handed down and no real major reforms were proposed. "This conspiracy has led not only to the unjust enrichment of certain brokers and persons who control the original source of tickets," said the report, "but to a dual system of distribution — one for persons with wealth or access; the other for the rest of the population who camp out in front of the box office all night only to find out that the best seats to an event are gone before you get to the window." The Manhattan hotel concierge pled guilty to speculation and was fined $150; three unlicensed brokers who were arrested pled guilty to mis-demeanor charges and were fined $250 each. Koppell said his office had been negotiating with the New York Hotel Association to end the practice of concierges commonly going to unlicensed brokers for seats but the talks collapsed when the group said it could not bind its members.[29]

In an effort to determine whether box office employees at Broadway theaters were diverting seats to unlicensed brokers, Koppell's investigators interviewed and examined box office records for hit shows and, with search warrants, seized the records of four illegal brokers in New York and New Jersey and those records, declared the report, "reflect extensive transactions with Broadway box offices." Licensed brokers, from their records, trafficked back and forth with their unlicensed counterparts and even purchased seats from out-of-state scalpers.[30]

A few months later, after Dennis Vacco had replaced Koppell as New York State Attorney General, an editorial in the *New York Times* wondered why seats to a Broadway show cost $75 each and why ordinary citizens could not buy tickets over the phone, even when a show played to a half-filled house. While admitting the answers were complex the editor did conclude, "Attorney General Dennis Vacco can help by taking on the street's most blatant villain: the ticket scalper." Pointing out the law limited ticket premiums then to $5 or 10 percent, he added that overcharges happened all the time, "Scalping is no longer merely the province of individuals who buy tickets in advance and sell them for a huge profit on the sidewalk. Ticket wholesalers buy up huge blocks of tickets and resell them at illegally high prices." If Governor George Pataki wanted to preserve the Broadway theater and the $900 million a year it brought the region in tourist dollars, argued the editorial, "he can start by encouraging Mr. Vacco to take up aggressively where Mr. Koppell left off."[31]

Apparently, though, Vacco took no action for a little while, until the spring of 1998 (he was running for re-election that fall) when he announced results from his own inquiry into ticket speculation. David Corvette, a spokesman for the Attorney General's office declared, "We think that ice is rampant in the industry, and that it's a major reason people have to pay so much to go to Broadway or concerts these days." An anonymous official with a firm that dealt in theater tickets observed, "I have no doubt ice exists. It does exist, it always has existed and it always will exist. But I think you have about as much chance of stamping it out as you have of outlawing prostitution." He added, "We see these kinds of investigations all the time, particularly in election years, but I don't think it's likely to change anything." Corvette denied the two-year-old probe had more to do with publicity than law enforcement, saying, "Just because this sort of thing has gone on for years does not make it right or justify the impact it has on exorbitant prices for tickets that consumers have to pay. If we can put a dent in that, we've accomplished something."[32]

As part of the Vacco probe, investigators checked allegations that employees in the box office for the United States Open tennis tournament illegally diverted prime seats to scalpers who in turn resold the tickets at vastly inflated prices. An undercover agent paid $1,700 for a ticket to a women's semi-final match ($80 face). Tournament officials acknowledged, in August 1998, that scalping was a widespread problem for the U.S. Open but said they doubted people working in the box office of the National Tennis Center in Flushing Meadows, where the tournament was held, were to blame. David Meehan, director of operations for the tennis center, maintained scalped seats probably originated with long-term box holders, who paid as much as $26,000 for 150 tickets. Gerard Nahay and his wife Janet Rosenblatt were convicted on August 13, 1998, on 19 counts of ticket scalping and tax evasion. During an August 1996 raid on the home of the couple, agents seized more than 1,000 tickets to the Open and hundreds of tickets to Mets, Yankees, and Jets games. In February 1998, the tennis center was fined $40,000 for failing to comply with a rarely enforced 1965 law that required ticket sellers to register with the state.[33]

Broadway's biggest theater group, the Shubert Organization (it controlled 16 theaters), was fined $25,000 in September 1998 for failing to register its ticket sellers with the state. Admitting no wrongdoing, the concern agreed to pay the fine. Vacco said enforcing the registration law, which had been on the books since 1965, was central to an investigation of ticket scalping because, "The ticket distributor registration law is a powerful tool in our arsenal to fight illegal ticket diversion and the high-stakes scalping that invariably results from it."[34]

Sports events drew a lot of scalping attention in this period, also, with the National Football League's premier event, the Super Bowl, becoming one of the scalping world's premier events.

18

Sports, 1950–2005

"The Super Bowl is the single biggest scalping event since Little Bighorn."
anonymous ticket broker, 1981

A big blitz against speculators took place in November 1970 at Ohio State University in Columbus when it was discovered that hundreds of scalpers were receiving as much as $100 for $5 seats to the upcoming game between Ohio State and Michigan. Said Robert Ries, director of the Ohio State athletic ticket office, "We have no scalping law in the state. It's gotten completely out of hand this week, and we've already traced better than 200 violations.... It's never been this bad as long as I've been here." That surge in scalping had prompted the university to investigate the situation. Ries said violators could lose future ticket-buying privileges.[1]

Jackie Sherrill, University of Pittsburgh football coach, suspended one of his assistants on December 15, 1981, for a month without pay for having engaged in a scalping scheme involving tickets to the Sugar Bowl, where Pittsburgh was to play Georgia on January 1. It was reported assistant coach George Pugh bought 50 seats to the game at the box office price of $17 each and then sold them, at that price, to a friend named Ray Bonner who resold them in the Atlanta area for $35 each. At the time, the scalping of sports tickets was prohibited by Georgia law. Bonner succeeded Pugh as the football coach at Columbia High School in Decatur, Georgia, in 1980, and Pittsburgh was then recruiting two Columbia High players. In helping Bonner to profit by around $900, Pugh created at least the appearance that Pittsburgh's ability to seek Bonner's assistance in that recruitment had been enhanced. "This has caused considerable embarrassment to our program," said Sherrill.[2]

In a 1989 newspaper book review of *Big Red Confidential: Inside Nebraska Football* (authored by Armen Keteyian) reviewer Allen Barra said of the situation at the University of Nebraska, "Mr. Keteyian also reports ticket-scalping by players. Some players made a solid living selling blocks of tickets for up to $100 apiece. The Heisman Trophy winner Mike Rozier said he would simply 'trade for a radio, stereo, something like that.'"[3]

In the professional football area, Robert Brown was arrested in Los Angeles at the Coliseum on August 27, 1954, when the Cleveland Browns played the Los Angeles Rams. Police said they saw Brown sell three 75 cent student seats for $2 each. Brown later pled guilty before Municipal Judge Parks Stillwell on September 24. It was his sixth conviction for scalping and Stillwell sentenced him to a jail term — the duration of which was not reported in the account.[4]

For the 1969 Super Bowl game held in Miami, all seats had a face value of $12. However, bellhops at one luxury hotel in Miami were selling them earlier in the week for $50 each and then for up to $125 each as game day neared. Played at the Orange Bowl with a capacity of 75,354, ticket allocation was as follows: 22,000 sold to the public in Miami; 14,000 to Miami Dolphin season ticket holders; 8,000 to out-of-towners by mail; 10,000 in total to the two competing teams; 4,800 in total to the other National and American League teams; 5,000 to the NFL Commissioner's office; 1,100 to the press; 10,000 to airlines (for package deals) and ticket brokers. At the public sale each person in line could buy up to 20 tickets. Speculators, reportedly, hired people to get in line early and buy a full complement, and it was those tickets that were said to be then commanding the high prices.[5]

Washington Redskins' officials announced the team planned to crack down on scalpers for an upcoming playoff game, in December 1972, against the Green Bay Packers at RFK Stadium in Washington. Edward Bennett Williams, president of the team, stated that season-ticket holders who engaged in scalping would lose the privilege of renewal for the next year. Newspapers had run ads from people seeking to sell seats at a premium.[6]

With the Super Bowl back in Miami in 1979, $30 seats were scalped for as much as $100. Also, counterfeit tickets were being circulated and sold by speculators. Miami's Police Department was checking local bars on the lookout for ticket transactions and promised a major patrol on Super Sunday at the game.[7]

Late in 1980, Al Davis, CEO of the Oakland Raiders, charged that Georgia Frontiere, owner of the Los Angeles Rams, sold tickets to the previous season's Super Bowl (played at Pasadena's Rose Bowl on January 20, 1980, between the Rams and the Pittsburgh Steelers) at above face value, and that NFL Commissioner Peter Rozelle may also have profited from such sales. Ticket scalping was then a violation of California law. Those accusations came in depositions taken from Davis and two others— Harold Guiver, a former Rams official and Melvin Irwin, onetime secretary to the family of Carroll Rosenbloom. They were both dismissed from their jobs by Mrs. Frontiere, Rosenbloom's widow. She inherited ownership of the team when he died in April 1979. The depositions were to be used in the antitrust trial launched by Davis resulting from the NFL's refusal to allow the Raiders to move south to Los Angeles.

According to the allegations Frontiere sold tickets to brokers for amounts above their $30 face value. Both Rozelle and Frontiere dismissed the accusations as nonsense. For that game the Los Angeles Rams were allocated 27,500 of the 104,000 tickets.[8]

At the time this story broke it was widely remarked that there was a long-standing hostility of some 15 years between Al Davis and Pete Rozelle. The latter's story was that Georgia came to him about 10 days before the Super Bowl and that she told him Carroll had agreed to sell Guiver 1,000 seats for the game. Although Rozelle said he didn't like the idea he believed she was under a moral and ethical obligation to honor the promise of her dead husband. Guiver reportedly stated in his disposition that Georgia charged him $100 each for the 1,000 seats, each with a face value of $30. She told him, according to Guiver, the $100,000 was to cover a $48,000 loan from the late Rosenbloom (which Guiver claimed had already been forgiven), $22,000 as payment for a football-club owned Mercedes car Guiver had been driving, and $30,000 to cover face value of the seats. Guiver reportedly wrote her a check for $100,000 but later stopped payment on it and wrote another for $30,000. Rozelle said he was only aware of the $30,000 payment.[9]

All the scandal and publicity that surrounded the story caused various law enforcement agencies and the IRS, probing the tax consequences of the underground economy generated by Super Bowl scalping, to take notice. Unreported scalping revenue for the Super Bowl alone was estimated in this account to be as high as $7 million a year. "There is a sickness about the whole thing," said Rozelle. "You feel a sickness in your stomach. There hasn't been anything like this in my 21 years as commissioner. We've had a problem, sure, but not of such a serious internal nature. It does make you sick." Rozelle conceded he had known for years that Super Bowl tickets were resold at premium prices. He recalled Tex Schramm, president of the Dallas Cowboys, getting up at one NFL meeting and describing how buyers met Cowboys fans moments after they picked up their Super Bowl tickets and offered to purchase them for more than face value. Also, Rozelle admitted he had seen ads in newspapers offering to buy and sell Super Bowl seats and knew that tickets reached travel agencies at premium prices. But he insisted he never dreamed the volume of premium sales was as large as it apparently was.[10]

Tickets for the 1981 Super Bowl were distributed by the NFL as follows: 16,425 to each of the competing teams (Philadelphia Eagles and Oakland Raiders); the Eagles allotted 12,000 to season subscribers, the Raiders 10,000. Rozelle's written guidelines, in the wake of the Davis allegation, suggested the Super Bowl competitors should establish a "firm policy" regarding the number of seats made available to players, coaches and staff members, with a maximum of 15 per individual. Both the Raiders and Eagles ignored Rozelle's suggestion, offering each player 30 and 20 seats, respectively, at face value. The host team, the New Orleans Saints, got 7,300 tickets; 876 seats went to each of the other 25 NFL teams (each NFL player was entitled to purchase a minimum of two tickets at face value); 2,500 to the owners of luxury suites in the Superdome; 10,950 to the NFL office. Except for the two tickets they had to offer to each of their players, NFL teams were not bound by any official rules as to the distribution of their supply; they just had Rozelle's guidelines. Usually owners kept what they wanted, dispersing the balance among executives, coaches, scouts, season-ticket holders, local media, and office workers.[11]

Rozelle said the NFL office used its allotment to provide seats at face value for various groups involved with the league such as NFL Properties, NFL Films, and the NFL Players Association, and for representatives of the three television networks, the print media, and for league office personal, including Pete Rozelle. A rookie NFL player said he was approached in the fall of 1980 by three different players and a coach, all of whom wanted to buy his two Super Bowl tickets. They offered varying amounts and he sold them to the player who offered him $300 for the pair—the highest offer. Murray's Tickets, located across from the Los Angeles Memorial Coliseum, usually had a lot of Super Bowl seats. In the previous year Murray's bought and sold some 6,000, buying for between $150 and $300 each and selling them for between $200 and $450. Since demand always exceeded supply in the case of Super Bowl tickets, Murray's, during the playoffs, opened what it called "remotes"—hotel rooms that functioned as offices—in several NFL cities, those whose teams had a chance to play in the Super Bowl. Once a team was eliminated from the playoffs the remote closed up. When a remote was in operation, buy and sell ads were placed in the classified section of local newspapers and contacts were established. According to Rozelle, his office would investigate all suggestions that NFL owners scalped tickets. He also said that when the owners held their annual meeting in March 1981 he hoped to introduce tough new NFL laws designed to better control the movement of Super Bowl seats.[12]

Journalist William Nack remarked that the January 1981 game in New Orleans at the Superdome would draw a crowd of 75,000. He estimated 50,000 would have paid the face value of $40 for their seats while the remaining 25,000 would have paid $150 to $500 for their tickets. Nack described ticket scalping as "a traditional American enterprise." One unidentified ticket broker told the reporter, "The Super Bowl is the single biggest scalping event since Little Bighorn. It's a single event scheduled at least two years in advance to take place in a certain city on a certain day. It can't be rained out. And it's a national event, the single most popular sporting spectacle of the year."[13]

With the Al Davis allegations still fresh and as seats for the January 1981 Super Bowl were scalped for up to $500 each, Rozelle came under increasing pressure to do something about the situation. "We're trying to come up with a system that will help us resolve the problem," he said, "but it's a tough problem. It's not healthy for the league, but it's part of the Super Bowl Phenomenon." A published report in the Los Angeles Times declared there was a "nationwide black market" dealing in Super Bowl seats. According to the report, NFL players, coaches and team officials had been involved in scalping. A source close to the NFL office said, "The league has been aware of a situation like that for some time. The league is aware that players and people who have options on tickets available in the host city are two of the main sources of tickets to ticket brokers." According to the piece in the *Los Angeles Times*, competing ticket scalpers had organized ticket captains on NFL teams. Those captains collected tickets from their team-mates and received more than face value from runners, who worked for the brokers. Those brokers then sold the seats at still higher prices to tour packagers that entertained clients with trips to the Super Bowl. "I've heard stories for years," said Rozelle, "about runners showing up at training camps lining up ticket purchases for December. I don't feel there's a big ring involved but rather a series of brokers who are independent operators."[14]

Acting on its own the Baltimore Colts tried to protect against the resale of its 1981 Super Bowl tickets by insisting their players pick up their seats at the will-call window in New Orleans. But the NFL Players' Association filed a grievance, contending the rule was a violation of the collective agreement; the rule was dropped. A former NFL assistant coach observed, "What else is new? There is very little a team can do to control this kind of thing. After all, many of the players had ticket deals in colleges, and they're accustomed to making a little something on tickets. Hey, what's the big deal?"[15]

Also in January 1981, Dallas Cowboys general manager Tex Schramm ordered that henceforth players and executives who bought Super Bowl tickets would have to sign statements that they would not resell their seats to scalpers. Schramm explained the affidavits were in reaction to the recent reports of NFL player and executive involvement in the practice. For the previous couple of years the Cowboys mailed out a letter to all personnel telling them it was against club policy to scalp tickets and if they did they would lose their ticket privilege. "We are very concerned about ticket scalping," said Schramm. "Now we're going one step further." The Dallas Cowboys, who distributed about 1,000 Super Bowl seats to players, coaches and staff that year, had hired a private investigator to monitor ticket transactions.[16]

With tickets for the January 1985 Super Bowl being scalped in some cases for over $600 and up to $1,000 for the best locations, the NFL said it might consider adopting stronger guidelines for how each club distributed its allotment of seats, but only to the extent of bringing the matter up at the owners' meeting in March. Under the distribution rules 25 of the 28 NFL teams each received one percent of the tickets, the team in or nearest the host city got 10 percent and the competing teams got 25 percent each. Because the San Francisco 49ers were both host and participant that year the NFL decided to give them and the Miami Dolphins 29.5 percent each. Face value that year was $60 per seat.[17]

    The Davis story recaptured the headlines in October 1986 when it was announced entertainment industry figure Dominic Frontiere (an Emmy Award–winning composer) had agreed to plead guilty to federal criminal charges that he failed to report to the IRS hundreds of thousands of dollars he made scalping tickets to the 1980 Super Bowl. It was agreed by the parties that Dominic and his wife Georgia reported income of $397,000 in 1980 on their joint income tax return while Dominic knew he should have reported much more. Georgia was not charged in the case. He admitted he lied to IRS investigators when he told them he personally had received only about 200 Super Bowl tickets, most of which he had given to friends, when the truth was that he received thousands of seats and sold most of them for more than face value through Raymond Cohen, a convicted thief. At the time the government made the announcement no other details were released. Maximum penalty faced by the composer was eight years in jail and/or a fine of $15,000; minimum penalty was probation.[18]

    Federal prosecutors released more details in the case at the beginning of December. Besides not being charged in the case, prosecutors made no allegations that Georgia knew her husband Dominic was scalping seats. She and Dominic were engaged at the time of the Super Bowl, married later in 1980, and filed a joint income tax return for that year. Prosecutors described Dominic as a "major white-collar criminal" who made $500,000 from the scalping. They added that in arranging for the scalping the composer told an intermediary, Raymond Cohen, that he expected to have access to Super Bowl seats for years to come and that if all went well, he could supply Cohen with tickets to sell for a long time.[19]

    According to prosecutors, in the weeks before the 1980 Super Bowl, Georgia ordered the boxes containing all 27,000 of the Rams tickets to be delivered to the Bel-Air estate she shared with Dominic. The composer then gave one box containing 5,000 tickets to Cohen, although he later retrieved 2,500 of those seats from Cohen after a Rams season-ticket holder, annoyed because he could not get a ticket, threatened to file a class-action lawsuit. Georgia's lawyer, Michael Hanrahan, learned about the threatened litigation and met with Rams ticket manager Don Nims, who told him he did not have enough tickets to satisfy all season ticket holder requests. Hanrahan met with Georgia and Dominic to tell them the potential lawsuit had merit. Georgia told her lawyer that she and her husband would make other tickets available. A day later Dominic told Cohen he needed 2,500 tickets back and later in the week he delivered those seats to Hanrahan.[20]

    Prosecutors maintained that Cohen, and others not identified who acted as salesmen for Cohen, sold the seats to various ticket brokers in Los Angeles and New York. Tyson's agency purchased "a large block," the Al Brooks agency was said to have taken 500, and Murray's Ticket Agency in Los Angeles bought between 1,000 and 1,500. Still, 3,216 tickets were left unaccounted for on the

Rams' books. According to the prosecutors Georgia had ordered that no complimentary seats be given to anyone, not even employees. Even Los Angeles Mayor Tom Bradley paid his own way to the game, as did Georgia's brother. Two months after the game Georgia told Clyde Gibson, then comptroller for the team, that the unaccounted for tickets had been given out on a complimentary basis. Dominic was said to have initiated the scalping scheme in the fall of 1979, before the Rams were assured of a Super Bowl berth, by meeting with a long time friend, Daniel Whitman, a restaurateur who then owned Cyrano's on the Sunset Strip in Los Angeles. Dominic asked Whitman if he knew anyone who could sell the Super Bowl seats if Dominic could get some. Whitman suggested his long time associate Cohen. In accounts filed with the courts by his own lawyer, Dominic had said he gave Cohen 1,800 tickets and told him to get as much money for them as he could, and that Cohen sold most of the seats and gave him a paper bag containing about $100,000.[21]

Later in December, Dominic was sentenced to a year and a day in jail and fined $15,000 for failing to report income from the sale of the seats and for lying to the IRS. He had pled guilty to two of three charges against him in a plea bargain. At the conclusion of the case the NFL office announced it intended to conduct an "administrative review" of the 1980 Super Bowl seat scalping incident.[22]

Reporter Eugene Kiely observed that just before a playoff game between the Philadelphia Eagles and New York Giants in January 2001 (played at the Meadowlands facility in New Jersey) fans had turned eBay, the online auction house, into a "virtual scalping site" for seats to the game until the company agreed to shut down any illegal auctions. Kevin Pursglove, spokesman for the San Jose, California, based eBay, said his firm had reached an agreement with the New Jersey Attorney General's office to remove any postings that violated the state's anti-scalping law. New Jersey law then prohibited the resale of tickets for more than $3 or 20 percent of face value, whichever was greater. Tickets with a face value of $72 or $77 (a legal resale limit of $86.40 or $92.40) were routinely auctioned off on eBay for $150 or more. Pursglove said the company required sellers to list the face value of tickets and a legal description of New Jersey's anti-scalping law. EBay adopted those rules in late 1999 after law enforcement officials complained that the site was being used to scalp tickets during the 1999 World Series, Pursglove said. Sellers, however, circumvented the new rules by posting inflated prices for the face value of Eagles-Giants seats.[23]

The NFL announced in March 2005 that it was investigating Minnesota Vikings Coach Mike Tice for scalping Super Bowl tickets, which he admitted he did as a Vikings assistant coach from 1996 to 2001 but denied doing as a head coach. The league required all players, coaches, and club personnel who bought Super Bowl tickets to sign a release stating they would not resell them for profit. For a few hours Tice denied all charges but then he told ESPN that he had been involved in Super Bowl scalping as an assistant coach — "just as all the coaches in this league have done." He also admitted that in that year he gave his assistant coaches the name of a California ticket agency that he had long dealt with for selling Super Bowl tickets, and that he had scalped 12 of his own tickets to the game. In June 2005 the NFL announced it had fined Tice $100,000 for scalping Super Bowl tickets. Vikings assistant coaches Dean Dalton and Rusty Tillman were each fined $10,000 by the league for the same offense.[24]

Baseball, especially the World Series, remained a favorite sport for speculators. Nine men were arrested near Ebbets Field in October 1953 and charged with scalping World Series tickets. That brought the total of arrests in two days to 22. Each man arrested had only a few tickets on him but police were of the opinion that each had concealed more seats with confederates in the neighborhood, thus limiting the number of seats confiscated if they were arrested. The Embassy Theatre Ticket Service in New York was also charged with scalping and faced a license revocation. Undercover police paid $170 for six seats to the game at the Embassy firm, when the total face value was $42.[25]

Sixteen men who sold tickets to baseball's All-Star Game in St. Louis in 1957 for as much as $30 were fined up to $50 and costs in police court in St. Louis. The men were arrested outside Busch Stadium for selling tickets without a city license.[26]

In August 1958 in Los Angeles three men appeared in court accused of trying to sell seats at face value to a Dodger baseball game in violation of the city ordinance prohibiting ticket scalping within 250 feet of a ticket window. However, the charges against all three were dismissed by municipal Judge E. Younger who declared it was unfair to classify as lawbreakers persons who found themselves with seats they could not use because of a change of plans, and tried to get out even by selling the seats at cost.[27]

Federal government agents moved in on baseball ticket scalpers in Los Angeles in July 1960 and arrested 30 suspects just before the start of a game between the Dodgers and the San Francisco Giants. The raid was a cooperative effort by U. S. Treasury agents and the local police department. Although a city ordinance prohibiting scalping had been held recently as unconstitutional in a court test, it was pointed out that federal law made it a violation if an individual failed to register to pay the amusement tax due on profits made on the sale of tickets. Dodger vice president E. Bavasi applauded the crackdown, saying the scalping situation had gotten out of hand. "We asked for the aid of the Treasury agents and the police," he said. "Once we sold tickets we were unable to prevent the re-selling of them." Bavasi warned that the federal agents would continue to monitor the stadium.[28]

New York City License Commissioner Bernard O'Connell announced in December 1963 penalties against broker firms and employees in connection with the scalping of 1963 World Series tickets. The licenses of Liberty Ticket Corporation (and employee Harvey Slater) and the Famous Theater Ticket

Corporation (and employee Bert Schneider) were all suspended for 30 days; the license of Alfred Leffler (an employee of Piccadilly Ticket Services) was suspended for 15 days. Leffler offered World Series seats for $20 each ($8 face, legal maximum $9.65) while the other two men sold undercover police seats at $40 each.[29]

Thirty-two people were arrested on charges of ticket scalping at baseball's All-Star Game on July 26, 1972, in Atlanta. Ten undercover police officers infiltrated the crowd. A state law prohibited the sale of seats at more than the regular purchase price. Police said the $12 tickets were offered for as much as $50.[30]

Journalist David Ferrell painted a picture of the sidewalk men who worked Los Angeles Dodger baseball games in 1994 as being small-time operators who made very little money out of the trade. Ferrell said Dodger Stadium was worked by more than 50 independent, unlicensed scalpers and that those men played a season-long cat-and-mouse game with Los Angeles Police Department vice officers, "winning just often enough to survive — though not in great numbers, or in lavish style. Most are poor street hustlers, moonlighting from blue-collar jobs or using scalping as a sole source of income." Almost all used the same hand-printed cardboard sign reading, "I need tickets" — meaning, of course, they sold tickets. They got seats from anywhere they could find them such as box offices, licensed brokers, and season-ticket holders. Sometimes the police shooed them away if not cited but if they were cited (caught in the act) their tickets were confiscated. Under California law, tickets could not be resold, even at face value, on the premises of an arena. Also, it was a misdemeanor to resell seats off-site without a license. A couple of the scalpers Ferrell ran into at Dodger Stadium were described as so poor that they did not have cars; they had to use the city bus system to get to the stadium.[31]

Plainclothes police officers were out in force to arrest scalpers around Yankee Stadium late in September 1998 as baseball's post-season got underway They were there under an order from New York City Mayor Rudolph Giuliani; it was another part of his clean-up New York campaign. On September 29, 64 people were arrested on scalping charges, 44 on the next day. In addition to the hundred or so officers in street clothes looking for scalpers, the police said, some officers had been trained to identify counterfeit tickets, which were said to have become more common. David Corvette said the Attorney General's office was running down the chain of purchases for each ticket they confiscated to see if blocks of seats were being sold illegally to speculators by box office employees. One of those arrested on September 29 was Jacob Levin, a lawyer with the City Corporation Counsel's office. Levin tried to sell his $35 seat to an undercover cop for $50, said the police.[32]

After two weeks of the crackdown the New York City police patrolling outside Yankee Stadium had arrested 242 people for scalping offenses. At the time the law limited the resale premium to $5 or 10 percent and banned completely the resale of seats within 1,000 feet of the venue. Jules Polonetsky, the New York City Consumer Affairs Commissioner, said he was also trying to find seven brokers who were charging as much as $2,500 for seats to the World Series. Subpoenas had been issued to get the addresses from telephone companies, he explained, since newspaper ads for the brokers listed 1-800 numbers but no addresses. "They've gotten a bit smarter," commented Polonetsky. "they used to advertise their names."[33]

The Boston Red Sox announced their crackdown on scalpers in late September 2004, just in advance of a weekend series in which they hosted the New York Yankees. For the following playoffs the Red Sox experimented with a so-called scalp-free zone outside Fenway Park, similar to one at Camden Yards in Baltimore, where fans could buy or sell seats at face value. Buyers who purchased seats in the scalp-free zone were required to enter the park immediately to prevent the buyer from going back to the street and perhaps selling for a premium or to a scalper. Red Sox season ticket holders agreed when they bought their tickets that they would not scalp them. If caught doing so, the team could revoke the tickets. For the first time, in 2004, the Red Sox sold out all 81 home games— Fenway was the smallest ball park in the major leagues, with the highest ticket prices, $43 on average. But the asking price of Boston online ticket brokers was much higher. Boston's Ace Ticket, for example, was offering four dugout-level seats ($250 to $300 face each) for $900 each for the Saturday night game in that end-of-season series with the Yankees. Four seats in a private suite that had a face value of $70 and were mostly sold to corporations were offered at $825 each. During the 2003 season the Red Sox responded to online scalpers with an online site of its own. Called Red Sox Replay, the site allowed season ticket holders to resell their seats at face value. Other fans (looking to buy) could subscribe to the service for $49.95 a year and buy seats at face value plus 24 percent. About 5,000 fans had reportedly signed up. However, the site had few tickets available for fans to buy. Ace Ticket listed online more than 170 tickets for that Yankee weekend series while Red Sox Replay had none posted.[34]

Basketball also drew its share of attention. Back in 1951 Eugene Nixon, a former Pomona College coach and athletic director, wrote, in the wake of an attempt to fix a college basketball game, about some of "the shady methods" employed in colleges to reward athletes without professionalizing them. He maintained, "Most colleges encourage their players to engage [in] ticket scalping." Practically every college gave out a definite number of game tickets to each player for every game. Ostensibly those tickets enabled the player to invite his relatives and friends to be his guests but, "It is nearly always tacitly understood between the athlete and the college, that, if he wishes to do so, the boy is at liberty to sell the tickets to the highest bidder and to pocket the money," noted Nixon. "Since the colleges condone this practice I do not see how we can condemn the boy. Thousands of our most respected athletes have done the same thing."[35]

Four college basketball coaches were arrested in April 1988 in Kansas City, Missouri, for trying to scalp seats to the Final Four tournament. The four were nabbed (13 were arrested in total) as part of a Kansas City Police Department undercover operation that concentrated on the lobbies of hotels in the city. According to William Frazier, commanding officer of the department's fraud and forgery division, all but one of the 13 were arrested in hotels, the other on the street; all arrested were described as "out-of-town professionals," except for the coaches. Generally coaches received their seats through the National Association of Basketball Coaches, although it was not then known if the tickets of those arrested came from that complement.[36]

Reporter Brett Pulley observed at the end of March 1996, from Trenton, New Jersey, that intense scalping was going on for that weekend's NCAA Final Four basketball tournament. Tickets were said to have been sold for up to 35 times face value ($2,500 for a $75 seat). Of the 18,000 seats in the venue, only 1,000 were made available to the public and those through a lottery conducted by the NCAA. The remainder went to the four colleges competing in the tournament, NCAA officials, coaches, local organizers, politicians (New Jersey Governor Whitman got 50, for example), and so on. Said John Scher, president of Metropolitan Entertainment, a New Jersey concert promoter, "People get these tickets and they try and sell them because they figure they can buy a car, pay a year's tuition, or pay the mortgage. I think the scalping that's going on now for the Final Four is repugnant."[37]

For the NCAA Final Four tournament in April 2001, each of the four competing teams was allocated 4,500 tickets (games were played in Minneapolis). One of the teams was the University of Arizona. Scalping was legal in Arizona with the only restriction being a ban on selling a seat for more than face value within 200 feet of an event venue. Many of the tickets for the tournament ended up on web sites like finalfourtickets.com, where they were offered for $400 to $5,500. In Tucson, 3,000 of those 4,500 seats went to members of the Wildcat Club, an athletic booster club. Another 1,000 went to players, coaches, the alumni association, and university administration and support staff; the remaining 500 were sold to students. Members of the Wildcat Club earned points each time they bought season tickets or made donations, and those with the most points earned got to purchase Final Four seats. When one member got his four (face value about $400 in total) he sold them for a total of $2,100.[38]

Just before Phoenix hosted the NBA All-Star game in February 1995, City Council legalized ticket scalping, as long as scalpers worked at their trade on a designated slab of concrete just outside the arena that was home to the National Basketball Association's Phoenix Suns. The practice had been illegal. With respect to that move a reporter commented, "Never before has an American city encouraged scalping and attempted to create a scalper safe haven." Said Stephen Happel, an economics professor and catalyst of the new law, "There's nothing more stupid in the free market system than to outlaw ticket scalping.

It's a waste of police power, and you never get a conviction anyway because no one will testify against a scalper." Scalpers, reportedly, disliked the new law because with all of them squeezed together into a small space they found too much competition, price comparisons, and falling prices. For several days before the All-Star game, tickets ($100 face value) sold on the street for $450. But when the law went into effect on game day and the speculators were herded together in the same area prices fell rapidly to $300 and then to $150. Rich Dozer, the Suns' chief operating officer, worried the law would encourage more activity by scalpers, especially out-of-town professionals. At first his team lobbied against the legislation but later determined to give it a chance. Every home game of the Phoenix Suns was sold out with most of the 19,023 seats in the hands of season-ticket holders.[39]

Journalist Gerald Eskenazi did an extensive investigation around the sports scalping situation in New York late in 1970. When he arrived at Madison Square Garden he found about 20 speculators working the sidewalk around the venue; men who rarely received summonses, but had perhaps a few hundred seats to sell for each Knicks or Rangers game — at prices ranging from $1 profit to 10 times face value. A ticket to see one of New York's football, basketball or hockey teams was said by Eskenazi to be a very hard item to obtain as the Giants and Jets football games were always sold out while the basketball Knicks and hockey Rangers had close to a full house for each game. He felt little action was ever taken against the scalpers (licensed brokers were limited to a maximum premium then of $1.50 while sidewalk sales were barred). The New York City Bureau of Consumer Affairs with a small staff of investigators could do little while the police who handed out summonses complained about "revolving-door justice." Judges who levied the fines were overworked and had what they considered to be more pressing matters. Madison Square Garden's (home to the Knicks and Rangers) own security force had little or no arresting power. Both the Giants and the Jets discovered that many scalped seats came from season-ticket holders who all said the tickets were lost or given to a friend. There was a waiting list of 25,000 seats for season tickets to Jets' games, 11,000 for the Giants.[40]

The New York Rangers had sold 12,500 of their 17,250 seats to season-ticket holders while the Knicks had some 9,000 season-ticket subscribers out of a potential 19,000. Since neither team had sold out to season subscribers it meant game tickets were available through the mail and at the box office, which meant diggers could go to work, and false names and/or false addresses could be used by speculators trying to accumulate tickets from the box office line or through the mail. Of the remaining 4,750 seats for Rangers' games, 600 went to Ticketron; another 150 to licensed brokers; 300 to the private Madison Square Garden Club (a long-time tenant of the Garden); 700 were set aside as courtesy (house) seats for Rangers' players, Garden executives, visiting teams, VIPs, the press, and so on. Thus, about 2,800 seats were left for the fans. According to the Garden, a scalper might put as many as 20 diggers in a box office line, picking up two to four seats for each event. The venue's security force used plainclothesmen to monitor the line. Rarely, continued Eskenazi, would a scalper have more than two tickets on his person. That way he could tell a police officer he was only selling his own seats and perhaps escape arrest. Even if he was arrested he would not have his entire stock confiscated. Even if he was arrested and found guilty the fine was often as little as $5 or $10.[41]

Of the 10,000 tickets available for each New York Knicks game 2,000 went to Ticketron; 250 to licensed brokers; 300 to the Madison Square Garden Club; 500 courtesy seats; 7,000 available for the regular fan. One charge that had been made was that up to 1,000 tickets per game came from the Garden's own ticket sellers who held that many back. However, a Garden lawyer maintained that no scalped seat had ever been traced to an employee. For New York Giants games there was a capacity of 64,600, with 63,550 sold as season seats. Ticket manager Harry Bachrach was left with a little over 1,000 seats to dispense, and they, of course, were all house seats (for visiting teams, players, press, VIPs, and so on). To the best of the club's knowledge no ticket brokers were on the list of season subscribers — they were taken off in 1956 when the team left the Polo Grounds. Bachrach believed most scalped seats for Giants' games were taken from mailboxes after the tickets were mailed to subscribers. The New York Jets had a capacity of 61,000 at Shea Stadium with 59,000 out to season subscribers. Team ticket manager Leo Palmieri admitted to a scalping problem and said the biggest problem was that the fines were so small. Palmieri said most scalped seats that turned up had originally been in the visiting teams' allotment (they got about 500 of the 2,000 house seats) with many others coming from the press complement (1,000 of the 2,000) and "very few" from season-ticket holders. In the one-year period ending in October 1970, the police issued 2,308 summonses at the Garden. From October 30 to December 15, 215 summonses were issued, but only 300 tickets were seized. On average, the number of tickets seized had dwindled from about five per scalper down to under two.[42]

A few months later Eskenazi reported the Muhammad Ali–Joe Frazier boxing match at Madison Square Garden "had created the most feverish demand and most outlandish ticket-scalping in sports history. Although the face value of the 20,455 tickets for the heavyweight title bout was $1,352,961, it is probable that close to $3 million actually was spent to acquire the seats." A scalper gave the reporter the mark-up he had made on his ticket sales: $150 face value seats for $400 to $600; $100 seats for $200 to $300; the $75, $50, $40, and $20 tickets went for 2.0 to 2.5 times the face value. Because of that activity, Alvin Cooperman, executive vice president of Madison Square Garden Center, was asked why he did not charge more for tickets in the first place. "We're an ongoing institution. We'll be here after the fight, and we've got to try and make the tickets available to the public at a decent price," he replied. In light of all the publicity that scalping at the Garden had generated in the previous few months, the facility sent a letter to each of its ticket holders advising them that scalping was illegal, and that the purchaser ran the risk of buying stolen tickets that would not be honored.[43]

Diggers who worked the Garden box office lines in April 1972, according to journalist Eskenazi, were usually teenage boys who were paid 50 cents to $1 for each seat they dug out. Garden security officials estimated 15 percent to 20 percent of public sales went to diggers. On a day before wrestling started, the Garden staff picked up a scalper with 188 wrestling seats—about one percent of the arena's capacity. Yet when they called up the District Attorney to find out a charge to book him on the District Attorney said to release him.[44]

About one year later, in June 1973, New York Attorney General Louis Lefkowitz revealed a six-month old probe of an alleged multimillion-dollar black market in "hot" sports tickets in New York, including those for the Knicks, Rangers, Giants, and Jets games. It was an inquiry said to have been prompted by repeated complaints from sports fans. One source explored was window number seven at the Garden from which, according to the Attorney General, eight ticket sellers were subpoenaed. All invoked the constitutional privilege against testifying and refused to answer questions. One ticket broker examined was William Malament, said to have amassed 66 season tickets to Jets football games and to have tried to evade the New York law by moving to New Jersey to operate his brokerage. He did so after compiling a criminal record for illegally selling tickets in New York City.[45]

Writing in *Sports Illustrated* in early 1979, Roy Blout Jr. remarked that although dealing with a scalper tended to leave a bad taste in the mouth, "the transaction is a kind of wildcat grassroots capitalism." Blout argued scalping was especially prevalent in sports, "the Super Bowl, the World Series, the NCAA basketball playoffs, the big college football games, the Masters golf tournament, the Kentucky Derby and the Indianapolis 500" were all major scalping events, among others. He thought a full-time scalper might mail in eight or 10 different orders for seats to a big event (using different addresses)—even if a limit of two per order was imposed it could still yield a speculator almost two dozen seats. A large operator might employ kids as diggers and scalpers sometimes made deals with ticket managers, ticket sellers and other front-office personnel to let them buy seats before they went on public sale.[46]

Blout noted that in college sports, students got cut-rate tickets as did faculty members and staff. Some of those found their way to the scalping market. Players got seat allotments and at a big-time college an alumnus could arrange with a player to buy all his tickets throughout the season. When a visiting team arrived at an airport for a game, local scalpers would be waiting to take extra seats off the players' hands. Most seats obtained from the inside, explained Blout, were scalped before game day to regular clients such as functionaries charged with fixing things for VIPs. Still, most sports scalping was described as small business. In most cities scalpers got away with a small fine and uniformed police usually ignored scalpers who exercised minimal discretion.[47]

In 2002 the Chicago Cubs held back some tickets and sold them just before game time through a ticket broker, for more than face value. There was much anger from fans, some of whom joined in a class action lawsuit that claimed the team violated the Illinois Ticket Scalping Act, which banned the selling of tickets above their face value. By 2004 that suit had been dismissed and was under appeal. Also, at that time, there was a hodgepodge of anti-scalping laws on the books in 31 states. More professional sports teams joined the Cubs. By 2004 eight teams, including the Seattle Mariners and the Green Bay Packers, had gone online to direct home town season ticket holders to offer their unused seats on stubhub.com — and taking about a 10 percent cut when the seats were sold. Eighteen other professional football, basketball or hockey teams had put up their own sites to do much the same thing, with the help of Ticketmaster. When the Cleveland Cavaliers and their superstar LeBron James came to Phoenix in November 2003, the Suns site got $300 for seats with a face value of $75. Los Angeles Clippers auctioned seats to their final basketball game of the season on April 14, 2004, on eBay. A similar auction was run that same week by the Orlando Magic with Ticketmaster.[48]

And then there was scalping at music events, especially at rock concerts.

19

Concerts, 1950–2005

"If you've gotta pay $200 to buy a ticket that's marked $12.50, it's not right, and you shouldn't stand for it. Tickets should go to the fans, not the scalpers."
                                                    Bruce Springsteen, 1981

"Every single show by a major act is scalped [by insiders]. I know it happens in every single city."
                                        Miles Copeland, Sting's manager, 1990

Four persons were charged with attempted ticket scalping on July 9, 1965, at the sold-out Frank Sinatra concert at Forest Hills Stadium in Queens, New York. City License Commissioner Joseph DiCarlo announced his inspectors issued two summonses outside the stadium and the Police Department the other two. One man was charged with offering eight $10 face value seats at $15 each while a second man offered two $5.95 tickets for $10 each. The License Commission's entire night force of 17 inspectors and two supervisors were assigned to the stadium by DiCarlo, after complaints of scalping activities from the public.[1]

When the Rolling Stones played Madison Square Garden on July 24, 1972, a new ticket distribution system was put in place in an effort to reduce scalping and to eliminate long lines— postcard requests were received for one week only, from June 11 to June 16. From 560,000 postcard requests for tickets, 20,000 were selected in a lottery drawing to determine who would get the seats and where they would sit. Winners could buy up to four tickets on a "first drawn best seat" basis for $6.50 each, a price limit set by the Stones. To that point their concert tour had been marked by sold out crowds but marred by sporadic violence on the part of fans that could not get tickets and those who found the seats they bought from scalpers were bogus. Phony tickets led to riots at tour stops in San Diego, Tucson, and Vancouver, BC, with scalpers' prices in Los Angeles reaching $75 per ticket and more.[2]

When the Rolling Stones returned to New York City in November 1981 for a series of concerts, tickets had a face value of $30 and were, again, obtained by lottery. Richard Shapiro sent in 20 letters, inside of which were 20 self-addressed envelopes. He got back one voucher that entitled him to stand in line for two hours to buy two seats. When he purchased them he was offered $250 for the pair. Mark Neston sent in 50 envelopes but did not win. Scalpers who wished to buy seats placed ads in newspapers that said, "Bids starting $500," and "No offer under $400 for pair."[3]

Police were out in force for each of the two Stones' concerts that year, with some 250 officers at the venue. On the night of the first concert over 80 people were arrested on charges that included narcotics violations, purse snatchings, assault, criminal trespass, and weapon possession. Forty of those were issued summonses for ticket scalping. Twenty-one people were arrested on drug charges the night of the second concert; 44 others were issued summonses for ticket scalping. As a capacity crowd of 20,000 streamed in warnings were delivered over the public address system that counterfeit tickets were being sold openly, some of them for "hundreds of dollars," and that they would not be honored at the doors.[4]

In May 1979, rock concert promoter Jim Rissmiller and David Krebs (manager of Aerosmith and Ted Nugent) announced the formation of a state-wide committee to place an anti-scalping proposition on California's June 1980 ballot. KMET, the highest-rated FM rock radio station in Los Angeles, also joined in the committee's formation. California state law then prohibited scalping on the premises of an event, but the only effect was that the speculators worked outside of the immediate area of an event. Tickets for several upcoming Rod Stewart concerts at the Inglewood Forum, just outside Los Angeles, had a face value of $10.50, $11.50, and $12.50 yet Good Time Tickets agency was asking $27.50 to $80 while Front Row Center brokers asked for $20 to $100. Several sources told reporter Salley Rayl that many of the scalped seats came from promoters, concert-hall personnel, and security guards. It was an allegation Rissmiller hotly denied, "None come from this office. As a promoter you'd be a fool to make a deal with scalpers. The first time you got caught you'd lose your credibility with everyone, and this business is based upon appealing to the masses."[5]

Bruce Springsteen's 1980-1981 concert tour was one of the major concert events of the year. Each night of his four-show stand at the Los Angeles Sports Arena in the fall of 1980 Springsteen lashed out at scalpers, declaring from the stage, "If you've gotta pay $200 to buy a ticket that's marked $12.50, it's not right, and you shouldn't stand for it. Tickets should go to the fans, not the scalpers." Incensed by the situation Springsteen's promoter, Ron Delsener, hired private investigators to probe the ticket distribution system in New York and Los Angeles. Barry Bell, Springsteen's booking agent, explained the scalpers ended up with blocks of eight to 10 tickets in a row for every show, "and you can't do that by mailing in requests." In Los Angeles Springsteen recorded a radio spot urging fans to support an anti-scalping bill that had been introduced in the California State Assembly. Meldon Levine, author of that bill, remarked, "The scalpers' lobby is one of the strongest in the state. When I introduced my first antiscalping bill in 1977, colleagues came up to me saying, 'That bill of your hurts my friends.' Unless we get support from the entertainment industry, we'll never overcome that."[6]

Bill Meister was a 23-year-old grade 10 dropout living in Cincinnati who, in a little over two years (ending in 1985), by buying and reselling concert tickets, became what one reporter called "the country's biggest ticket broker." Scalping had been legal in Cincinnati since 1982. Meister's empire fell when the Ohio Division of Securities took over his assets after alleged improprieties over the way he raised money from investors so he would have the amounts of cash necessary to buy large amounts of tickets. One example was Prince's Purple Rain tour that played three shows at Cincinnati's Riverfront Coliseum in January 1985. The 42,948 tickets, which went on sale in December, sold out in record time. Despite the eight-seat-per-buyer limit, Meister bought more than 12,800 tickets, saying he did so by hiring people to wait in line. Meister claimed to have paid these diggers—usually high school and college students—$40 to $100 each, depending on the quality of the seats. He also bought blocks of seats from other scalpers; he sold his Prince tickets ($15.50 and $17.50 face value) for $35 and up, stating he grossed $640,540 from Prince's Cincinnati concerts with $120,000 of it being personal profit. Not surprisingly, the Prince organization was angry. "In the end, it's the kids who suffer," said Steven Fargnoli, Prince's manager. When Meister's assets were seized 2,000 unsold Prince tickets were found.[7]

Rhonda Stofko and June Iacovello lined up early in the New Rochelle Mall in the suburbs of New York one August morning in 1988 to get seats for a Rod Stewart concert; they said they were first in line and expected good seats. But they ended up with tickets in the upper reaches of Madison Square Garden, in the third tier. Later in the day they phoned a ticket broker who had somehow acquired second-row seats he was selling for $250. Ticketmaster CEO Fred Rosen argued his records showed the women were not first in line, but fifth. According to Rosen, all Ticketmaster outlets were linked to the same single ticket bank and Ticketmaster could sell up to 1,000 tickets a minute in the New York area. Conceivably, by 9:09 A.M. (when the two women got their seats), Ticketmaster could have sold more than 8,000 of the best seats at the 20,000-capacity Garden.[8]

Reporter Michael Goldberg remarked that the women's experience was not unique and it had become extremely difficult in some cities, especially Los Angeles and New York, for the average person to obtain a decent concert seat without paying an exorbitant fee to a broker. On a recent Sunday, 25 ticket brokers had ads in the *Los Angeles Times* entertainment section offering tickets to various concerts at prices ranging from $125 to $400. Rosen claimed brokers got most of their tickets by employing kids as diggers, or purchasing from legitimate fans as they left the box office. Yet Rosen admitted he did have problems with the occasional ticket seller who worked at a Ticketmaster outlet. But he insisted most seats that fell into speculators' hands did so from the public, "The public causes the problem, and they're the ones who pay for the problem," he said. Concert promoter Danny Scher agreed he was familiar with the digger theory of ticket acquisition but laughed, "If you're gullible enough to believe that, you won't last long in this business." Said Seth Hurwitz, a Washington, DC, concert promoter, "This business about brokers claiming they had people standing in line is horse manure. They've got deals with people in ticket agencies, they've got deals with promoters, sources in the box office." Peter Mensch, co-manager of Def Leppard, suggested fans would have to make a lot more noise before the situation changed. "People never write letters about this to Def Leppard or the other groups we manage," he said. "It would seem that no one gives a shit."[9]

Goldberg returned with another lengthy piece on scalping in the concert business in November 1990. He recounted the story of Billy Joel's tour manager, Jim Miner, who received a call from a professional scalper in the fall of 1989, just before the start of Joel's U.S. tour. The scalper wanted to purchase several thousand choice seats and he told Miner to name his own price. At a later meeting in Joel's New York office, the speculator indicated to Miner that in the past he'd bought many tickets from a member of Joel's business staff. But that individual no longer worked for Joel so the scalper needed a new connection; he wanted to buy 500 tickets a night for each of five shows in New York. Joel, with Miner's cooperation, had a private investigator tape the conversation. The scalper planned to split the profit with Miner, whose share could have amounted to nearly $200,000. According to Tom Ross (he headed the music department at the Creative Artists Agency), scalping then involved some of the biggest concert promoters and insiders. Said Sting's manager Miles Copeland, "Every single show by a major act is scalped [by insiders]. I know it happens in every single city."[10]

Contracts between artists and their agents, promoters or managers, continued Goldberg, usually prohibited the artist's representative from providing tickets to a scalper. "For someone to pay more than $30 to see my show is outrageous," said Billy Joel. "My show isn't worth $150." Seats for the Rolling Stones in Milwaukee in 1989 were scalped for as much as $600; tickets for David Bowie in Philadelphia in 1990 went for $550. Said Larry McCain, a former scalper who worked for Murray's Tickets in Los Angeles, "You cannot buy a good seat by standing in line at an authorized ticket outlet in Los Angeles. All the good seats go to brokers." A report from Philadelphia concluded that in that city as many as one-third of all tickets never made their way into the hands of ordinary people who paid ordinary prices. ICM agent Troy Blakely said, "The scalpers are getting tickets from at least one of three sources; the promoter, the building or the ticket agency. And they are probably getting them from one, two or all three sources in just about every market."[11]

The Rolling Stones Steel Wheels tour in the 1980s was handled by promoter Michael Cohl (through his company BCL). According to an internal report prepared by one of Cohl's employees, a total of 150,000 tickets—including more than 25,000 in one city—were withheld from normal sale by BCL. Seats were routinely withheld from sale by concert promoters to accommodate the performer, the record company, the media, the tour sponsor, the press, other VIPs, and so on (house seats). But, according to insiders, the hold in each city on the Steel Wheels tour was excessive. A typical hold for a headliner playing an arena in Los Angeles might be 1,000 to 2,000 tickets while the number for a city like St. Louis would be in the range of 300 to 500. For the Stones tour, BCL held about 13,000 seats for one Los Angeles show and more than 7,000 for a single show in St. Louis. Scalpers approached many individuals connected with the Stones tour. One tour insider turned down an offer of $100,000 for 400 choice seats.[12]

At least 70,000 of the tickets BCL held from normal sale, all for seats in the best 50 percent of the venues, were delivered to Event Transportation Systems (ETS), a firm specializing in package deals that included a concert ticket and a bus ride to and from the show. For its Stones packages, ETS charged an average of $79.95, but a number of ETS outlets contacted by Goldberg's *Rolling Stone* magazine during the tour said seats were available for $89.95—with or without the bus ride. ETS president Donald McVie maintained his firm did not provide scalpers with tickets, yet in a letter written to a promoter (and obtained by *Rolling Stone*) a Milwaukee woman complained that she and her husband paid $1,200 for two Stones seats that were traced to the ETS allotment. Asked about those two tickets, McVie checked his records and claimed they were sold for less than $100 each to a Chicago hotel that purchased around 100 ETS ticket-and-transportation packages.[13]

Tickets-R-Us agency in Rhode Island obtained hundreds of Stones seats for shows in Philadelphia, Boston, and New York City, advertised for sale at $85 and up. Asked if the company could sell a caller 400 tickets for the Boston and New York shows, one Tickets-R-Us agent replied, "No problem." The North American Promoters Association (NAPA) had voted not to deal with ETS "whenever possible." Said NAPA director Carl Freed, "ETS is persona non grata with us." Stones promoter Cohl said he was philosophically opposed to scalping and vehemently denied any involvement in it and contended his ticket holds were not excessive. He also defended the ETS deal as an established part of the modern concert business and felt it was a value added service for fans—such as in providing a bus ride. In a statement issued during the tour Stones business manager Joe Rascoff declared, "All methods of ticket distribution through BCL have been approved by the Rolling Stones."[14]

An agent at one Los Angeles broker firm told Goldberg that scalping was a new profit center for promoters and that a promoter could make more money from scalping seats than from his legitimate share of the profits. For example, a sold out concert at the Forum in Los Angeles might net a promoter $28,000 or less, yet by selling 1,000 seats to brokers at an average of $70 over face, the promoter could pocket an extra $70,000. Some promoters used concert clubs, or season-ticket programs, as a cover for their dealings with scalping. For a yearly fee to the promoter — sometimes hundreds of dollars — a member of a concert club could purchase tickets before they were made available to the general public. In many instances, according to several major promoters, ticket brokers had joined those clubs. Brian Harlig of Good Time Tickets, one of the biggest agencies in Los Angeles, said he bought season tickets at Irvine Meadows and the Forum (which called them Senate seats). Harlig then resold those seats for many times over face value. One factor that fueled the scalping business in the past decade, thought Goldberg, was the introduction of computerized sales — it had become much easier for insiders to abuse the system.[15]

Ticket sellers at agencies also sometimes made black-market sales to speculators, unbeknownst to their employer. Ticketmaster president Fred Rosen said that in the previous year 40 of his seat sellers were caught dealing with scalpers and were quickly fired. Goldberg felt scalping probably could not be stopped and, in any event, there were strong anti-scalping laws in only a few states, such as New York and Pennsylvania. In California promoter Bill Graham was heading a group, Californians Against Ticket Scalping, that hoped to get anti-scalping legislation introduced. "Everybody knows that [it] is unethical and immoral. What we intend to do is make it illegal," said Graham. Concluding strong federal legislation was needed or a coordinated state effort and that neither seemed likely, Goldberg said, "There has, as yet, been no public outcry for antiscalping legislation. And, of course, it is a segment of the public that keeps the scalpers in business by continuing to pay outrageous prices for tickets." Earlier in 1990 Aerosmith manager Tim Collins decided it was time to do something about scalping. So he started calling other managers, hoping they would want to join forces to fight and defeat it. But he was wrong, finding that no one he spoke to wanted to rock the boat. No one wanted to alienate the promoters, the venue managers and the others who would be needed to do business with on the next tour. Said Collins, "There's no interest. Nobody seems to give a fuck."[16]

Tickets for Sting's two concerts in March 1994 in New York City were priced at $35 with "limited gold circle seating available" as the promoters introduced premium pricing in an effort to reduce scalping activities. For $30 more a concert-goer could join a couple of hundred other fans in the best seats in the 5,600-capacity house. Until about 1990, remarked reporter Sheila Rule, rock concerts had been without the type of first-class seats long common at the opera or on Broadway, but which were becoming more common at rock concerts. In 1993 Paul Simon's month-long engagement in New York had a top seat price of $100, as did Bette Midler's 30 shows at Radio City Music Hall. Concert promoters and others said those high-priced seats were being offered largely in response to the success of scalpers. Ben Liss, executive director of the North American Concert Promoters Association (which contained America's leading promoters), explained, "Scalping indicated that for certain artists, the audience was willing to pay a premium for the ticket. With scalping, the money was not going to the artist or promoter.... If people are willing to pay those prices, why not let the money go through the proper channels to the artist."[17]

According to journalist Eric Boehlart in 1996, a new generation of rock acts, including Smashing Pumpkins, Nine Inch Nails, the Black Crowes, and Pearl Jam "whose members recall what it was like to stand in line at the box office only to be told that the best tickets had all been snatched up" had beaten back scalping with new ticket distribution systems. The method used by the Pumpkins in New York; Los Angeles; Toronto; San Diego; San Francisco; and Washington, DC catered to motivated fans. In each city, local radio stations announced three hours in advance when and where $25 cash-only seats would go on sale. Tickets were limited to two per buyer, and fans needed to present identification when buying. After paying, they received vouchers marked with their name and a corresponding number from the ID (such as a driver's license or Social Security card). On the concert night the buyers' names and ID numbers were checked off a master list at the door. The Pumpkins' system was devised by band leader Billy Corgan and first tested at Chicago's Double Door nightclub in early 1995, as a variation of another method. As part of his small-hall tour in late 1994 Eric Clapton teamed with Ticketmaster for a voucher-only system. But Clapton's seats were available only by phone, required a credit card on the part of the fan, and sales were restricted to people over the age of 20.[18]

Three years earlier, in 1993 continued Boehlert, the Black Crowes required fans purchasing seats in the first 10 rows to sign for them and produce ID. In the fall of 1995, after their arena tour with David Bowie, Nine Inch Nails headlined a two-week club tour and sold vouchers with an ID system. "We wanted to make sure true fans got the tickets," said band manager John Malm. A problem with voucher systems was that they were cumbersome. A source close to Clapton said his small-hall tour was a "logistical nightmare" due to the ticket system. Such methods were also costly for venues as they required more staff to spend long hours verifying IDs, and so on. In Austin, Texas, where a first-come, first-served system was in place for a Bruce Springsteen concert, brokers paid the homeless $50 each to stand in line and buy seats. A former worker at a Chicago Ticketmaster outlet said he routinely pocketed $5 to $15 for every ticket he funneled to scalpers and he averaged 10 seats per concert. At the time Boehlert was writing, scalping was outlawed or restricted in just 20 states, including New York, Pennsylvania, Minnesota and Massachusetts. Major lobbying campaigns launched by ticket brokers had paid dividends in Illinois and New Jersey where legislators had recently eliminated anti-scalping laws over the objections of consumer advocates. Boehlert found that promoters and scalpers blamed each other. Promoters lobbied for tougher laws, insisting scalpers gouged and damaged the concert industry's reputation. Brokers contended the promoters withheld the best seats for their own gain.[19]

Trying to take a stand against rampant ticket scalping at rock concerts, Hootie and the Blowfish said in July 1996, that it would not honor hundreds of tickets for its concerts at Jones Beach, New York, that got into the hands of scalpers. Seat holders who bought the 534 seats in the first 10 rows for concerts on August 3 and 4 were reimbursed at the $25 face value of the seats. However, those seats had been sold by scalpers for as much as $150, according to the band. Under the terms of its contract, the first 10 rows of seats had to be sold on a first-come, first-served basis. Band officials received word, and a printout, that on May 10, the night before seats went on sale, someone in the main box office at Jones Beach held back the first 10 rows of seats for both shows. Between that date and the announcement by Hootie and the Blowfish two Jones Beach box office employees were dismissed.[20]

Only 135 of the original 534 seats were returned for a face value refund leaving the band with a $10,000 windfall. With that money the group made a $10,000 donation to create a music scholarship at the State University at Stony Brook, Long Island.[21]

On June 11, 1997, the box office manager of Jones Beach Theater was indicted on charges of grand larceny and computer tampering after allegedly selling more than 14,000 tickets to scalpers for a personal profit of $360,000. Joseph Nekola, who ran the box office at Jones Beach for 15 years, pled not guilty to all charges. Allegedly, the scam took place at 38 Jones Beach shows in the summer of 1996, including performances by Alanis Morissette and Sting. It was Hootie and the Blowfish who blew the whistle on Nekola after the band's tour accountant uncovered sales discrepancies and stumbled onto the scam. Tipped off by the band the New York State Attorney General's office began a probe and discovered the Hootie incident was not an isolated event.[22]

According to the charges in the indictment, the venue's computerized box office records showed on May 10, 1996, the night before seats for Jones Beach's summer concert season went on sale, Nekola logged on to the ticketing system. He then changed the status of every Hootie seat in the first 10 rows from "open" (available to the public) to "hold" (not available to the public). Thus, the first person to buy Hootie tickets on May 11 when the public sale began got 11th row seats at the best. After both of Hootie's shows sold out, it was alleged Nekola logged back on, printed out the held tickets and within five minutes bought all 534 seats, which he was charged with later selling for a profit to various ticket brokers. He allegedly repeated the process for some three dozen concerts. It was only a fluke that the scam was discovered. Following most concerts managers or tour accountants sign off on a general audit — presented by the promoter — that confirmed the number of tickets sold and the amount of money due the artist. Since Nekola paid for his seats in cash the books appeared balanced and an ordinary audit would have revealed nothing. On a whim, though, Hootie's tour accountant, Michael Loric, requested from Jones Beach officials a copy of the show's ticket journal, a little-used but highly detailed computer printout generated by Ticketmaster that chronicled when, where and by whom each ticket for a show was sold.[23]

20

Conclusion

Ticket scalpers and those who engaged in the practice have been reviled and vilified by editorial writers and general commentators from at least 1850 to the present time. Luminaries from superstar Jenny Lind in 1850 to legendary showman Flo Ziegfeld much later, and to rocker Bruce Springsteen much later still, have tried to deal with the problem. Legislators at the state and local level in dozens of jurisdictions have passed a large amount of legislation that tried to abolish or regulate the practice. Various entertainment industry figures such as venue owners, managers, producers, promoters, and sports team officials have declared innumerable "wars" against scalping over the past century and a half. Victories have even been declared, on occasion, over the practice. However, all such victories have been short lived at best, but more usually they have been illusory. Police have often expended a great deal of effort in trying to eradicate scalping, and at other times have been accused of not doing enough. Courts all over the country have fined people throughout this period for scalping tickets; they have even sent some to jail. Those fines, though, were regularly for trivial amounts of money. Yet despite all those efforts, and more, the practice of scalping remained, seemingly undiminished. Mainly that was because too many people involved in the ticket distribution system made far too much money by continuing the scalping system. All too often when entertainment industry figures railed against the practice they did not mean a word they said; it was all rhetoric.

During the latter half of the 1800s the sidewalk men were the main speculators, who were very well entrenched all through that period. Agencies, or brokers, who sold tickets from fixed places not at the entertainment sites, got started around the 1860s but were only a minor part of the industry during the 1800s. Also, scalping was well established in sports events, mostly at boxing matches and at college football games. Students at the universities were usually blamed for the practice and much was made of the idea that it was morally bad for the students. Many arrests of the sidewalk men took place, usually on a charge of disorderly conduct or blocking the sidewalk or some such charge when specific anti-scalping laws were absent. Laws were in place at the state level as early as 1884 in Pennsylvania and at the local level in 1873 in the city of Boston. Virtually all of the early laws against the practice focused on the sidewalk men, ignoring the activity of the agencies, most of which were then located in the lobbies of the better class of hotels.

Producers and managers of entertainment regularly fought the practice with the most frequently employed tactic in the 1800s and into the early 20th century being the use of private security guards and/or local police officers to patrol the area on the street directly around the venue. When those spotters saw a scalper selling seats to a customer that buyer was pointed out to the door staff who subsequently denied entry to the buyer. A flood of letters to the editor indicated the public was overwhelmingly annoyed by speculators, both at the prospect of having to pay a premium over the box office price in order to get tickets, and annoyed in a more general sense by what they viewed as harassment and unwanted contact with loud and obnoxious scalpers.

The idea that speculators were in collusion with managers—even while those managers decried the practice in public—was already well established. Indeed, evidence existed for such collusion and usually it involved the venue using its own sidewalk men, who later split their profits with the venue. Scalpers got their tickets during this period mostly by using proxies to stand in line and buy seats for them. New York City tried to control the problem by passing a licensing law in 1880. However, it ended up giving the speculators and their profession a degree of legitimacy they had always previously lacked. Having licensed them and soon realizing it had been a mistake, New York City tried many times over many years to eliminate that law.

From 1900 to near the end of World War II New York City stood out prominently as the worst city in the world with respect to ticket scalping, but the practice was common in many other American cities and in foreign locales. The practice received more media coverage in this period than in the past as the ticket agencies and brokers became more pervasive and their role in the practice became more prominent. For the first time pre-event financing deals between agencies and producers were mentioned in accounts, along with their potential for corruption, and so on. As a tactic for obtaining tickets, the use of proxies in line-ups began to fade, as did the role and importance of the sidewalk men. The status of the speculator, to the public, remained that of a loathsome pariah. While the sidewalk men became less important, relative to the agencies, they bore the brunt of public criticism and wrath because they were far more visible to the public, and a much easier target.

Management tactics in the period 1900 to 1917 remained much the same as in the past; most of the efforts were directed against the sidewalk men. While very few people could be found with a good word to say about the sidewalk men, quite a few were willing to defend the agencies, at least to some extent. New York City banned all sales of tickets on the streets but a proposal to banish agencies was quashed. More media attention was also devoted to scalping at sports events, especially at baseball games and during the World Series. Owners of sports teams strongly condemned the practice publicly, as did theatrical managers, but, like the latter, seemed to be powerless to prevent it.

During the period 1918 to 1949 the practice became more entrenched and more pervasive. In rare cases people came forward to defend speculating, usually employing supply and demand economic rationales. More observers also publicly blamed the public for the situation; that is, if the public refused to patronize the scalpers the practice would quickly die out. Agencies became still more powerful and dominant in this period and managers determined to fight the practice in a public way were more likely to tackle the agencies than they were the sidewalk men. Laws enacted by various jurisdictions focused more on those agencies. New York State and New York City both enacted measures that limited the amount of premium that an agency could add to the price of a ticket. For the first time governments at different levels instituted official probes of the scalping situation. Such probes always produced dramatic results showing collusion between ticket brokers and producers. Also exposed was graft on the part of box office personnel and treasurers who sold seats in blocks to ticket brokers. Such revelations always drew lots of media attention and garnered plenty of positive publicity for the man heading the probe (who regularly was heading into a re-election campaign) but never seemed to have any effect on the practice. Public sentiment by prominent producers, observers, editors, and so forth, remained overwhelmingly against the practice.

By the modern era, 1950–2005, scalping remained well entrenched within American society and was practiced openly, even in places where anti-scalping laws were in place. The existence of house (or courtesy) seats and how they contributed to scalping was acknowledged much more than it had been in the past. Economic rationales in favor of speculating were advanced more than ever before, even bizarre ones. One economist argued that standing in line to buy seats favored those with free time (the poor) and thus discriminated in their favor; that is, scalping simply evened things out for the rich. Laws continued to be enacted here and there but more and more the futility of such measures was acknowledged. As the capitalist mantras of free markets and deregulation took tighter hold on society the enactment of such laws became less likely. Football's Super Bowl was added to the list of important sporting events for scalpers. Rock concerts also were regularly scalped and major rock stars such as Billy Joel and Bruce Springsteen publicly attacked the practice, like so many prominent entertainment figures in the past, but also seemingly had no effect.

People advancing economic arguments in favor of scalping inevitably brought up the concept of supply and demand, and blamed the public for patronizing the scalpers. However, they did not point out that the supply was manipulated before the fact. The average concertgoer or playgoer could not get a good seat by standing in line for hours or by mailing in a request months in advance because the best seats were all put in the hands of scalpers before the public had a chance at them. If the public dealt with speculators to buy a good seat it may not have been through choice but only because the speculator alone had control of the good seats.

Scalping often seemed like a very innocuous event, one in which no one got hurt. However, in some cases, a huge amount of money was siphoned away from the people who created and/or promoted an entertainment event and given to people with no connection with the event. It was the creators and promoters who expended the time and effort, who took the risk, and it was possible they made less money in the end than did the speculators.

More recently it seemed that many observers felt, whether they were for or against the practice, that scalping could not be stopped or prevented. Back in the 1850s the scalping "evil" was divided into two streams; one was in the entertainment industry. That other stream was in the transportation field, specifically it had to do with railroad tickets. Suppose that Detroit was exactly midway between New York and Chicago and a one-way ticket to Detroit from New York cost $10 while a one-way ticket to Chicago from Detroit cost $10. That was logical given the distance covered. But a one-way ticket from New York to Chicago cost $16 (not the $20 one might have expected), which was not logical considering the other fares. Someone saw the possibilities and bought a ticket from New York to Chicago even though he was only going to Detroit. When he arrived in the Michigan city he sold the rest of his ticket to his brother-in-law, who wanted to go from Detroit to Chicago, for $8. Each man paid $8 instead of $10 and was happy. The railroad was not. Since most people did not have a friend or relative going on to a specific city at the right time brokers arose who dealt in those tickets. In that case the mythical traveler, when he arrived in Detroit, sold his ticket to the broker for $7. He had paid $9 instead of $10 to go from New York to Detroit and was happy. The broker sold the other part of the ticket for $9 to a stranger in Detroit going to Chicago. He saved a dollar and the broker made a profit of $9 minus $7, less his expenses.

As the scalping of train tickets became pervasive in the late 1800s— it was as common as the scalping of entertainment tickets in the period — the railroads got angrier and angrier even though it was their illogical and inconsistent pricing system that was at the root of the situation. They felt all the above hypothetical riders should have paid $10 for their tickets. Rather than alter that pricing system they lobbied the government to legislate against the practice and to enforce that legislation. It was done and by very early in the 1900s that practice was more or less eradicated. A major difference between the two streams of scalping was that in the case of railroads all the lines were united against the practice. None of the railroads made a cent from the train ticket scalping that was taking place and none of them colluded in any way with those scalping the seats.

Scalping continued undiminished in the entertainment industry precisely because there was so much collusion involved. A few methods tried in the entertainment industry to control the problem reportedly worked. Yet, none of those methods were adopted anywhere else or apparently used again, one reason being that the system of ticket distribution used in America since 1850 (a changing system, of course), which fostered scalping, has been one that provided too much extra money to too many people.

Chapter Notes

Chapter 1

1. "Ticket scalpers present their side." *New York Times*, October 15, 1908, p. 2.
2. "Jenny Lind worried over ticket prices." *New York Times*, May 2, 1929, p. 27.
3. Robert Sylvester. "Broadway ticket scandal." *Collier's* 124 (July 2, 1949): 26.
4. "The ticket speculator." *New York Times*, August 22, 1870, p. 8; "Eccentric Joseph Siegrist." *New York Times*, June 29, 1892, p. 2.
5. "The Booth-Barnett season." *New York Times*, September 29, 1887, p. 1.
6. "Amusements." *New York Times*, September 8, 1856, p. 1.
7. Ad. *New York Times*, October 30, 1858, p. 3.
8. "Theatre nuisances." *New York Times*, August 27, 1874, p. 4.
9. "A carnival of crime." *New York Times*, November 20, 1876, p. 4.
10. No title. *New York Times*, September 11, 1883, p. 4.
11. "Speculation in tickets." *New York Times*, September 23, 1885, p. 5.
12. "Gossip of the theatres." *New York Times*, September 25, 1885, p. 3.
13. "The speculation evil." *New York Times*, January 1, 1893, p. 12.
14. "Ticket scalpers in Paris." *New York Times*, February 18, 1900, p. 9.
15. "Mr. Sullivan's failure." *New York Times*, July 18, 1882, p. 1.
16. "Off day at Morris Park." *New York Times*, June 4, 1891, p. 3.
17. "Seats for the big game." *New York Times*, November 25, 1890, p. 5.
18. "Student ticket speculators." *New York Times*, November 24, 1893, p. 9.
19. "Students get the seats." *New York Times*, November 28, 1894, p. 7.
20. "Yale in good condition." *New York Times*, November 24, 1899, p. 9.

Chapter 2

1. "General city news." *New York Times*, September 28, 1868, p. 7.
2. "War upon the ticket speculator." *New York Times*, August 20, 1870, p. 4.
3. "The troubles of the ticket speculators." *New York Times*, August 23, 1870, p. 8.
4. "The ticket speculators." *New York Times*, August 24, 1870, p. 3.
5. "The ticket speculators." *New York Times*, August 27, 1870, p. 3.
6. "A theatre-ticket speculator in trouble." *New York Times*, November 26, 1870, p. 2.
7. "Troubles of theatre-ticket speculators." *New York Times*, April 12, 1872, p. 2.
8. "A ticket speculator fined in Boston." *New York Times*, April 19, 1873, p. 1.
9. "The ticket speculators." *New York Times*, August 22, 1870, p. 8.
10. "The Albany legislators." *New York Times*, January 24, 1884, p. 2.
11. "The steam-heating job." *New York Times*, December 15, 1880, p. 3.
12. "Ticket speculators discharged." *New York Times*, January 12, 1881, p. 8.
13. "Opposed to ticket speculators." *New York Times*, April 4, 1882, p. 8.
14. "The ticket speculator." *New York Times*, April 11, 1882, p. 8.
15. "War on ticket speculators." *New York Times*, May 21, 1882, p. 12.
16. "Theatre ticket speculation." *New York Times*, June 3, 1882, p. 8.
17. "Woes of ticket speculators." *New York Times*, January 1, 1883, p. 8.
18. "Ticket speculators." *New York Times*, September 22, 1883, p. 4.

19. "The ticket speculator evil." *New York Times*, April 12, 1884, p. 8.
20. "All about licenses." *New York Times*, January 9, 1885, p. 8.
21. "In favor of the ticket speculators." *New York Times*, March 17, 1885, p. 8.
22. "A ticket speculator fined." *New York Times*, July 5, 1885, p. 12.
23. "Spoiling for a fight." *New York Times*, December 21, 1885, p. 2.
24. "This is a free country." *New York Times*, March 19, 1886, p. 8.
25. "Harrigan was a witness." *New York Times*, March 3, 1891, p. 8.
26. "For theatre-ticket speculators." *New York Times*, June 5, 1895, p. 8.
27. "Ticket speculators win." *New York Times*, October 7, 1899, p. 7.
28. No title. *New York Times*, January 23, 1884, p. 4.
29. "The Booth-Barrett season." *New York Times*, September 29, 1887, p. 1.

Chapter 3

1. "Amusements." *New York Times*, November 9, 1869, p. 5.
2. "The ticket speculators." *New York Times*, August 22, 1870, p. 8.
3. "The Bernhardt tickets sold." *New York Times*, October 2, 1880, p. 10.
4. "Ticket speculators and the opera." *New York Times*, February 28, 1881, p. 2.
5. "Ticket speculators and the opera." *New York Times*, March 4, 1881, p. 2.
6. "High prices for Patti tickets." *Washington Post*, November 26, 1881, p. 2.
7. "Night waiting at Wallack's." *New York Times*, November 13, 1882, p. 5.
8. "The ticket speculators will not redeem." *New York Times*, January 9, 1883, p. 4.
9. "Nine men on camp stools." *New York Times*, October 1, 1883, p. 8.
10. "Seats for the Irving season." *New York Times*, October 4, 1883, p. 8.
11. "Mr. Daly and the speculators." *New York Times*, May 24, 1885, p. 4.
12. "The Arion out $7,000." *New York Times*, February 19, 1895, p. 13.
13. "William Turnbull killed." *New York Times*, March 23, 1890, p. 1; "A coroner's jury exonerates Hyde." *New York Times*, March 28, 1890, p. 3.
14. "The ticket speculators." *New York Times*, August 22, 1870, p. 8.
15. "The speculation evil." *New York Times*, January 1, 1893, p. 12.

Chapter 4

1. Ad. *New York Times*, September 11, 1860, p. 7.
2. "Wallack's new theatre." *New York Times*, December 30, 1881, p. 5.
3. "Low prices the rule." *New York Times*, April 20, 1882, p. 5.
4. "The ticket speculators." *New York Times*, August 22, 1870, p. 8.
5. "Ticket speculators balked." *New York Times*, May 21, 1881, p. 2.
6. "War with ticket speculators." *New York Times*, January 28, 1882, p. 1.
7. "Ticket speculators." *New York Times*, January 31, 1882, p. 4.
8. "Gossip of the theatres." *New York Times*, October 22, 1885, p. 3.
9. "The ticket speculator's a nuisance." *New York Times*, October 27, 1885, p. 2.
10. "Gossip of the theatres." *New York Times*, October 30, 1885, p. 3.
11. "Annoyed by speculators." *New York Times*, December 6, 1885, p. 2.
12. "A fair show for all." *New York Times*, August 27, 1887, p. 8.
13. "The speculators couldn't work." *New York Times*, July 19, 1888, p. 8.
14. "Operagoers defrauded." *New York Times*, January 14, 1889, p. 5.
15. "The speculator nuisance." *New York Times*, March 14, 1889, p. 5.
16. Ibid.
17. "Fighting ticket speculators." *New York Times*, May 2, 1889, p. 3.
18. "Harrigan was a witness." *New York Times*, March 3, 1891, p. 8.
19. "Fighting the speculators." *New York Times*, January 3, 1893, p. 8.
20. Ibid.
21. "Ticket speculator nuisance." *New York Times*, April 8, 1894, p. 12.
22. "Ticket speculators kept away." *New York Times*, September 23, 1894, p. 8.
23. "Ticket speculator arrested." *New York Times*, June 19, 1896, p. 8.
24. "Ticket speculators foiled." *Washington Post*, February 26, 1896, p. 7.
25. "Amusements." *New York Times*, November 9, 1869, p. 5.
26. "Theatre ticket speculators." *New York Times*, April 28, 1875, p. 4.
27. "War with ticket speculators." *New York Times*, January 28, 1882, p. 1.
28. "Ticket speculators." *New York Times*, January 31, 1882, p. 4.
29. "The engagement of Patti." *New York Times*, April 23, 1882, p. 9.
30. "More complaints about ticket speculation." *New York Times*, December 10, 1883, p. 4.

31. "The man in the lobby." *New York Times*, December 13, 1883, p. 9.

32. Ibid.

33. Ibid.

34. "The man in the lobby." *New York Times*, December 13, 1883, p. 4.

35. "Dividing the pudding." *New York Times*, December 14, 1883, p. 5.

36. "The theatre ticket abuse." *New York Times*, December 15, 1883, p. 5.

37. "The three men in the lobby." *New York Times*, December 16, 1883, p. 2.

38. "The ticket speculators." *New York Times*, December 17, 1883, p. 5.

39. "How to fight the lobby man." *New York Times*, December 21, 1883, p. 3.

40. No title. *New York Times*, January 16, 1884, p. 4.

41. "The speculation evil." *New York Times*, January 1, 1893, p. 12.

Chapter 5

1. F. Scott Fitzgerald. *The Beautiful and Damned*. Middlesex, England: Penguin, 1966, p. 26.

2. "The ticket speculator nuisance and some suggested remedies." *New York Times*, January 13, 1907, p. X1.

3. "One-price tickets at Paris theatres." *New York Times*, July 5, 1908, p. C3.

4. "Rush to hear Caruso." *New York Times*, October 25, 1908, p. C2.

5. "Riot outside Royal Theatre." *New York Times*, October 26, 1910, p. 1.

6. "Bayreuth ticket pledge." *New York Times*, March 31, 1912, p. C3.

7. "Alter theatre ticket plan." *New York Times*, December 3, 1909, p. 8.

8. "Sidewalk ticket speculator." *New York Times*, August 10, 1910, p. 10.

9. "Chicago opera hurt by ticket scalping." *New York Times*, November 23, 1911, p. 11.

10. "Profits of ticket scalping." *New York Times*, January 7, 1912, p. 17.

11. "Ticket speculators busy." *New York Times*, April 27, 1914, p. 20.

12. "Sell soda checks as theatre tickets." *New York Times*, September 21, 1915, p. 11.

13. "Ticket status in theatres of Boston is told." *Christian Science Monitor*, September 4, 1915, p. 6.

14. Ibid.

15. "Theater ticket question is again brought to fore." *Christian Science Monitor*, February 26, 1916, p. 16.

16. Ibid.

17. "In line at theatre door." *New York Times*, October 15, 1900, p. 7.

18. "Was a losing speculation." *Los Angeles Times*, May 20, 1904, p. A4.

19. "Many victims of swindling game." *Los Angeles Times*, September 21, 1907, sec 2, p. 1.

20. "Theatre tickets in hotels." *New York Times*, January 25, 1907, p. 8.

21. "Metropolitan drops rates to agents." *New York Times*, March 22, 1910, p. 11.

22. Ibid.

23. "New way in hotel ticket distribution by theatres." *Variety*, November 4, 1911, p. 3.

24. Ibid.

25. "Ticket speculation reduced to system and economy basis." *Variety*, January 24, 1913, p. 12.

26. Ibid.

27. "Educating the managers says cut-rate speculator." *Variety*, April 30, 1915, p. 11.

28. "Ticket deal now working: no cut-rates this week." *Variety*, September 10, 1915, pp. 3, 6.

29. "Theatre managers' agreement is not sufficiently binding." *Variety*, September 17, 1915, p. 11.

Chapter 6

1. "No theatre ticket scalpers in Chicago." *New York Times*, January 5, 1906, p. 1.

2. "Arrest theatre managers." *New York Times*, March 27, 1907, p. 9.

3. "Ticket speculator freed." *New York Times*, June 4, 1907, p. 1.

4. "Logical but not satisfactory." *New York Times*, December 21, 1907, p. 8.

5. "To banish ticket scalpers." *New York Times*, November 5, 1910, p. 1.

6. "Ticket scalping checked." *New York Times*, March 21, 1912, p. 11.

7. "Ticket scalping causes stir in Chicago Council." *Christian Science Monitor*, March 6, 1915, p. 16.

8. "Chicago managers see joker in latest anti-scalping law." *Variety*, January 7, 1916, p. 11.

9. "Chicago theatre notes." *Christian Science Monitor*, January 11, 1916, p. 4.

10. "Ticket speculators held." *New York Times*, February 8, 1907, p. 1.

11. "Jail ticket speculators." *New York Times*, January 28, 1912, p. 15.

12. "To fine Yale speculators." *New York Times*, September 1, 1907, p. C4.

13. "Speculators hard hit." *New York Times*, October 15, 1907, p. 7.

14. "For obstructing the street." *Washington Post*, March 5, 1900, p. 8.

15. "Ticket speculator fined $10." *Washington Post*, March 6, 1900, p. 10.

16. "Circus-ticket scalping." *Los Angeles Times*, September 26, 1905, sec 2, p. 10.

17. "May now scalp opera tickets." *Los Angeles Times*, April 1, 1906, sec 2, p. 2.

18. "Theatre ticket speculators." *New York Times*, March 21, 1902, p. 5.

19. "To stop theatre ticket speculation." *New York Times*, January 16, 1907, p. 1.

20. "Theatre managers accused by Saxe." *New York Times*, February 26, 1907, p. 11.

21. "Defend ticket speculators." *New York Times*, March 22, 1907, p. 5.

22. "Wagner bill passed." *New York Times*, April 4, 1907, p. 9.

23. "For anti-speculator bill." *New York Times*, April 5, 1907, p. 7.

24. "His theatre tickets costly." *New York Times*, March 21, 1911, p. 7.

25. "Would license a nuisance." *New York Times*, May 18, 1911, p. 10.

26. "See loophole for ticket speculators." *New York Times*, February 18, 1915, p. 6.

27. "Speculators' license fee." *New York Times*, November 16, 1901, p. 8.

28. "License for speculators." *New York Times*, December 11, 1901, p. 3.

29. "Ticket speculators lose." *New York Times*, November 26, 1901. p. 9.

30. "Ticket speculators are highwaymen." *New York Times*, December 2, 1901, p. 14.

31. "Have right to sell tickets." *New York Times*, December 6, 1901, p. 2.

32. "To stop ticket speculation." *New York Times*, February 15, 1902, p. 2.

33. "Ticket speculator fined." *New York Times*, April 18, 1905, p. 11.

34. "Says theatre gets half." *New York Times*, August 28, 1905, p. 7.

35. "Ticket speculator fined." *New York Times*, September 1, 1905, p. 9.

36. "Theatre managers win in speculator's test." *New York Times*, December 6, 1905, p. 11.

37. "Circus bars speculators." *New York Times*, May 20, 1906, p. 16.

38. "The ticket speculator nuisance and some suggested remedies." *New York Times*, January 13, 1907, p. X1.

39. "Theatre ticket speculators hit." *New York Times*, March 20, 1907, p. 16.

40. "Ticket speculators safe." *New York Times*, April 24, 1907, p. 18.

41. "Ticket speculation ordinance passes." *New York Times*, December 2, 1908, p. 1.

42. "Ticket speculators now off the street." *New York Times*, January 15, 1909, p. 5.

43. "Speculators rush to buy tickets." *New York Times*, January 16, 1909, p. 6.

44. Ibid.

45. "Speculators run foul of the police." *New York Times*, January 17, 1909, p. 11.

46. "Speculators talk of appeal to managers." *New York Times*, January 18, 1909, p. 9.

47. "Aldermen not to blame." *New York Times*, January 19, 1909, p. 4.

48. "Ticket seller in a cell." *New York Times*, January 24, 1909, p. 16.

49. "Arrest ticket vendors." *New York Times*, January 28, 1909, p. 3.

50. Ibid.

51. "Mulqueen upholds ticket speculation." *New York Times*, October 3, 1909, p. 9.

52. "Law too mixed to fine speculators." *New York Times*, December 13, 1909, p. 16.

53. "War on speculators in theatre tickets." *New York Times*, February 2, 1910, p. 7.

54. Ibid.

55. Ibid.

56. "Aldermen insincere theatre man says." *New York Times*, February 4, 1910, p. 7.

57. "Klaw gives warning in speculator fight." *New York Times*, February 11, 1910, p. 11.

58. "Blacklist invoked in speculator war." *New York Times*, February 17, 1910, p. 7.

59. "Arrest twelve speculators." *New York Times*, February 21, 1910, p. 1.

60. "A nuisance to be suppressed." *New York Times*, February 16, 1911, p. 10.

61. "Ticket speculators to fight law today." *New York Times*, March 20, 1911, p. 9.

62. "Ticket speculators begin test of law." *New York Times*, March 21, 1911, p. 7.

63. "Speculators renew their annoyances." *New York Times*, March 22, 1911, p. 11.

64. "Ticket speculator loses court case." *New York Times*, March 29, 1911, p. 22.

65. "Drive off speculators." *New York Times*, March 31, 1911, p. 11.

66. "The ticket speculators." *New York Times*, April 16, 1911, p. 10.

67. "Warns ticket speculators." *New York Times*, June 6, 1911, p. 2.

68. "Ticket vendor discharged." *New York Times*, June 11, 1911, p. 8.

69. "Ticket speculator to jail." *New York Times*, May 13, 1913, p. 11.

70. "Trap ticket speculators." *New York Times*, March 28, 1916, p. 22.

71. "Theatre ticket premiums part of gross receipts?" *Variety*, January 16, 1915, p. 10.

72. Howard Taubman. "Time for tax repeal." *New York Times*, December 6, 1964, p. X5.

Chapter 7

1. "Refuse to honor tickets." *New York Times*, August 21, 1900, p. 12.

2. "Speculators keep away." *New York Times*, August 22, 1900, p. 7.

3. "War on ticket speculators." *New York Times*, September 24, 1900, p. 7.

4. "Theatregoer's complaint." *New York Times*, May 26, 1901, p. 19.

5. "Ticket speculators' attack." *New York Times*, February 9, 1902, p. 10.

6. "Ticket speculator fined." *New York Times*, February 10, 1902, p. 9.

7. Ibid.

8. "Fierce riot on Broadway." *New York Times*, February 16, 1902, p. 1.

9. "Ticket sellers active." *New York Times*, February 27, 1902, p. 6.

10. "Sidewalk ticket speculators harassed." *New York Times*, March 16, 1902, p. 14.

11. "Can revoke theatre tickets." *New York Times*, April 26, 1902, p. 8.

12. "Ticket speculators' case." *New York Times*, April 27, 1902, p. 11.

13. "War on ticket sellers." *New York Times*, May 1, 1902, p. 9.

14. "War against speculators." *New York Times*, September 2, 1902, p. 9.

15. "Ticket broker arrested." *New York Times*, September 5, 1902, p. 3; "Notes of the theatre." *New York Times*, September 10, 1902, p. 9.

16. "War on ticket speculators." *New York Times*, March 31, 1906, p. 9.

17. "Circus war on speculators." *New York Times*, April 5, 1903, p. 11.

18. "Conreid to fight ticket speculators." *New York Times*, February 24, 1904, p. 9.

19. "Theatre manager punches speculator." *New York Times*, September 27, 1904, p. 9.

20. "Erlanger leads war on the speculators." *New York Times*, August 30, 1905, p. 9.

21. "To foil ticket speculators." *New York Times*, October 13, 1905, p. 9.

22. "War on speculators at the Hippodrome." *New York Times*, December 30, 1906, p. 15.

23. "The ticket speculator nuisance and some suggested remedies." *New York Times*, January 13, 1907, p. X1.

24. "Ticket speculators hit." *New York Times*, January 16, 1907, p. 7.

25. "Speculators on hand." *New York Times*, October 22, 1907, p. 9.

26. "To fight speculators." *New York Times*, October 23, 1907, p. 11.

27. "Movement to oust ticket speculators." *New York Times*, September 10, 1908, p. 9.

28. "Speculators to go, managers decree." *New York Times*, September 11, 1908, p. 9.

29. "Managers act on speculators." *New York Times*, September 12, 1908, p. 7.

30. "Ticket scalpers accuse managers." *New York Times*, September 15, 1908, p. 18.

31. "Politics block speculator fight." *New York Times*, September 16, 1908, p. 7.

32. "A campaign with mysteries." *New York Times*, September 16, 1908, p. 8.

33. "Managers call scalpers pests." *New York Times*, September 17, 1908, p. 7.

34. "Theatre men meet ticket scalpers." *New York Times*, September 29, 1908, p. 9.

35. "Ticket scalpers present their side." *New York Times*, October 15, 1908, p. 9.

36. "To end speculation in theatre tickets." *New York Times*, November 17, 1908, p. 7.

37. "War on speculators in theatre tickets." *New York Times*, February 2, 1910, p. 7.

38. "Blacklist invoked in speculator war." *New York Times*, February 17, 1910, p. 7.

39. "Ticket speculator fined $3." *New York Times*, December 17, 1910, p. 22.

40. "Managers to fight ticket speculators." *New York Times*, January 6, 1911, p. 7.

41. "Ticket speculators still to the fore." *New York Times*, November 28, 1905, p. 8.

42. "Conreid and speculation." *New York Times*, March 9, 1906, p. 8.

43. "The ticket speculator nuisance and some suggested remedies." *New York Times*, January 13, 1907, p. X1.

44. "A chance to end an abuse." *New York Times*, January 24, 1907, p. 8.

45. "Theatre managers accused by Saxe." *New York Times*, February 26, 1907, p. 11.

46. "Shubert accused of ticket deal." *New York Times*, October 9, 1907, p. 11

47. "The circus." *New York Times*, April 5, 1908, p. SM11.

48. "Cry from the speculators." *New York Times*, November 29, 1908, p. 2.

49. "Wait all night at the Polo Grounds." *New York Times*, October 14, 1911, pp. 1–2.

50. "The theater and the scalper." *Christian Science Monitor*, January 13, 1912, p. 40.

51. "The ticket scalping nuisance." *Christian Science Monitor*, May 2, 1917, p. 20.

Chapter 8

1. "Yale students fined." *New York Times*, December 13, 1902, p. 3.

2. "In the football world." *New York Times*, November 5, 1903, p. 10.

3. "Speculators hard hit." *New York Times*, October 15, 1907, p. 7.

4. "Ticket speculators fined." *New York Times*, November 22, 1908, p. 2.

5. "Harvard and Yale ready for battle." *New York Times*, November 20, 1909, p. 9.

6. "Probe ticket scalping." *New York Times*, November 27, 1910, p. C6.

7. "Army and Navy ticket scandal." *New York Times*, November 21, 1911, p. 10.

8. "Outwit ticket scalpers." *New York Times*, November 28, 1916, p. 14.

9. "Censure Chicago club." *New York Times*, December 19, 1908, p. 10.

10. "Ebbets after ticket speculators." *New York Times*, April 26, 1909, p. 8.

11. "Speculators blamed." *Washington Post*, October 6, 1909, p. 8.

12. "Plans for world's baseball series." *New York Times*, October 4, 1910, p. 9.

13. "To foil speculators." *New York Times*, October 8, 1910, p. 9.

14. "Ticket speculators caught." *New York Times*, October 15, 1911, p. 4.

15. "Harvest for speculators." *New York Times*, October 17, 1911, p. 2.

16. "Arrest ticket scalper." *Washington Post*, October 17, 1911, p. 2.

17. "Johnson and Brush on ticket scandal." *New York Times*, November 4, 1911, p. 9.

18. "Ticket scandal inquiry falls flat." *New York Times*, December 12, 1911, p. 13.

19. "Leagues war over ticket scandal." *New York Times*, December 13, 1911, p. 9.

20. "National League sidesteps trouble." *New York Times*, December 15, 1911, p. 14.

21. "No collusion in world's series." *New York Times*, January 6, 1912, p. 14.

22. "Pirates spring plans." *New York Times*, January 7, 1912, p. C7.

23. "Baseball rows caused by talk." *Los Angeles Times*, February 4, 1912, sec 7, p. 6.

24. "World Series opens in New York Oct. 8." *New York Times*, September 26, 1912, p. 9.

25. Ibid.

26. "Fans pay $250,000 to see first game." *New York Times*, October 9, 1912, p. 4.

27. "Seats are scarce." *New York Times*, October 7, 1913, p. 10.

28. "Players waiting for prize money." *New York Times*, October 13, 1913, p. 7.

29. "Seven fined for ticket scalping." *New York Times*, October 13, 1916, p. 8.

30. "Comiskey after scalpers." *New York Times*, September 29, 1917, p. 8.

31. "Acts to head off big show scalpers." *Los Angeles Times*, October 4, 1908, sec 6, p. 4.

32. "Trendall and Welsh." *Los Angeles Times*, October 4, 1908, sec 6, p. 4.

33. "Good order kept in throng outside." *New York Times*, March 26, 1916, p. 22.

Chapter 9

1. Ad. *New York Times*, November 3, 1929, p. X3.

2. Frank S. Nugent. "The screen." *New York Times*, October 16, 1937, p. 22.

3. "Specs and high prices." *Variety*, December 31, 1920, p. 12.

4. "Ticket speculating future." *Variety*, November 24, 1922, p. 9.

5. "Ticket scalpers." *Los Angeles Times*, February 29, 1924, p. A4.

6. "Declares war on scalpers." *Los Angeles Times*, March 5, 1924, p. B2.

7. Morrow Mayo. "Ticket-scalping fine art for brokers, worry for owners—but public pays." *Los Angeles Times*, March 29, 1925, p. C1.

8. Ibid., pp. C1, C3.

9. "Union official assails films." *Los Angeles Times*, June 9, 1926, p. 4.

10. "Equity to boycott ticket plan rebels." *New York Times*, January 8, 1930, p. 27.

11. "Moscow jails 2 theatre ticket speculators." *New York Times*, February 9, 1935, p. 1.

12. "Moscow jails ticket scalpers." *New York Times*, September 12, 1948, p. 30.

13. "Mexico seizes ticket scalpers." *New York Times*, April 8, 1945, p. 7.

14. "Russians sweep Czech movie fete prizes." *New York Times*, August 8, 1949, p. 11.

15. "Ticket speculation defended by Weber." *New York Times*, December 4, 1929, p. 33.

16. "In the dramatic mailbag." *New York Times*, December 8, 1929, p. X4.

17. Heywood Broun. "It seems to Heywood Broun." *Nation* 129 (December 18, 1929): 741.

18. Ibid.

19. Brock Pemberton. "Ticket, ticket, who's got the ticket?" *Theatre Arts Monthly* 17 (December, 1933): 945–7.

20. Ibid., p. 948.

21. Ibid., pp. 948–949.

22. Ibid., pp. 950–951.

23. Paul Gallico. "Ticket scalper curse thriving, unbridled." *Washington Post*, March 18, 1934, p. 19.

24. Paul Gallico. "Ticket speculators a worry; they're cats, we're mice." *Washington Post*, March 14, 1935, p. 21.

25. Warren P. Munsell, Jr. "Box-office bugaboo." *Theatre Arts* 32 (February, 1948): 1.

Chapter 10

1. "Ziegfeld fights brokers." *New York Times*, June 17, 1918, p. 11.

2. "Calls it a defeat for speculators." *New York Times*, June 25, 1918, p. 11.

3. Ibid.

4. Ibid.

5. "Ziegfeld routs the specs." *Washington Post*, June 30, 1918, p. SM2.

6. "Ziegfeld says he has won." *New York Times*, July 8, 1918, p. 9.

7. "Specs stuck with tickets are hard hit by epidemic." *Variety*, October 18, 1918, p. 12.

8. "The ticket specs." *Variety*, December 27, 1918, p. 12.

9. Ibid., p. 162.

10. "The cut-in of cut rates." *Variety*, December 27, 1918, p. 13.

11. Ibid.

12. Ibid.

13. "More than $250,000 in buys for this week's six new shows." *Variety*, October 10, 1919, p. 3.

14. "Chicago ticket deal." *Variety*, August 29, 1919, p. 3.

15. "Scalping system makes Chicago highest priced theatre town." *Variety*, October 3, 1919, p. 3.

16. Ibid.

17. "Mrs. Couthoui advertises." *Variety*, October 17, 1919, p. 3.

18. "Chicago's woman spec trying to scale theatres." *Variety*, August 19, 1921, pp. 1, 9.

19. "Chicago's scalping queen gives display of power." *Variety*, September 9, 1921, pp. 14, 60.

20. "The queen of the scalpers." *Variety*, December 30, 1921, p. 1.

21. Ibid.

22. "Couthoui agencies in Chicago barred by syndicate houses." *Variety*, December 29, 1922, p. 1.

23. "Tickets at box office bunk uncovered by Chicagoans." *Variety*, March 15, 1923, p. 11.

24. "Shuberts bar Couthoui's." *Variety*, August 17, 1927, p. 47.

25. "Theatre tickets again." *New York Times*, November 24, 1920, p. 15.

26. "Uncle Sam after ticket scalpers." *New York Times*, November 10, 1920, p. 3.

27. "Limit seats to brokers." *New York Times*, December 21, 1922, p. 22.

28. "Gyp ticket stands under current secret investigation." *Variety*, March 4, 1925, pp. 1, 13.

29. "Brokers to fight ticket speculator." *New York Times*, December 25, 1925, p. 22.

30. "Theatre prices up to $16.50 New Year's Eve." *New York Times*, December 30, 1926, p. 1.

31. "Scalping charged to Jacobs agency." *New York Times*, June 13, 1946, p. 12.

Chapter 11

1. "Chicago fights scalpers." *New York Times*, July 12, 1918, p. 11.

2. "Ticket spec evils rouse both Chicago and New York." *Variety*, December 13, 1918, p. 13.

3. "Illinois theatre spec bill signed by Governor Small." *Variety*, July 12, 1923, pp. 12, 16.

4. "Scalper ordinance out." *Variety*, April 2, 1920, p. 13.

5. "Ticket profiteering small; one fined $50." *Washington Post*, June 6, 1923, p. 2.

6. "Bills aim to stop ticket speculator." *Christian Science Monitor*, March 15, 1924, p. 3.

7. "Bay state court declares scalping can be prohibited." *New York Times*, April 24, 1924, p. 21.

8. "Ticket agency law effective." *Christian Science Monitor*, September 4, 1924, p. 3.

9. "Council votes new blow to scalpers." *Los Angeles Times*, May 27, 1941, p. 18.

10. "Scalper measure ruled invalid by Baltimore judge." *Washington Post*, October 29, 1948, p. B7.

11. "Swann goes slow in arresting idlers." *New York Times*, July 2, 1918, p. 24.

12. "Round up idlers in night raid." *New York Times*, July 7, 1918, p. 17.

13. "Calls ticket speculators." *New York Times*, September 22, 1918, p. 21.

14. "Says speculators get tickets for opera." *New York Times*, September 24, 1918, p. 6.

15. "Signs bill abolishing ticket speculators." *New York Times*, February 27, 1921, p. 6.

16. "Urge bills to check ticket speculators." *New York Times*, March 31, 1922, p. 11.

17. "Says law can't set ticket sale profit." *New York Times*, January 6, 1923, p. 23.

18. "Court upholds curb on ticket brokers." *New York Times*, December 1, 1923, p. 15.

19. Ibid.

20. Ibid.

21. "Banton opens war on ticket gougers." *New York Times*, December 5, 1923, pp. 1, 9.

22. "57 ticket brokers listed for arrest." *New York Times*, December 19, 1923, p. 26.

23. "Raid unlicensed ticket brokers." *New York Times*, December 21, 1923, p. 19.

24. "Anti-scalping law upheld on appeal." *New York Times*, February 20, 1924, p. 19.

25. "Sees ticket gouging." *New York Times*, February 28, 1924, p. 23.

26. "Anti-gouging law on theatre tickets declared invalid." *New York Times*, March 1, 1927, pp. 1, 12.

27. "Ticket case — and opinions." *Variety*, March 16, 1927, p. 37.

28. "The ticket scalper now free to scalp." *Literary Digest* 92 (March 19, 1927): 14.

29. "The Constitution shelters the ticket speculator." *New Republic* 50 (March 16, 1927): 84, 86.

30. "All kinds of suckers." *Saturday Evening Post* 200 (August 13, 1927): 26.

31. "More bills aimed at ticket agencies." *New York Times*, March 4, 1927, p. 23.

32. "Bloch bolsters bill to end ticket gouging." *New York Times*, February 22, 1928, p. 7.

33. "Senate passes ticket bill." *New York Times*, March 13, 1928, p. 3.

34. "State to add 10,000 to civil service." *New York Times*, April 22, 1940, p. 15.

35. "Praise ticket ordinance." *New York Times*, November 21, 1918, p. 8.

36. "Wants a limit on ticket profits." *New York Times*, November 30, 1918, p. 9.

37. "Tax ticket speculators." *New York Times*, December 18, 1918, p. 19.

38. "New York adopts measure to curb ticket brokers." *Variety*, December 20, 1918, p. 12.

39. Ibid.

40. "Ticket speculator ordinance signed." *New York Times*, December 29, 1918, p. 9.

41. "Ticket speculators fined." *New York Times*, March 1, 1919, p. 13.

42. "5 ticket brokers arrested in raid." *New York Times*, July 13, 1919, p. 7.

43. "Brokers in theatre tickets arrested." *New York Times*, November 8, 1919, p. 18.

44. "Swann blames managers." *New York Times*, November 9, 1919, p. 18.

45. "Theatre men urge war on speculator." *New York Times*, November 14, 1919, p. 13.

46. "Condemns scalping evil." *New York Times*, November 17, 1919, p. 27.

47. "Speculators again in danger." *New York Times*, November 17, 1919, p. 14.

48. "Ticket speculator gets limit of law; six months in workhouse for the next one." *New York Times*, November 18, 1919, p. 17.

49. "Fines ticket speculator." *New York Times*, November 30, 1919, p. 12.

50. "Ticket ordinance killed by court." *New York Times*, January 6, 1919, p. 1.

51. "Specs can charge any price if they keep off sidewalk." *Variety*, January 9, 1920, p. 7.

52. "Ticket speculator upheld." *New York Times*, January 28, 1920, p. 13.

53. "Whalen opens war on ticket scalpers." *New York Times*, February 1, 1929, p. 19.

54. "Ticket scalpers jailed." *New York Times*, February 2, 1929, p. 36.

55. "43 seized near circus." *New York Times*, April 5, 1934, p. 25.

56. "Bars ticket speculators." *New York Times*, August 10, 1937, p. 22.

57. "New rules curb ticket scalpers." *New York Times*, July 4, 1940, p. 17.

58. "Moss on new tack against scalpers." *New York Times*, December 22, 1943, p. 19.

59. "Broadway's best." *Business Week*, January 13, 1945, pp. 22, 24.

60. "Raids ticket speculators." *New York Times*, May 24, 1927, p. 27.

61. "New tax regulations hit ticket scalpers." *New York Times*, November 11, 1936, p. 24.

Chapter 12

1. "Republicans in Washington to assist Bloom's spec bill." *Variety*, January 31, 1924, p. 10.

2. "Sees theatre men forced to graft." *New York Times*, July 8, 1927, p. 8.

3. Ibid.

4. Ibid.

5. "Trade board aids in ticket inquiry." *New York Times*, July 10, 1927, p. 19.

6. "Sees play in grip of ticket brokers." *New York Times*, July 15, 1927, p. 19.

7. "Shuberts' dealings with ticket men and treasurers detailed by Long." *Variety*, July 20, 1927, p. 37.

8. "Deep stuff in ticket inquiry; Ziegfeld blames forced buys." *Variety*, July 27, 1927, p. 43.

9. Ibid.

10. "Theater ticket graft in New York." *Literary Digest* 94 (July 30, 1927): 11.

11. "Theatre ticket bamboozle." *Variety*, September 21, 1927, p. 46.

12. "Jail and $5,000 fine for ticket gouger." *New York Times*, October 12, 1927, p. 29.

13. "Ticket agents lose appeal in test case." *New York Times*, December 13, 1927, p. 31.

14. "Again B'way ticket gyps." *Variety*, October 12, 1927, pp. 1, 41.

15. "Tuttle replies to Brady." *New York Times*, January 2, 1929, p. 27.

16. "New drive begins on ticket gougers." *New York Times*, May 4, 1929, pp. 1, 35.

17. "Scalper holding 18 *South Pacific* tickets." *New York Times*, May 10, 1949, p. 27.

18. Murray Schumach. "On the trail of the specs." *New York Times*, May 15, 1949, p. X3.

19. "*South Pacific* theatre, facing license loss, ousts treasurer." *New York Times*, May 19, 1949, pp. 1, 34.

20. "Murtagh to hear Lee Shubert today." *New York Times*, May 20, 1949, p. 23.

21. Murray Schumach. "*Kiss Me, Kate* date sought; broker faces license loss." *New York Times*, May 23, 1949, pp. 1, 50.

22. "2d broker faces lose of license." *New York Times*, May 25, 1949, p. 31.

23. "Brokers map plan to end ticket evil." *New York Times*, May 28, 1949, p. 17.

24. "Pearl again balks on theatre data." *New York Times*, June 2, 1949, p. 29.

25. "Shubert is vague on ticket sales." *New York Times*, June 3, 1949, p. 22.

26. Richard Maney. "Advice to those who want two on the aisle." *New York Times*, June 5, 1949, p. SM19.

27. Murray Schumach. "Ticket men meet; one loses licenses." *New York Times*, June 8, 1949, p. 31.

28. Ibid.

29. "2d ticket agency loses its license." *New York Times*, June 10, 1949, p. 29.

30. "Producers launch drive on scalping." *New York Times*, June 10, 1949, p. 33.

31. "9 hotels accused in ticket inquiry." *New York Times*, June 15, 1949, p. 39.
32. Murray Schumach. "Ticket agency ban asked by Murtagh." *New York Times*, June 18, 1949, p. 1.
33. "Every broker now in Murtagh's sights." *New York Times*, June 28, 1949, p. 29.
34. Robert Sylvester. "Broadway ticket scandal." *Collier's* 124 (July 2, 1949): 26, 64.
35. "Ban on 8 brokers asked by Murtagh." *New York Times*, July 13, 1949, p. 29.
36. "Ticket men ask Murtagh ouster." *New York Times*, July 20, 1949, p. 30.
37. "Court upholds city in revoking license." *New York Times*, July 21, 1949, p. 5.
38. "2 more ticket men out." *New York Times*, October 8, 1949, p. 8.
39. "Mayor pledges aid to city's theatres." *New York Times*, September 2, 1949, p. 14.
40. "O'Dwyer's postscript to a probe." *New York Times*, September 11, 1949, p. X1.
41. Murray Schumach. "Ticket sale code." *New York Times*, March 5, 1950, p. 99.
42. Ibid.

Chapter 13

1. "Producing managers will take action against speculating evil." *Variety*, November 7, 1919, p. 3.
2. "Managers striving to regulate ticket speculating gypping." *Variety*, November 12, 1920, p. 10.
3. "Belasco opens war on speculators." *New York Times*, February 13, 1921, p. 16.
4. Ibid.
5. "Ziegfeld attacks new agency plan." *New York Times*, December 16, 1922, p. 23.
6. "Theatres modify ticket agency plan." *New York Times*, April 11, 1923, p. 16.
7. "Keith's Palace starts drive against ticket speculators." *Variety*, April 5, 1923, p. 1.
8. "Banton goes after ticket gougers." *New York Times*, June 18, 1924, p. 22.
9. "Theater wars on scalper." *Los Angeles Times*, March 10, 1925, p. A2.
10. Ibid.
11. "War launched on scalpers." *Los Angeles Times*, May 27, 1930, p. A5.
12. Ibid.
13. "Smith asks public to aid ticket plan." *New York Times*, April 17, 1930, p. 26.
14. "Defends plan to curb ticket speculators." *New York Times*, April 20, 1930, p. 2.
15. "7 producers assail theatre ticket plan." *New York Times*, April 23, 1930, p. 31.
16. "Ziegfeld attacks plan again." *New York Times*, June 21, 1930, p. 20.
17. "Postal ticket plan is called a success." *New York Times*, November 11, 1930, p. 1.

18. "Will close affairs of theatre league." *New York Times*, January 16, 1931, p. 7.
19. "Theatre pact bans ticket speculation." *New York Times*, July 27, 1938, pp. 1, 15.
20. "Theatre ticket scalping code is revised giving new curbs and better distribution." *New York Times*, November 15, 1939, p. 25.
21. "The world and the theatre." *Theatre Arts Monthly* 18 (December, 1934): 887–888.
22. "Opera opens drive on scalpers who sell tickets on sidewalks." *New York Times*, March 13, 1937, p. 21.
23. George Jean Nathan. "That ticket mess." *Newsweek* 14 (August 28, 1939): 24.
24. "Trouble in Shubert offices evident from resignations." *Variety*, December 19, 1919, p. 14.
25. "Keith war on specs causes Palace box office shake-up." *Variety*, April 9, 1920, p. 6.
26. "Scalpers got 3,500 tickets weekly." *Variety*, July 30, 1920, p. 4.
27. "The cure for ticket speculating." *Variety*, November 19, 1920, p. 9.
28. "Huge ticket graft paid, says Brady." *New York Times*, January 27, 1924, p. 19.
29. John F. Wharton. "Wharton looks at scalping." *New York Times*, March 18, 1962, p. 3.
30. "Equity hits inequity." *Literary Digest* 103 (December 7, 1929): 20.
31. "$365,000 in graft on theatre tickets charged to police." *New York Times*, December 3, 1930, p. 1.

Chapter 14

1. "Recommends expulsion for student ticket speculators." *New York Times*, November 18, 1920, p. 22.
2. "Few ticket speculators." *New York Times*, December 9, 1921, p. 24.
3. "Ticket scalpers face rocky road." *New York Times*, November 2, 1922, p. 24.
4. "Profiteering in Army-Navy game tickets as in theatre seats, agency canvas shows." *New York Times*, November 23, 1923, p. 1.
5. "Scalpers trapped, told to leave Annapolis." *Washington Post*, November 19, 1926, p. 13.
6. "Stanford student ticket scalpers under fire." *Los Angeles Times*, November 21, 1929, pp. A13, A15.
7. "Scores taken in police drive on ticket scalpers." *Los Angeles Times*, December 11, 1932, p. 19.
8. Allison Danzig. "102,000, East's largest football crowd, will see Army-Navy clash today." *New York Times*, November 28, 1936, p. 9.
9. "Md. legislator plans bill to ban scalp-

ing." *Washington Post*, December 3, 1944, p. M3.

10. "Inquiry promised on ticket scalping." *New York Times*, November 2, 1945, p. 14.

11. "Col. Jones says Army and Navy strive to avert tickets scalping." *New York Times*, November 19, 1945, p. 16.

12. "Ticket disgrace hit by service bulletin." *New York Times*, November 30, 1946, p. 24.

13. "Thirteen fined as scalpers." *Los Angeles Times*, November 25, 1947, p. 2.

14. "Judge finds Navy lax in ticket sale." *New York Times*, October 29, 1948, p. 32.

15. "New plan of selling." *New York Times*, December 22, 1949, p. 32.

16. "Police arrest eight for ticket scalping." *Washington Post*, December 9, 1940, pp. 17, 19.

17. "Illegal grid ticket sales cost man $50." *Washington Post*, November 23, 1943, p. B1.

18. "Ticket speculators active at school football game." *New York Times*, November 30, 1928, p. 31.

19. "Demand $100 for seats." *New York Times*, October 1, 1919, p. 13.

20. "Arrest alleged scalpers." *New York Times*, October 4, 1919, p. 14.

21. "Ebbets after scalpers." *New York Times*, September 28, 1920, p. 20

22. "Cleveland's mayor asks fans' support." *New York Times*, October 8, 1920, p. 23.

23. "Scalpers reap profit." *New York Times*, October 10, 1920, p. 19.

24. "Arrest Marquard for speculating." *New York Times*, October 10, 1920, p. 1.

25. "Marquard's days with Robins ended." *New York Times*, October 13, 1920, p. 21.

26. "Scalpers driven from park." *New York Times*, October 1, 1925, p. 24.

27. "If Dreyfuss can raise prices, scalpers can, says magistrate." *New York Times*, October 8, 1927, p. 9.

28. "Scalpers' tickets barred at the park." *New York Times*, October 12, 1929, p. 19.

29. "Eleven ticket speculators get summonses from revenue agents outside Ebbets Field." *New York Times*, May 12, 1930, p. 1.

30. "Questions ticket sellers." *New York Times*, May 13, 1930, p. 12.

31. "18 scalpers arrested." *New York Times*, October 3, 1930, p. 32.

32. "Ticket scalpers holding sack." *Los Angeles Times*, October 3, 1935, p. A9.

33. "Ticket speculators held." *New York Times*, May 31, 1940, p. 25.

34. "Ticket scalper out $26." *New York Times*, September 8, 1941, p. 17.

35. "Landis to urge elimination of ticket scalping." *Christian Science Monitor*, October 3, 1942, p. 14.

36. "Fans have court friend." *New York Times*, October 4, 1947, p. 19.

37. "Baseball ticket scalper is fined $520 in Boston." *New York Times*, September 10, 1948, p. 28.

38. "To fight scalpers of boxing tickets." *New York Times*, December 6, 1920, p. 22.

39. "Ringside tickets are sold for $150." *New York Times*, September 13, 1923, p. 17.

40. "Mob fights for tickets." *New York Times*, September 15, 1923, pp. 1–2.

41. "Charges Rickard aided speculator." *New York Times*, February 20, 1924, p. 15.

42. "Baxter digs deep for fake tickets." *Los Angeles Times*, September 12, 1924, p. 13.

43. "Counterfeit tickets printed for bout here." *Los Angeles Times*, April 17, 1936, p. A11.

44. "Cops nab Jacobs' tickets scalpers." *Los Angeles Times*, June 7, 1946, p. A9.

45. Arthur Daley. "Sports of the Times." *New York Times*, May 10, 1949, p. 34.

46. "Wars on speculators." *New York Times*, December 7, 1928, p. 35.

47. "Students beat scalpers." *New York Times*, February 28, 1930, p. 30.

48. "Daro spurns offer of ticket scalper." *Los Angeles Times*, September 3, 1924, p. B3.

49. "Five tennis match ticket scalpers given jail terms." *Los Angeles Times*, February 18, 1937, p. A2.

50. "11 seized as scalpers." *New York Times*, February 11, 1945, p. 41.

51. "Fined $25 for ticket scalping." *New York Times*, March 21, 1946, p. 26.

Chapter 15

1. "Is it true you can't get tickets for the New York theatres?" *Good Housekeeping* 143 (October, 1956): 53.

2. Ibid.

3. "John McBride, 84, of ticket agency." *New York Times*, November 29, 1961, p. 41.

4. Austin C. Wehrwein. "Chicagoans recall Jack Ruby as ticket scalper and chiseler." *New York Times*, November 25, 1963, p. 12.

5. John F. Wharton. "Wharton looks at scalping." *New York Times*, March 18, 1962, pp. 1, 3.

6. "Moscow ticket scalping a lucrative business." *New York Times*, October 25, 1981, p. 21.

7. John Corry. "Some theater people say that skimming profits and the scalping of tickets persist on Broadway." *New York Times*, November 23, 1980, p. 66.

8. Ibid.

9. Ibid.

10. Ibid.

11. Ibid.

12. Jeremy Gerard. "*Phantom* scalpers' bonanza." *New York Times*, January 20, 1988, p. C15.

13. Ibid.

14. Jesse McKinley. "For the asking, a $480 seat." *New York Times*, October 26, 2001, p. A1.

15. Ibid., pp. A1, D11.

16. John Tierney. "Tickets? Supply meets demand on sidewalk." *New York Times*, December 26, 1992, pp. 1, 24.

17. Ibid.

18. Janina de Guzman. "Ticket scalpers making enemies of some White House tourists." *Washington Post*, August 2, 1997, p. B1.

Chapter 16

1. "Scalpers given freedom to peddle ducats." *Los Angeles Times*, December 19, 1958, p. 18.

2. Robert Blanchard. "War declared on ticket scalpers." *Los Angeles Times*, February 7, 1961, p. C1.

3. "City council backs Unruh scalping bill." *Los Angeles Times*, February 8, 1961, p. C6.

4. Art Ryon. "Nicholas says box office sellers helping scalpers." *Los Angeles Times*, February 9, 1961, pp. C1, C3.

5. "Ticket scalping now illegal at Coliseum." *Los Angeles Times*, May 24, 1961, p. C1.

6. "City-wide ban slated on scalping." *Los Angeles Times*, September 13, 1961, p. 26.

7. "Ban on ticket scalping now law by default." *Los Angeles Times*, November 16, 1981, p. A3.

8. "Ticket-scalping still no crime for Kentuckians." *Washington Post*, February 19, 1966, p. C1.

9. Albert J. Parisi. "New Jersey journal." *New York Times*, February 5, 1984, p. NJ3.

10. Brett Pulley. "Final four is not the final word on scalping experiment." *New York Times*, March 30, 1996, pp. 25, 29.

11. Rob Karwath. "Legislator, sports teams urge crackdown on ticket scalpers." *Chicago Tribune*, June 20, 1990, Chicagoland section, p. 6.

12. Ibid.

13. "Producers upset by ticket ruling." *New York Times*, April 27, 1957, p. 33.

14. "Theatre ruling is lifted by city." *New York Times*, May 6, 1957, p. 24.

15. Arthur Gelb. "City seeks to end ticket scalping." *New York Times*, February 9, 1962, pp. 29, 60.

16. Milton Esterow. "Broadway quiet on Dowling plan." *New York Times*, February 10, 1962, p. 14.

17. Arthur Gelb. "Dowling shocked by ticket clause." *New York Times*, February 21, 1962, pp. 47, 57.

18. "Writer defends clause on tickets." *New York Times*, February 22, 1962, p. 49.

19. Louis Calta. "Theatre leaders discuss tickets." *New York Times*, May 25, 1962, p. 29.

20. "Broadway ticket scalper fined $500 on two charges." *New York Times*, December 19, 1964, p. 24.

21. "Father and son fined for ticket overcharging." *New York Times*, February 11, 1965, p. 45.

22. "State's high court annuls city ruling on ticket scalping." *New York Times*, May 15, 1969, p. 43.

23. "Scalper fined $250 and jailed 30 days." *New York Times*, June 27, 1972, p. 49.

24. Charles Mahtesian. "Two on the aisle?" *Governing* 8 (October, 1994): 25.

25. Ibid.

26. Ibid.

27. William H. Honan. "Anti-scalping law: mixed impact likely." *New York Times*, August 8, 1991, p. C13.

28. Clifford J. Levy. "A new deal for brokers of tickets?" *New York Times*, May 1, 1995, pp. B1, B5.

29. Raymond Hernandez. "Albany legislature votes to reinstate law on ticket scalping for one year." *New York Times*, September 23, 1997, p. B10.

30. Raymond Hernandez. "Albany bill passed to extend current ticket-scaling law." *New York Times*, June 2, 1999, p. B6.

31. Jayson Blair. "Attorney General favors elimination of state ticket-scalping law." *New York Times*, April 22, 2001, p. 38.

32. "New state law on ticket scalping." *New York Times*, June 7, 2001, p. B6.

33. Howard Taubman. "Time for tax repeal." *New York Times*, December 6, 1964, p. X5.

Chapter 17

1. "City investigates ticket-scalping." *New York Times*, May 2, 1956, p. 24.

2. "Ticket sale inquiry on." *New York Times*, May 25, 1956, p. 27.

3. Murray Schumach. "Who's got the tickets?" *New York Times*, April 14, 1957, pp. X1, X3.

4. Ibid.

5. Ibid.

6. Milton Esterow. "Ticket scalping netting millions to be bared at theater inquiry." *New York Times*, December 2, 1963, pp. 1, 44.

7. Louis Calta. "Broadway split on ticket inquiry." *New York Times*, December 3, 1963, p. 51.

8. "Scalpers' profit on shows put at $10 million." *New York Times*, December 11, 1963, pp. 1, 54.

9. Ibid.

10. Ibid.

11. "Scalpers at work." *New York Times*, December 15, 1963, p. 17.

12. "Scalpers scalped." *Newsweek* 62 (December 23, 1963): 46.

13. Sydney H. Schanberg. "Indictments sought by Hogan's office in theater inquiry." *New York Times*, December 21, 1963, pp. 1, 17.

14. Sydney H. Schanberg. "More are silent at ticket inquiry." *New York Times*, December 24, 1963, p. 7.

15. Sydney H. Schanberg. "State is watching *Dolly* box office." *New York Times*, January 24, 1964, p. 29.

16. Sydney H. Schanberg. "Jersey is joining drive on scalping." *New York Times*, February 1, 1964, p. 12.

17. Sydney H. Schanberg. "Theater inquiry sifts Weiss death." *New York Times*, February 12, 1964, p. 30.

18. Milton Esterow. "Lefkowitz urges $25 for shows." *New York Times*, June 10, 1964, pp. 1, 51.

19. Milton Esterow. "State is pressing fight on scalping." *New York Times*, August 29, 1964, p. 23.

20. Jack Roth. "2 Broadway ticket brokers held as scalpers." *New York Times*, November 10, 1964, p. 55.

21. Milton Esterow. "Ice bill passage gets mixed notice." *New York Times*, May 20, 1965, p. 53.

22. Milton Esterow. "Lefkowitz opens new hunt for ice." *New York Times*, March 22, 1966, p. 33.

23. Frank Rich. "An inspector calls." *New York Times*, May 1, 1994, p. E17.

24. Ian Fisher. "Where do tickets go?" *New York Times*, May 8, 1994, p. 32.

25. John Tierney. "Scalping, fair and square." *New York Times*, June 26, 1994, p. SM16.

26. "Hotel worker held in ticket scalping." *New York Times*, August 11, 1994, p. B7.

27. Thomas J. Lueck. "Inquiry finds ticket scalping pervasive." *New York Times*, August 17, 1994, p. B3.

28. "2 companies settle in ticket inquiry." *New York Times*, December 23, 1994, p. C35.

29. Ralph Blumenthal. "Investigation finds complex network of ticket scalping." *New York Times*, December 22, 1994, pp. C7, C12.

30. Ibid.

31. "Broadway robbery." *New York Times*, March 25, 1995, p. 22.

32. Peter Applebome. "State presses inquiry into corruption in Broadway ticket sales." *New York Times*, July 28, 1998, pp. E1, E6.

33. Terry Pristin. "Inquiry on ticket scalping at Tennis Center's box office." *New York Times*, August 29, 1998, p. B2.

34. "Shubert organization is fined in ticket inquiry." *New York Times*, September 14, 1998, p. B4.

Chapter 18

1. Neil Amdur. "Ticket scalpers put on a big blitz at Ohio State." *New York Times*, November 19, 1970, p. 59.

2. "Scalping brings ban." *New York Times*, December 16, 1981, p. B11.

3. Allen Barra. "Scoring for dollars." *New York Times*, October 22, 1989, p. BR29.

4. "Ticket scalping lands football fan in jail." *Los Angeles Times*, September 25, 1954, p. B2.

5. Frank Litsky. "Super Bowl game boon to business." *New York Times*, January 12, 1969, p. S2.

6. "Redskins try to stymie scalpers." *Washington Post*, December 19, 1972, p. D1.

7. "Miami set for Super gold week." *New York Times*, January 25, 1979, p. C8.

8. William N. Wallace. "Ram owner, Rozelle deny bowl scalping." *New York Times*, December 11, 1980, p. B18.

9. Dave Anderson. "Rozelle-Davis war." *New York Times*, December 21, 1980, p. S7.

10. William Nack and Robert Sullivan. "Football's little bighorn?" *Sports Illustrated* 54 (January 26, 1981): 33.

11. Ibid., pp. 33–34.

12. Ibid., pp. 34–36.

13. Ibid., p. 33.

14. Murray Chass. "$40 Super Bowl tickets go legally for $500." *New York Times*, January 15, 1981, pp. D19, D22.

15. Ibid.

16. "Cowboy players, staff are warned on scalping." *New York Times*, January 18, 1981, p. S9.

17. "N.F.L. concerned by scalping." *New York Times*, January 17, 1985, p. B10.

18. Ted Rohrlich. "Frontiere agrees to plead guilty in ticket scalping." *Los Angeles Times*, October 21, 1986, p. 1.

19. Ted Rohrlich. "Prosecutors detail plot of ticket scalping plan." *Los Angeles Times*, December 2, 1986, sec 2, p. 3.

20. Ibid.

21. Ibid.

22. Michael Janofsky. "N.F.L. to review 1980 ticket scalping." *New York Times*, December 10, 1986, p. D31.

23. Eugene Kiely. "Tickets taken off eBay." *Dallas Morning News,* January 6, 2001, p. 1B.

24. Sam Farmer. "NFL is investigating Vikings' coach Tice." *Los Angeles Times,* March 10, 2005, p. D3; "Tice fined for scalping." *Times Colonist* (Victoria, BC), July 1, 2005, p. C9.

25. "9 arrested in scalping." *New York Times,* October 4, 1953, p. S2; "Scalping hearing put off." *New York Times,* October 6, 1953, p. 37.

26. "16 ticket scalpers arrested." *New York Times,* July 11, 1957, p. 30.

27. "Trio freed in case of ticket scalping." *Los Angeles Times,* August 5, 1958, p. 4.

28. "U.S. accuses 13 in ticket scalping." *Los Angeles Times,* July 8, 1960, p. B1.

29. Milton Esterow. "Subpoenas given in ticket inquiry." *New York Times,* December 6, 1963, p. 38.

30. "Ticket scalpers arrested at Atlanta." *New York Times,* July 27, 1972, p. 24.

31. David Ferrell. "Ticket tricks." *Los Angeles Times,* May 27, 1994, p. B1.

32. Kit R. Roane. "More arrests at stadium in scalping crackdown." *New York Times,* October 1, 1998, p. B6.

33. Terry Pristin. "State sues 2 brokers accused of scalping Yankee tickets." *New York Times,* October 17, 1998, p. B3.

34. Steve Bailey. "Red Sox crack down on scalping." *Boston Globe,* September 27, 2004, p. D1.

35. Eugene Nixon. "Attempted fix reveals practice of ticket scalping by players." *Los Angeles Times,* March 7, 1951, p. C3.

36. Dave Sell. "Valvano out of running as UCLA coach." *Washington Post,* April 3, 1988, p. C12.

37. Brett Pulley. "Final four is not the final word on scalping experiment." *New York Times,* March 30, 1996, pp. 25, 29.

38. Tiffany Kjos. "Carefree scalpers sell tickets with zeal." *Arizona Daily Star,* March 31, 2001, p. A1.

39. "Scalping goes legit in Phoenix experiment." *Miami Herald,* March 2, 1995.

40. Gerald Eskenazi. "Scalpers: shadowy profiteers in sports." *New York Times,* December 28, 1970, p. 1.

41. Ibid., p. 49.

42. Ibid.

43. Gerald Eskenazi. "A $1,000-a-seat bid is rejected." *New York Times,* March 9, 1971, p. 30.

44. Gerald Eskenazi. "Ticket scalping at Garden is big business." *New York Times,* April 5, 1972, p. 55.

45. Francis X. Clines. "Sports ticket scalpers get millions, state says." *New York Times,* June 8, 1973, pp. 1, 50.

46. Roy Blout Jr. "Hey, I got the ducks." *Sports Illustrated* 50 (February 5, 1979): 32–34.

47. Ibid., p. 34.

48. Brian Crow. "Don't scalp us. We'll scalp you." *Business Week,* April 19, 2004, p. 44.

Chapter 19

1. "4 charged with scalping tickets at Sinatra concert." *New York Times,* July 10, 1965, p. 14.

2. Les Ledbetter. "Rock fans set for Stones to roll in." *New York Times,* July 13, 1972, p. 28.

3. Anna Quindlen. "About New York." *New York Times,* November 11, 1981, p. B4.

4. "Policeman arrested in theft of a ticket for Stones concert." *New York Times,* November 14, 1981, p. 26.

5. Salley Rayl. "Drive to stop ticket scalping under way in California." *Rolling Stone,* May 31, 1979, p. 10.

6. Steve Pond. "Bruce Springsteen takes on scalpers, wins bootleg suit." *Rolling Stone,* February 5, 1981, p. 48.

7. Larry Nager. "America's largest ticket scalper." *Rolling Stone,* May 9, 1985, pp. 9, 78.

8. Michael Goldberg. "Scalped: why you can't get good concert seats." *Rolling Stone,* November 17, 1988, p. 41.

9. Ibid.

10. Michael Goldberg. "Ticket rip-off." *Rolling Stone,* November 1, 1990, p. 21.

11. Ibid.

12. Ibid., p. 22.

13. Ibid.

14. Ibid., pp. 22, 40.

15. Ibid., pp. 40–41.

16. Ibid.

17. Sheila Rule. "Gold circle strategy is bid to scalp scalpers." *New York Times,* December 15, 1993, p. C19.

18. Eric Boehlert. "Rick & roll ticket masters." *Rolling Stone,* March 7, 1996, p. 12.

19. Ibid., p. 13.

20. "In move to discourage scalping, rock band won't honor tickets." *New York Times,* July 2, 1996, p. B5.

21. "School gets scholarship after a scalping scandal." *New York Times,* August 7, 1996, p. C15.

22. Eric Boehlert. "Scalping the scalpers." *Rolling Stone,* August 7, 1997, p. 28.

23. Ibid.

Bibliography

"Acts to head off big show scalpers." *Los Angeles Times*, October 4, 1917, p. 5.

Ad. *New York Times*, October 30, 1858, p. 3.

Ad. *New York Times*, September 11, 1860, p. 7.

Ad. *New York Times*, November 3, 1929, p. X3.

"Again B'way ticket gyps." *Variety*, October 12, 1927, pp. 1, 41.

"The Albany legislators." *New York Times*, January 24, 1884, p. 2.

"Aldermen insincere theatre man says." *New York Times*, February 4, 1910, p. 7.

"Aldermen not to blame." *New York Times*, January 19, 1909, p. 4.

"All about licenses." *New York Times*, January 9, 1885, p. 8.

"All kinds of suckers." *Saturday Evening Post* 200 (August 13, 1927): 26.

"Alter theatre ticket plan." *New York Times*, December 3, 1909, p. 8.

Amdur, Neil. "Ticket scalpers put on a big blitz at Ohio State." *New York Times*, November 19, 1970, p. 59.

"Amusements." *New York Times*, September 8, 1856, p. 1.

"Amusements." *New York Times*, November 9, 1869, p. 5.

Anderson, Dave. "Rozelle-Davis war." *New York Times*, December 21, 1980, p. S7.

"Annoyed by speculators." *New York Times*, December 6, 1885, p. 2.

"Anti-gouging law on theatre tickets declared invalid." *New York Times*, March 1, 1927, pp. 1, 12.

"Anti-scalping law upheld on appeal." *New York Times*, February 20, 1924, p. 19.

Applebome, Peter. "State presses inquiry into corruption in Broadway ticket sales." *New York Times*, July 28, 1998, pp. E1, E6.

"The Arion out $7,000." *New York Times*, February 19, 1895, p. 13.

"Army and Navy ticket scandal." *New York Times*, November 21, 1911, p. 10.

"Arrest alleged scalpers." *New York Times*, October 4, 1919, p. 14.

"Arrest Marquard for speculating." *New York Times*, October 10, 1920, p. 1.

"Arrest theatre managers." *New York Times*, March 27, 1907, p. 9.

"Arrest ticket scalper." *Washington Post*, October 17, 1911, p. 2.

"Arrest ticket vendors." *New York Times*, January 28, 1909, p. 3.

"Arrest twelve speculators." *New York Times*, February 21, 1910, p. 1.

Bailey, Steve. "Red Sox crack down on scalping." *Boston Globe*, September 22, 2004, p. D1.

"Ban on 8 brokers asked by Murtagh." *New York Times*, July 13, 1949, p. 29.

"Ban on ticket scalping now law by default." *Los Angeles Times*, November 16, 1961, p. A3.

"Banton goes after ticket gougers." *New York Times*, June 18, 1924, p. 22.

"Banton opens war on ticket gougers." *New York Times*, December 5, 1923, pp. 1, 9.

Barra, Allen. "Scoring for dollars." *New York Times*, October 22, 1989, p. BR29.

"Bars ticket speculators." *New York Times*, August 10, 1937, p. 22.

"Baseball rows caused by talk." *Los Angeles Times*, February 4, 1912, sec 7, p. 6.
"Baseball ticket scalper is fined $520 in Boston." *New York Times*, September 10, 1948, p. 28.
"Baxter digs deep for fake tickets." *Los Angeles Times*, September 12, 1924, p. 13.
"Bayreuth ticket pledge." *New York Times*, March 31, 1912, p. C3.
"Bay state court declares scalping can be prohibited." *New York Times*, April 24, 1924, p. 21.
"Belasco opens war on speculators." *New York Times*, February 13, 1921, p. 16.
"The Bernhardt tickets sold." *New York Times*, October 2, 1880, p. 10.
"Bills aim to stop ticket speculator." *Christian Science Monitor*, March 15, 1924, p. 3.
"Blacklist invoked in speculator war." *New York Times*, February 17, 1910, p. 7.
Blair, Jayson. "Attorney General favors elimination of state ticket-scalping law." *New York Times*, April 22, 2001, p. 38.
Blanchard, Robert. "War declared on ticket scalpers." *Los Angeles Times*, February 7, 1961, p. C1.
Bloat, Roy Jr. "Hey, I got the ducks." *Sports Illustrated* 50 (February 5, 1979): 32–35.
"Bloch bolsters bill to end ticket gouging." *New York Times*, February 22, 1928, p. 7.
Blumenthal, Ralph. "Investigation finds complex network of ticket scalping." *New York Times*, December 22, 1994, pp. C7, C12.
Boehlert, Eric. "Rock & roll ticket masters." *Rolling Stone*, March 7, 1996, pp. 12–13.
Boehlert, Eric. "Scalping the scalpers." *Rolling Stone*, August 7, 1997, p. 28.
"The Booth-Barrett season." *New York Times*, September 29, 1887, p. 1.
"Broadway robbery." *New York Times*, March 25, 1995, p. 22.
"Broadway ticket scalper fined $500 on two charges." *New York Times*, December 19, 1964, p. 24.
"Broadway's best." *Business Week*, January 13, 1945, pp. 22, 24.
"Brokers in theatre tickets arrested." *New York Times*, November 8, 1919, p. 18.
"Brokers map plan to end ticket evil." *New York Times*, May 28, 1949, p. 17.
"Brokers to fight ticket speculator." *New York Times*, December 25, 1925, p. 22.
Broun, Heywood. "It seems to Heywood Broun." *Nation* 129 (December 18, 1929): 741.
"Calls it a defeat for speculators." *New York Times*, June 25, 1918, p. 11.
"Calls ticket speculators." *New York Times*, September 22, 1918, p. 21.
Calta, Louis. "Broadway split on ticket inquiry." *New York Times*, December 3, 1963, p. 51.
Calta, Louis. "Theatre leaders discuss tickets." *New York Times*, May 25, 1962, p. 29.
"A campaign with mysteries." *New York Times*, September 16, 1908, p. 8.
"Can revoke theatre tickets." *New York Times*, April 26, 1902, p. 8.
"A carnival of crime." *New York Times*, November 29, 1876, p. 4.
"Censure Chicago club." *New York Times*, December 19, 1908, p. 10.
"A chance to end an abuse." *New York Times*, January 24, 1907, p. 8.
"Charges Rickard aided speculator." *New York Times*, February 20, 1924, p. 15.
Chass, Murray. "$40 Super bowl tickets go legally for $500." *New York Times*, January 15, 1981, pp. D19, D22.
"Chicago fights scalpers." *New York Times*, July 12, 1918, p. 11.
"Chicago managers see joker in latest anti-scalping law." *Variety*, January 7, 1916, p. 11.
"Chicago opera hurt by ticket scalping." *New York Times*, November 23, 1911, p. 11.
"Chicago theater notes." *Christian Science Monitor*, January 11, 1916, p. 4.
"Chicago ticket deal." *Variety*, August 29, 1919, p. 3.
"Chicago's scalping queen gives display of power." *Variety*, September 9, 1921, pp. 14, 60.
"Chicago's woman spec trying to scale theatres." *Variety*, August 19, 1921, pp. 1, 9.
"The circus." *New York Times*, April 5, 1908, p. SM11.
"Circus bars speculators." *New York Times*, May 20, 1906, p. 16.
"Circus-ticket scalping." *Los Angeles Times*, September 26, 1905, sec 2, p. 10.
"Circus war on speculators." *New York Times*, April 5, 1903, p. 11.
"City council backs Unruh scalping bill." *Los Angeles Times*, February 8, 1961, p. C6.
"City investigates ticket-scalping." *New York Times*, May 2, 1956, p. 24.
"City-wide ban slated on scalping." *Los Angeles Times*, September 13, 1961, p. 26.

"Cleveland's mayor asks fans' support." *New York Times*, October 8, 1920, p. 23.

Clines, Francis X. "Sports ticket scalpers get millions, state says." *New York Times*, June 8, 1973, pp. 1, 50.

"Col. Jones says Army and Navy strive to avert ticket scalping." *New York Times*, November 19, 1945, p. 16.

"Comiskey after scalpers." *New York Times*, September 29, 1917, p. 8.

"Condemns scalping evil." *New York Times*, November 17, 1919, p. 27.

"Conreid and speculators." *New York Times*, March 9, 1906, p. 8.

"Conreid to fight ticket speculators." *New York Times*, February 24, 1904, p. 9.

"The Constitution shelters the ticket speculator." *New Republic* 50 (March 16, 1927): 84–86.

"Cops nab Jacobs' ticket scalpers." *Los Angeles Times*, June 7, 1946, p. A9.

"A coroner's jury exonerates Hyde." *New York Times*, March 28, 1890, p. 3.

Corry, John. "Some theater people say that skimming profits and the scalping of tickets persist on Broadway." *New York Times*, November 23, 1980, p. 66.

"Council votes new blow to scalpers." *Los Angeles Times*, May 27, 1941, p. 18.

"Counterfeit tickets printed for bout here." *Los Angeles Times*, April 17, 1936, p. A11.

"Court upholds city in revoking license." *New York Times*, July 21, 1949, p. 5.

"Court upholds curb on ticket brokers." *New York Times*, December 1, 1923, p. 15.

"Couthoui agencies in Chicago barred by syndicate houses." *Variety*, December 29, 1922, p. 1.

"Cowboy players, staff are warned on scalping." *New York Times*, January 18, 1981, p. S9.

Crow, Brian. "Don't scalp us. We'll scalp you." *Business Week*, April 19, 2004, p. 44.

"Cry from the speculators." *New York Times*, November 29, 1908, p. 2.

"The cure for ticket speculating." *Variety*, November 19, 1920, p. 9.

"The cut-in of cut rates." *Variety*, December 27, 1918, pp. 13, 60.

Daley, Arthur. "Sports of the Times." *New York Times*, May 10, 1949, p. 34.

Danzig, Allison. "102,000, East's largest football crowd, will see Army-Navy classic today." *New York Times*, November 28, 1936, p. 9.

"Daro spurns offer of ticket scalper." *Los Angeles Times*, September 3, 1924, p. B3.

"Declares war on scalpers." *Los Angeles Times*, March 5, 1924, p. B2

"Deep stuff in ticket inquiry; Ziegfeld blames forced buys." *Variety*, July 27, 1927, p. 43.

"Defend ticket speculators." *New York Times*, March 22, 1907, p. 5.

"Defends plan to curb ticket speculators." *New York Times*, April 20, 1930, p. 2.

de Guzman, Janina. "Ticket scalpers making enemies of some White House tourists." *Washington Post*, August 2, 1997, p. B1.

"Demand $100 for seats." *New York Times*, October 1, 1919, p. 13.

"Dividing the pudding." *New York Times*, December 14, 1883, p. 5.

"Drive off speculators." *New York Times*, March 31, 1911, p. 11.

"Ebbets after scalpers." *New York Times*, September 28, 1920, p. 20.

"Ebbets after ticket speculators." *New York Times*, April 26, 1909, p. 8.

"Eccentric Joseph Siegrist." *New York Times*, June 29, 1892, p. 2.

"Educating the managers says cut-rate speculator." *Variety*, April 30, 1915, p. 11.

"18 scalpers arrested." *New York Times*, October 3, 1930, p. 32.

"11 seized as scalpers." *New York Times*, February 11, 1945, p. 41.

"Eleven ticket speculators get summonses from revenue agents outside Ebbets Field." *New York Times*, May 12, 1930, p. 1.

"The engagement of Patti." *New York Times*, April 23, 1882, p. 9.

"Equity hits inequity." *Literary Digest* 103 (December 7, 1929): 20.

"Equity to boycott ticket plan rebels." *New York Times*, January 8, 1930, p. 27.

"Erlanger leads war on the speculators." *New York Times*, August 30, 1905, p. 9.

Eskenazi, Gerald. "A $1,000-a-seat bid is rejected." *New York Times*, March 9, 1971, p. 30.

Eskenazi, Gerald. "Scalpers: shadowy profiteers in sports." *New York Times*, December 28, 1970, pp. 1, 49.

Eskenazi, Gerald. "Ticket scalping at Garden is big business." *New York Times*, April 5, 1972, p. 55.

Esterow, Milton. "Broadway quiet on Dowling plan." *New York Times*, February 10, 1962, p. 14.

Esterow, Milton. "Ice bill passage gets mixed notice." *New York Times*, May 20, 1965, p. 53.

Esterow, Milton. "Lefkowitz opens new hunt for ice." *New York Times*, March 22, 1966, p. 33.

Esterow, Milton. "Lefkowitz urges $25 for shows." *New York Times*, June 10, 1964, pp. 1, 51.

Esterow, Milton. "State is pressing fight on scalping." *New York Times*, August 29, 1964, p. 23.

Esterow, Milton. "Subpoenas given in ticket inquiry." *New York Times*, December 6, 1963, p. 38.

Esterow, Milton. "Ticket scalping netting millions to be bared at theater inquiry." *New York Times*, December 2, 1963, pp. 1, 44.

"Every broker now in Murtagh's sights." *New York Times*, June 28, 1949, p. 29.

"A fair show for all." *New York Times*, August 27, 1887, p. 8.

"Fans have court friend." *New York Times*, October 4, 1947, p. 19.

"Fans pay $250,000 to see first game." *New York Times*, October 9, 1912, p. 4.

"Father and son fined for ticket overcharging." *New York Times*, February 11, 1965, p. 45.

Ferrell, David. "Ticket tricks." *Los Angeles Times*, May 27, 1994, p. B1.

"Few ticket speculators." *New York Times*, December 9, 1921, p. 24.

"Fierce riot on Broadway." *New York Times*, February 16, 1902, p. 1.

"57 ticket brokers listed for arrest." *New York Times*, December 19, 1923, p. 26.

"Fighting the speculators." *New York Times*, January 3, 1893, p. 8.

"Fighting ticket speculators." *New York Times*, May 2, 1889, p. 3.

"Fined $25 for ticket-scalping." *New York Times*, March 21, 1946, p. 26.

"Fines ticket speculator." *New York Times*, November 30, 1919, p. 12.

Fisher, Ian. "Where do tickets go?" *New York Times*, May 8, 1994, p. 32.

Fitzgerald, F. Scott. *The Beautiful and Damned*. Middlesex, England: Penguin, 1966.

"Five tennis match ticket scalpers given jail terms." *Los Angeles Times*, February 18, 1937, p. A2.

"5 ticket brokers arrested in raid." *New York Times*, July 13, 1919, p. 7.

"For anti-speculator bill." *New York Times*, April 5, 1907, p. 7.

"For obstructing the street." *Washington Post*, March 5, 1900, p. 8.

"For theatre-ticket speculators." *New York Times*, June 5, 1895, p. 8.

"4 charged with scalping tickets at Sinatra concert." *New York Times*, July 10, 1965, p. 14.

"43 seized near circus." *New York Times*, April 5, 1934, p. 25.

Gallico, Paul. "Ticket scalper curse thriving, unbridled." *Washington Post*, March 18, 1934, p. 19.

Gallico, Paul. "Ticket speculators a worry; they're cats, we're mice." *Washington Post*, March 14, 1935, pp. 19, 21.

Gelb, Arthur. "City seeks to end ticket scalping." *New York Times*, February 9, 1962, pp. 29, 60.

Gelb, Arthur. "Dowling shocked by ticket clause." *New York Times*, February 21, 1962, pp. 47, 57.

"General city news." *New York Times*, September 28, 1868, p. 7.

Gerard, Jeremy. "*Phantom*: scalpers' bonanza." *New York Times*, January 20, 1988, p. C15.

Goldberg, Michael. "Scalped: why you can't get good concert seats." *Rolling Stone*, November 17, 1988, p. 41.

Goldberg, Michael. "Ticket rip-off." *Rolling Stone*, November 1, 1990, pp. 21–23, 40–41.

"Good order kept in throng outside." *New York Times*, March 26, 1916, p. 22.

"Gossip of the theatres." *New York Times*, September 25, 1885, p. 3.

"Gossip of the theatres." *New York Times*, October 22, 1885, p. 3.

"Gossip of the theatres." *New York Times*, October 30, 1885, p. 3.

"Gyp ticket stands under current secret investigation." *Variety*, March 4, 1925, pp. 1, 13.

"Harrigan was a witness." *New York Times*, March 3, 1891, p. 8.

"Harvard and Yale ready for battle." *New York Times,* November 20, 1909, p. 9.

"Harvest for speculators." *New York Times,* October 17, 1911, p. 2.

"Have right to sell tickets." *New York Times,* December 6, 1901, p. 2.

Hernandez, Raymond. "Albany bill passed to extend current ticket-scalping law." *New York Times,* June 2, 1999, p. B6.

Hernandez, Raymond. "Albany legislature votes to reinstate law on ticket scalping for one year." *New York Times,* September 23, 1997, p. B10.

"High prices for Patti tickets." *Washington Post,* November 26, 1881, p. 2.

"His theatre tickets costly." *New York Times,* March 21, 1911, p. 7.

Honan, William H. "Anti-scalping law: mixed impact likely." *New York Times,* August 8, 1991, p. C13.

"Hotel worker held in ticket scalping." *New York Times,* August 11, 1994, p. B7.

"How to fight the lobby man." *New York Times,* December 21, 1883, p. 3.

"Huge ticket graft paid, says Brady." *New York Times,* January 27, 1924, p. 19.

"If Dreyfuss can raise prices, scalpers can, says magistrate." *New York Times,* October 8, 1927, p. 9.

"Illegal grid ticket sales cost man $50." *Washington Post,* November 23, 1943, p. B1.

"Illinois theatre spec bill signed by Governor Small." *Variety,* July 12, 1923, pp. 12, 16.

"In favor of the ticket speculators." *New York Times,* March 17, 1885, p. 8.

"In line at theatre door." *New York Times,* October 15, 1900, p. 7.

"In move to discourage scalping, rock band won't honor tickets." *New York Times,* July 2, 1996, p. B5.

"In the dramatic mailbag." *New York Times,* December 8, 1929, p. X4.

"In the football world." *New York Times,* November 5, 1903, p. 10.

"Inquiry promised on ticket scalping." *New York Times,* November 2, 1945, p. 14.

"Is it true you can't get tickets for the New York theatres?" *Good Housekeeping* 143 (October, 1956): 52–53.

"Jail and $5,000 fine for ticket gouger." *New York Times,* October 12, 1927, p. 29.

"Jail ticket speculators." *New York Times,* January 28, 1912, p. 15.

Janofsky, Michael. "N.F.L. to review 1980 ticket scalping." *New York Times,* December 10, 1986, p. D31.

"Jenny Lind worried over ticket prices." *New York Times,* May 2, 1929, p. 27.

"John McBride, 84, of ticket agency." *New York Times,* November 29, 1961, p. 41.

"Johnson and Brush on ticket scandal." *New York Times,* November 4, 1911, p. 9.

"Judge finds Navy lax in ticket sale." *New York Times,* October 29, 1948, p. 32.

Karwath, Rob. "Legislator, sports teams urge crackdown on ticket scalpers." *Chicago Tribune,* June 20, 1990, Chicagoland section, p. 6.

"Keith war on specs causes Palace box office shake-up." *Variety,* April 9, 1920, p. 6.

"Keith's Palace starts drive against ticket speculators." *Variety,* April 5, 1923, pp. 1, 7.

Kiely, Eugene. "Tickets taken off eBay." *Dallas Morning News,* January 6, 2001, p. 1B.

Kjos, Tiffany. "Carefree scalpers sell tickets with zeal." *Arizona Daily Star,* March 31, 2001, p. A1.

"Klaw gives warning in speculator fight." *New York Times,* February 11, 1910, p. 11.

"Landis to urge elimination of ticket scalping." *Christian Science Monitor,* October 3, 1942, p. 14.

"Law too mixed to fine speculators." *New York Times,* December 13, 1909, p. 16.

"Leagues war over ticket scandal." *New York Times,* December 13, 1911, p. 9.

Ledbetter, Les. "Rock fans set for Stones to roll in." *New York Times,* July 13, 1972, p. 28.

Levy, Clifford. "A new deal for brokers of tickets?" *New York Times,* May 1, 1995, pp. B1, B5.

"License for speculators." *New York Times,* December 11, 1901, p. 3.

"Limit seats to brokers." *New York Times,* December 21, 1922, p. 22.

Litsky, Frank. "Super Bowl game boon to business." *New York Times,* January 12, 1969, p. S2.

"Logical but not necessary." *New York Times,* December 21, 1907, p. 8.

"Low prices the rule." *New York Times,* April 20, 1882, p. 5.

Lueck, Thomas J. "Inquiry finds ticket scalping pervasive." *New York Times*, August 17, 1994, p. B3.
Mahtesian, Charles. "Two on the aisle?" *Governing* 8 (October, 1994): 25–26.
"The man in the lobby." *New York Times*, December 13, 1883, pp. 4, 9.
"Managers act on speculators." *New York Times*, September 12, 1908, p. 7.
"Managers call scalpers pests." *New York Times*, September 17, 1908, p. 7.
"Managers striving to regulate ticket speculating gypping." *Variety*, November 12, 1920, p. 10.
"Managers to fight ticket speculators." *New York Times*, January 6, 1911, p. 5.
Maney, Richard. "Advice to those who want two on the aisle." *New York Times*, June 5, 1949, pp. SM19–20+.
"Many victims of swindling game." *Los Angeles Times*, September 21, 1907, sec 2, p. 1.
"Marquard's days with Robins ended." *New York Times*, October 13, 1920, p. 21.
"May now scalp opera tickets." *Los Angeles Times*, April 1, 1906, sec 2, p. 2.
Mayo, Morrow. "Ticket-scalping fine art for brokers, worry for owners—but public pays." *Los Angeles Times*, March 29, 1925, pp. C1, C3.
"Mayor pledges aid to city's theatres." *New York Times*, September 2, 1949, p. 14.
McKinley, Jesse. "For the asking, a $480 seat." *New York Times*, October 26, 2001, pp. A1, D11.
"Md. Legislator plans bill to ban scalping." *Washington Post*, December 3, 1944, p. M3.
"Metropolitan drops rates to agents." *New York Times*, March 22, 1910, p. 11.
"Mexico seized ticket scalpers." *New York Times*, April 8, 1945, p. 7.
"Miami set for super gold week." *New York Times*, January 15, 1979, p. C8.
"Mob fights for tickets." *New York Times*, September 15, 1923, pp. 1–2.
"More bills aimed at ticket agencies." *New York Times*, March 4, 1927, p. 23.
"More complaints about ticket speculators." *New York Times*, December 10, 1883, p. 4.
"More than $250,000 in buys for this week's six new shows." *Variety*, October 10, 1919, p. 3.
"Moscow jails ticket scalpers." *New York Times*, September 12, 1948, p. 30.
"Moscow jails 2 theatre ticket speculators." *New York Times*, February 9, 1935, p. 1.
"Moscow ticket scalping a lucrative business." *New York Times*, October 25, 1981, p. 21.
"Moss on new tack against scalpers." *New York Times*, December 22, 1943, p. 19.
"Movement to oust ticket speculators." *New York Times*, September 10, 1908, p. 9.
"Mr. Daly and the speculators." *New York Times*, May 24, 1885, p. 4.
"Mr. Sullivan's failure." *New York Times*, July 18, 1882, p. 1.
"Mrs. Couthoui advertises." *Variety*, October 17, 1919, p. 3.
"Mulqueen upholds ticket speculation." *New York Times*, October 3, 1909, p. 9.
Munsell, Warren P. Jr. "Box-office bugaboo." *Theatre Arts* 32 (February, 1948): 1, 6.
"Murtagh to hear Lee Shubert today." *New York Times*, May 20, 1949, p. 23.
Nack, William, and Robert Sullivan. "Football's little bighorn?" *Sports Illustrated* 54 (January 26, 1981): 32–36.
Nager, Larry. "America's biggest ticket scalper." *Rolling Stone*, May 9, 1985, pp. 9, 78.
Nathan, George Jean. "That ticket mess." *Newsweek* 14 (August 28, 1939): 24.
"National league sidesteps trouble." *New York Times*, December 15, 1911, p. 14.
"New drive begins on ticket gougers." *New York Times*, May 4, 1949, pp. 1, 35.
"New plan of selling." *New York Times*, December 22, 1949, p. 32.
"New rules curb ticket scalpers." *New York Times*, July 4, 1940, p. 17.
"New state law on ticket scalping." *New York Times*, June 7, 2001, p. B6.
"New tax regulations hit ticket scalpers." *New York Times*, November 11, 1936, p. 24.
"New way in hotel distribution by theatres." *Variety*, November 4, 1911, p. 3.
"New York adopts measure to curb ticket brokers." *Variety*, December 20, 1918, p. 12.
"N.F.L. concerned by scalping." *New York Times*, January 17, 1985, p. B10.
"Night waiting at Wallack's." *New York Times*, November 13, 1882, p. 5.
"9 arrested in scalping." *New York Times*, October 4, 1953, p. S2.
"9 hotels accused in ticket inquiry." *New York Times*, June 15, 1949, p. 39.

"Nine men on camp stools." *New York Times*, October 1, 1883, p. 8.

Nixon, Eugene. "Attempted fix reveals practice of ticket scalping by players." *Los Angeles Times*, March 7, 1951, p. C3.

"No collusion in world's series." *New York Times*, January 6, 1912, p. 14.

"No theatre ticket scalpers in Chicago." *New York Times*, January 5, 1906, p. 1.

No title. *New York Times*, September 11, 1883, p. 4.

No title. *New York Times*, January 16, 1884, p. 4.

No title. *New York Times*, January 23, 1884, p. 4.

"Notes of the theatre." *New York Times*, September 10, 1902, p. 9.

Nugent, Frank S. "The screen." *New York Times*, October 16, 1937, p. 22.

"A nuisance to be suppressed." *New York Times*, February 16, 1911, p. 10.

"O'Dwyer's postscript to a probe." *New York Times*, September 11, 1949, pp. X1, X3.

"Off day at Morris Park." *New York Times*, June 4, 1891, p. 3.

"One-price tickets at Paris theatres." *New York Times*, July 5, 1908, p. C3.

"Operagoers defrauded." *New York Times*, January 14, 1889, p. 2.

"Opera opens drive on scalpers who sell tickets on sidewalks." *New York Times*, March 13, 1937, p. 21.

"Opposed to ticket speculators." *New York Times*, April 4, 1882, p. 8.

"Outwit ticket scalpers." *New York Times*, November 28, 1916, p. 14.

Parisi, Albert. "New Jersey journal." *New York Times*, February 5, 1984, p. NJ3.

"Pearl again balks on theatre data." *New York Times*, June 2, 1949, p. 29.

Pemberton, Brock. "Ticket, ticket, who's got the ticket?" *Theatre Arts Monthly* 17 (December, 1933): 945–952.

"Pirates spring plans." *New York Times*, January 7, 1912, p. C7.

"Plans for world's baseball series." *New York Times*, October 4, 1910, p. 9.

"Players waiting for prize money." *New York Times*, October 13, 1913, p. 7.

"Police arrest eight for ticket scalping." *Washington Post*, December 9, 1940, pp. 17, 19.

"Policeman arrested in theft of ticket for Stones concert." *New York Times*, November 14, 1981, p. 26.

"Politics block speculator fight." *New York Times*, September 16, 1908, p. 7.

Pond, Steve. "Bruce Springsteen takes on scalpers, wins bootleg suit." *Rolling Stone*, February 5, 1981, p. 48.

"Postal ticket plan is called a success." *New York Times*, November 11, 1930, p. 1.

"Praise ticket ordinance." *New York Times*, November 21, 1918, p. 8.

Pristin, Terry. "Inquiry on ticket scalping at Tennis Center's box office." *New York Times*, August 29, 1998, p. B2.

Pristin, Terry. "State sues 2 brokers accused of scalping Yankee tickets." *New York Times*, October 17, 1998, p. B3.

"Probe ticket scalping." *New York Times*, November 27, 1910, p. C6.

"Producers launch drive on scalping." *New York Times*, June 10, 1949, p. 33.

"Producers upset by ticket ruling." *New York Times*, April 27, 1957, p. 33.

"Producing managers will take action against speculating evil." *Variety*, November 7, 1919, p. 3.

"Profiteering in Army-Navy game tickets as in theatre seats, agency canvas shows." *New York Times*, November 23, 1923, p. 1

"Profits by ticket scalping." *New York Times*, January 7, 1912, p. 7.

Pulley, Brett. "Final four is not the final word on scalping experiment." *New York Times*, March 30, 1996, pp. 25, 29.

"The queen of the scalpers." *Variety*, December 30, 1921, pp. 1–2.

"Questions ticket sellers." *New York Times*, May 13, 1930, p. 12.

Quindlen, Anna. "About New York." *New York Times*, November 11, 1981, p. B4.

"Raid unlicensed ticket brokers." *New York Times*, December 21, 1923, p. 19.

"Raids ticket speculators." *New York Times*, May 24, 1927, p. 27.

Ranzal, Edward. "State ticket law upheld by court." *New York Times*, November 21, 1964, p. 32.

Rayl, Salley. "Drive to stop ticket scalping under way in California." *Rolling Stone*, May 31, 1979, p. 10.

"Recommends expulsion for student ticket speculators." *New York Times*, November 18, 1920, p. 22.

"Redskins try to stymie scalpers." *Washington Post*, December 19, 1972, p. D1.

"Refuse to honor tickets." *New York Times*, August 21, 1900, p. 12.

"Republicans in Washington to assist Bloom's spec bill." *Variety*, January 31, 1924, p. 10.

Rich, Frank. "An inspector calls." *New York Times*, May 1, 1994, p. E17.

"Ringside tickets are sold for $150." *New York Times*, September 13, 1923, p. 17.

"Riot outside Royal Theatre." *New York Times*, October 26, 1910, p. 1.

Roane, Kit R. "More arrests at stadium in scalping crackdown." *New York Times*, October 1, 1998, p. B6.

Rohrlich, Ted. "Frontiere agrees to plead guilty in ticket scalping." *Los Angeles Times*, October 21, 1986, p. 1.

Rohrlich, Ted. "Prosecutors detail plot of ticket scalping plan." *Los Angeles Times*, December 2, 1986, sec 2, p. 3.

Roth, Jack. "2 Broadway ticket brokers held as scalpers." *New York Times*, November 10, 1964, p. 55.

"Round up idlers in night raid." *New York Times*, July 7, 1918, p. 17.

Rule, Sheila. "Gold circle strategy is bid to scalp scalpers." *New York Times*, December 15, 1993, pp. C19–20.

"Rush to hear Caruso." *New York Times*, October 25, 1908, p. C2.

"Russians sweep Czech movie fete prizes." *New York Times*, August 8, 1949, p. 11.

Ryon, Art. "Nicholas says box office sellers helping scalpers." *Los Angeles Times*, February 9, 1961, pp. C1, C3.

"Says law can't set ticket sale profit." *New York Times*, January 6, 1923, p. 23.

"Says speculators get tickets for opera." *New York Times*, September 24, 1918, p. 6.

"Says theatre gets half." *New York Times*, August 28, 1905, p. 7.

"Scalper fined $250 and jailed 30 days." *New York Times*, June 27, 1972, p. 49.

"Scalper holding 18 *South Pacific* tickets." *New York Times*, May 10, 1949, p. 27.

"Scalper measure ruled invalid by Baltimore judge." *Washington Post*, October 29, 1948, p. B7.

"Scalper ordinance out." *Variety*, April 2, 1920, p. 13.

"Scalpers at work." *New York Times*, December 15, 1963, p. 17.

"Scalpers driven from park." *New York Times*, October 1, 1925, p. 24.

"Scalpers given freedom to peddle ducats." *Los Angeles Times*, December 19, 1958, p. 18.

"Scalpers got 3,500 tickets weekly." *Variety*, July 30, 1920, p. 4.

"Scalpers' profit on shows in year put at $10 million." *New York Times*, December 11, 1963, pp. 1, 54.

"Scalpers reap profits." *New York Times*, October 10, 1920, p. 19.

"Scalpers scalped." *Newsweek* 62 (December 23, 1963): 46.

"Scalpers' tickets barred at the park." *New York Times*, October 12, 1929, p. 19.

"Scalpers trapped, told to leave Annapolis." *Washington Post*, November 19, 1926, p. 13.

"Scalping brings ban." *New York Times*, December 16, 1981, p. B11.

"Scalping charged to Jacobs agency." *New York Times*, June 13, 1946, p. 12.

"Scalping goes legit in Phoenix experiment." *Miami Herald*, March 2, 1995.

"Scalping hearing put off." *New York Times*, October 6, 1953, p. 37.

"Scalping system makes Chicago highest priced theatre town." *Variety*, October 3, 1919, p. 3.

Schanberg, Sydney H. "Indictments sought by Hogan's office in theater inquiry." *New York Times*, December 21, 1963, pp. 1, 17.

Schanberg, Sydney H. "Jersey is joining drive on scalping." *New York Times*, February 1, 1964, p. 12.

Schanberg, Sydney H. "More are silent at ticket inquiry." *New York Times*, December 24, 1963, p. 7.

Schanberg, Sydney H. "State is watching *Dolly* box office." *New York Times*, January 24, 1964, p. 29.

Schanberg, Sydney H. "Theater inquiry sifts Weiss death." *New York Times*, February 12, 1964, p. 30.

"School gets scholarship after a scalping scandal." *New York Times*, August 7, 1996, p. C15.

Schumach, Murray. "*Kiss Me, Kate* date sought; broker faces license loss." *New York Times*, May 22, 1949, pp. 1, 50.

Schumach, Murray. "On the trail of the specs." *New York Times*, May 15, 1949, p. X3.

Schumach, Murray. "Ticket agency ban asked by Murtagh." *New York Times*, June 18, 1949, pp. 1, 7.

Schumach, Murray. "Ticket men meet; one loses licenses." *New York Times*, June 8, 1949, p. 31.

Schumach, Murray. "Ticket sale code." *New York Times*, March 5, 1950, p. 99.

Schumach, Murray. "Who's got the tickets?" *New York Times*, April 14, 1957, pp. X1, X3.

"Scores taken in police drive on ticket scalpers." *Los Angeles Times*, December 11, 1932, p. 19

"Seats are scarce." *New York Times*, October 7, 1913, p. 10.

"Seats for the big game." *New York Times*, November 25, 1890, p. 5.

"Seats for the Irving season." *New York Times*, October 4, 1883, p. 8.

"2d broker faces loss of license." *New York Times*, May 25, 1949, p. 31.

"2d ticket agency loses its license." *New York Times*, June 10, 1949, p.29.

"See loophole for ticket speculators." *New York Times*, February 18, 1915, p. 6.

"Sees play in grip of ticket brokers." *New York Times*, July 15, 1927, p. 19.

"Sees theatre men forced to graft." *New York Times*, July 8, 1927, p. 8.

"Sees ticket gouging." *New York Times*, February 28, 1924, p. 23.

Sell, Dave. "Valvano out of running as UCLA coach." *Washington Post*, April 3, 1988, p. C12.

"Sell soda checks as theatre tickets." *New York Times*, September 21, 1915, p. 11.

"Senate passes ticket bill." *New York Times*, March 13, 1928, p. 3.

"Seven fined for ticket scalping." *New York Times*, October 13, 1916, p. 8.

"7 producers assail theatre ticket plan." *New York Times*, April 23, 1930, p. 31.

"Shubert accused of ticket deal." *New York Times*, October 9, 1907, p. 11.

"Shubert is vague on ticket sales." *New York Times*, June 3, 1949, p. 22.

"Shubert organization is fined in ticket inquiry." *New York Times*, September 14, 1998, p. B4.

"Shuberts bar Couthoui's." *Variety*, August 17, 1927, p. 47.

"Shuberts' dealings with ticket men and treasurers detailed by Long." *Variety*, July 20, 1927, p. 37.

"Sidewalk ticket speculator." *New York Times*, August 10, 1910, p. 10.

"Sidewalk ticket speculators harassed." *New York Times*, March 16, 1902, p. 14.

"Signs bill abolishing ticket speculators." *New York Times*, February 27, 1921, p. 6.

"16 ticket scalpers arrested." *New York Times*, July 11, 1957, p. 30.

"Smith asks public to aid ticket plan." *New York Times*, April 17, 1930, p. 26.

"*South Pacific* theatre, facing license loss, ousts treasurer." *New York Times*, May 19, 1949, pp. 1, 34.

"Specs and high prices." *Variety*, December 31, 1920, pp. 12, 35.

"Specs can charge any price if they keep off sidewalk." *Variety*, January 9, 1920, p. 7.

"Specs stuck with tickets are hard hit by epidemic." *Variety*, October 18, 1918, p. 12.

"The speculation evil." *New York Times*, January 1, 1893, p. 12.

"Speculation in tickets." *New York Times*, September 23, 1885, p. 5.

"The speculator nuisance." *New York Times*, March 14, 1889, p. 5.

"Speculators again in danger." *New York Times*, November 17, 1919, p. 14.

"Speculators blamed." *Washington Post*, October 6, 1909, p. 8.

"The speculators couldn't work." *New York Times*, July 19, 1888, p. 8.

"Speculators hard hit." *New York Times*, October 15, 1907, p. 7.

"Speculators keep away." *New York Times*, August 22, 1900, p. 7.

"Speculators' license fee." *New York Times*, November 16, 1901, p. 8.

"Speculators on hand." *New York Times*, October 22, 1907, p. 9.
"Speculators renew their annoyances." *New York Times*, March 22, 1911, p. 11.
"Speculators run foul of the police." *New York Times*, January 17, 1909, p. 11.
"Speculators rush to buy tickets." *New York Times*, January 16, 1909, p. 6.
"Speculators talk of appeal to managers." *New York Times*, January 18, 1909, p. 9.
"Speculators to go, managers decree." *New York Times*, September 11, 1908, p. 9.
"Spoiling for a fight." *New York Times*, December 21, 1885, p. 2.
"Stanford student ticket scalpers under fire." *Los Angeles Times*, November 21, 1929, pp. A13, A15.
"State to add 10,000 to civil service." *New York Times*, April 22, 1940, p. 15.
"State's high court annuls city ruling on ticket scalping." *New York Times*, May 15, 1969, p. 43.
"The steam-heating job." *New York Times*, December 15, 1880, p. 3.
"Student ticket speculators." *New York Times*, November 24, 1893, p. 9.
"Students beat scalpers." *New York Times*, February 28, 1930, p. 30.
"Students get the seats." *New York Times*, November 28, 1894, p. 7.
"Swann blames managers." *New York Times*, November 9, 1919, p. 18.
"Swann goes slow in arresting idlers." *New York Times*, July 2, 1918, p.24.
Sylvester, Robert. "Broadway ticket scandal." *Collier's* 124 (July 2, 1949): 26.
Taubman, Howard. "Time for tax repeal." *New York Times*, December 6, 1964, p. X5.
"Tax ticket speculators." *New York Times*, December 18, 1918, p. 19.
"The theater and the scalper." *Christian Science Monitor*, January 13, 1912, p. 40.
"Theater ticket graft in New York." *Literary Digest* 94 (July 30, 1927): 11.
"Theater ticket question is again brought to fore." *Christian Science Monitor*, February 26, 1915, p. 16.
"Theater wars on scalper." *Los Angeles Times*, March 10, 1925, p. A2.
"Theatre manager punches speculator." *New York Times*, September 27, 1904, p.9.
"Theatre managers accused by Saxe." *New York Times*, February 26, 1907, p.11.
"Theatre managers' agreement is not sufficiently binding." *Variety*, September 17, 1915, p. 11.
"Theatre managers win in speculator's test." *New York Times*, December 6, 1905, p. 11.
"Theatre men meet ticket scalpers." *New York Times*, September 29, 1908, p. 9.
"Theatre men urge war on speculator." *New York Times*, November 14, 1919, p. 13.
"Theatre nuisances." *New York Times*, August 27, 1874, p. 4.
"Theatre pact bans ticket speculation." *New York Times*, July 27, 1938, pp. 1, 15.
"Theatre prices up to $16.50 for New Year's Eve." *New York Times*, December 30, 1926, p. 1.
"Theatre ruling is lifted by city." *New York Times*, May 6, 1957, p. 24.
"The theatre ticket abuse." *New York Times*, December 15, 1883, p. 5.
"Theatre ticket bamboozle." *Variety*, September 21, 1927, p. 46.
"Theatre ticket premiums part of gross receipts?" *Variety*, January 16, 1915, p. 10.
"Theatre ticket scalping code is revised giving new curbs and better distribution." *New York Times*, November 15, 1939, p. 25.
"Theatre ticket speculation." *New York Times*, June 3, 1882, p. 8.
"A theatre-ticket speculator in trouble." *New York Times*, November 26, 1870, p. 2.
"Theatre ticket speculators." *New York Times*, April 28, 1875, p. 4.
"Theatre ticket speculators." *New York Times*, March 21, 1902, p. 5.
"Theatre ticket speculators hit." *New York Times*, March 20, 1907, p. 16.
"Theatre tickets again." *New York Times*, November 24, 1920, p.15.
"Theatre tickets in hotels." *New York Times*, January 25, 1907, p. 8.
"Theatregoer's complaint." *New York Times*, May 26, 1901, p. 19.
"Theatres modify ticket agency plan." *New York Times*, April 11, 1923, p. 16.
"Thirteen fined as scalpers." *Los Angeles Times*, November 25, 1947, p. 2.
"This is a free country." *New York Times*, March 19, 1886, p. 8.
"$365,000 in graft on theatre tickets charged to police." *New York Times*, December 3, 1930, pp. 1, 7.

"The three men in the lobby." *New York Times*, December 16, 1883, p. 2.
"Tice fined for scalping." *Times-Colonist* (Victoria, BC), July 1, 2005, p. C9.
"Ticket agency law effective." *Christian Science Monitor*, September 4, 1924, p. 3.
"Ticket agents lose appeal in test case." *New York Times*, December 13, 1927, p. 31.
"Ticket broker arrested." *New York Times*, September 5, 1902, p. 3.
"Ticket case — and opinions." *Variety*, March 16, 1927, p. 37.
"Ticket deal now working: no cut-rates this week." *Variety*, September 10, 1915, pp. 3, 6.
"Ticket disgrace hit by service bulletin." *New York Times*, November 30, 1946, p. 24.
"Ticket men ask Murtagh ouster." *New York Times*, July 13, 1949, p. 29.
"Ticket ordinance killed by court." *New York Times*, January 6, 1919, p. 1.
"Ticket profiteering small; one fined $50." *Washington Post*, June 6, 1923, p. 2.
"Ticket sale inquiry on." *New York Times*, May 25, 1956, p. 27.
"The ticket scalper now free to scalp." *Literary Digest* 92 (March 19, 1927): 14.
"Ticket scalper out $26." *New York Times*, September 8, 1941, p. 17.
"Ticket scalpers." *Los Angeles Times*, February 29, 1924, p. A4.
"Ticket scalpers accuse managers." *New York Times*, September 15, 1908, p. 18.
"Ticket scalpers arrested at Atlanta." *New York Times*, July 27, 1972, p. 24.
"Ticket scalpers face rocky road." *New York Times*, November 2, 1922, p. 24.
"Ticket scalpers holding sack." *Los Angeles Times*, October 3, 1935, p. A9.
"Ticket scalpers in Paris." *New York Times*, February 18, 1900, p. 9.
"Ticket scalpers jailed." *New York Times*, February 2, 1929, p. 36.
"Ticket scalpers present their side." *New York Times*, October 15, 1908, p. 9.
"Ticket scalping causes stir in Chicago Council." *Christian Science Monitor*, March 6, 1915,
     p. 16.
"Ticket scalping checked." *New York Times*, March 21, 1912, p. 11.
"Ticket scalping lands football fan in jail." *Los Angeles Times*, September 25, 1954, p. B2.
"Ticket scalping now illegal at Coliseum." *Los Angeles Times*, May 24, 1961, p. C1.
"The ticket scalping nuisance." *Christian Science Monitor*, May 2, 1917, p. 20.
"Ticket-scalping still no crime for Kentuckians." *Washington Post*, February 19, 1966, p. C1.
"Ticket scandal falls flat." *New York Times*, December 12, 1911, p. 13.
"Ticket seller in a cell." *New York Times*, January 24, 1909, p. 16.
"Ticket sellers active." *New York Times*, February 27, 1902, p. 6.
"Ticket spec evils rouse both Chicago and New York." *Variety*, December 13, 1918, p. 13.
"The ticket specs." *Variety*, December 27, 1918, pp. 12, 162.
"Ticket specs plying trade under new law supervision." *Variety*, February 28, 1919, p. 12
"Ticket speculating future." *Variety*, November 24, 1922, p. 9.
"Ticket speculation defended by Weber." *New York Times*, December 4, 1929, p. 33.
"Ticket speculation ordinance passes." *New York Times*, December 2, 1908, pp. 1–2.
"Ticket speculation reduced to system and economy basis." *Variety*, January 24, 1913, p. 12.
"The ticket speculator." *New York Times*, April 11, 1882, p. 8.
"Ticket speculator arrested." *New York Times*, June 19, 1896, p. 8.
"The ticket speculator evil." *New York Times*, April 12, 1884, p. 8.
"A ticket speculator fined." *New York Times*, July 5, 1886, p. 12.
"Ticket speculator fined." *New York Times*, April 18, 1905, p. 11.
"Ticket speculator fined." *New York Times*, September 1, 1905, p. 9.
"A ticket speculator fined in Boston." *New York Times*, April 19, 1873, p. 1.
"Ticket speculator fined $10." *Washington Post*, March 6, 1900, p. 10.
"Ticket speculator fined $3." *New York Times*, December 17, 1910, p. 22.
"Ticket speculator gets limit by law; six months in workhouse for the next one." *New York
     Times*, November 18, 1919, p. 17.
"Ticket speculator loses court case." *New York Times*, March 29, 1911, p. 22.
"Ticket speculator nuisance." *New York Times*, April 8, 1894, p. 12.
"The ticket speculator nuisance and some suggested remedies." *New York Times*, January 13,
     1907, p. X1.

"Ticket speculator ordinance signed." *New York Times*, December 29, 1918, p. 9.
"Ticket speculator to jail." *New York Times*, May 13, 1913, p. 11.
"The ticket speculators." *New York Times*, August 22, 1870, p.8.
"The ticket speculators." *New York Times*, August 24, 1870, p. 3.
"The ticket speculators." *New York Times*, August 27, 1870, p. 3.
"Ticket speculators." *New York Times*, January 31, 1882, p. 4.
"Ticket speculators." *New York Times*, September 22, 1883, p. 4.
"The ticket speculators." *New York Times*, December 17, 1883, p. 5.
"The ticket speculators." *New York Times*, April 16, 1911, p. 10.
"The ticket speculator's a nuisance." *New York Times*, October 27, 1885, p. 2.
"Ticket speculators active at school football game." *New York Times*, November 30, 1928, p. 31.
"Ticket speculators and the opera." *New York Times*, February 28, 1881, p. 2.
"Ticket speculators are highwaymen." *New York Times*, December 2, 1901, p. 14.
"Ticket speculators' attack." *New York Times*, February 9, 1902, p. 10.
"Ticket speculators balked." *New York Times*, May 21, 1881, p. 2.
"Ticket speculators begin test of law." *New York Times*, March 21, 1911, p. 7.
"Ticket speculators busy." *New York Times*, April 27, 1914, p. 20.
"Ticket speculators' case." *New York Times*, April 27, 1902, p. 11.
"Ticket speculators caught." *New York Times*, October 15, 1911, p. 4.
"Ticket speculators discharged." *New York Times*, January 12, 1881, p. 8.
"Ticket speculators fined." *New York Times*, February 10, 1902, p. 9.
"Ticket speculators fined." *New York Times*, November 22, 1908, p. 2.
"Ticket speculators fined." *New York Times*, March 1, 1919, p. 3.
"Ticket speculators foiled." *Washington Post*, February 26, 1896, p. 7.
"Ticket speculators freed." *New York Times*, June 4, 1907, p. 1.
"Ticket speculators held." *New York Times*, February 8, 1907, p. 1.
"Ticket speculators held." *New York Times*, May 31, 1940, p. 25.
"Ticket speculators hit." *New York Times*, January 16, 1907, p. 7.
"Ticket speculators kept away." *New York Times*, September 23, 1894, p. 8.
"Ticket speculators lose." *New York Times*, November 26, 1901, p. 9.
"Ticket speculators now off the street." *New York Times*, January 15, 1909, p. 5.
"Ticket speculators safe." *New York Times*, April 24, 1907, p. 18.
"Ticket speculators still to the fore." *New York Times*, November 28, 1905, p. 8.
"Ticket speculators to fight law today." *New York Times*, March 20, 1911, p. 9.
"Ticket speculators upheld." *New York Times*, January 28, 1920, p. 13.
"The ticket speculators will not redeem." *New York Times*, January 9, 1883, p. 4.
"Ticket speculators win." *New York Times*, October 7, 1899, p. 7.
"Ticket status in theatres of Boston is told." *Christian Science Monitor*, September 4, 1915, p. 6.
"Ticket vendor discharged." *New York Times*, June 11, 1911, p. 8.
"Tickets at box office bunk uncovered by Chicagoans." *Variety*, March 15, 1923, pp. 11, 23.
Tierney, John. "Scalping, fair and square." *New York Times*, June 26, 1994, p. SM16.
Tierney, John. "Tickets? Supply meets demand on sidewalk." *New York Times*, December 26, 1992, pp. 1, 24.
"To banish ticket scalpers." *New York Times*, November 5, 1910, p. 1.
"To end speculation in theatre tickets." *New York Times*, November 17, 1908, p. 6.
"To fight scalpers of boxing tickets." *New York Times*, December 6, 1920, p. 22.
"To fight speculators." *New York Times*, October 23, 1907, p. 11.
"To fine Yale speculators." *New York Times*, September 1, 1907, p. C4.
"To foil speculators." *New York Times*, October 8, 1910, p. 9.
"To foil ticket speculators." *New York Times*, October 13, 1905, p. 9.
"To stop theatre ticket speculators." *New York Times*, January 16, 1907, p. 1.
"To stop ticket speculation." *New York Times*, February 15, 1902, p. 2.

"Trade board aids in ticket inquiry." *New York Times*, July 10, 1927, p. 19.

"Trap ticket speculators." *New York Times*, March 28, 1916, p. 22.

"Trendall and Welsh." *Los Angeles Times*, October 4, 1908, sec 6, p. 4.

"Trio freed in case of ticket scalping." *Los Angeles Times*, August 5, 1958, p. 4.

"Trouble in Shubert offices evident from resignations." *Variety*, December 19, 1919, p. 14.

"Troubles of theatre-ticket speculators." *New York Times*, April 12, 1872, p. 2.

"The troubles of the ticket speculators." *New York Times*, August 23, 1870, p. 8.

"Tuttle replies to Brady." *New York Times*, January 2, 1929, p. 27.

"2 companies settle in ticket inquiry." *New York Times*, December 23, 1994, p. C35.

"2 more ticket men out." *New York Times*, October 8, 1949, p. 8.

"Uncle Sam after ticket scalper." *New York Times*, November 10, 1920, p. 3.

"Union official assails films." *Los Angeles Times*, June 9, 1926.

"Urge bills to check ticket speculators." *New York Times*, March 31, 1922, p. 11.

"U.S. accuses 13 in ticket scalping." *Los Angeles Times*, July 8, 1960, p. B1.

"Vikings' Tice admits to scalping Super Bowl tickets." *Washington Post*, March 11, 2005, p. D2.

"Wagner bill passed." *New York Times*, April 4, 1907, p. 9.

"Wait all night at Polo Grounds." *New York Times*, October 14, 1911, pp. 1–2.

Wallace, William N. "Ram owner, Rozelle deny bowl scalping." *New York Times*, December 11, 1980, p. B18.

"Wallack's new theatre." *New York Times*, December 30, 1881, p. 5.

"Wants a limit on ticket profits." *New York Times*, November 30, 1918, p. 9.

"War against speculators." *New York Times*, September 2, 1902, p. 9.

"War launched on scalpers." *Los Angeles Times*, May 27, 1930, p. A5.

"War on speculators at the Hippodrome." *New York Times*, December 30, 1906, p. 15.

"War on speculators in theatre tickets." *New York Times*, February 2, 1910, p. 7.

"War on ticket sellers." *New York Times*, May 1, 1902, p. 9.

"War on ticket speculators." *New York Times*, May 21, 1882, p. 12.

"War on ticket speculators." *New York Times*, September 24, 1900, p. 7.

"War on ticket speculators." *New York Times*, March 31, 1903, p. 9.

"War upon the ticket speculators." *New York Times*, August 20, 1870, p. 4.

"War with ticket speculators." *New York Times*, January 28, 1882, p. 1.

"Warns ticket speculators." *New York Times*, June 6, 1911, p. 2.

"Wars on speculators." *New York Times*, December 7, 1928, p. 35.

"Was a losing speculation." *Los Angeles Times*, May 20, 1904, p. A4.

Wehrwein, Austin C. "Chicagoans recall Jack Ruby as ticket scalper and chiseler." *New York Times*, November 25, 1963, p. 12.

"Whalen opens war on ticket scalpers." *New York Times*, February 1, 1929, p. 19.

Wharton, John F. "Wharton looks at scalping." *New York Times*, March 18, 1962, pp. 1, 3.

"Will close affairs of theatre league." *New York Times*, January 16, 1931, p. 7.

"William Turnbull killed." *New York Times*, March 23, 1890, p. 1.

"Woes of ticket speculators." *New York Times*, January 1, 1883, p. 8.

"The world and the theatre." *Theatre Arts Monthly* 18 (December, 1934): 886–888.

"World Series opens in New York Oct. 8." *New York Times*, September 26, 1912, p. 9.

"Would license a nuisance." *New York Times*, May 18, 1911, p. 10.

"Writer defends clause on tickets." *New York Times*, February 22, 1962, p. 49.

"Yale in good condition." *New York Times*, November 24, 1899, p. 9.

"Yale student fined." *New York Times*, December 13, 1902, p. 3.

"Ziegfeld attacks new agency plan." *New York Times*, December 16, 1922, p. 23.

"Ziegfeld attacks plan again." *New York Times*, June 21, 1930, p. 20.

"Ziegfeld fights brokers." *New York Times*, June 17, 1918, p. 11.

"Ziegfeld routes the specs." *Washington Post*, June 30, 1918, p. SM2.

"Ziegfeld says he has won." *New York Times*, July 8, 1918, p. 9.

Index

257

www.ingramcontent.com/pod-product-compliance
Lightning Source LLC
Chambersburg PA
CBHW020242290326
41929CB00045B/1481